Barnaby Williams, a one-time motorbike racer, journalist and pilot, is now studying for his History PhD. He is the author of the acclaimed *Revolution*, an epic novel of twentieth century Russia, and *Crusaders*, the story of modern Israel.

Also by Barnaby Williams

Revolution

ANNO DOMINI

THE CRUCIFIXION OF THE TRUE FAITH

POCKET BOOKS

New York   London   Toronto   Sydney   Tokyo   Singapore

First published in Great Britain by Simon & Schuster Ltd, 1995
First published by Pocket Books, 1996
An imprint of Simon & Schuster Ltd
A Viacom Company

Simon & Schuster Ltd
West Garden Place
Kendal Street
London W2 2AQ

Simon & Schuster of Australia Pty Ltd
Sydney

A CIP catalogue record for this book is available from the British
Library.

ISBN 0-671-85182-9

This book is a work of fiction. Names, characters, places and
incidents are either the product of the author's imagination or are
used fictitiously.

Printed and bound in Great Britain by Caledonian International
Book Manufacturing, Glasgow

FOR SUSAN CARRDUS, HEADMISTRESS
EXTRAORDINAIRE

WITH THANKS:

As always, to my splendid, supportive and far-sighted publisher, Nick Webb, for letting me do it, and for all his help.

To my skilful and talented editor Jenny Olivier, for much hard work and good ideas. Also for meeting dreadful deadlines while on her way to getting married!

To my superb agent, Anne Dewe, for all her help, advice and expertise; and also to Debbie and Tina, wonderful ladies all.

To Anne, Abbey and Philippa, without whom there would be no point in doing it.

As always, to my mother, with whom Connell could have an interesting chat, as one double-first at Oxford to another.

And to pagans everywhere, whose time will return.

1

Jabal Mountains, Upper Egypt

The wind was from the south, and Abercrombie was a little hard of hearing, so when the helicopter came over the ridge above him he saw it before he heard it. He was out in the open, a water flask that he was carrying from the Toyota four-wheel drive hidden amidst the scrub in his hand, he had no option but to stand and wait as the pilot circled once and let down into a hover over the arid ground.

The thudding of the blades penetrated the still, parched air in the cave up in the cliff and brought Connell cautiously forward to peep outside. He was in time to see Abercrombie hurry behind a great boulder as the cloud of dust swept towards him, saw him bend quickly, taking a paper from inside his jacket and stuffing it in a crevice under a rock.

The helicopter was various shades of brown and yellow, it settled on to the ground like a particularly ugly insect, its turbine hissing to itself as the long, drooping wings slowed. Abercrombie came out from behind his boulder, brushing dust from the lapels of his linen jacket. A door opened in the side of the machine and an Egyptian in camouflaged military clothing got out and came over to him.

'This is a prohibited area,' he said sharply. He spoke in English.

'I'm so sorry,' Abercrombie said apologetically, 'I had no idea.'

'There are signs on the road.'

'I was trying out the four-wheel drive. So exciting, going off the roads.'

The officer glanced sharply at the Toyota, near invisible in the scrub.

'Why have you hidden your vehicle?'

'I haven't,' Abercrombie said baldly.

'Let me see your passport.'

The older man reached inside his jacket and handed it over.

'You are a bookseller,' the Egyptian said accusingly.

'That's right.'

'What sort of books?'

'I sell what the publishers print,' he said blandly, 'all kinds of things.'

'The climate here is very dry. It rarely rains. Did you know that?'

'It certainly looks like it.'

'It means that very ancient objects do not deteriorate here. Things buried by our ancestors, Mr Abercrombie.'

He tapped himself on the chest.

'*My* ancestors. Not yours. Things made by the Pharaohs belong to Egypt. They may not be taken out of Egypt, by international law.'

'I assure you, all I wish to take from Egypt are happy memories of my holiday.'

'Very good. So it would be best if you get back to the parts of Egypt that are suitable for holidaymakers. Come. I shall escort you out of this area. It is a military area, Mr Abercrombie, it is not safe for strangers.'

He went over to the helicopter and spoke briefly with the pilot, then joined Abercrombie by the Toyota.

Looking down from the rim of the cave, Connell saw them get inside the four-wheel drive, saw it bump away over the rough ground. The helicopter's hiss increased into a powerful, metallic whine, the blades whirled about it and it lifted away in a blast of dust. Very soon it was out of earshot. The brown Toyota blurred with the harsh terrain of the valley, went around some rocks and vanished from his sight. Connell sat up on the floor of the cave and fumbled in the pockets of his jacket for his packet of cheroots. He ignited one with a brass Zippo lighter and inhaled the smoke.

'Blast,' he said.

He sat smoking his thin black cigar in silence. It was completely quiet, high up in the deserted mountains. When he had finished he rubbed out the glowing ember on the sole of his leather climbing boot and pocketed the stub. He got up, the cave was high enough to allow him to stand. Light permeated its rear and Connell went down there, leaving his small bag of tools on the smooth floor, his boots marking the dust of its surface, proof of centuries of dessication.

At the back of the cave a fissure had opened the rock to the air. Looking up he could see a clear, cloudless blue sky. He pulled himself up through the gap the way that he had come and shortly afterwards stood at the head of the cliff. A black kite wheeled patiently overhead, small stones rattled down the slope as he made his way down.

The tracks of the Toyota were still visible, heading away through the harsh-leaved scrub, as dry and brown as the rock it clung to. Connell bent by the boulder and found, stuffed into a crevice, a crumpled roll of paper. A green lizard the length of his thumb stared at him before skittering into hiding.

He squatted down and spread the paper out flat upon a rock. He was very familiar with it, but examined it once again. At one corner it bore a series of letters and numbers in the manner of a very exact map reference or the coordinates of a global positioning grid. The paper appeared to be painted with colours, in the manner of a scanning machine, with whorls and peaks of red heat, rivulets and pools of ice, dark and deep ravines and canyons. Connell's eyes flicked from his chart to the cliff face above him, where the rock was pierced by the mouths of the caves. He nodded to himself and got up, a lean figure in climber's cord trousers and baggy-pocketed jacket. His hair had fallen over his eyes and he pushed it back as he made his way back up the hill, the kite above watching his progress.

Back in the cave he took out a builder's measure in a circular case and began marking out the floor. The cave was long, broader in the middle, like an alligator's belly, narrowing at neck and tail. He appeared to settle upon an area towards the rear, close to the wall. Taking a small stiff brush from the bag he carefully swept it clear of dust, and the accumulation of centuries of wind-blown debris, sand, seed and guano, finally exposing the rock beneath.

The yellow-grey rock was fissured into a mosaic. Connell took a short-handled climber's ice axe from his bag and began to tap gently on the surface he had uncovered, his head cocked as attentively as a woodpecker's. The triangular blade of the axe moved across and down, across and down as Connell tapped with a regular cadence, like a musician playing a particular piece. Gradually his area became circular. He stopped tapping, and struck the rock with a blow.

The blade bit into the fissures, Connell levered at it using the handle to gain purchase and chunks of flat rock came out with a deceptive ease. They had been placed there, as a man might make a stone wall. Connell felt his heart suddenly thump in his chest, and using his axe carefully, he began to excavate, the pile of broken rock building up beside him.

The axe ground on something that was not solid, not rock, but hollow, and Connell put it down, using his fingers to retrieve the stones and chunks in the hole. Slowly the head of a jar came into view. Its clay was still red from its firing, its surface still ridged from the fingers of its potter. Its neck was sealed with a clay plug that bore ochre streaks of the cement that bound it to the jar. Staring in wonder at its surface Connell saw delicate ochre fingerprints, the marks of a woman's hands desperately tamping the plug into place.

He felt a sudden prickle of fear that was century upon century old.

'She was in a hurry,' he whispered. 'They were hunting her.'

Very carefully, he resumed his task of exhuming the jar from its ancient resting place. Once he was certain that it was free completely about its sides he put his hands about its neck and lifted it from the hole.

Holding it as though it were made of thin glass he put it down upon his rucksack, which he had spread out by the wall, and for many minutes he sat, simply staring at it in wonder. It was a big jar, almost eighteen inches across at its widest point and about two and a half feet high. Examining it, he could see that it was completely intact, and that it was wholly sealed. The ochre cement around its neck had been smeared into the join time and again. With hands that trembled slightly, he tipped it to one side and felt something move, and tap the inner wall. He stood it up once again.

The light filtering into the cave was beginning to dim as the sun hastened towards the ridge above. Connell was suddenly aware of being both hungry and thirsty, but he shrugged wryly to himself. The provisions were in the Toyota.

He dropped all his tools into the hole that had held the jar and put the stones on top of them. By the fissure that led up to the cliff top he found a seamed and weathered pile, and realised there were the original excavations. Working extremely carefully, he worked the jar into his rucksack and secured the straps. He pulled it on to his back and climbed cautiously up into the air. The sun was going down in a ball of orange fury, on the horizon the white sickle of the moon was already visible. With it came the first sharp fingers of the chill night, and Connell, aware of the dangers of a night in the desert unequipped, began to walk down the slope, his prize upon his back.

It was downhill all the way, coming out of the mountains. There was only one way, the wings of the valley soon gathered him up, the walls of the ravine rising around him. As the dark descended upon him his eyes adapted to the pale illumination of the thin moon and her stars. He was fit, he kept moving in the cold air, and when his parched throat reminded him of its thirst he promised it a beer from the coldbox in Abercrombie's truck.

Near midnight by his watch the wings of the ravine began to fall away, and through the crystal-clear air he could see the sharp yellow and white lights of habitation in the distance. Somewhere out there was the Nile.

Without warning, a cluster of powerful lamps exploded the dark, pinning him in the middle of his trail. He threw up an arm against the sudden impact, shielding himself from the blow. Instead he heard the clunk and creak of a metal door opening, from somewhere behind the glare.

'Hullo, Connell,' said a voice, 'I've been waiting for you.'

It was the voice of a woman. The lights suddenly dimmed, leaving only the glow of the side lamps. He could see her, in what was left of his night vision, standing by the door.

'Get in,' she said, 'I'll give you a lift.'

He went round to the passenger side, as she bid, and climbed cautiously up on to the bench-seat of the pick-up truck, turning sideways to allow for his big pack. As he sat down his feet began to throb from all the walking he had done.

'Out hiking?' she asked, slightly amused.

'Training for the marathon,' he said.

'That must be why you have the pack on your back,' she said dryly. He could see her vague outline in the darkness.

'How did you know I'd be coming?'

'This is the only way down from the mountain,' she said. 'I saw George Abercrombie driving through here earlier today, with an Egyptian official. And I said to myself, where George Abercrombie, antiquarian bookseller and crook is, can Dr Frank Connell be far behind? And so I waited for you.'

Connell patted his pockets and located his cheroots. He put one in his mouth and lit it with the Zippo. In the sudden yellow flame he could see her, tall and aquiline, long black hair pulled back into a high ponytail. About thirty.

'Want one?' he asked.

'I like my lungs clean,' she said.

'I like the nicotine. You have the advantage of me. You seem to know me, but I don't know you.'

'Of course I know you. I used to go to all your lectures.'

The sudden, old stab of pain.

'You were at Oxford?' he said levelly.

'I was at St Anne's. And I went to your lectures. You were brilliant, you know.'

'Yes, I know,' he said honestly.

'Dr Frank Connell, double-first, M.A., D.Phil. A brilliant young don. A star at Merton College,' she said cruelly, 'headed straight for a chair. Arrested, charged with fraud and theft of archaeological artefacts, the biggest stink seen in the University for years. Chucked out on his ear.'

'The Israelis have no sense of humour,' he quipped. 'Their patch of the world is stuffed with scrolls. They could spare me some. All their bloody generals and cabinet ministers are at it all the time.'

'*Their* generals and cabinet ministers,' she pointed out, 'not an English academic on the make.'

'Irish. An Irish academic on the make. My pa was a broth of a boy from Dublin.'

'Why did you do it, Frank? For the money?'

Connell drew on his cheroot.

'Of *course* I did it for the money. Why else would you do such a thing?'

'Is it important?' she asked, her voice soft.

'My parents divorced because there was no money,' he said quietly. 'My mother died because she didn't have the money for an operation they said would wait. I have thought money important ever since. Yes, I thought it was important. But you still have the advantage of me.'

'Berridge,' she said. She held out her hand, it was cool, the skin slightly callused. 'Juliana Berridge.'

'You're an archaeologist,' he said, 'you've got the hands.'

'Yes. Fairy Liquid doesn't work for us.'

'On a dig?'

'Yes,' she said shortly. 'Not far from here. What's in the bag, Frank?'

'What if I don't want to tell you?'

'What if I snitch on you if you don't tell me?' she said, with a laugh. 'Come on, Frank, maybe we can help each other. Walking out of the Egyptian mountains in the middle of the night you're hardly delivering groceries. George Abercrombie is somewhere in the area, and he is an influential, if rather shady, dealer in antiquities. You can't go to the Dead Sea any more because the Israelis will sink you in it. You've turned to Egypt. You've got some artefacts.'

'Yes, all right, I have. A large pottery jar.'

'You just went off with your little pick and spade and found it.'

'No. We used subsurface interface radar. You know it?'

Juliana nodded.

'Like sonar. It can see a hollow space underground. Like a big jar.'

'Yes.'

'But you can't just wander about with it hoping to hit on something under your feet.'

'No,' he agreed. 'But I had an idea of where to look.'

'How?'

'What's my field?'

'Early religious history.'

'Right. When the Orthodox Christian Church – what became the Catholic Church – finally gained power as the religion of the Roman Empire it became increasingly intolerant of alternative religions. The later stages of the fourth century see a great deal of smashing of "pagan" temples, or their conversion into churches. The bishops didn't like people worshipping the old gods and goddesses. But even less did they like people following alternative forms of Christianity, most especially the Gnostic Churches which they had managed to have Constantine ban by edict back in 325 – the Council of Nicaea when they consolidated their power.

'Towards the end of the century the plight of any Church promulgating an alternative view of Christianity was roughly speaking equivalent to running that of the dissident movements in Stalinist Russia. They were crushed with the utmost ruthlessness. They would have been driven out of the major centres and it is my guess that they took to the mountains. There are a number of monasteries up here which the Orthodox Church took over after it drove the original occupants out. When the time came that the alternative Churches could survive no longer they would have sought to bury their liturgy and histories against the day when they could find them again, in better times. Those days never came for them, of course. The Orthodox Church never did lose its grip. But my theory was that up there is where such artefacts would be found. And, I thought, in the caves – the last hiding place of persecuted people.'

'And that's where you found your jar.'

'Yes. It took us a lot of searching with the radar. Plenty of little pots and jars, and then this. Which is when the bloody helicopter landed.'

'They're having manoeuvres.'

'Why can't they stay in barracks?' he said testily.

'Well,' she said, 'we'd better open the jar. You won't be doing whatever is inside any good by marching it across country. I've got a temperature- and humidity-controlled room over at the dig.'

Connell was quiet for a moment, feeling the weight of the jar on his back.

'If there are scrolls inside, what will you do with them? Will you sell them to some rich American?'

Her voice took on a sharp edge.

'No,' he said quietly, 'although I'd want a lot of money.'

'What for?'

'A foundation. It could buy me back in.'

'Professor Connell,' she said.

'Yes,' he smiled and in the darkness she saw his teeth shine. 'Once an academic always an academic. I want to go home.'

'I understand that,' she said evenly, 'I certainly do. So let's go and open the jar.'

The room was cool and dry. Filtered air seeped gently through the vents. The jar stood on a white table, held by an archaeologist's cradle. Connell drilled a small hole, running the metal between the ochre-streaked clay plug and the side of the jar, and inserted the slim blade of an electric saw. It buzzed in his hand, sucking up the fine dust it made, and he very slowly ran the blade around the neck of the jar, cutting the plug free. As he cut he inserted small hooked wires behind him.

He came full circle, and the plug moved. He put down the drill and he and Juliana carefully lifted the plug out with the wires, putting it down on a cloth spread out on the table.

They looked inside.

Filling the bottom of the jar were scrolls, codices like old books, and a thick silt of fragments of papyrus with black writing on. On top lay a torn piece of parchment, and Connell, reaching in with a gloved hand, took it out, lying it reverently on the cloth. The sable ink stared up at them in the light.

'That's Coptic,' Juliana said, with excitement in her voice.

'Yes,' Connell whispered. He slowly read aloud.

'*They have killed us all. The Children of Jeshua are no more. I, Maria am the last of the one true faith. They search for me, they will find me soon.*

'*Here lie the words of those who sought to bring the words of Jesus to the land of Satan. Whosoever may find them, we who have died command you not to let them die with us.*

'*I see them down in the valley. I must seal the jar and bury it. They are coming. The evil ones are coming.*

'*Be there one among you that will put on the robe of glory. Be there one who will say the prayer for me. Be there one who will dance by the fire in the silver smoke as the robe of glory sings for me.*'

Connell looked at the clay plug of the jar. Gently, he touched the desperate ochre streaks, the delicate fingerprints of her hands.

'Maria,' he said. 'Her name was Maria.'

'You read Coptic really well,' Juliana said judiciously.

'Thank you. I have to. In my position I have to be able to read Greek, Latin, Aramaic, Hebrew and Coptic. Not to mention dialects various and wonderful. At a guess all the documents in the jar here are later translations into Coptic.'

'Not old Coptic – the demotic characters from the first century are missing – but well-developed standardised Coptic. Hieratic script, no corrections. Written by a master scribe.'

'Yes, it's very nice to look at, isn't it? It certainly makes it easier to read. My guess would be a translation from Aramaic made in the late third or early fourth century.'

She pointed a finger at the black script.

'I would say that part there translates as stronger than just "the evil ones". The way its framed carries an even more hideous connotation.'

'Mmm. You could be right.'

'Demons. The denizens of Hell.'

'Now it's my turn to say how well you read.'

'Oh,' she said casually, 'I should. For my doctorate I traced the development of the Sahidic dialect of the Coptic language to its origins in Thebes.'

She pointed to the scrap of parchment.

'*That's* Sahidic.'

She peered into the jar and murmured to herself for a moment before looking up at Connell.

'So's what's in there.'

'Yes, it is.'

'I'm very good at jigsaw puzzles,' she said artlessly.

He was puzzled.

'You are?'

'I've always liked them. I can remember Granny coming to stay, when I was about six, and I was doing one on the kitchen table – it was raining, and we couldn't go out to play. Granny came in to sit in the window seat. My sister Mary came by and she stopped her. "Go ask your sister," she said, "if she knows what day it is." And she took out her rosary.'

Green eyes flashed up at Connell.

'It was Sunday,' she said. 'You were not to take pleasure in anything but the Lord on Sunday. I was brought up as a Catholic, but then, I suppose, so were you.'

'I wasn't, actually. I was brought up by my aunt, who married a divorced man, and wouldn't go to church at all because the vicar refused to perform the service with her there.'

She looked intently over the jar at him.

'So what does someone who's good at jigsaw puzzles, was trained in the Catholic faith and is totally fluent in the Sahidic dialect mean to you, Connell?'

She pointed at the jar.

'At a guess there must be two or three thousand fragments in there. Who are you going to have piece them together? You'll want the codices and scrolls, won't you?'

'*You* want to do them?'

'I challenge you to get anyone better.'

He waved a hand about him.

'What about this dig here?'

'Dead,' she said bitterly. 'A minor temple of the god Amun. Cleared clean by robbers a very long time ago. It all looked so good when he started, too.'

She smiled pleasantly.

'But it leaves me free for alternative work.'

'You know that I got into trouble,' he said slowly. 'I've been helping George Abercrombie for ten years or more, identifying and translating, authenticating various texts and scrolls that appear in the underground trade. Mostly from the Dead Sea area and Jerusalem. The Bedouin rent the land when they find a promising site and put up one of their very large black tents over it. Then they excavate. Some of what they find, I would authenticate. It never gets into the "official" world of archaeology and biblical scholarship, you know. A lot gets sold to private collectors and investors. I identified a letter by Simeon bar Kochba, the Son of the Star, the last great Jewish warlord a year or so back. I haven't seen it come up anywhere official.

'This, though, looks like it is in a different class. If it is, there's bound to be some kind of stink, when we come out in public with it. If it's good enough, though . . .'

He looked hungrily at the jar.

'We need to make photographs of everything to work from and keep the originals safe in a temperature- and humidity-controlled environment. George has such a room in Oxford. He has all the photographic equipment there. Let's get them home. Then we can start work.'

Juliana was peering intently into the jar, she reached out and adjusted a lamp to shine down into it, and suddenly the thick silt of papyrus and parchment sparkled with lights.

'Connell, look,' she said excitedly. 'The parchment, the last thing Maria wrote, she put it on top of something else.'

She reached inside with slim fingers, and drew out a tiny gold bell. Still attached to it were wisps of ancient cloth, as fine as a spider's web. In the light, they shimmered like the reflection of the sky in a lake, like the stars in the heavens. The tiny bell rang softly in her fingers, a pure, shining note.

'Oh, it's beautiful,' she whispered.

Connell could see hundreds of tiny bells, gold and silver, lying there.

'The robe of glory,' he said softly.

2

Oxford

Outside in the narrow, ancient road, bounded by the high walls of the college, the old car stood parked, its tall radiator and curving wings symbols of an earlier age. Its reflection sparkled in the wood-framed window where leather-bound books stood awaiting a buyer. Out of sight in a back room, Connell stood filing piles of large, high-resolution photographs. As he worked, one caught his eye and he held it up to the light. He sat down, studying the close-knit lines of cursive script intently. Fumbling in his jacket for a pen and, pulling paper towards him, he began to make notes.

'Here are those zealous for the Law,' said the priest. 'They are the *zelotai*, is this not their house?'

The crowd below him, dressed in their woollen tunics, murmured in agreement. The sun was rising over the temple wall, casting long shadows over the great paving slabs of ochre stone. Smoke was on the air, and the smell of charring flesh from the altar where the sacrifices were made.

'Do they not come from the wilderness, like the sons of Mattathias Maccabeus?' said Zaddik, the Just. 'Are they not purified, are they not undefiled, as they were. When the sons of Mattathias captured this temple, they made it pure, they cleansed it of its pagan defilement.'

Zaddik, the Just, indicated the high walls of the courtyard about them. Wisps of incense were tickling their nostrils from the central building at his back.

'This is not the temple of Maccabeans, the priests and kings of Israel made clean. This is what was made by another, by one who was not zealous for the Law, as we are. He was called Herod, he slaughtered those of the line of Mattathias, and the unclean ones called him King. The Zaddikim, the righteous ones he killed, those who now infest this holy place were put here by him, corrupt, unclean, and without zeal.'

The people could hear the chinking of coins, the steady accumulation of wealth on the tables of the money-changers as men bought favour from their god, and the smoke rose from the brands under the altar. Their faces grew hard and angry.

'Once again the Children of Israel suffer under the tyranny of pagans. Once Egypt, now Rome. How can this be?'

Zaddik looked over the men and women beneath him. He held out his arms and the long linen sleeves of his rainment fell down like wings.

'The *zelotai* have failed. It must be that the Law is not enough. It must be that the Children of Israel have forgotten their true worship. Where were we led astray? Who commanded us to build this – '

In his back room, Connell peered intently at the photograph, taking a magnifying glass in an attempt to decipher the blurred and flaked image over sixteen hundred years old. He looked up as a board creaked, and saw Abercrombie coming in from the front of the shop, dressed in a tweed hacking jacket and cavalry twill trousers.

'You're on to something,' he said, and smiled. He sat down in a battered armchair, crossing his worn tan brogues. Through

the open window came the cries of some undergraduates bounding off towards the pub. Connell pushed back his chair and
began to stride about the little room, deftly avoiding the small
hills of manuscripts, the copses of books and essays.

'It *is* George, it is. It's a new sect, I know it,' he said, the
words tumbling out. 'Whoever they were, they *knew*. They
were close to the real action.'

He paused at the desk, picking up the big oblong photographs and looking thirstily at them again.

'The High Priest is preaching to a group of his followers in
the Jerusalem Temple. I place this at perhaps Anno Domini
66. He is wearing the linen robes and mitre of the high priest,
but he is not Caiaphas, the Herodlian Sadducee. He is called
Zaddik, meaning the Just, or the Righteous. And I know who
he is, George.'

'Who?' the antiquarian asked quietly.

'He has to be James, the sibling of Jesus – "the Lord's
brother", to quote Acts. The acknowledged leader of the community in Jerusalem – this is in the few years after the crucifixion of Jesus – which becomes known to a later tradition as
the "Early Church".'

'That's one of his texts?' George asked, indicating the small
sheaf of photographs.

'*No.*' Connell said gleefully. 'He is preaching. If he is the
James that we think of – leader of the Jerusalem church – he
ought to be a hard-line exponent of Zeal for the Law, a
descendant of the Maccabees, messianic, rigorous, fundamen-
talist and xenophobic, the agent of Yahweh, whipping up hatred
against the corrupt Herodian administration, its puppet priests
and – by implication – the ultimate authority, the occupying
pagan power of Rome.'

Connell frowned, looking back again at the photograph.

'There's something very funny about this, George. Zaddik

seems to be questioning the *concept* of the Law itself. I wish this section wasn't so faded, I'm going to have to do some work on the original to try and bring it up. And there's something else. They are in the temple. Women and men mixed, and yet I think it's the men's court, which doesn't fit with the prohibitions at all. In there, foreigners, women and dogs have already been excluded.'

He looked up, his eyes glittering.

'We're on to something, George, we're definitely on to something.'

Boards creaked outside, and Abercrombie peered around some books.

'Aha,' he said, 'an American. Let me go and relieve him of some dollars while you find out what Zaddik is up to.'

He went out and Connell bent over his text again.

'He will pronounce it good when we pull you into pieces!'

The heavy high doors of the gate in the wall crashed back as a man came swaggering in, his followers about him like a swarm. Smoke streamed from a long brand of wood he had taken from the fire.

'There is the enemy!' cried Zaddik. 'Saul the Liar, Saul of the one ear is amongst us.'

'God does not want you here with your jabbering,' Saul sneered. His followers were streaming in, outnumbering the worshippers about Zaddik. He wore a fine-woven white tunic with red markings, charcoal stained it where the brand rested on his shoulder. His guards were about him with drawn swords and spears.

'We have priests enough here,' he said.

'We need no priests,' Zaddik said clearly.

Saul looked about him, his eyes glittering.

'Well, why do we wait?' he cried, and the young toughs with him grinned. 'Are we hesitating?'

The worshippers were moving across the courtyard, and up the steps.

'No!' he cried. 'Let us lay our hands on them.'

He swung the great brand of wood and the flames crackled. Blood fountained from a man's skull and he screamed. Saul laid about him, yelling with excitement, his guards striking out with their swords, and the worshippers ran about the courtyard like rats in a pen. Saul saw Zaddik scrambling up the steps, the woman that was with him was fighting with her sword to remain close to him. He threw his branch of wood at her. She fell, and Saul ran after Zaddik, snatching a spear from his bodyguard. The mitre he had cast aside lay burning on the step.

Saul saw him clear, he cast the spear up at Zaddik, catching him in the side. Zaddik fell and as his guards held the steps Saul ran up, drawing his sword. He struck at Zaddik, and the woman who had been with Zaddik hewed at his guards and he heard them scream. Then he ran, the woman after him, her sword running red to the hilt with blood.

'*Satan!*' she screamed. 'I see you at last.'

Connell sat at the table deep in thought. The tinkling of the bell brought him back to the present, the Abercrombie returned.

'Well?' he said eagerly.

'All right. I still can't make out the middle section. But towards the end of Zaddik's peroration a man bursts in on them, with superior numbers of followers. He starts a full-scale riot, flailing about him with a great burning brand of wood he has pulled out of the altar fire. A lot of blood is shed, and the man, whose name is Saul, attacks Zaddik, with spear and sword.'

Connell reached out and pulled another photograph to him.

'This text was next to the one I'm reading. If it follows on, then James – Zaddik – is not dead. It says so here, in this last passage. His followers carried him away to his house in Jerusalem, and before dawn the next day off to Jericho, to recover from his wounds. The choice of Jericho is significant. Only a few miles from Qumran, the Essene stronghold where the Dead Sea Scrolls were found. We know that, broadly speaking, those who are zealous for the Law are the same as the Essenes, the Zealots, the Nazarenes. They all share the same religious and political impetus that suffuses the Holy Land at this time. James has gone to get help from his fellows, the Essenes, probably the best healers of their day. And here's more proof, and the identity of the man, Saul.'

Connell flipped deftly through the photographs. From the street below came the metallic rolling of beer barrels heading to the college bar.

'Here it is.' "After three days one of the brethren came to the followers of James from Gamaliel, bringing secret tidings that Saul the enemy, who hated the true Jesus all his life, had received a commission from Caiaphas, the chief priest, that he should arrest all those who had known Jesus, and who were zealous for the Law, and should go to Damascus with his letters . . .'"

Connell's eyes glittered in delight.

'There! Who was called Saul, but changed his name on the road to Damascus, where he was travelling with arrest warrants?'

'Paul,' said Abercrombie. 'It supports your contention that "Damascus" is the code-name for Qumran.'

'It has to be! Saul of Tarsus, who become Paul, is, even on

the basis of what we are shown in the New Testament, the enforcer, the assassin of the high priest. He admits himself that he had persecuted his victims "to death". Caiaphas sends him to "Damascus" to do his business. *He cannot possibly be going to Syria.* Syria is a separate Roman province, governed by a Roman legate, who will react very negatively, indeed, very brutally, to any attempt by a foreign priest to interfere in his affairs by sending assassination squads to his province. Within *Palestine*, however, Caiaphas's writ runs. "Damascus" is the Essene community in Qumran, on the Dead Sea. It is on the way there that Saul has his vision and becomes Paul. It is in Qumran that Paul joins the Essenes, spending the three years there that was mandatory probation and training.'

The antiquarian was frowning slightly. 'What was that phrase about hating Jesus?'

Connell picked up the photograph with its black, reed-nib writing.

'They're talking about Saul. They have an agent within the temple, and he reports to them that: "Saul the enemy, who hated the true Jesus all his life, had received a commission from Caiaphas, the chief priest." To go to "Damascus", on the road to which he suffers his famous conversion.'

'A peculiar way of putting it, isn't it?' George queried. 'To say: who hated the true Jesus *all his life.*'

'I assume that the author of the text means all his life, *as Saul.*' Connell said thoughtfully. 'It's admitted, even in Acts, that as Saul, he "worked for the total destruction of the Church". As *Paul*, of course, he becomes a new man.'

So what is the significance of this text?' George asked quietly.

'It's significant on its own, and most certainly as a part of a whole corpus of knowledge, which is what I suspect it is. The Acts of the Apostles has Saul engineering an attack on the Early Church which results in the death of Stephen – Acts

9.21. Rather improbably, he watches over the clothes of those who stone Stephen. What this text is – in my opinion – is the true story. Stephen is an invented figure, created to disguise the fact that Saul, who becomes Paul, in fact attacked James, "the Lord's brother", leader of the Early Church. Acts simply cannot admit that, given Paul's later pivotal role in Christianity.'

Connell reached out, picking up the first photograph.

'We're on to it, George,' he said triumphantly. 'But who is this? "The woman that was with Zaddik." He appears to have had a woman bodyguard of some description. She has a sword, and she pursues Saul with it after the attack. It must be there somewhere, what happens. I must find out . . .'

'How are you going to tackle it?' Abercrombie said in a businesslike fashion.

'I've got a room set up at my place over at Hook Norton. Two long tables we can work at. Juliana Berridge is coming up next week. She has a flat in Oxford, she's going to drive out every day. I'm going to handle the texts, she's going to do the fragments.'

'Do you know where you're going to start?'

'With a whole codex. I've identified one. There's something interesting about these texts, from what I can see, George. There's women in them.'

Abercrombie raised an interrogatory eyebrow.

'*Women*. In positions of power. "Let the woman learn in silence with all subjection. But I suffer not a woman to teach nor to usurp authority over the man, but to be in silence." Who wrote that, now? Paul himself, it's I Timothy. And also, the women must "keep silence in the churches: for it is not permitted unto them to speak; but they are to be commanded to be under obedience, as also saith the law. And if they will learn anything, let them ask their husbands at home: for it is a shame for women to speak in the church." Corinthians, that one. Those who ran the early Catholic Church certainly found texts like that useful. Once the notion that it was only possible for the people to worship the Christian God through the office of the Catholic Church's own servants – its bishops and priests – was put forward as dogma then women had only one place to be. Except as worshippers, women were shut out of the Church for nearly two thousand years.

'But that was in the Catholic Church. Which was, for some three centuries, only one – albeit an increasingly powerful one – of hundreds, if not thousands of Jesus-based cults. What I think we have is the devotional library of one of those cults. What we're reading is their story. *Their* knowledge of Jesus. And women seem to have been far more important in this sect than the Catholics would allow. Why? Were women more important in the religious organisation of the living Jesus too?'

'Have you started reading your codex?'

'Yes. It's called the Gospel of Maria. It's the story of a young girl – maybe thirteen – in Antioch. About the year sixty two – the first century. In Rome, the Emperor is Nero.'

3

Antioch, A.D. 62

The *horologium ex aqua* gave a throaty whistle as it registered the hour and its float threw a pebble into the waiting dish with a musical note. It was sufficient to wake Maria, in the small bedroom off the open *peristyle* of the villa. A little light leaked around the edge of the heavy leather curtain across the entrance, whether from the last of the moon or the approaching dawn she was not sure. The vibration of the clock disturbed the fish in the pool, she heard the swirl of water as one took an insect and then it was quiet. Her mother always kept fish. The fish and the Fisherman, she explained, were the same. Quiet, cold, unseen. Deadly.

She was hungry. She slipped silently from underneath the *lodix*, moving gracefully in the dim light. Dancing masters had trained her from an infant, she could dance before a king. Her tunic was at the end of the bed and she pulled it over her head. They were always ready, her mother, her brother and she.

She was completely silent as she moved in the room, her dancer's feet kissing the cold tiles. Mary her mother had taught her to walk along a line of upturned jars without making a sound. When she failed she had been punished, and she learned the grace of a cat.

She slid around the leather curtain. The open *peristyle* was lit by the dim light of the young moon, it was not yet dawn.

The marble tiles were damp with dew under her feet. Light glinted faintly on the surface of the pool, it was smooth. The fish moved when they felt vibrations from outside, the upturned jars had been arranged in a circle about their pool. If the water swirled as she made her way about them she had felt the slap of her mother's thong.

Her mother loved her. The world was cruel, it would do terrible things to her if she could not master the arts of survival.

She slipped through the darkness towards the kitchen, passing the bedroom where her mother and brother slept. She could hear Jeshua snoring softly. She slept as a servant would, in the little room outside. When they went out, she acted in the manner of a servant, not a daughter or sister. Mary their mother had explained that it was to be so, and the two children were used to special rules, for they were not as others were.

In the kitchen a medley of scents tickled her nostrils – fading, cold charcoal from the cook's fire, chopped parsley and crushed rosemary. Garlic. The salty tang from the empty mussel shells. The smell of the honey used to sweeten the wine.

Her mouth was watering. Her nose guided her to the dish of mutton and she lifted the lid. She quickly cut off some slices and speared them on the blade of her knife. Then she went back outside into the *peristyle*. Sosias the cook lay sleeping, he would not miss the meat.

It was quiet, there in the open centre of the villa, which sat in the best part of the city. Down towards the sea, where the fabulous marble street ran straight as a sword blade for two miles, there was noise day and night, of people buying and people selling, people drinking and eating, worshipping and taking their pleasure, delivering and taking away, building and demolishing again. You could have anything you wanted in Antioch. Any pleasure, any vice. Any contact, any information. If it was not there it was because it did not exist.

They lived half a mile from the bustle. Walled, gardened grounds surrounded the villa. *Rus in urbs*, her mother would say, with that peculiar, twisted smile on her face that came whenever she spoke Latin. Their two great wolfhounds had the gardens for their own at night.

The moon came out from behind a cloud and its light glittered on the ripples of the pool. The fish were moving.

She frowned, the last piece of meat half-way between her dagger and her mouth. Then she slipped along by the wall, where the shadows were deep. The *peristyle* was open to the air, all the other covered rooms led off it. The atrium led to the vestibule that guarded the main door. There by the wall was the household shrine. It was the *lararium*, where Romans would keep the collection of household gods that kept hearth and home safe. The shrine had a platform for the ceremonial libations, bowls for the collection of blood, a concealed brazier for the offering of sacrifice.

Theirs lay empty and dusty. Her mother would not have it cleaned. Their deities could not be seen.

A faint light illuminated the atrium. It came from the vestibule, where Samuel the freedman sat at guard in the night hours. She crept forward.

He sat in the big, armed chair. A bronze lamp was burning on a shelf next to him. It was in the shape of a dolphin, and nearby was a small jar of oil for its replenishment.

He sat still, his head upon his chest, his broad-bladed spear in his hand. He was asleep. She felt her mother's flare of anger and stepped forward to strike him awake.

The floor was wet and sticky. She glanced down at the mosaic. It was decorated with a very realistic representation of a fierce dog. *Cave canem* was the message, beware of the dog.

She stood on his savage face, and it was blotted out. A cold breeze was tickling her ankles, the great door with its heavy lock and chain stood ajar. She was standing in Samuel's blood.

She felt a shriek rising up from within her and bit down on her hand. Her breath snorted in terror. Samuel held his spear in a stiffening grasp, she saw the rent in his throat, smelled the spreading gore. In the *peristyle*, a fish swirled in the pool. She whirled, turning back into the house.

Men moved through the shadows. They were outside the bedroom with its curtain of leather, their heads cocked, listening. They could hear Jeshua's light snore. A cloud scudded past the moon and in the fresh light savage metal glistened in their hands. A glow suddenly lit cupped hands, she heard a man blow on the coal and a torch of twisted faggots burst into flame.

They frightened naughty children with tales of the dark monster who would come for them if they were not good. She had always tried to be good. She could run around a ring of upturned jars and the fish would not move.

He had come anyway. In the flare of the torch she saw the face of the Fisherman.

She opened her mouth to scream a warning. On a harsh bellow of command, the men rushed forward. She saw the interior of the bedroom splash yellow with light, heard shouting, a curse, a cut-off scream. She grabbed the spear from Samuel's fixed hand, and as they dragged her mother and brother from the bedroom, she hid inside the alcove of the *lararium*. It was musty in there, she disturbed the ash of dead sacrifices.

Blood was streaming down her mother Mary's face, blackening her tunic. One of the men was clutching his shoulder, seeking to stem the flow from a wound. Her mother slept with a *sica* under the hard pillow. Another man held Jeshua, twisting his arms behind him.

The Fisherman howled in triumph, holding the crackling torch high.

'We have you, Magdalene! Blasphemer!'

His voice was harsh and rough, uneducated, as her mother had always said. He capered in ecstasy, the torch spitting glowing fragments into the air.

In the darkness of the alcove, she felt about her. A brick in the fire of the altar shifted slightly in her head. It shifted slightly. A weapon, a missile. She was trained, she could use a sling. Her slim fingers eased it out. There was something behind it. A leather bag, tied with a drawstring. Without thinking, she slipped it about her neck and let it fall inside her tunic. She gripped the brick in one hand, the spear in the other, and crept out of the dark hole.

Mary stood up straight, the blood still spilling down her face.

'You shall not harm the King,' she said, and her voice rang from the walls. Maria slipped along the wall in the gloom, on her silent dancer's feet.

'The King is Almighty God!' the Fisherman bellowed. Above the open *peristyle*, the sky was lightening.

'He is coming,' the man crooned. 'He is coming to see his work done.'

'You were ever stupid,' Mary said contemptuously. The man, whose hair and ragged beard were streaked with grey, snarled, hitting her with the torch, and she screamed in pain as her hair blazed. Jeshua struggled in the grip on the man holding him and in the commotion, Maria flitted along the wall, behind the plants.

The Fisherman indicated to the two henchmen holding Mary.

'Let us be quick about it,' he ordered. 'Let Mary leave us, for women are not worthy of life. Then we shall attend to the bastard whelp.'

They bent her over a stone bench, face up, quickly lashing her hands to it. Behind them, where the *peristyle* walls fell open towards the East, the sky was pale.

The Fisherman was looking at the approaching dawn.

'She did not believe in you, Lord,' he howled.

Her mother spoke, through the blood that ran from her mouth.

'Who betrayed him?' she said viciously, and spat, spraying his white tunic with blood.

There was a knife in his hand, a strange, shining weapon with a hooked blade. He trembled, and it was with joy.

'He comes, he comes.'

Maria heard her mother's voice again.

'It's cold,' she said, 'so cold. Your master is here, Fisherman.'

They were all staring at the dawn. The pillars, the trellises on which the plants climbed were in her way. She saw the knife in the Fisherman's hand and knew she was too late.

The first ray of the rising sun fell into the *peristyle*.

'*The unbeliever is yours.*'

She stood, and hurled the spear. The blade flashed and blood spurted from her mother's throat.

The spear impaled the man holding Jeshua, spitting him. She flung the brick at the Fisherman and he howled as it smacked him in the head. Maria ran into the uproar, grabbing her brother, and they fled.

At the wall she bent over to make a step for Jeshua and he reached down to help pull her up. She looked back – one of the younger men was coming after them. They jumped down into the lane. There people were beginning to move in the early light, Greeks and Romans, Phrygians and Jews, the air was filled with the squeak of cart axles, the braying of donkeys and flung curses as they pushed their way through.

By a market stall she crouched down, pulling Jeshua to her, looking back the way they had come. He was not there. Against the eggshell-blue sky a pillar of smoke was rising, black and roiling. Somehow she understood that the villa had become both altar and pyre, that her mother burned in the smoke rising towards the sky. The breath was heaving in their chests, Jeshua's eyes were wide and blank with shock.

'Come,' she urged, 'we have to get away.'

He got up, obeying her, and they slipped across the great arrow-straight strip of marble, shining like a sword-blade in the light all the way to the Circus, set with shops and bazaars, stalls and bars. She went along a columned arcade, the rising sun at her back.

'*There! There they are.*'

The rough Hebrew attracted little attention in a city where most spoke Greek. In a city where you could get anything, a running young couple pursued by determined men attracted little notice either. Runaway slaves; two of the thousands of *hetarii*, boys and girls, available for a man's pleasure, and ready to pick his purse; sneakthieves. They watched indifferently, the traders, the whores, the men coming out of the Venusian bars into the light of day with stale wine in their throats.

All it took was a knife between the ribs to kill a man in a crowd, she knew.

'*Get them.*'

The smell of the sea hit her, she pushed Jeshua towards it and they ran through the gate where the muleteers and porters were moving between the great warehouses, shifting the multitude of goods that poured into the great city through its port. She dodged round a wagonload of pepper and ginger from

Arabia, colliding with a stevedore carrying tallow. A babel of curses followed them as their pursuers also knocked into the workmen unloading and storing the goods of the ships at the wharf.

One was moving, its square sail bellying out, the helmsman at the quarter-rudders, the bands off, a sailor blowing the horn from the bow to alert those on the surface of the water to the passage of the ship. They were behind, she could hear their panting breath at her shoulder, feel a brushing hand grabbing at her tunic.

'*Jump for it, Jeshua,*' she yelled, and at full tilt she let herself drop, right under the pounding feet of the men. She felt the impact of their *caligae*, heard the thump and curse as they went down, and then she was up again, sprinting for the dockside.

She saw Jeshua leap, flying over the water, saw him land on the great wooden rubbing strake that ran around the hull, clinging on for his life, the breath knocked out of him. The wharf was upon her, she took off at full speed, her hands reaching for the retreating ship. She landed with a crash next to Jeshua.

From behind, she heard a curse, a sudden grunt of effort. The air hissed, there was a thump and her brother suddenly cried out. The spear transfixed him, he began to slip from the hull to the dirty, swilling water beneath, and she grabbed him with one hand.

The helmsman was conning the big grain-carrier out into the channel. As it gathered way the sea began to foam into a hissing bone in its teeth.

'*Help me.*'

On the quay, the two men turned, running, vanishing into the crowd.

Blood ran scarlet down the side of the ship, like sacrifice.

4

Oxford

'I have a name for them,' said Juliana. Connell put down a half tankard of Hook Norton bitter on the wooden table in front of her, and she picked it up. He raised his pint.

'Cheers,' he said. 'Who?'

She carefully wiped a small moustache of creamy foam from her lip. Across the welt-high green grass a punt was gliding along the river. A girl giggled.

'The sect. You were right. What we have is a part of what must be an extensive devotional library. Some larger fragments I have fit together – the grain of the papyrus is different, they were easy to spot. I can date the epistle, because Telesphorus is Bishop of Rome. We are in the 130s.'

'*Fantastic!*' Connell took a celebratory swallow of the nutty beer. 'What do they call themselves?'

'Jeshua's Children.'

'Ah-*ha*. So we have the supposition that the two, brother and sister, Maria and Jeshua, succeeded in their escape to Rome, and there founded one of the many Jesus-based cults. But I am running on ahead, I'll have to see. It'll be interesting to know whether it is Jeshua the son or Jeshua – Joshua's the Hebrew, Jesus is Greek, but it's the same name – that they mean.'

'Jeshua the son of whom?' she asked, acutely.

'Ah, that's it, isn't it?' Connell said gleefully. 'What we have

33

in the first part of the codex is confirmation of the terrible hatred that existed between Peter the fisherman – St Peter – and Mary the Magdalene. There is plenty of evidence in the scrolls and the Nag Hammadi codices to show that it was very real. Mary feared Peter and, we now see, with reason. She is in hiding in Antioch, and somehow Peter finds her and murders her – ritually, calling her an unbeliever. May we take it from what she says that she was the wife of Jesus? I think we can, given all the other evidence that supports that contention. But what of the children? Her son, Jeshua, she calls "the King". The "King" of Israel? Is Mary herself a Jewish aristocrat? Is her husband Jesus – if the role of the Essenes is what we think it is – descended from the Davidic line.'

'But hold on a minute,' Juliana objected. 'We're dating the codex at sixty two. Nero is Emperor. The boy Jeshua is no more than nine or ten. With Jesus crucified in thirty-six he really can't be the son of Jesus.'

'Not unless Jesus didn't die on the cross,' Connell said quietly. He held up his hand as she opened her mouth to object.

'No, really. All the circumstances surrounding the crucifixion are suspicious, even in the Gospels which were written, you'll recall, during and after the Jewish revolt of A.D. 68 to 74, when organised Judaism had effectively ceased to exist.'

He tipped back his glass.

'Another, in a minute? I'll get some sandwiches. Sunday is a day of rest, after all. It didn't used to be, the sabbath was Saturday, in line with Judaism, but the Catholic bishops changed it to oblige Constantine back in 321. Constantine worshipped the sun, Sol Invictus, but in the interests of unity didn't mind Mithras and Jesus Christ joining in – that's why Jesus has a halo on stained-glass windows, it's the sun of Sol Invictus and Mithras.'

'Frank, do you know what an iconoclast is?' Juliana asked dryly.

'Certainly,' Connell said unabashedly, and grinned, 'someone like me. Another beer? A couple of rounds of beef? Brown bread?'

'Brown bread,' she said, 'and a half.'

He came back from the old pub, threading his way through the tourists and undergraduates, and unloaded a tray. They busied themselves with salt, mustard and horseradish and nibbled the cress and celery garnish.

'The crucifixion,' she said.

'Right,' Connell mumbled, through a mouthful of sandwich. 'Even on the evidence of the Gospels – which are slanted, politically motivated accounts, at best – the story is suspicious. Firstly, it wasn't a public affair. It was witnessed from "afar off" – Luke 23:49. Now, *where?* "In the place where he was crucified there was a garden; and in the garden a new sepulchre, wherein was never man yet laid." – John 19:41. A private garden and a private tomb. We even know whose it was. Matthew 27:60 tells us it belonged to Joseph of Arimathea, a rich man and a secret disciple of Jesus. And a friend of Pontius Pilate, who was himself corrupt and susceptible to bribes. As we may surmise, for once Jesus is pronounced "dead", Pontius Pilate expresses his amazement at the rapidity of that death – crucified men usually lasted for some days, not an hour or two – but then grants the body to Joseph of Arimathea! Totally, flagrantly against the Roman Law! Relatives of crucified men were *never* allowed the body, which was left up there for the birds to peck at. Crucifixion was for the enemies of the Roman Empire, it was meant to be horrible, even after death.

'So, yes, I think that everything points to a stage-managed affair which not only saved the life of Jesus, but made real the old Testament prophecies of a Messiah, thus keeping going whatever complex political stratagems were in motion at the time. And so the boy Jeshua, brother of Maria and son of Mary the Magdalene could easily have been the son of Jesus, in my book. I see Mary Magdelene as a prime mover, a devious and capable political operator. However, whatever plans she may have had seem to have been halted by Peter in Antioch, since, as we see, he murders her.'

'I can see why the boy is so important – his sister throws the spear to save *him*, not her mother, on Mary's own specific instructions. Jeshua is the heir to the throne. But why the sister? It's made clear that Maria is equally important. Mary has taken the trouble to hide her away, if you like. She is presented in public as a servant – clearly Mary is fearful of Peter and those like him. She cannot hide the son, for his status must be known, but she hides the girl from harm.'

'I know,' said Connell, 'and I don't yet know why.'

'Why does Peter hate Mary so much?'

'While Jesus is alive, sheer jealousy? In the Nag Hammadi Gnostic gospels it is suggested that Jesus raises Mary up to be foremost amongst his disciples – and furthermore, kisses her often upon the mouth! Peter is a pretty unattractive character – narrow-minded, a religious bigot, prone to violence – he's a Zealot – and undoubtedly what they would now call a male chauvinist pig. He would see a woman's role as being *kinder* and *kuche*, child-bearing and menial tasks for men. Mary was most probably beautiful, she was educated, she was an aristocrat and Jesus gave her status above the others. Peter would have loathed her. And *afterwards*, after the crucifixion, and after Jesus rises from the dead – if that's what he did – you may have had this really elemental clash between the two sectors that made up Jesus's political movement in his lifetime. Firstly, the small group of prime movers, the real operators, whose objective is to get Jesus to the throne of Israel. Perhaps Mary is one of these. Secondly, the rank and file, the *lumpenproletariat* whose support they require, and who must – and did – believe that Jesus was the Messiah, come to deliver the people of Israel from their bondage. Peter is one of the foremost amongst these, he is one of the sergeants.

'Now we know that the political campaign of Jesus came badly unstuck. At which point the interests of the two factions become increasingly divergent. If this theory is correct, then for Mary and perhaps a small group of advisers, the important thing is to keep the royal bloodline intact. This has been the obsession of noble and royal families forever. But for those who believed in the ideology of Jesus, in his message, the important thing is to keep his teaching alive, and for them, the bloodline is at most irrelevant, and at worst, a threat. Mary Magdalene is preparing her son Jeshua for the throne of Israel. Perhaps he was a pretender, perhaps he wasn't. But either way, she is threatening the movement of the Messiah. As I say, Peter was a man of narrow but clear vision, a man used to solving problems by violence. And, it seems, he did. Except, of course, he didn't manage to kill the offspring, because we have your Jeshua's Children some seventy years later.'

Connell began dabbing crumbs and fragments of beef up with a horseradish-sticky finger. He glanced up.

'You're not looking happy about them,' he observed.

'They *hate* each other!' she burst out.

'Who do?'

'The early Catholics and Jeshua's Children. They not only say the vilest things about each other, they spy on each other, they actually come to blows!'

'They did, you know,' Connell observed. 'There were a great number of Jesus-based sects in the early centuries and they were all in competition with each other. Pagans were pagans, but someone who believed in a different version of Christ was there to be hated with a will.'

'I was brought up to believe that the Early Church was composed of good, Christian people,' she said quietly. 'People who shared their belongings, who helped each other, whose rule for life was *Agape*, which meant "love".'

She looked down at the dark clover, where polished brown honey-bees were tending the cones of white flowers.

'They told me that they all worked for good in a wicked world, just like those bees work, making honey. It was a beautiful image. I don't much like what I'm reading.'

'Many of the sects did just that. And would bury the dead decently and say prayers – which brought adherents in an age when if you couldn't afford a proper burial the corpse was taken off by the refuse collectors. But sect still hated sect.'

Across the meadow came the sound of church bells ringing a peal.

'The winners,' said Connell. 'Survival of the fittest.'

'But Jeshua's Children really hate the Catholics. Paul is called the Wicked Priest, the Christ-Killer.'

'A nice piece of symbolism. Paul *did* hijack the early Christian movement, and turned it into something entirely different that could no longer accommodate those, like James, the brother of Jesus, who were zealous for the Law. In that sense Paul did kill the original message of Christ. Perhaps Jeshua's Children saw themselves as keepers of the flame.'

He tipped back his tankard.

'Have you had enough? Come on then, I want to read your text. I'm in the mood for a bit of early priest-bashing.'

'Don't joke about it,' she said soberly.

'Let's see. Telesphorus, one of the very early bishops of Rome. A Pope, if you like, although they didn't use the title then. The second Jewish Revolution is either in progress or over.'

'Over,' she said. 'Telesphorus is gloating over what has happened to them.'

Her face looked as though she had swallowed something bitter.

'He shouldn't have,' she said.

'You're judging him – nearly two thousand years ago – by the standards of today. And *your* standards at that,' Connell said reprovingly. 'That's not professional. You wouldn't do that to one of your pharaohs, would you?'

'No, of course not. But it just isn't seemly.'

'Because of God? If the history of organised religion is anything to go by, there is nothing God likes better than dancing on the bloody corpses of his enemies, and howling with triumph as he does so.'

'Don't.'

They walked across the grass to where the old car stood parked. She looked at its huge, flowing form with puzzled amusement.

'Why can't you have a car like everyone else, Frank?'

'I'm a historian. Some people are musicians, or poets, or artists. They live what they do. I live what I do.'

He pointed to the gleaming form with pride.

'Restored by me, too. That's a Jaguar Mark IX. What strikes you about it from a historical point of view?'

'I don't know,' she said. 'It's an antique that smells nice when you get into it.'

'It's *imperial!* It's an updated Mark VII, and it was designed in the early 1950s, when Great Britain was still an imperial power. Look at that radiator grille, it's columned and fluted, it's the direct kin of the great buildings of empire. It's high and mighty, ornamented with grandeur. What did Jaguar make after that? The 3.4 Marks 1 and 2, which were rounded and svelte, and not imperial at all. The XK120 was imperial, the E-type wasn't. Because the Empire was gone by then.'

'You could have a modern car,' she suggested mischievously. 'They do fifty to the gallon and park on a shoebox.'

'Bleak and soulless,' he said dismissively. 'Like the age. It was something to see a Mark IX rumbling by. Now everyone has a tin box to go about in, like a mobile prison, and there are so many of them we all get gassed.'

He reached in his pockets for a cigar.

'You should talk,' she said.

'I'm a historian,' he said breezily. 'History is all about inconsistency and prejudice.'

From the church the pealing bells showered clear notes over them as he opened the door.

'Want to go?' he said, smiling. 'Have a quick prayer?'

'That's an Anglican church. Anyhow, I've already been to Mass.'

He was surprised.

'You actually go?'

'Don't sound so incredulous. Yes, I believe in God. I nearly became a nun, you know, when I was younger. Then I went to Oxford instead. But I go to worship in church. You ought to go too. You can't just believe in Frank Connell.'

'Believe in God?' he mused. 'But which one? That arid stretch of hot rocks gave birth to three, and they all hate each other. The place has been soaked in blood for millennia. I'll stick with Frank Connell. I'm fairly harmless. Telesphorus, now, he was an activist, he believed in God – *his* God, of course, not anyone else's. Not that it did him any good, he came to a sticky end, all right.'

Anno Domini

Rome, A.D. September 135

The light that leaked through the transparent curtain of the litter was sufficient to see one's companion, but if Claudius the priest had not seen the cinnamon and cassia anointing Telesphorus's greying hair with youth he could have smelled it. It was not unpleasant, it tickled his nostrils and kept the smell of sweat away as the *cursores* beneath bore them through the crowded streets. Although it was still early, the populace of the city was about, thronging the *viae* and *vici*. It was a festival day.

The two, the Bishop of Rome and his priest, wore their *amictae*, lighter and easier than the toga to put on. They were in plain white, but as the litter slowed and halted, swaying as the slaves put it down, and Telesphorus pulled back the curtain, a blaze of colour confronted them. Women dazzled and shimmered like peacocks in their brilliantly embroidered *stola* tunics and *palla* cloaks, dyed every shade of the rainbow with saffron and reseda, woad for brilliant blue, madder and archil for scarlet and purple. Their cloaks and shawls and mantles were pinned with glittering brooches of silver and gold, their wrists a-clink with bracelets of bronze and bone, their throats adorned with necklaces of bead, glass, coral and amber, jet, ivory and shell.

The shimmering women and their consorts and companions were overshadowed by the massive walls of the vast amphitheatre towering above them. Its doors were open and they were hurrying inside. Telesphorus looked about him with twinkling eyes, in high good humour.

'Come, Claudius, we don't want to miss the parade.'

They left the slaves sitting by the litter. The brightly painted stone pillars and arches of the amphitheatre housed a multitude of shops and taverns, handy for the hungry and thirsty, for eating and drinking was not allowed within; shrines, where one could communicate with one's god, and agree to offer a sacrifice if the deity would oblige by favouring one's betting, that day; whorehouses for those suitably excited by the events within – *fornixes* where common *prostibuli* worked wooden bunks under the *licencia stupro* listing their cheap charges, and the far finer *lupanars* where the pick of women earned great sums catering to the tastes of the élite.

Holding their pottery *tesserae* they found the archway closest to their seats, the numerals clearly incised in the travertine limestone. The archways each side were occupied, in one a man – middle-aged, paunchy – coupled with a prostitute in full view, his *amictus* hitched up about his waist, in the other the ancient god Mutinus waited, life-size and seated, phallus erect, for a living woman to come and give him sacrifice. They went through into the amphitheatre, passing a *Hermes* at the entrance – a short stone pillar of Hermes furnished with a penis every bit as big and stiff as his rival's next door, prepuce painted a brilliant red. As the two men went in a young woman ahead of them caressed it briefly as she passed by, for it was known to bring luck to all – a husband for the virgin, a child to the barren.

Out in the sun she opened and twirled her green parasol, making light flash from its polished ornamental stones over the wood and stone of the seats, over the colourful clothing of the people filling them. On the fresh raked sand of the arena a band was playing, rousing military music from the syrinx, the *tibia*, the tuba and *lituus*, the trumpeters and pipers standing before the big hydraulic organ set in the stand, the organist commanding his keyboard while two slaves pumped the air.

As they settled themselves down, adjusting their dress, placing their cushions for comfort, out on the sand more slaves were hurrying, miraculously converting the arena into a lush garden of living vegetation with great pots of trees and shrubs. Rocks there were too, for cover. In this garden clowns and cripples were fighting with wooden swords, along with dwarves and obese women, fat awobble, and gusts of laughter came here and there from the filling crowd at the antics of the ridiculous creatures and their pantomime of death. The Emperor was earnest that no hour of the day of the festival he had provided for his people should lack for amusement.

Latecomers hurried in, having left even the gulp of water and few mouthfuls of bread and cheese of their breakfast behind in their anxiety not to miss the fun. As they settled puffing into their seats, one of the fat women threw herself to the sand in an extravagant paroxysm of simulated death, a hunchbacked dwarf capered in victory, a cripple crawled across the sand like a crab, tormented by pole-wielding clowns. Next to Claudius, Telesphorus put back his head and guffawed with mirth.

Down where the sloping *vomitoria* abutted against the retaining wall of the arena the bookies stood, bags of *denarii* bulging, scribes at their side ready to take the bets on fresh wax boards. The young woman who had squeezed the *Hermes* was there in her shimmering green *palla*, her long shining black hair held back by a crimson *vitta* band. While Telesphorus was watching the horseplay on the sand, Claudius had been eyeing the spectators. He was a handsome young man, with a clipped black beard and his hair in tight ringlets. The young woman paused on the smooth passageway between the seats and he smiled at her, rising from his seat to make room, and she nodded graciously. He attentively adjusted her silk cushion for her, and she rearranged the folds of her tunic in a brief flash of crossing legs.

'May I?' Claudius smiled, and the girl handed him her green parasol. Her hand was soft, she smelled of fresh rose-water. He held up the delicate umbrella and shaded her from the rays of the sun, now climbing over the high side of the amphitheatre to the upper galleries, where the *pullati*, the poor folk clad in brown stuff, rubbed elbows, milling in excited anticipation.

A roar suddenly went up and white cloths broke out from the crowd, fluttering like a cloud of disturbed butterflies. In the imperial *pulvinar* a slim figure in pure white entered, surrounded by men and women.

He saluted to the crowd as the shouts of 'Long Life!' and 'Hail to the Emperor!' echoed from wall to wall.

The brass mouths of the *cornu* blasted and the gladiators' chariots burst into the arena.

They were magnificent men in purple and gold cloaks, their muscled bodies shining, oiled, slaves in their wake carrying the glittering tools of their trade, their bright shields and plumed helmets. They toured the arena before dismounting and standing tall and proud before the Emperor's box. As one, they thrust their arms forward from their naked chests in salute.

'Ave, Imperator, morituri te salutant!'

The bellowed salutation crashed against the wall and they marched in order out through the gate. The eyes of the young woman glittered.

Telesphorus leaned forward in his place, smiling with anticipation.

'Bring on the heretics,' he crooned. 'Let us see their insides, *ad maiorem Dei gloriam.*'

'You're in luck,' said the procurator. 'The Emperor's going to let you live.'

Some of the faces of the prisoners in the long, stone holding cell under the ground lit with a sudden hope. Through the rock came the approving laughter of the crowd as the cripples and monsters capered on the sand.

'He's going to let two of you live,' he said, and smiled grimly to see the hope change to desperation. 'You're to team up in pairs, one man, one woman. You'll be chained together and given weapons. The last pair standing gets to walk out.'

'I'm an architect,' a middle-aged Syrian wailed. 'What do I know of fighting?'

'Then you shouldn't have quarrelled with the Emperor,' the procurator said severely.

'What does he know of design?' retorted the man. 'I am Appollodorius, I designed the Forum, I put up the column of Trajan.'

'You are Appollodorius who should have kept his mouth shut in exile,' said the official. 'Now get yourselves organised, they will be here to chain you together in a minute.'

Simon and Ruth were sitting together already. Some scores were being settled; Appollodorius should have known better than to criticise the Emperor Hadrian's taste in temple design, and the Emperor's young lover should most definitely have known better than to fall in love with a beautiful girl and be found in her bed. Hadrian liked his boys faithful. His imperial sense of humour had propelled the happy couple to the cell, where they sat unhappily, side by side.

The Jews had had a new Messiah, the Son of the Star. The lost king had come into his own, and Palestine and Judea become aflame as the Jews proclaimed the freedom of Israel, killing all not of God in their path. The Emperor had sent troops, who killed all the Jews they could. Some they captured had been sent back, for the Emperor's entertainment. It had been a strange war, not all the Jews believed in the same god.

Two who worshipped the old deity sat amid the unclean, dark eyes burning, a man and a woman, young, soldiers. Simon had heard them talking quietly to each other, the man was called Jahucal, the woman Penninah.

About half the women, and the same proportion of men, were clearly sword-fodder. There had been complaints of poor service from the temple prostitutes at the shrine of Aphrodite and the priests had bought some fresh girls. Those cast out had objected: their protests had been noted, and two sat dejectedly on the bench, looking as listless as their annoyed patrons had claimed.

Three stood out as potential winners; one was the Jewish girl from Palestine, Penninah, an experienced fighter, she would be with her partner. The second was a strange, savage-looking creature, chalk-white of face and with hair like autumn leaves. Big and powerful she was, and a long way from home. Caledonia was her country, a strange land where blue mists hid icy lakes and deer bounded across heaths set under lonely mountains. Her kind came, every so often, to kill and pillage in the south, and the border legionaries had caught them coming back.

Ruth was at his side. They gripped hands.

Across the cell the Palestinian Jahucal spat.

'Galileans,' he said contemptuously, 'many of you have we given a meal of steel since we arose.'

'You will find us harder work,' said Simon. 'We are the Children of Jeshua.'

The woman captive Penninah glared at him.

'Idolator,' she hissed. 'When we kill you we shall anoint ourselves with your blood, in honour of God. Apostate, on your way to Hell.'

The arena was suddenly filled with fabulous beasts, appearing as if from the very bowels of the earth, and the music of the band was drowned by their bellowing, roaring and howling. With them came the *venatores*, tumbling from the partitioned turnstiles, whips and spears, lances and daggers and glowing firebrands in their hands, packs of powerful Scotch hunting hounds running before them.

Next to Claudius, his pretty neighbour's face lit up. The animals were even more exotic than the ones depicted in the garish posters which hung in the streets, with small crowds of gawping slaves and idlers always about them. Close by a huge, tawny cat was engaged by a *venatore*, firebrand in one hand, spear in the other. As many of its fellow beasts ran about in panic, this one gripped the cold sand with mighty paws, its ears flat on a furrowed head, huge yellow teeth bared as its tail lashed from one side to the other. It had been here before, with prey in front of it.

It charged, giving a cough of rage. Claudius and the girl shivered with a shared thrill of fear that went down the spine, and into the loins. Like an acrobat, the *venatore* tumbled backwards into a round spiked basket behind him, thrusting the blazing torch into the face of the cat as he did so. It screamed with fury and pain. Great dogs suddenly appeared, urged on by other *venatores*, and it whirled, turning away from the *ericius* basket. As it did so, the *venatore* popped his head out of the porcupine and threw his spear into the cat's ribcage. The crowd roared with laughter. The girl with the crimson bandeau in her hair put back her head in innocent merriment, her white teeth, polished with powdered horn that morning, shining in the sunlight. Claudius held the parasol attentively over her, his other arm supportively around her waist.

The cat was dying, some thrashing bodies of its killers lying about it, gutted by its terrible claws. The *venatores* were organising two great beasts to fight each other – a brown bear that reared up, higher than a man could reach, and a buffalo, heavy-shouldered, its long horns sharp as spears – using the fire in their hands to drive them on, enrage them.

The buffalo was a bull, hugely endowed, it swung as the animal wheeled around the padding bear, and the girl turned to Claudius, her eyes exaggeratedly large, and her hand over her laughing mouth.

The buffalo charged, as fast as a panther, and as unexpectedly, catching the bear on all fours, bowling it over. Sand flew gold in the air as the terrible head sought to impale its victim. It bellowed in agony, and reared away. The bear rolled on to its feet and stood up.

Half of the buffalo's face was torn away. Fearful claws slashed at the air, blood was on the bear's mouth, blood splattered on to the clean sand as the buffalo tottered. Fire thrust at its loins and it screamed. The bear loped forward.

The woman was on her feet, shouting with excitement.

'*Verbera!* Strike him! *Iugula!*'

Claudius's arm was around her, standing up with her, his hand squeezed her breast.

'*Iugula*! Slay him!'

Now it was the bear's turn. It moved fast, to the side where an eye dangled amidst the gore. Terrible jaws closed like iron behind the great head, the buffalo staggered in a short circle, sand flying from its hooves, a deep, awful groaning rising from its chest. There was a snap like a bough breaking, and it collapsed like a marionette. The girl jumped for joy, and Claudius's hand felt her breasts freely.

A huge, panic-stricken bird came running past, taller than a man, with a great long neck and big legs. A waiting *venatore* swung an expert blade and the big head with its poppy eyes flew in the air. The running body continued to run!

It ran round and round in circles, headless, until it fell over with its legs kicking and they laughed so much they thought they might be sick, and had to use their *mappas* to wipe the tears from their eyes. As the slaves moved into the arena to haul the corpses away the woman took a small and rare lead-backed glass mirror from the leather bag she carried – green, to match her *palla* and parasol – and checked her make-up, to be sure the powdered antimony around her eyes had not run.

Below slaves were teaming horses to drag the great corpse of an elephant from the arena. The rhinoceros had gouged it deep, its blood flowed into the sand like a lake.

'Now,' said Telesphorus, 'the heretics are coming. Now we shall see their gore.'

Chains were clanking, men brought them in and locked them about their waists, a loop some five feet long holding each pair together, and they went out and up the smooth sloping corridor to the arena.

Then they were pushed out of the gate and into the great arena, the sun's glare in their eyes, the sand hot under their bare feet. How huge it was, how high the tiers of seats holding the crowd, baying with pleasure at the new spectacle, approving. It was important not to let them be bored, to vary the spectacle.

They were paraded about the rim of the oval fighting area, and Simon could see a bustle of activity among the men gathered about the bookies above, hear their womenfolk shouting advice as they passed. By the gate of the dead a man stood waiting in the uniform of Charon, ferryman of souls into Hades, leaning on his heavy hammer, its head sticky with blood.

Looking up at the great crowd that was waiting for his death

Simon saw a lean, middle-aged man with dyed hair rising from his seat, pointing excitedly down at them.

'There,' Telesphorus barked, up in the stand, and Claudius glanced away from his companion.

'There, Claudius. See them. There are the Jews and there the heretics, the filthy Children of Jeshua. How we suffer with heresy!'

He watched in satisfaction as the pairs of chained prisoners went by below, long *spathae* shining in their hands.

'One day, one day all men will be pure, Claudius, they will believe in the true faith.'

His voice dropped, so that only Claudius could hear him.

'The Emperor is a pagan, but a tool of the Lord nevertheless. When the war against the Jews was won, and their Messiah dead, he set up a stone pig, as high as the trees on the Bethlehem Gate, and crucified all the rabbis facing it, sacrificing them to pork!'

Telesphorus chuckled, and wiped tears of happiness from his eyes.

'Heresy, all heresy,' he murmured, and sat back to watch the show.

On the sand, the guards, all instructors from the *ludus magnus* gladiatorial school on the Via Labicana, separated the prisoners up into four groups, situated in the four corners of the arena so that all the spectators might get a good view of the blood flying.

Simon and Ruth were marched to their segment along with the architect Appollodorius and one of the prostitutes from the temple of Aphrodite. The designer looked resigned, the woman simply weary, her spirit broken by years as a mattress to relays of fat-bellied worshippers.

'Right,' said the instructor briskly, a tough young man with a long red scar running up his forearm, and a whip in his hand which he brandished, 'if there's one thing they can't stand it's prisoners who won't fight. Give them a good show. Two of you get to walk out, it can be you. I've done it. Now, form up against each other and when the trumpet blasts, no quarter.'

Simon went close to Ruth and whispered in her ear. She nodded; the *cornu* sounded and the crowd howled for blood.

'*Acheruntis pabulum!*' Telesphorus yelled. 'Send them to Hell.'

Appollodorius and the whore were facing them, the length of their chain apart to keep away from each others' blades, their swords gripped in both hands, tips forward. Simon and Ruth ran round the woman so that momentarily their chain crossed hers like a capital letter T. The architect was slow, wheeling in the dust, the whore fended Simon's sword away in desperation and Ruth skewered her from behind. They advanced on Appollodorius from both sides and he dragged the gargling body over the sand. Simon attacked him as he retreated and Ruth hacked at him. He fell moaning to the sand, one leg half-severed, and Simon chopped off his head.

Up on the stand the crowd was on its feet. Claudius and his companion jumped with joy as the blood spouted high in the air, they were clinging to each other, his hand was down the front of her tunic, her breasts were free, smooth and taut with excitement. Telesphorus leaned on the stone balustrade, smiling malevolently.

The two Palestinians had made short work of their opponents and were cutting their throats noisily on the sand. The big woman from the far north of Britain was teamed with a tall Dacian, and they were matched with the two young lovers who had so displeased the Emperor.

There was a tremendous clang as the swords of the two women clashed, and the *spatha* of the Scot tumbled flashing in the air. She went after it, and jumping forward the young girl whirled her blade back with both hands in preparation for her final strike. The whistling blade caught her lover just under the chin and his body fell to the ground, blood spraying up from the stump of his neck like a scarlet fountain, his head tumbling over the sand. The dead weight of his body held her back, and her stroke missed. On her knees she looked at him in horror, and then they slashed her to pieces. In the box above, the homosexual Emperor smiled.

Across the arena one man stood, while three others lay dying on the sand. The *cornu* sounded, the *libitinarii* came out to clear away the dead and the instructors moved the survivors forward. Simon and Ruth were teamed against the Scot and the Dacian. As they went across the sand Simon tripped and fell. He pushed himself up and heard the Palestinian Jew Jahucal laugh.

'You'll not last long,' he said, as the pair marched menacingly across to the sand towards the single survivor standing chained to the corpse of his companion.

In the stands they were sitting back down. The young woman watched the moving gladiators with sparkling eyes and smiled brilliantly at Claudius. Her upper lid was dewed with tiny beads of perspiration.

Simon held his sword in one hand and clasped sand in the other. The bookies were busy taking fresh bets, now they were down to half. No one was putting money on the lonely figure confronting the Jews.

'Same again?' murmured Ruth.

'Yes. But these two are fast.' He put his mouth close to her ear, whispering, and she nodded. Her black hair was sodden with sweat, sticking to her skull. She wiped it clear of her eyes and gripped the sword with both hands.

When the horn brayed they ran again, but the pair against

them wheeled as well. Simon passed close enough to the tall, white-faced woman to fling the sand in her eyes and she shrieked a terrible Gaelic curse. Ruth slashed at her as she backed away, crashing into the Dacian, and blood ran down her side in a steady stream.

They shuffled about them after that, keeping their distance. The crowd howled abuse and their backs ran with blood from the lash of the instructor.

'*Verbera!* Strike! Burn them! *Ure!*' the young woman screamed furiously.

On the sand the Scot slumped slowly to the ground. The tall Dacian howled in his own language; he picked up her sword and threw it.

It caught Ruth on the thigh and tumbled to the ground. The Dacian was trapped by the dying woman; Simon picked her sword back up and they advanced on him. Simon threw it with all his strength from a matter of feet away and they rushed him as it thudded into his flesh.

'*Hoc habet!* Now he's got him!' she shrieked. They were on their feet again, howling for blood. The hem of her tunic was just above her knees, as she jumped with exhilaration Claudius slipped his hand under it and between her thighs, feeling the heat of her loins. The gore flew and she wriggled in ecstasy.

Blood glistened all down Ruth's leg; she left a single gory footprint as they went to the centre of the sand where the Jews were waiting. Behind them the attendant dressed as Charon came up, his heavy mallet in hand. He smashed the forehead of the dying Dacian with it, and summoned his *libitinarii*, who carried the dead man out on a stretcher through the gate, where Libitina, goddess of death, watched her offerings being brought to her.

Their chests heaved as they dragged the air into their lungs. They were sprayed and streaked with gore from the fighting, it ran slowly amidst the sweat that glistened on their bodies. The roar of the crowd above crashed over them like surf beating on rock. The brass horn brayed brutally, and they manoeuvred about each other, their chains clinking.

The crowd bellowed, swaying and shouting. Claudius was behind the woman as she leaned over the balustrade. Her tunic rode up over her thighs, he went with her, his arm about her and his other hand lifted the skirt.

The *spathae* blasted sparks from their blades, the impact jarring their arms. Slippery with sweat, Simon's sword twisted in his hand, and Jahucal leaped at him. Ruth had slipped on her own blood, the Jews were above them. As the blade came down Simon hit at it with his free arm; the woman Penninah slashed at Ruth, her teeth shining a snarling white in her face, and his sword tip smashed through them into her mouth. At that moment he felt the sword slice into him without pain.

Claudius thrust into her. All was hidden in the tumult of the crowd. She shuddered in joy. On the sand, blood flew and figures tumbled.

On her knees, Ruth hacked at Jahucal's legs as he advanced on Simon, and he went down with a scream of slashed hamstrings. Simon was on the sand, clutching the stump of his arm. She pushed herself up and the sword of the instructor brought her up short as she advanced to finish the job. On the bloody beach Jahucal held up his palm, asking the Emperor for mercy.

They were here, the joyous climax to the battle, when the spectators chose who should live, and who die. The roar of the crowd beat against the *pulvinar* and Hadrian stood to hear their wishes.

'*Iugula!* Kill him! *Iugula!*'

Jahucal looked up at the Emperor. It was a delicious moment for them all, would the defeated man show fear, beg?

Jahucal stared at the *pulvinar*, expressionless. One of the *confector*'s men was standing nearby, bowl in hand.

The crowd was not unreasonable, it could show mercy. But the war was barely over. Nobody much felt like pardoning a Jew.

'*Iugula! Iugula!*'

Hadrian bowed to their wishes, smiling to left and right, a calm thumb turned to his chest, *pollice verso*.

The short sword thrust, blood fountaining. The *confector*'s man quickly thrust his bowl into the stream to catch it. The woman's body twanged like a bow string, thrumming like an arrow. The *libitinarii* threw the dying bodies on to their bloody stretchers and hurried to the gate of the dead, following Jahucal with the bowl of steaming blood. Fresh from a dying gladiator, it was possessed of magical qualities. There were people waiting to buy juglets of it, outside. The woman slumped back in her seat, tugging her tunic back over her knees. She was flushed, her chest heaving as though she had been running. Claudius leaned back against the stone, as though drunk.

On the sand, Ruth tore a long strip from her dress, binding the stump of Simon's arm. Supporting each other, they staggered out of the *Sanavivaria*, the gate for the living, and the cheers of the crowd broke around them.

Telesphorus looked at the darkness of the tunnel in fury.

'They are not dead,' he said furiously. He turned on his priest. 'Not dead, Claudius!'

Ruth watched detachedly as the doctor from the gladiators' school passed the slim bone needle through both lips of the wound in her leg, expertly pulling the gut thread taut with a single knot and securing it with a second. He was a young man, a Greek, well-rewarded for his tasks. Gladiators were valuable, they made a lot of money for their owners, it paid to keep them in fighting condition.

The smell of tar was in the air, a small pot of it bubbled on a brazier. The stump of Simon's arm shone black as it dried in the sun, the doctor had dipped it, swiftly and efficiently, into the molten tar, sealing the wound. Then he had thrust a glass beaker of unwatered wine into his hand and bid him drink it. Simon sat by the wall. The *libitinarii* were dragging in corpses and piling them up on the other side of the courtyard, ready for the refuse carts to take them to the marshes. Simon looked up.

'My arm will be there,' he observed. 'There is a ring on the hand I would have saved, but I have no doubt that one of them will have snatched it from the finger.'

'Take the teeth from your head, they will,' the doctor agreed. Ruth lifted her head sharply.

'We are the survivors,' she said, 'we are to have our belongings back, the Emperor has said so.'

'Ask in the guardroom,' the man said. 'They dice for the things of value from the dead in there.'

'We are the survivors,' Simon said to the legionary at the door. From below came a snarling and coughing of feral animals, and a smell of blood and ordure.

'Of a kind,' said the tough young man, eyeing their wounds.

'We are to have our belongings back,' said Ruth. 'The Emperor says so. There, I see them in the pile. The bags there.'

The legionary peered inside the leather sacks.

'Parchment,' he said contemptuously. 'Are you scribes?'

'Of a kind,' she replied, and they took what they owned and limped outside. In the shadow of the great walls they paused at a fountain to drink. Simon scooped up the chill water, using his one hand.

'I shall have to get used to this,' he said.

'The Lord has saved us, saved the Children of Jeshua,' Ruth commented. 'Now we have to decide where to begin spreading his word.'

'He allowed the Romans to drive us out of Palestine, but now he has saved us from death in there. It must be that he wishes us to go out into the world, all about the great sea.'

Ruth straightened up. Her leg was almost on fire, but she made herself ignore it.

'There. We have my scars and your arm to show how God saved us for his work. Let us get out of this city and down to the port.'

They left the great killing-ground behind them, making their way through the narrow *actae* towards the left bank of the Tiber. The streets of shops and houses were dim, light filtering in through the narrow gap between the *insulae*, eight stories up where the poorest slept, amidst dirt, mice and insects. They did not attract any attention as they passed through the traders and shopkeepers; the beggars and snake-charmers, with their crowds of idlers, shoppers and slaves; the schoolteachers instructing their cramped semicircles of pupils; the whores outside the drinking booths. Cripples and maimed people were not rare in Rome.

Their senses had become heightened during their ordeal. The sudden swirling rush of men that should have left them bloodied and dying in the alley outside the baths found them at the top of a small flight of steps. The tough *cursores* recoiled as their leader fell back into their midst, clutching a shoulder rapidly staining scarlet with blood, and they stared resentfully at the short, shining blade in Simon's hand.

'I have but one now,' he called triumphantly, 'but it is still good.'

From the shadows, Telesphorus came forward, with the priest Claudius at his elbow.

'*Apage Satanas*,' Ruth hissed. 'Get you gone, slave of Satan, servant of the Antichrist.'

'I?' Telesphorus said menacingly. 'I serve the Lord my God, I am here to keep his house clean from sin.'

'With slaves such as these? Do you not know that our Lord Jeshua commanded any that owned slaves to set them free?'

'He did not!' Telesphorus said, momentarily alarmed.

'It is easier for a camel to pass through the eye of a needle than for a man who enslaves another to pass into the Kingdom of Heaven.' Ruth said coldly.

'Heresy,' Claudius shouted furiously. 'All heresy.'

'What do you have in your bags?' Telesphorus asked softly.

'Holy gospels,' answered Simon. He waved his knife. 'You may come up and read them, Bishop, if you will.'

'Heretical scriptures. Give them to me, and I shall burn them for you.'

'We are taking them from this city of evil. We shall bring them to those in need. They shall be as a draught of pure spring water, bringing faith and life to the pure in heart.'

From down the narrow way came the cries of alarm and of sudden pain, and the heavy tramp of hobnailed *caligae*. The column of soldiers marching down the centre of the road was visible from the top of the steps.

'Stay away from us, son of Satan!' Ruth cried. 'We are as doves before the Lord, but as ravening wolves to the ungodly.'

As the soldiers approached, Simon and Ruth suddenly jumped down, running away up the street in front of it. Telesphorus held back, pressing against the wall, and when the column had gone through the two had vanished from sight.

'We shall not risk going to the magistrate with them,' he muttered, and Claudius looked relieved. Telesphorus snarled a command at the *cursores*, and they began to slouch up the alley. The one whose shoulder was stained with blood turned to the bishop.

'Is it so, master, that the Lord Jesus forbade men to own slaves?'

Telesphorus slashed at him with his whip, and fresh blood ran from his face. The bishop looked furiously down the lane.

'We shall find them again, one of these days,' he promised.

5

Hook Norton

Connell looked up from the sheets of text, with its joins and gaps, painstakingly put together. Outside, the evening sun was falling over the garden, the whites and blues of the roses and campanulas were beginning to glow. He heard the burble of a kettle.

'I'll have some tea, if there is any,' he called, and went outside through the open French windows on to the brick terrace, where the Oxford blue clematis was falling down in sheets. Juliana appeared with two mugs, and they went on to the lawn.

'I must mow this, sometime,' said Connell. 'You could graze sheep here.'

He sipped his tea, appreciatively.

'They certainly hated each other,' he commented. 'And it's really well dated. The second Jewish revolt has been defeated, the rabbis who believed that Simeon bar Kochba was the new messiah have been crucified in front of a giant stone pig by the Romans, in an unusual display of a sense of humour. Simon and Ruth were clearly involved, but as a part of the new Jewish heresy that believed in Jesus. The two traditional Jews, Jahucal and his wife hate them – they are the Galileans. And yet Simon and Ruth still consider themselves Jewish – they haven't made the complete break to considering themselves Christians.'

'How do you know that?'

'It's the way Ruth threatens Telesphorus. She warns him that she and Simon are as doves before the Lord, but as ravening wolves to the ungodly. That's a Jewish rallying cry from the war – they said "heathens", Ruth says "ungodly", but then, she specifically associates Telesphorus with Satan. She calls him his servant, and slave of the Antichrist.'

'Isn't that a bit extreme?' Juliana protested.

'Well, she *has* just come out of the arena where she has been fighting for her life, and had Telesphorus howling to see her insides while his priest had it off with the young vulture at his side,' Connell said reasonably.

'That was horrible.'

'Not uncommon, though. Ovid knew what the sight of blood did to young Roman ladies. They all of them, men and women, had a highly developed appetite for the slaughter of the *munera* – the games. We of the late twentieth century are hardly in a position to throw stones at them when we watch murder, torture and pornography on television on a daily basis.'

'I don't watch television,' she said austerely.

'No, I don't much either. I like the cricket, but it's just as good on the radio.'

Over the river at the end of the garden something brightly coloured swooped. Water flew, gold in the sunlight, and the kingfisher rose back up into the air, a minnow in its beak.

'Telesphorus is very anxious to eradicate the Children of Jeshua. When they aren't killed in the circus, he wants to burn their gospels.'

'Well, of course. He's showing an extremely good grasp of the rules of propaganda.'

'He's the Bishop of Rome. He's trying to spread the word of God,' she protested.

'So are *they*,' Connell pointed out, 'and anyway, what is propaganda? It's the transmission of ideas and values from one person, or group of persons, to another, with the specific intention of influencing the recipients' attitudes in such a way that the interests of its authors will be enhanced. Telesphorus, on behalf of the God he serves, whoever that may be, is seeking to gain power over people by having them believe in what he tells them. But successful propaganda has to go hand in hand with rigorous censorship. The two are Siamese twins. This transmission and acceptance of ideas and values can only be successful provided no competing ideology is allowed on stage. Telesphorus understands this very well.'

Connell tipped back his mug.

'I wonder if they did meet again, as Telesphorus threatened.'

'Oh, yes. They did,' she said positively. 'I've been putting together another text. Telesphorus and Claudius have been travelling in the Mediterranean, evangelising.'

'Ah ... the Church of Rome, still in its infant stage, is suffering from severe competition. From the Gnostics, Marcion and Valentinus, right? And, one assumes, from the Children of Jeshua.'

'That's right,' she said. 'What do we know about Telesphorus?'

'Not a great deal. What we do know comes from Eusebius. Bishop of Caesarea from about 313 A.D., he wrote an enormous Ecclesiastical History – the history of the Early Church. He lived long enough to see the Emperor Constantine accept Christianity – in a sort of *mélange* with Sol Invictus and Mithras – as the religion of the Empire. It's a very *useful* history, if rather like reading that wonderful Communist Party *History of the Civil War, The Great Proletarian Revolution*, edited by such scholars as Vyacheslav Molotov and Joseph Stalin.'

She looked at him, suddenly angry. He shrugged.

'It isn't objective, Juliana, is what I mean. It's very biased.'

'I wish you weren't so cynical about all this. Don't you realise, you're going to upset a lot of people? You upset *me*.'

'How can the truth upset anyone?' he said breezily. 'We are historians, only the truth matters. But anyway, you were asking about Telesphorus. Bishop of Rome after Sixtus. Eusebius says he was martyred.'

Gortyna, Crete, A.D. September 136

And the Lord Jesus looked down upon the Children of Jeshua, and he saw that what they did was good.

Claudius came down the hill and his feet sent up puffs of dust that drifted away in the dry air. The very leaves of the grey olive trees drooped, the fruits small and hard. A thin and meagre juice they would provide for men used to pressing out rich gold. The rain had not come.

Claudius continued on his way through the parched hillsides to the capital, the money stuffed tight in the belt about his waist. Twenty miles had he walked, setting out at dawn to cross the island from the port of Phoenix, where Telesphorus was. It had been a hard year, the heretics grew in strength all the time, Valentinus and Basilides voyaged up and won the Mediterranean, writing, preaching, discussing and founding groups and communities of their Gnostic movements without hindrance.

The decision had been taken, and the Bishop himself had gone out even before the safe sailing season had begun. He had been aboard ship in April, braving storm and shipwreck to defeat the wicked. Hyginus remained in Rome in his place.

It had been a long summer, spent in Alexandria and Antioch,

Salamis and Seleucia, Miletus, Myra and many more cities about the sea where the faithful needed support; the port of Phoenix was their last call on their way home. Soon the freighters and grain-carriers would be tying up for the winter. It was time to be gone.

But first, one last mission. The messenger had come stumbling in, footsore, thirsty and weary, and at dawn Claudius had set out to cross the island.

He came over the hill and the city was there before him on the north coast, the sea a gleaming blue beyond. And there was the amphitheatre. It was the time of the annual Provincial Games.

The heat was still great. It had not rained all summer on this island. His feet sent up puffs of dust that spread out in the dry breeze, and those who were waiting for him saw him coming.

As he came into the capital itself they slipped out of the shadows of the trees, and walked with him.

'Where are you going?' one man asked.

'I am to see Proconsul Clemens,' Claudius replied. 'I have business with him.'

'We shall take you to him,' said a voice, 'for we know where he is.'

Claudius turned, and saw a man with only one hand.

'Do you know me?' asked Simon. 'You watched while I lost this.'

He held up his puckered stump.

'Who are these people?' Claudius demanded.

'Followers of Jesus,' he said proudly. 'We, the Children of Jeshua, have brought the truth to them.'

'Where is the woman?'

'Here,' said Ruth.

Their followers were with them, they did their bidding.

They seized Claudius and took him to the oval amphitheatre. The annual games lasted three days, the second was ending. The yellow sand was darkly stained.

The proconsul was in his *pulvinar*. Simon slipped in. Standing with his hands tied at the entrance Claudius saw a man stumble and fall, heard the roar of the crowd. The governor turned his thumb to his chest, *pollice verso*, and they yelled with delight.

Simon was whispering in his ear, he beckoned and the men guarding Claudius gave him a shove. He stumbled in, and stood at the side of the governor. Simon was holding out the money-belt they had taken from about his waist.

'Another priest from Rome, governor,' he said, 'come to try to bribe you to release the ones waiting for the beasts. Not of course that he would have succeeded.'

'He might be an innocent merchant,' said the proconsul. He was a man in middle age, educated, one of the wide Empire's many servants who saw to it that the wishes of Rome were carried out.

'One must not jump to conclusions.'

He turned to Claudius.

'What say you?'

'I had hoped to request a meeting with you at your house, once this day's games were over.'

'He wished to try to bribe you in private,' Simon said. He put the heavy belt down by Clemens.

'*Aurei*, sir.'

Clemens was an *equite*, a knight, he allowed not a flicker of satisfaction to appear on his face, but Claudius knew that Simon had hit the mark. The point was, as he, Telesphorus, and Clemens all knew, the Empire was run on corruption. Those who ran it made money from those who did not, or in the case of the Emperor, from both. In private, it was possible to make a deal. Men for gold. In public, not. And not now the gold had changed hands without effort.

The governor's next question confirmed it.

'You are a follower of this Christ?' he said abruptly.

'I am,' said Claudius.

'How very tiresome of you.'

He looked balefully down at the arena and the wooden stands. Claudius could see Ruth and her followers moving about down there, could hear a rising swell of anger coming from the people. Next to the governor a centurion, his face seamed by twenty years' worth of service to the Emperor in far-flung lands, shifted uneasily on his bench, his hand slipping to the hilt of his sword.

'This frightful island has had a drought,' Clemens said shortly. 'Sacrifice to all the gods has brought no relief and the crops have died in the field. Clearly if the gods will not be appeased something must be wrong.'

Clemens talked stone-faced, and Claudius wondered at the level of his belief. A man like him would do what was required, keeping his true thoughts to himself.

'The priests conducted a search, and found a strange sect busy worshipping a condemned criminal. Clearly a repellent crew, on investigation they were found to conduct strange rites including cannibalism, incest and other forms of vice.'

He held up a hand.

'While revolting, it is not necessarily enough for arrest and trial, let alone a one-way trip into that arena down there. This is the Roman Empire, we offer tolerance to the gods of those we conquer. No, what clearly has set these Christians aside is the fact that they are *atheists*. They refuse formal acknowledgement of the gods of the community in which they live.'

There was a noise down there, a growing tumult. The two

67

gladiators fighting paused and slowed, wondering what was up, the centurion frowned.

'We worship the one true God, whose son was Jesus Christ.'

'Do not offend my ears with this piffle,' said Clemens. 'I as a man trained in philosophy, I have had enough from the miserable lot due for the wild beasts on the morrow without you repeating the experience. What you claim to believe in is mere *superstitio*, not *religio*.'

It was a storm, a yelling of angry voices, of shaking fists and bared teeth.

'They're all drunk, of course,' said Clemens, 'and very, very angry. With you.'

He looked down upon those whom he ruled in the name of Rome.

'Greek peasants,' he said disparagingly, 'like the fools waiting for the beasts.'

'And as you say, Governor, angry ones,' the centurion grunted, 'we don't have the troops to deal with a full-scale riot.'

'Look. Those of your sect down in the cells I cannot save and would not anyway. But you are of Rome, as I am. Agree to sacrifice to the local gods – down there in the arena where these Greeks can see you – and I can get you off. There is no point in dying for a bunch of Greeks, I assure you.'

It had arrived, as he had wondered if it would. He licked dry lips.

'I cannot,' he whispered, 'for my God sees all I do.'

He saw Simon smile.

'But why are we being singled out?' he asked angrily. 'What of these who have brought me here? They do not make sacrifice either. Put them in the arena.'

'We are Jews. We are *religio licita*,' said Simon, 'the Emperor Antonius Pius has said so.'

'It is so. The Jews are the exception, for their antiquity. Are you Jewish? No. But come now. We have little time, these drunken Greeks will climb up here in a minute and deal with you themselves and I do not want my toga splashed with your blood. Sacrifice. I will have the herald announce it and they will be most happy. Then you can get you gone back to Rome, which is where I wish I was. I'll tell you what. You look like a man of the world. Sacrifice, and you can come back with me for *cena*. I have some pretty slaves you can enjoy.'

He could hear what the mob was calling – 'Kill the atheist. Kill the atheist.' They roared it at the tops of their drunken voices.

Claudius shook his head.

'I cannot,' he said again. 'It is commanded of me that I recognise only the one true God. Hell awaits me should I do otherwise.'

They took him down and when the crowd saw him brought out, and the tall tripod set up, they shouted with joy and went back to their places. The centurion leaned back on the bench and took his hand from the hilt of his *gladius*.

They were quiet, looking into the bright arena with glittering eyes. When he was stretched out on the tripod the first of the two men at each side swung the long rod. They saw the spout of blood, heard the rod's smack and the cry of the unbeliever. They nodded in satisfaction, for the gods would have heard it too. They swigged *trimma* from the wine-skins they sat on, and settled back to enjoy the spectacle with their deities.

When the thing in the arena hung still like a dripping bloody sack from the tripod, Simon leaned forward by Clemens's ear.

'There is another on the island, Excellency,' he murmured respectfully. 'The one who leads all the other sinners. A bishop.'

'But what are you *doing* out in these ghastly places?' Clemens asked querulously. 'I'm here because the Emperor has sent me here, but the sooner I am home, the better I shall like it. I hunger for Lucrine oysters, and thirst for Falernian. Here they eat goat and drink adulterated muck. But you, you are a Roman. You left to come out here. Why?'

Telesphorus stared down into the arena where men were gathering up fragments of flesh and bone, strings of intestine and hanks of hair from blood-soaked sand. The beasts had been chased back into their masonry cages for another day. A full-grown lion or panther was an expensive thing, this far out in the Empire.

'I work for the Lord,' he said grimly. 'I do battle with those who seek to besmirch his holy name.'

Clemens shifted in his chair. The annual games were, without doubt, an unmitigated pain, and expensive to boot. And what with the drought, there was little hope of recouping his costs from those under him this year.

He wiped his face irritably. It had clouded over and the damp heat was stifling.

'Look, old fellow Roman. Just between you and me, this thing about the gods is all for the peasants, the simpletons. I do what is required of me. Pay homage to the *genius* of the Emperor? Certainly. Cut a bull's throat? Here I am, your man. I don't care if the Emperor has a statue of his backside made and demands we all kiss it. If that's the state requirement, I'll go along with it. So should you. What good has it done those poor fools to believe in your Church? There they rest, underneath our feet, in the stomachs of beasts. Off I go to a good supper – as good as this wretched place can produce, at any rate – and a fuck. It has to be better that what they had.'

'They are with God,' said Telesphorus. 'But listen, Proconsul. I too wish to be with God, but there is still much to be done. I am no Ignatius, I will die if I have to, but I do not hunger for the teeth of the beasts to grind me into God's flour, as he did. I would rather get on with the business of running my Church. We have money, I can send for it. These games must have cost you plenty, would you not like to recoup your losses?'

'I should indeed,' said Clemens. Below, the amphitheatre was emptying, but on the sand a crowd had gathered. At its head stood Simon.

'What do you want?' yelled Clemens. 'The games are finished.'

'We want the atheist,' called Simon.

'The sports are closed, the beasts back in their cages.'

'We still want him.'

'What for?'

'Give him to us, and you will see.'

They rushed to get logs and faggots from the workshops and public baths, and those who had left the amphitheatre, thinking all sport over, hurried back so as not to miss it.

They nailed him to a post, for it was known that the lick of the flames could give a man extraordinary strength, and piled up the wood, dry after the long summer, all about him.

They heard him calling out a prayer to his god.

'I bless you, Lord, for counting me worthy of this day and hour.'

Yes, yes, the hour had come all right, they agreed, and tossed on a few more faggots for luck.

'In the number of the martyrs I may partake of Christ's cup.'

That confused them a bit, but they drank to it anyway.

'May I be received into your presence today, a rich and acceptable sacrifice.'

'Rich and acceptable indeed,' said Ruth. He saw her standing by the pyre, a burning bundle in her hand.

'Go back to your master, slave of Satan.'

She plunged in the torch.

'God of truth, you cannot lie,' he shouted.

The logs crackled and the flames burned with a clean yellow flame.

He screamed, the fire roared and the clouds above opened. The peasants danced about the flames.

'See!' Ruth cried. 'The Lord Jesus looks down upon us, and shows us his love.'

6

Hook Norton

'I wish we knew why they hate each other so,' said Juliana. Under her slim fingers fragments of script were slowly turning into recognisable sections of text.

Connell glanced up from his desk and put down the pen he had been using to translate, flexing his stiff fingers.

'It's a feud,' he suggested, 'and a religious one at that. The Mediterranean has been notorious for blood feuds since time immemorial – the Mafia didn't invent it, they just carried it to extreme lengths.'

He tapped the page he was reading.

'Maria and Jeshua – the children of murdered Mary of Magdalene – have escaped from Peter in Antioch, they're on the grain-carrier to Rome. The Greek captain knows they're running. He says it must be a blood feud. He understands that.'

'There's more to it,' she persisted. 'The Children of Jeshua are fighting a *war*. Over centuries. They keep it up, and it's not simply blind hate. They're convinced that the Orthodox Church is wholly evil, that they must do anything to stop it. Something must have triggered it all off.'

'Peter murdering Mary might do for a start,' Connell said laconically.

Juliana stretched, getting up and staring out of the window, allowing her eyes to focus on infinity.

'Jeshua didn't die, then?' she said, interested. 'I thought Peter's men nailed him with a spear.'

'They did. His sister appears to be an adept with herbs and healing. He's still ill, but alive. They're in Malta, making a sacrifice after a storm. Going to Rome. I want to see what happens to them there. It's an interesting time, of course. Nero is Emperor, and well off the wall by now.'

'How big would the Christian community be?'

'Pretty small. A heretical Jewish splinter group for anyone not familiar with the technical detail. Just one of a seething mass of cults. Paul was there in 61 A.D., sent by Festus after his row with the *zelotai*. To read Acts you'd think the place was decorated with bunting to greet him, but in reality just about nobody would know he was there. Peter was there too, apparently. Reading the texts we have here we know why. He went to murder Mary's children.

Malta, A.D. 62

She saw Thasos coming from the town huddled about the natural stone harbour. He bore a goat under his arm, which he carried up the gangplank. The captain and helmsman smiled at her, seated with a mortar on her knee, as he came abroad.

'You are still with us, little blue-eyes?'

She had thought of changing ships. Thasos had explained how the voyage of this vessel would be recorded both at the offices of the *magnarii* whose grain was filling the hull, and at those of the *domini navium*, the shippers whose craft the *Charis* was. The Fisherman knew where she was headed, to be sure. But the end of the shipping season was near. The storm that had sprung their planks was a harbinger of fiercer ones to come. She feared isolation, a winter in which the Fisherman could trace them, and come for them with his crooked knife in the spring.

Thasos put the goat down with a thud by the deck-house behind the goose's head on the prow, and it bleated and scraped its tied hooves.

'You shall be with Isis soon,' he told it, not unkindly.

'We shall travel with you to Rome,' she agreed. On his pallet, under the sailcloth she had rigged for shade and shelter, Jeshua rested, his face white from the blood he had lost. She took some seeds and added them to the ground root in the mortar. She picked up the stone pestle and began to grind with practised movements. Now she had her herbs, Jeshua would be well again.

'Other vessels travel from Antioch to Rome, is it not so?' she asked.

'More than you can imagine. From all over the Great Sea. Everything goes to Rome. At the port the warehouses are bigger than whole towns, you will see.'

'Those who ran after us, those who tried to kill my brother. They could send word, or even travel on another vessel. Now that we have been delayed, they could be there before us, be waiting.'

'They could,' he agreed. He eyed her shrewdly, she had talked little on the journey.

'What is it? Not happy with their choice of husband, I'll be bound.'

He was from Phrygia, his olive skin like leather from his years at sea.

'That's it,' she said.

'Marry a sailor! My wife's happy – I'm gone half the year. When I come back I have gold in my purse and by the time we get to arguing again it's time for voyaging. Listen, I have a son, a fine young lad. Come back with me and marry him. Bring your brother, I'll find a strapping girl for him.'

She shook her head.

'I cannot.'

She was a princess.

He was quick.

'There is blood, isn't there?'

He understood what a blood feud was.

'You could do one thing for us,' she said. 'When we come to Rome, if they are waiting for us, you could say we left ship here.'

He laughed. 'And have them running off the wrong way? Yes, little blue-eyes, I'll do that for you.'

A breeze ruffled her hair, Thasos brought out a bronze bowl. Behind them at the stern fine grey smoke came from the little galley. Both god and supplicant dined from sacrifice.

'But what will you do?' he asked. 'Have you somewhere to go? No? You will find Rome a hard place without money, without friends. People enslave themselves there, simply to live. Come back to Phrygia with me, become a sailor's wife, it is not so bad.'

'I am a dancer, I can sing, I play music.'

'You know the rites of the gods?'

'Yes.'

He eyed her briefly, appreciating her beauty.

'Always work in Rome for that. The gods like pretty girls.'

He paused.

'Want to tell me who's after you? If you want me to send them the wrong way?'

'Very well.'

She added a little wine to the mortar, mashing the herbs into a smooth paste.

'He is a man called Peter, that we know as the Fisherman. He is a Jew, from Palestine. He believes a man called Jesus, that the Romans crucified like a criminal, is God.'

'A god, eh? Many strange things come out of Palestine.'

'No. Not *a* god. God.'

'*One* god?' Thasos mused. A thoughtful look came over his face. 'I have heard of this Jesus. There's a fellow I know in Rome now, knows about Jesus. I picked him up here early this year, he'd been shipwrecked. Took him to Rome. Saul, his name was. He did nothing but talk about the gods, and Jesus. He was running from some Jews, too. They didn't like what he said about this Jesus. Yes, I'll send your Peter the wrong way.'

'Thank you,' she said. She gestured at the goat with her pestle. Under the awning Jeshua stirred and gasped in his sleep as his wound pained him.

'You, too, know about the gods.'

Thasos pointed to the pile of cracked and shattered planking on the quayside.

'That's a god's work. Done with a sleepy flick of a fingernail. No, before we sail, Isis on our prow must have proof.'

He turned, coming close to her, so that she smelled the salt and sweat, the garlic and the wine and tar of him.

'In my village, before it is time to sail, as the first shoots begin to push through after the winter, we thank Dionysus. The Romans too know Dionysus, they call him Bacchus, and like him for he is the god of wine. A merry fellow, they think.'

A wine-skin hung in the shady side of the wheel-house, Thasos took it and poured some, almost purple, into two cups, and handed one to Maria.

'Wine. There is nothing like it. It will ease all pain – the pain of the mind and the pain of the body. For some it brings exaltation, for others new belief from loss of hope. It will make you well. Give it to your brother, when he awakes.'

He tipped back the cup.

'It makes the stupid Romans drunk,' he said derisively, 'and they drink to Bacchus, and yet do not know they are drinking the blood of the god.'

He pointed to the cup still in her hand.

'Every year the god dies. His body is torn and crushed. His blood flows out, his vines stand bare and lifeless. And every year as we prepare to sail again the miracle happens, he who was dead is reborn. The shoots of his life appear once more, and we drink his blood to thank him, who died for us.'

She sipped the wine in the warm sunshine. It bit pleasantly at her mouth, the breeze tugged at the furled sail above her. Thasos wagged a gnarled, scarred finger.

'But you must believe,' he said solemnly. 'Gods punish those who do not believe. When Dionysus came to be with us, to bring us wine, people did not believe. The king did not believe. So Dionysus made his women mad, and sent them into the hills to dance. And Dionysus tempted the king to come after them, to climb up into a tree, to see what they were doing. And then the god talked to the women.

' "Maidens," he shouted, "I bring and offer up to you the one who laughs at you. At me. And at my secret rites. Avenge yourselves on him." The women pulled the king down from the tree, pulled off his head. They believed they had hunted and killed a mountain lion, and the mother took the head home and nailed it to the wall. Then Dionysus allowed them to see what they had done. They were destroyed by grief, but not he. Gods do not care about our pain.'

He looked back at her.

'Drink,' he said brusquely. 'The gods punish those who do not believe.'

He pulled the goat up on to the tiled deck-house. The crooked knife glittered in his hand and she closed her eyes. When she opened them again blood was running down over the godhead of the prow.

Rome

Finely powdered chaff from the sacks was rising in thin, spreading lines up through the planks of the decking of the deck-house. She lay next to Jeshua under the wooden shelf that served Thasos as a bed, and felt them tickling her nose. It was salty there, from the sea's spray, and musty, too, from the dried blood of a hundred sacrifices.

She could hear the rhythmic tramp of the *geruli* stevedores as they came up the gangplank, and down the ladder into the hold. She heard them curse the weight of the sack as they pulled each expertly upon their backs. Through a tiny crack in the wall she could see them going back down the plank with their curious, mincing gait, past the *custodiarius* with his waxed tally tablet, carrying the sacks away into the warehouse of the merchant. Slowly the ship was rising. The gangplank, that had been flat, now ran up at an angle.

Away on the far side of the Forum men sat under the shade of the long portico, where the various corporations of the port had their offices. Two were there, their gaze fixed upon the ship. They had been there when they docked. Peeping through her crack, she saw one rise and walk across the esplanade where the stevedores and porters streamed like ants, where the *muliones* whipped up their laden mule teams and the drovers assembled their herds. Jeshua peeped through the crack too, saw him come, ignoring the coasters and rafts and boats that thronged the quay. The boy shivered in remembered pain.

'It is him. The one who threw the spear,' he whispered. She put her arms around him to comfort him, and felt him hot, the fever of his wound still not extinguished.

'Hullo, the *Charis.*'

He was a young man, he spoke good Greek, she saw his teeth white in the sun as he smiled up at Thasos supervising the unloading. He had stood on the quay at Antioch, staring at her.

'Are you out of Antioch?' he called, above the din. On the banks of the Tiber the boats and ships loaded and unloaded, took on ballast, were caulked and painted and repaired, there their ropes and sails were made, all about was the noise of tools, of the rushing and hustle, the creak and squeal of carts, the panting and swearing of men.

'Are you out of Antioch?'

'We are,' agreed Thasos.

'You took on two passengers just as you set sail. A young woman and a boy.'

'Aye, I remember them.'

'They are runaway slaves, guilty of the worst crime. They killed her master.'

'I knew nothing of that.'

'There is a reward,' the young man said silkily, 'much gold.'

'I would that you had told me that as we were sailing. I should have stopped and handed them to you.'

'Where are they?'

'We put in at Malta for repairs. They left ship there. They owe me money for their fare.'

'The boy still lived, then . . . Did they say where they were bound?'

'No . . .' Thasos said regretfully, 'but, see now, I fare all over the Great Sea. It might be I should chance upon them again. Who are you, and how should I find you to get my reward?'

'I am Mark of Jerusalem. I am here in Rome about other affairs as well as these runaway slaves. See, over there, where the port corporations are. See the *statio* of the *piscatores*. They know of me there. Leave word, and one will come for them, if not I.'

'You travel about, then? Jerusalem, Antioch, Rome.'

'Yes,' the young man said quietly, and his voice was barely audible above the din of the port. 'My business takes me all about the lands of the Great Sea.'

'If I find them on my travels I shall bring them to you. If the gold is waiting.'

The man Mark was turning away, now he spoke over his shoulder.

'It will be. Much gold.'

Through her crack in the planking she saw him walk back to the portico. He paused there in the dim shade and when two came out she could see the flash of silver hair on his companion. They vanished in the crowd.

'Come back with me to my village,' Thasos said softly. They had come up and were sitting on the shelf of his bed. 'My son is not a bad fellow and I can always use another hand.'

'They would find us,' said Jeshua. 'In a small village such as yours we would be seen. There is money on our heads, as you heard. Someone would betray us and you, too, would pay. Here in Rome we can hide, for there are many who are foreigners.'

'You could not hide in Antioch,' Thasos said shrewdly.

'We were betrayed,' Maria said quietly. 'Besides, we are meant to stay in Rome, for that is where we were to go, not this year but next. We were to come here to meet our father. Now we shall wait for him.'

'Your father?' Thasos said interestedly. 'Should you not go to him?'

'We do not know where he is.'

'He is a powerful man,' said Jeshua. 'He moves in secret places. Soon, when I am a man, I shall join him. Then I too shall be powerful and we shall pay the account with Peter.'

Thasos looked at the young couple carefully, almost warily. 'It may be best, as you say. The sea is dangerous enough, without men coming to kill you in the night. But Rome is a large place, how will you know where to meet your father, now your mother is gone?'

'There is a day,' said Maria. 'His birthday. And a place. We know that.'

'But you will need somewhere to stay while you wait,' said the sea captain. His brow wrinkled momentarily in thought. 'I know, go see Saul, that was shipwrecked, that I brought here, who talks about this Jesus.'

Thasos got up, and went to the box under his bed. He opened it and took out some tightly wrapped scrolls.

'He pays me,' he said. 'He knows I travel all about the Great Sea. When I reach a far-off port there are those there, followers of this Jesus, that meet me and give me letters to take to Saul.'

He glanced up at the sky with an experienced grey eye.

'The seafaring season has not long to run,' he said. 'I must away, if I am not to be marooned over winter. I would see my wife again.'

He handed the small sheaf of scrolls to Maria.

'Here,' he said. 'Take these to Saul for me. You will find him near the Forum. He lives not far from the fishmarket. Ask at the sign of the Red Mullet, they know of him there.'

'Are you Saul of Tarsus?'

Quick, intelligent brown eyes set wide in the big head snapped on to them. Seeing two children, their sudden anxiety relaxed into mere alertness. As he turned they saw that he had only one ear. The left one was but a stump. The creased scar under the grey hair was white, it was an old injury.

'I am he,' the man said. He smiled at them both. 'But who wishes to know?'

'I am Maria and this is my brother Jeshua. We came on the grain-vessel of Thasos the Phrygian.'

She held out the small sheaf of rolled letters.

'He sent you these.'

All about them people swirled in the great open arena of the Forum, set in the middle of the city. Its margins had been roped off to make a roughly rectangular track. Close by, outside the temple of Venus and over at the Basilica Julia, slaves were raking smooth the golden sand cast down. From one of the streets came the sound of whinnying horses.

'Ahh . . . my letters,' said Saul, taking them.

'He begs your pardon, but the sailing season is soon to be gone. He is making sail for home.'

'I know too well what happens when you sail late in the year,' said Saul. He was speaking *koine* as they were, common Greek, the international language of the world.

'I am grateful to you for bringing me my correspondence. Now I have all winter to prepare my replies. Where did you come from?'

'From Antioch,' said Maria. She and Saul understood each other, although they had only just met. It was the accent, the way they stood and comported themselves, they were both educated, of good breeding, they were not of the *pullati*, those of the brown stuff, the plebs.

'We have come to meet our father here,' she explained. 'He is a man who travels, on important affairs.'

'Of course,' murmured Saul, 'I can tell that from speaking to you.'

Jeshua was looking around at the spectacle unfolding. All about them were the people of the city. Lawyers in full, purple-edged toga; the clients who could afford their services; young dancers and their mothers turned to fortune-telling; bankers and brokers; brassy Syrian whores, vivid in their bright clothes and make-up; idlers, swindlers and vagabonds; merchants and shopkeepers; bookies and betters.

'What is happening?' Jeshua asked.

Saul stowed his letters away inside his tunic and came between the two, putting his arms round their shoulders.

'You've arrived in time for the horse race,' he said, in a friendly fashion. 'It is October the fifteenth, the day of the ceremonial race.'

Light, high-stepping horses were prancing on to the raked track from the street, their slight riders bright in their finery. They began to trot round the track so that all might see them, and the bookies standing on their wooden steps started to shout the odds. Jeshua watched them with keen interest.

'We went to the circus in Antioch,' he said, 'but there they raced chariot teams. I have not seen men racing upon horses.'

'It is an old custom,' said Saul. 'The Greeks and Etruscans raced like this, before chariots. Choose a horse! Which one takes your fancy?'

'I think . . . that one, the black with the flaxen mane and tail. In the red and yellow colours,' Jeshua said.

The crowd was buzzing, men shouting, leaping up in the air to see their selection better, calling encouragement. It was exciting, the boy's face was alive. Saul smiled at him, watching his horse go by. The black stallion was bright of eye, his hooves polished with yellow, glossy skin bursting with health.

'It looks a good one,' Saul admitted. 'I shall take the piebald there, with the green ribbons. What about you, Maria?'

Maria had been watching the steps of the Vestal temple, on to which six virgins had come out in their ceremonial dress. Nearby, where the white tape marked the starting line, the high priest, the *flamen* of Mars, was waiting.

'Oh, I am not sure,' she said. 'I know little of horses. But . . . that one there, with white socks. I shall take her.'

'The horse of Venus,' said Saul. 'See, she prances outside the temple.'

Across the track they could see the statue of Venus inside her temple, her breasts decorated with pearls.

'Aphrodite, really,' Saul murmured, 'the Greek goddess of love. Now the Romans think of her as Venus, who was once the goddess of the fields. Strange, isn't it, how the gods can change their names, their very character. But come now, what about a wager on this race, now that we have chosen our horses?'

'We do not have much money to spare,' Maria said carefully, 'and we have to find somewhere to live while we are waiting for our father to meet us here.'

Saul glanced thoughtfully at her and then smiled.

'But for bringing letters there must be a fee,' he said. 'Here, I will pay for the bets.'

He reached inside his tunic for the *crumella* kept safe about his neck and fished out some coins. They followed him over to a bookie at his stand.

'Hoy, Timothy,' he called, 'what odds on the black with the flaxen mane?'

The bookmaker smiled, a slim Greek in his late twenties. He spoke with a surprisingly cultured accent.

'Three gets you five, Saul,' he said, and Saul handed over the money.

'These young people have brought the letters from Thasos,' he said, bringing them out with a flourish, and showing them to Timothy. Jeshua peered curiously at them once more.

'From so many different places!' he exclaimed, and Saul looked at him with interest.

'You can read, young master?'

'Why yes,' the boy said, 'my father is a learned man.'

'I know,' Saul murmured politely, 'that is what you said.'

'Our mother had us taught, for that was what he wanted.' Maria chimed in.

'Your mother is learned too?'

'Our mother is dead,' Maria said quietly, and the two men nodded. Many were the things that could kill, from men to evil humours in the air. Many were the children orphaned younger than the brother and sister in front of them.

'She had scribes instruct us,' Jeshua said.

'Timothy here is a scribe. When he is not making a book,' Saul said with a grin. 'He'll help you, if you need the practice.'

'Happy to,' said Timothy. He handed back the letters and took another bet.

'I'd like to read those later, make my copies,' he said.

'We have travelled, Timothy and I,' said Saul. He waved his sheaf of missives before tucking them away, 'all about the Great Sea, spreading the word of God. When we ran low on money we would go to the games and run a book from our tent. We made money. We know about winners, Timothy and I.'

Saul's eyes were suddenly far away. He massaged the stump of his ear in a habitual gesture. The two children watched him carefully until then he came back to them.

'Timothy is writing a history of all we have done,' he said, inconsequentially, and the scribe nodded.

From behind the temple of Mars, from the rookery of tall, swaying buildings at the foot of the Esquiline Hill came the sound of rough voices, shouting and singing. The first of them, a dun mob splashed with the bright colours of the strumpets, burst through the gap by the temple wall, pushing their way into the crowd and a howl of execration went up from a similar group of toughs and whores, men and women, gathered where the Sacred Way left the Forum. The two lots proceeded to exchange abuse, threats and waved fists.

'What's *happening?*' asked Maria.

'The lot that have just arrived live in the slum of Suburra, over there. The others live along the Sacred Way,' Timothy explained. 'One lot gets to keep the winner of the horse race.'

'They keep the horse? Why?'

'The gods,' Saul said with a smile. 'What else? The ones who keep the winning horse will be blessed by the gods with good luck for a whole year. It's a very old tradition, the gods have always enjoyed a horse race.'

They took their small pottery *tesserae* tokens from the bookmaker and moved away, towards the rope rail. Saul reached inside his tunic and pulled out one of the letters.

'I thought I saw the hand of Torlonia,' he murmured. 'Good, good.'

'The letters are marked to *Paul*,' Maria remarked. 'Yet Thasos called you Saul.'

Saul looked up, and smiled. 'I am one and the same,' he said. 'There are those that know me as Saul, and others as Paul.'

He pushed the letter back.

'Time enough for reading later, and all winter to pen a reply. The race is about to start!'

The steps of the temples were awash with people; Saul, Maria and her brother were in a favoured part against the rope rail. In front of them the horses pranced and shook their heads, their riders balanced on their backs.

From the steps, the *flamen* of Mars sounded a blast on the *cornu*, the white tape fluttered to the ground, pounded into the sand by the sudden pummelling hooves of the animals.

The sound of the horses was blotted out by the furious roar of the people, leaping and cavorting, raving and shrieking, beating themselves and each other in their passion as the pack of animals made for the first corner, sand dust flying.

By the Basilica Julia a grey and a roan collided and went down in a tumble of thrashing hooves. The grey scrambled back up on its feet, its young jockey still clinging to its mane. He struggled back on to his pad saddle, blood streaming from his nose, and rejoined the race. The roan got up, looked about and jumped over the rope, trotting away up the street. A man in the crowd gave a howl of anguish, flinging his shirt at the dazed jockey, leaping on to the track himself, beating and reviling him. He chased him down the sand as the horses came around again, and there was a sudden, short shriek as he vanished underneath the pack of animals.

'Your black is in the lead!' Saul cried to Jeshua, ignoring the tumbled, bloody corpse like everyone else. The *cornu* sounded again for the last lap and the black and a grey contested for first place. As his horse tired, the jockey of the black swerved across his opponent, but the grey had been expecting it, and went for the inside as the *meta* turning post came up. The black jockey had a counter to that, as the grey's thrusting head came through, he slashed at its eyes with his whip. There were no rules at the circus, only winners and losers.

The legs of the grey went stiff, its head came up and its jockey went over it. The thundering mob of horses behind crashed into it and the black trotted for the line, leaving the mêlée behind.

'*Naufragia!*' went the cry. 'Shipwreck!'

The *flamen* of Mars was waiting at the line in his heavy robes of office, he caught the flaxen mane in his hand as the jockey slid from the sweating animal. Two acolytes stood behind him, holding shining, ornate bowls. The people of the Sacred Way and Suburra surged about then, growling.

The *flamen* cried out in a great, clear voice.

'*Whence comes death, thence also life may rise again!*'

A glittering, hooked knife was in his hand. With the skill of constant practice he plunged it into the neck of the victorious horse, the hot blood gushing out over his hand and into the first of the ready bowls. The thumping heart of the fast horse pumped it out like a scarlet fountain, and the people roared their approval.

As the bowl was filled, the horse sank to its knees, its eyes glazing over in incomprehension. Its heart, that had taken it around the race course, continued to empty its body of blood. The acolyte reverently carried the heavy bowl over the Forum, to the palace of Numa, home of the Pontifex Maximus, ultimate religious authority of Rome. There the fire was burning in the hearth.

The second bowl was filling, on the Vestal steps the virgins waited for it.

It was full, the black horse with its now-bloody flaxen mane and its flaxen tail, had fallen on to its side. Working as the expert butcher he was, the *flamen* severed the head and held it high. Blood was dribbling down his arm and over his robes. The crowd stood in pent-up silence about him. All stared at the temple. A sudden gush of silver smoke rising in the clear autumn sky.

'*Whence comes death,*' the *flamen* howled a second time, '*thence also may life arise again!*'

With a powerful jerk of his arm he threw the small, neat

black head with its still-open eyes high up into the air. A roar erupted from the waiting horde of the Sacred Way and Suburra and he stepped smartly back on to the safety of the temple steps as the head vanished into a boiling scrum of screaming, fighting people.

'Get back!' Saul cried, pulling the children over towards the central fountain. They scrambled up on to its stone rim, watching the brawl. The head was not visible, its position only recognisable by a swirling in the fighting crowd, like a whirlpool that sucked in human bodies. As the centre of the battle moved about the Forum people lay like jetsam on the shore, groaning, pushing themselves to hands and knees, staggering after the fray.

'There it is!' Saul cried, and they saw it tumbling through the air, a hunk of torn and bloody meat. It was seized, thrown again, and some fleet-footed youths were running free in triumph towards the Suburra. A howl of rage and disappointment came from the dwellers of the Sacred Way, but it was gone. Saul, Maria and Jeshua climbed down.

'Well, good fortune for the people of Suburra,' Saul said genially.

'What will they do with it?'

'Hang it on a sacred wall in their quarter,' Saul replied knowledgeably. 'They nail it to a length of wood that is the tree of life, and hang it from their wall.'

He waved a hand at the temples.

'The blood of the horse has purified the city. Its bones will protect the inhabitants of Suburra.'

He smiled and gave a small, faintly mocking shrug.

'That is what they and their ancestors believe, and belief is all, is it not? Jeshua, do you have your *tessera*? Come, collect your winnings.'

They went through the thinning crowd, past men having

crushed fingers set, or pressing cloth wet from the fountain against gashed wounds; past women looking anxiously in polished metal mirrors at bruises and swollen lips; amongst those with empty purses and those ajingle, heading for the free baths to complain and the bars to celebrate.

'Hoy, Timothy,' said Saul, 'you owe this young man some money.'

The scribe who ran a book paid up willingly, his burly *apparitore* with his club guarding his fat bag of coins.

'I'm down at the pit next week, Saul,' he mentioned. 'Wolf will be there.'

'The usual day? I'll call by.'

Saul turned to the young couple.

'So you're waiting for your father? Where are you meeting him?'

'Here.'

Saul reached inside his tunic and with an evident show of delight pulled out a little *solaria*, a tiny sundial, half the size of a lady's pocket mirror. He held it level, raising up the little leaf of the *gnomon* and peering at its shadow as it incised the engraved *polos*.

'The *hora sexta*,' he pronounced with satisfaction, flipping the *gnomon* flat again and tucking his miniature timepiece away. 'When are you to meet your father?'

'Midsummer's day,' Maria said dryly, and Saul looked at her, nonplussed.

'But that is next year,' he protested. 'Why have you come so early?'

'We had no choice,' she said, and next to her Jeshua nodded in agreement, suddenly rubbing his wound, aching in memory.

'Men are trying to kill us,' she continued quietly. 'Men who killed our mother, in Antioch.'

'Men you know,' said Jeshua, his eyes large in his face. 'Thasos said so.'

Saul looked from one to the other in query.

'The Fisherman,' said Maria, and breath hissed through his teeth.

'Ahhh . . . Peter,' he said quietly. 'Yes, the Fisherman. Your mother, then, was an enemy of Peter. Do you know why? Why he killed her?'

'No,' Maria said firmly, and next to her, Jeshua's face was expressionless. 'We are but children.'

Saul eyed them thoughtfully.

'Yet an enemy of Peter must be a friend of mine,' he murmured. He rubbed the stump of his ear in his familiar way. 'The Fisherman is ever one ready to use a weapon. He it was that took off my ear . . . Have you anywhere to stay, while you wait for your father, on midsummer's day?'

'No. We ran, we have lived on the deck of the ship.'

'And little *denarii*, despite your winnings. You will find Rome a costly place . . .'

Maria cast a slender hand about at the temples ringing the great Forum.

'I am a dancer, a singer. I am trained in the ritual arts.'

Saul's face brightened.

'A maenad!' he said cheerfully. 'We shall find you work. The temples always need pretty girls. And you can stay with me, until you find somewhere better.'

On the bloody sand a team of butchers were expertly cutting up the horse, tossing the heavy joints on to a waiting cart. The city *vespillones* were moving through the Forum with a big wagon, clearing the rubbish. The butchers took the opportunity to throw the offal and flayed skin aboard. A flaxen mane flew through the air. The *vespillones* swept the bloody area clean and washed it down to purify it of demons. Water flowed freely in channels through the Forum, taking the blood of sacrifice away from the temples into the great *cloaca maxima*. A dead man lay unclaimed on the stone, they picked him up and tossed him on the rubbish. They were prohibited from leaving carcasses on the street, nor could they put them in the sewer, they had to be taken to the mass grave at the Esquiline.

'Come on,' said Saul, 'I live not far away.'

He led them across the Forum. They crossed the newly wet stone and their sandals left damp footprints behind them, steaming in the sun.

'Your mother,' Saul said casually, 'she must have known many people. People of the gods, for otherwise why would she have earned so much enmity from the Fisherman?'

'Perhaps,' Maria said cautiously.

'She knew, possibly, the Cowled Man?'

He stopped suddenly, looking from one to the other, searching their faces with his dark eyes.

'The Cowled Man,' he repeated. 'Have you heard that name?'

They shook their heads, watching him carefully.

'Or Zaddik. The Righteous. He is known as the Teacher of Righteousness by some. Zaddik.'

Jeshua glanced at his sister.

'No,' he said, 'we do not know that name.'

Saul relaxed, and began to walk on again.

'It is no matter,' he said. 'I thought you might know him.'

He reached inside his tunic, and felt the letters there.

'He is someone that Paul looks for.'

Trotting beside him, Jeshua looked up curiously.

'But *you're* Paul,' he objected.

'Only sometimes,' said Saul.

'Nice place you've got here,' said the man.

Saul eyed him carefully.

'I like it,' he said.

Slouched on a stone bench on the terrace with yellowing vine leaves, sheltering him from the autumn sun, the man looked out over the glittering Tiber. Down on the rocks men stood with short rods, there was a cry of triumph and a shimmering fish slapped water up into the air. The man shifted his position and broke wind.

'Yes, well I'd like it too,' he said, his dark eyes ran over Saul like knife blades. 'Living high and mighty at the Emperor's expense and doing nothing.'

Down in the water, the fish was fighting for its life and cries of encouragement came on the air as the fisherman struggled to bring it to shore.

'The Emperor has many living at his expense,' said Saul, 'and many who do little, except heap upon him extravagant praise, for which they receive their reward.'

The brown eyes widened slightly.

'Do you know who I am?' he inquired.

'You must be Tigillinus,' said Saul, watching him with the same attention as the fisherman gave his catch below. 'Horse-trader, spymaster and imperial confidant.'

'Pretty words,' Tigillinus sneered, in his coarse Sicilian accent, 'but of course, you're an educated man. Yes, I give the boss what he wants. And you have missed out a title. Imperial co-prefect.'

It was Saul's turn to express surprise.

'What has happened to Burrus?'

'Burrus is lying at home. Something's eating his throat. He always liked to talk too much. *I* have the job now. And I give the boss what he wants. Which all costs money. So I'm looking to make some savings. I'm in charge of re-housing. I'm going to re-house *you*. What do you fancy? Somewhere in Suburra? Or would you prefer a ticket back to Tarsus?'

His square, tanned, cruel face split into a seamed smile.

'Oh, yes, I know all about you. I know where you come from.'

'Not enough, it seems,' said Saul calmly. 'Have you talked to Burrus about me? Or to Seneca?'

'Fine fellows like them?' the Sicilian jeered. 'Men who read literature? They don't talk to the likes of me, mister Jew. But who's in charge now, then?'

He jerked a thick thumb at his chest.

'Me. Me and the boss, we understand each other. Nero, he's tired of being a statesman, he wants a bit of fun. A man can be frugal, or he can be Caesar. Well, lucky for him, he's Caesar. Lucky for me too. Just not so lucky for you. Now, you've got until tomorrow to piss off, so start getting your things ready. I've got this little number reserved for one of his favourite bugger-boys.'

Tigillinus inserted a finger into his mouth and began excavating from a tooth. A piece of meat appeared on the end of a yellow nail and he flicked it to the floor.

'Snipped it all off he did,' he said ruminatively. 'Looks just like a girl.'

'If you haven't spoken to Burrus or Seneca,' Saul said steadily, 'then I should tell you what you ought to know. You can't get rid of me. I'm very valuable to the Emperor.'

'Valuable?' Tigillinus let out a hoarse laugh. 'He doesn't even know who you are!'

He leaned forward, with his elbows on the polished stone table on Saul's balcony. Down on the rocks a man capered eagerly, a hook gleaming on the end of a pole as he waited for the pike to be dragged into range. A small crowd had gathered up on the bank, yelling encouragement.

'I'll tell you who's valuable to the Emperor. Pretty girls and boys. Actors and people why play the lyre. Anyone with money he can get hold of. Priests with a good religion.'

'I have a good religion,' Saul said quietly.

'You?' Tigillinus cried in disbelief. 'You mince about like some old dowager discussing etiquette. I'm talking about the real thing!'

His voice dropped.

'The Emperor has embarked on a personal journey of discovery, and he is taking Rome with him.'

'Does Rome wish to go?' Saul asked blandly.

'Don't get funny with me,' Tigillinus snarled. 'They'll do what they're told, if they know what's good for them.'

'The Emperor Nero believes the old order to be dead and ossified. I happen to agree with him, but I do not think that what he plans to replace it with will work . . .' Saul said, almost dreamily. 'However, while those of the old order most certainly hate him with a vengeance for what he is doing, for his orgiastic excesses and obsessions, not to mention his appropriation of their money – for is he not generous with other men's money as well as his own? – I think it not unlikely that he can hang on to his head for the time being, at least.'

Tigillinus looked at him through slitted eyes.

'Any more of this talk and you may find it difficult to hang on to yours,' he said threateningly.

'Pah!' Saul said dismissively. 'You know what I say is true. Isn't that what you are really for, Mister co-prefect? Don't you run the spies that seek out disaffection? Won't you be the one looking for "traitors"? Oh yes. But beware, having too many wealthy men, too many generals slit their own veins will cause the others to think deeply . . .'

There was a pause, and he seemed to be watching the ongoing contest in the water.

'Do you know where Judah is?" he said suddenly. 'Who lives there?'

'Of course I do,' Tigillinus grunted. Saul had a small glazed dish of olives on the table, glossy black in their oil. The Sicilian took one, chewing the plump flesh and spitting the stone out on to the people passing beneath.

'That's where all the prick-slicers live. The Hebes.'

'Not all the Jews, no,' Saul corrected him. 'It is, to be sure, the ancient land of the Jews, given to them by their god, Yahweh. But they don't all live there. Many, many of them are scattered all about the shores of the Great Sea, in Corinth and Ephesus, in Smyrna and Parthia, Laodicea and Galatia. There are Hebrews living here in Rome, there are others in Alexandria, in Antioch and Damascus. Jewish communities are everywhere.'

Tigillinus belched, and helped himself to another couple of olives.

'Do I care?'

'You should,' Saul said admonishingly. 'You should not restrict your spy intelligence to those in Rome. The Jews might cost your master his head, and yours also.'

Tigillinus's eyes widened.

'You see,' Saul pointed out acidly, 'you should have talked to Burrus after all.'

'All right, then,' the other said, more quietly, '*you* tell me about it.'

'Very well. Deranged though he is, like the Emperor Caligula before him, your master can probably survive offending most of the established old order, as he is doing, in the name of some bizarre oriental belief in personal liberation through excess.'

'You're a wordy bastard,' Tigillinus grunted, 'just like those pricks Burrus and Seneca.'

'We wordy *illegitimati* are keeping you and your master alive,' Saul observed sharply, 'so sit there and listen. What the Emperor will *not* survive is another major colonial uprising. The British tribesmen under their leader Boudicca, pushed the powers of the Roman Empire to the limit. Nero could not even send reinforcements to the governor, Suetonius Paulinus, because the situation in the more strategically vital provinces of Gaul and Germany appeared equally threatening. Indeed, he even considered giving up and pulling back the four British legions to bolster them. Had it not been for the military genius of Paulinus the island would now once more be the property of the British – and what message would *that* send to other conquered peoples of the Empire, answer me that?'

Saul stared savagely over his beaky nose at Tigillinus, but the former horse-dealer stayed warily silent.

'The cost of it all was appalling,' Saul went on. 'The British war turned the province from an asset into a liability.'

He leaned forward.

'It even caused devaluation of the currency,' he said softly. He reached into his purse and tossed a shiny silver coin on to the stone. It bore the likeness of Nero, with his thick neck and chariot-driver's hairstyle. 'There's *tin* in that. It's not worth what people think it is.'

'You aren't supposed to know that,' Tigillinus blurted.

'I know many things,' Saul said quietly and confidently. 'I know about gods, and I know about the Jews. What do you know about the Jews, Prefect?'

'Pig-worshipping, prick-slicing Hebes, as I told you,' Tigillinus said disagreeably.

'You omitted the part about the swine, I think,' Saul murmured. 'Let me enlighten you a little, then, since your future welfare may depend upon my people. I'll be brief, I can tell you are a busy man – have you not an apartment to find for the Emperor's catamite?

'Like most powerful forces it is easy to understand. Build your house close to the river in the summer and when the spring floods come they wash it away. We are the Jews. We do not believe in gods various, as do other peoples, but one God alone. He is a jealous God, who commands us to worship no other. In return for our worship, he has given us our own land, the land of Judea. This land, which the Jews believe has been given to us in trust by the only true God, is currently occupied by the Romans. It is a Roman province, a part of the Empire, and taxed and ruled as such.'

Saul stared steadily at Tigillinus, his eyes unwinking.

'The Jews believe that the Romans under their Emperor are countermanding the will of God. They believe that God will come, very very soon, to deliver his people from the yoke of Rome, as he did through Moses, delivering his people from the slavery of Egypt. Only this time he will come himself, wrapped in fire and surrounded by his angels, and he will bring Judgement Day. And to hasten that day, there are many in Judea who are ready to rise, sword in hand, against the Romans. And if they do, they shall be as doves before the Lord, but as ravening wolves to the heathens. It will make Paulinus's problems with Boudicca seem like a spring outing.'

Down at the river's edge, the pike was tiring, the waiting hook trembled, flickering in the sun.

'The rising can probably be put down, given the resources of Rome and its soldiers – unless the Almighty *does* come – but it will prove very costly. It will put the Emperor's position – given his known dislike of government – further under strain. He will require the services of a first-class general, a real fighting soldier like Corbulo, to put it down. Such a man, with the loyalty of battle-hardened troops to support him, may come to the realisation that emperors can be made elsewhere than Rome.'

'Yes, yes,' Tigillinus said testily, 'I understand all this. But what does it all have to do with *you*, and your strange little cult?'

'*I* stand between that devastating uprising with all its consequences, and you.'

The Sicilian raised his eyebrows in disbelief. One was split by an old scar.

'I have been a landlord in my time,' he commented. 'I have heard all the excuses for not coming up with the rent. Come on, you may as well just get out and let me get the little queer in here. *You* can prevent a Jewish revolt? You are their king, perhaps? Or their God?'

'No. I am his apostle,' Saul said steadily. 'Let me explain to you. The people of Israel believe that the coming of the Lord is nigh, that he will deliver them from their bondage. Unfortunately, his coming is hampered by a plethora of false prophets. Only a year or two ago we saw one in action. The Egyptian and his Chosen Ones. You remember? He claimed that he and his disciples had been sent by God to overthrow the Romans and restore Israel to the Jews. *He* very nearly ignited the whole province. Only swift and violent action by the troops of the procurator, Antonius Felix, kept the lid on, and they had to slaughter hundreds. *Nothing has changed*. Those who could bring out the entire population in war are there. It is not important what exact title one gives them – there are a number of groups – they are Essenes, they are Zaddokites, they are Nazoreans and Zealots. To Felix and the Romans they are brigands and outlaws. But they are but variations on a theme. They all want their land rid of Roman occupation, they want the old monarchy of Judea reinstated, together with its legitimate priesthood. In fact, they want more than that, for in the Book of Numbers does it not say: "a star from Jacob takes the leadership, a sceptre arises from Israel"? There are many who believe that the star is the Interpreter of the Law who shall come . . . as it is written . . . the sceptre is the prince. No, further than that, there are those, the *zelotai*, who believe that the star *has* come, that the prince, the Messiah, has already been amongst them, and they are the most dangerous of all . . . They prophesy that from Judea shall go forth men destined to rule the world.'

Saul stared at Tigillinus all the while, his eyes bright and unwinking. The prefect found it uncomfortable.

'Do you know who the Prince was? His name was Jeshua. He led a movement not unlike the Chosen Ones some twenty-five years ago. He entered Jerusalem in the state of a king. Before he could raise the land against the Romans he was betrayed to the Prefect of Judea, one Pontius Pilate. He was crucified and died.'

'So? Plenty of troublemakers in this world. Rome rules many people – Macedonians, Phrygians, Egyptians, Africans, Gauls, Britons, Germans, Jews. They're always throwing up rebel leaders. We crucify them too, that's what we do with trouble-makers. What's so special about this Jeshua?'

His mouth worked around the unfamiliar language.

'What's that in a decent tongue? Jesus, yes? Why is this Jesus important?'

'He died upon the crucifix, he was taken down and placed in a tomb – alone, for having died as a criminal his body was unclean by Jewish law. Three days later he rose from the dead. In visions he appeared to his disciples, and commanded them to continue his work. Then he ascended into Heaven.'

There was silence, only broken by an outburst of cheering

from the river. Held high from the iron hook on a pole, the long silver pike flapped wearily.

'Where I come from in Sicily the simple people see the Green Man at nightfall and think it good luck,' Tigillinus said stonily, 'others think that nymphs live in the woods. I believe that if you bite a gold coin it is hard. I believe that if you cut a man open he dies.'

'The man Jeshua, whom you call Jesus, was the Chosen One of God, the Messiah, the Anointed One, in Greek, the *Christos*. That is what his disciples believed. They formed themselves into a community that they called *The Way*, and led by Peter the Fisherman, and James, that they call the Just, the brother of Jesus – not that their importance matters to me – began to spread the gospel of the resurrection of Jesus.'

'And do all Jews agree with this – that their God has come in the guise of this preacher?'

'Ah,' Saul smiled approvingly. 'Good question. Certainly not. Is not a hanged man accursed in the sight of God?'

He peered enquiringly at Tigillinus. 'You are familiar with Deuteronomy? No? Ah well. No. Many Jews would say – how can this Jesus have been the Chosen One, come to liberate the people of Israel? *For he failed!*'

'That's right. We nailed him up. So?'

'But he was the son of God,' Saul said intensely, leaning forward over the table, 'for he rose from the dead.'

'I believe all this as much as I do in the Green Man,' Tigillinus muttered. 'So what, to you – since this is all about what you think, and *I* think you are mad from too much religion – does that mean?'

'It means that God is revealing his purpose to us,' Saul said softly. 'It means that he favours not just the people of Israel, but the people of the world, the gentiles too, such as yourself, who will come to *him*. Those who will believe in him, and will through their faith in him and his son Jesus, the *Christos*, sit at his right hand in Heaven.'

Tigillinus sighed wearily.

'So you and these fishing disciples go about getting people to believe all this? What is the point? And what good will it do *me*?'

'Ah,' said Saul. 'The disciples and I do *not* preach the same message. Not at all.'

His eyes glittered.

'They are but simple men. Their minds cannot encompass and grasp what has happened. *God has spoken to them.* He has spoken and they cannot hear, they stumble along the same rutted ways, their eyes fixed upon the ground. They preach adherence to the Law, that thicket of regulations that has guided the people of Israel for so long, when what God is saying is that those laws no longer apply!'

Saul rose from his bench and held up his clenched hands in the air in triumph.

'That is why God has turned to me, to be foremost amongst his apostles. No, to be his *only* apostle! For I did not receive my gospel from man, nor was I taught it. God himself spoke in my ear . . .'

Saul turned to Tigillinus, his tunic swinging. The sun was sinking, splashing the balcony with orange.

'What will my gospel do for you, Prefect? The Lord Jesus will return, and return soon. If you will believe in him, then he will deliver you from the wrath to come.'

Saul looked cynically down at the brutal figure in front of him.

'But I feel you would prefer worldly rewards, would you not? . . . Well, those I have too. We come back to the revolt of the people of Israel. Here those who believe that the Messiah is yet to come and those who believe he was the Lord Jesus, those of The Way, are as one. They are all *zaddikim*, they are zealous for the Law. They are waiting for the day when they will rise up and slaughter their Roman masters. But they are not fools, they know that to take on the might of Rome they require men. As many men as possible, and as trained in the art of war as possible. Where will they find them, outside Israel?'

Saul's voice sank to a whisper.

'They want the Jews that live all about the Great Sea, in Mesopotamia, in Syria, in Egypt and in Macedon and in Persia. Many are the Jewish officers in these armies, highly trained, highly experienced. For God, they will come. Those of The Way move all about the Great Sea, seeking to bring them into their new Church, which will call upon them when the day comes. I have knowledge of them . . . the Cowled Man, he dogs me . . .'

Saul stood looking out over the river at the far bank, his eyes a long way off.

'They are all wrong . . .' he whispered.

His voice rose into a howl, and those down at the water's edge looked up nervously.

'For God has revealed his purpose to *me!*' he shrieked. 'To me alone!'

Then his voice dropped, and he spoke normally.

'God is coming, the Lord Jesus will soon be back among us, his wondrous wounds for all to see. But he is not coming just for the people of Israel. He comes for all. Those of The Way, those servants of righteousness, who see only Israel and the Law of Moses, believe in another Jesus. They stumble when they should embrace the true Jesus. It is *my* Church that is the Church of God, and the people flock to *me*. He who believes *my* word, he who has faith in Christ and not fidelity to the Law shall be saved, and who is that man? He is not a gentile, not a Jew, but a new man, a Christian.'

'I get it,' Tigillinus said slowly. 'If they aren't Jews, they won't fight! You've chopped their balls off.'

Saul smiled.

'I knew we would understand each other . . . I'm so glad you came by. If Burrus is ill, then you can help me . . .'

'Burrus knows about all this?'

'How do you think I got here?' Saul murmured. 'I was a Pharisee, I worked for the High Priest, Ananas, I persecuted those of The Way. Then I joined them, in the community they call Damascus, to the east of Jerusalem, on the Dead Sea. I became one of them, so that I would know them. I was with them for three years. It was there in that desert place that God revealed his true plan to me . . .'

'You need some help, you said?' Tigillinus said briskly.

'Yes . . .' Saul murmured. 'The time is coming for God to move against those of The Way. I cannot yet myself return to Jerusalem, for fear of assassination. But I have agents, those who communicate with me. James, the brother of Jesus, that they call the Just, is a powerful man . . .'

'Let me know,' Tigillinus said shortly. 'I can make things happen.'

He frowned.

'How can you and he be talking so differently, if he is the brother of this prophet of yours?'

'He knew not the true Jesus,' Saul said dreamily. 'He knew *another* Jesus.'

Down at the water's edge the pike thrashed briefly as its captor opened its belly. Its insides drifted away on the stream and it was still. He hoisted it over his back on the short pole and began to climb up the steps. Tigillinus rose.

'You can stay here,' he said. 'I'll fix the little queer up somewhere else.'

By the door he turned.

'These people of yours,' he said, 'they actually believe all that stuff?'

Saul smiled. He heard Tigillinus's *caligae* clattering down the stairs to the street.

'Paul does,' he murmured.

Hook Norton

Juliana pressed the back of her neck with her hand, holding her head this way and that, a frown crinkling her high forehead. At his desk Connell peered at a sheet of text and made a note with his pen on the sheet of paper. It was quiet, she heard the soft scrape of the gold nib moving. She reached out and rearranged some cut-out sections, then sighed. Connell looked up. Cold coffee cups sat grey on the table,

'All right?' he enquired.

'I've got a headache,' she admitted. 'All the muscles in my neck have gone stiff.'

'It's an academic illness,' he said. 'We spend so much time poring over manuscripts and texts. Still, I suppose every profession has its drawbacks. Look what happened to the hatters.'

'Went mad,' she said. 'I think *I'm* going to go mad if I don't give myself a break from trying to make sense of this particular batch of Coptic letters.'

'Let's get a breath of air,' he suggested. 'We've been cooped up for hours.'

She picked up her bag, and they went out into the garden.

The autumn sun had burned off the mist, occasional russet leaves were drifting down from the chestnuts on the boundary.

'Mind if I smoke?' she said. 'It might help my head.'

'No.' he said, slightly surprised. 'Go ahead.'

She fumbled in her bag, taking out a home-made cigarette, and lit it with a small gold lighter. As the smoke drifted across his face, Connell's nostrils flared.

'I haven't smelled that since I was an undergraduate!' he exclaimed.

'I don't smoke much of it. Just every now and again. Want some?'

Connell took the joint cautiously, and inhaled.

'College dons arrested in drugs bust,' he muttered. 'God, that takes me back. Sitting stoned on the hill, believing I was the reincarnation of Darius, King of Prussia.'

She glanced at him quickly. 'Did you do that too? I started this when I was in Egypt, in the desert, out at the dig, and I *knew* the ghosts about me were real.'

'I know.'

'I get it now,' she said quietly. 'Reading the texts, I know the Children are here, or I'm there . . . The text you're working on, with Maria and Jeshua, is there a woman called Gaia?'

'I haven't come to her, if she's there.'

'I'm pretty sure it's the right time. It's certainly Nero's Rome. Maria's the right age, about fifteen. I put together some fragments.'

'The codex is a bit ragged, in parts.'

Juliana moved her head cautiously.

'I think it's getting a bit better.'

'Would you like me to massage your neck? I find that's often the only way.'

'Maybe . . . I think I'll lie down for a few minutes.'

'Go ahead. Take the spare room.'

She took a final pull at her cigarette and passed the stub to Connell. He inhaled as she went inside, then ground the end against the sole of his shoe. He walked thoughtfully around his garden, hearing his shoes rustle against the leaves, relaxed by the marijuana.

'This won't get the baby fed,' he muttered to himself, and went inside. As he closed the door, he heard Juliana's voice from the spare bedroom.

'Frank . . .'

The curtains were drawn, and the sunlight filtering through them was deep gold. She was lying on her stomach on the bed. She had untied her hair, and it lay over her shoulders in a raven sheet. She had taken off all her clothes, just a small hand towel was draped modestly over her hips. He knelt down by the bed, reaching into the thick, soft hair to massage the taut muscles of her neck.

'Oh,' she said quietly. 'That's lovely.'

He worked gently, feeling the cramp slowly easing. After some minutes she turned over, her black hair falling across the white pillow. Her eyes were closed. The gold light fell on her body and she was beautiful.

'Maria does this to Gaia,' Juliana muttered.

In the *thermae*, steam drifted across the great room, around the pillars, hiding the nooks and crannies with its soft heat. He bent and kissed the sweet sheen of her breasts. In the steam a hand could steal unseen up a smooth thigh, hidden from view under a modest towel, while through the doors were the calls of the bathers. He felt her shudder as his hand moved into her.

The herbs moved in his mind, the blood hot in his throat. A girl's hand slipping underneath the loincloth of her slave masseuse, allying them against the terrors that faced them both. He felt Juliana freeing him, the soft wetness of her lips upon him.

The sunlight streamed gold through the curtains, just as it had in the *thermae*, rich yellow shafts painting the moving stream.

7

Oxford

They could hear the eight coming. It was a strange, rythmical sound, of blades clopping in unison, of men gasping with effort, of other men exhorting them to do more, of water slipping over a shiny hull. Connell and Abercrombie stepped to one side as the coach on his bicycle came up the towpath, and the long racing-boat went by. The breath of the oarsmen hung briefly like mist in the cold air, and the morning sun glittered on the disturbed water. They stepped back on to the path and their brogues crunched the drying red leaves.

'Do you think we're getting ready to let something go public – in a limited sense?' Abercrombie murmured. 'Have you come across anything yet that might raise some interest?'

Connell looked slightly amused.

'Raise interest? I doubt if there'll be anything more controversial this century or next. This is explosive, George.'

'I'm so pleased,' the antiquities dealer said urbanely. 'That's just what I was hoping you'd say.'

The dark-blue racing-shell was disappearing around the bend of the river, pursued by the shouts of the coach.

'If you want to release a text won't we run the risk of Egyptians jumping in and demanding the originals?'

Abercrombie looked down the river, with its bare trees, shorn of branches, leaning over, looking at themselves.

'Who says the texts were discovered in Egypt?' he asked,

almost dreamily, his hands deep in the pockets of his green Barbour.

'It's a fair supposition,' said Connell. 'We have them dated to maybe 350 A.D., they're written in Coptic, the Egyptian language – translated from the original Greek, clearly – and must have been hidden shortly after that time. We are quite definitely dealing with the religious library of the sect we know of now as the Children of Jeshua, which was clearly hidden by them as a result of persecution by the by-then established Catholic Church of the Empire, which considered them heretics. My guess would be that they wound up working in Alexandria and Upper Egypt – hence the Coptic translations – and were then made extinct by the Catholics.'

'Your guess, yes,' George said patiently, 'but isn't there a valid case for saying that they might have surfaced *anywhere* in the old Roman Empire?'

'It's unlikely.'

'But possible. In which case, the Egyptian government would have no right to demand them.'

'Ah,' said Connell. Abercrombie looked across at him with liquid eyes, as sharp as a bird's.

'Which would be a different affair altogether. It would open up the market. You did say the texts were as controversial as anyone could hope for.'

'Oh, yes.'

'I'd say we can both of us think, off hand, of a dozen major institutions who could raise the kind of money required to acquire the entire collection.'

'Of course. Actually, what sort of money?'

'When we're ready, we're going to have an auction. We won't let people through the door unless they can start the bidding at twenty million.'

Abercrombie turned to look at him, and for a moment

Connell could see the naked ambition shining in his pale-blue eyes.

'I want to be a gentleman of leisure, Frank. I don't want to be dealing in fragments of Simeon bar Kochba's letters with strange Jews from Pittsburg for the rest of my life.'

'I can do without it,' Connell agreed.

'But we must establish a sound academic argument to prove the texts could have been found elsewhere than Egypt.'

'I think we can do that,' Connell said slowly.

'Well, that's splendid. I'll shuffle off, then. So we want a text or two that we can circulate to suitably interested parties, as a trial balloon. With more tempting stuff to follow.'

'I'm working on it. Juliana's putting a fragmented codex together right now.'

They left the towpath by the boathouse, where big young men in singlets and shorts were carrying craft down to the water.

'There's just one other thing. It would be terrible if you were to come across anything in the texts that really did link them to Egypt. Some note, put in by the people who hid them, maybe . . .'

'It's possible.'

Abercrombie smiled pleasantly, shaking his head.

'No, it isn't, Frank. Not possible at all.'

'No,' said Connell grinning boyishly, 'of course not.'

He climbed into his old Jaguar and lit a cheroot, winding down the window to let the smoke wisp out into the chill air as he drove out of the city. In the fields, sheep watched him go by, stolid in their warm round coats.

Near the village he turned off down the lane that crossed the old railway line, where the little steam train had pulled its two coaches through the countryside. Saplings and bushes grew all through the old cinder track.

At a half-hidden driveway he turned in, parking in the barn next to the old Morris Minor shooting brake he was restoring, and before going inside, paused feeling the strength of the varnish he had put on over the wood frame.

Juliana looked up from her table, sheets of script spread out in front of her. She looked very pale.

'What's the matter?' he asked.

'They were in Lyons,' she said simply, 'in 181.'

'Oh, God,' he said, understanding. 'So it was them. Of course. It had to be.'

Lyons, Gaul, A.D. May 181

They came, in the end, four of them, and sat themselves down on chairs in the simply furnished room. Irenaeus looked up from the table where he was working. Several sheets of papyrus were before him, covered in his neat Latin script. He put down his pen and shook some sand over the wet black ink.

'You are late,' he observed.

'We are here at the time of our choosing,' said one of the two young women. 'For it may seem to you that you have summoned us, but it is we who wish to interview you.'

There it was, the obdurate determination to stand the whole world on its head, the very first time they opened their mouths. He ignored her grimly.

'And you are not whom I summoned,' he ground out. 'I asked for no women, but your so-called bishop.'

'I am the bishop,' said the young woman.

'You are Paulina Marcellinus, daughter of Marius, and an empty-headed and frivolous young fool,' Irenaeus snapped. 'One who has got caught up with these heretics calling themselves the Children of Jeshua.'

Paulina smiled pleasantly. 'I am still the bishop. For today. But where is the one *you* call Bishop? We wish to speak with him.'

There it was again. He could feel the pulse drumming in his throat, and forced himself to be calm.

'Blessed Pothinus is much advanced in years. *I*, the senior presbyter, am to interrogate you on his behalf.'

'We had heard,' said one of the young men, who had red hair, 'that a new agent of the ungodly had been sent to persecute the righteous.'

Irenaeus stared balefully at him.

'I will teach you the meaning of godly, and ungodly, and, yes, persecution, before I am through,' he promised malevolently. 'For I have been sent from Rome to bring the wicked before Christ.'

'Then you may go back to Rome,' said the second young woman, a striking creature with long black hair and green eyes. 'For we bring the Lord Jesus to the people in these parts. You are not needed here.'

'There is but the one true Church, the Church of Rome, and can be no others,' he thundered. The young people smiled faintly at each other, and he flushed purple with rage.

After a few moments he brought himself under control.

'Let us begin,' he said. 'Your assertion that you are bishop of this nasty cult of yours for today interests me. The blessed Pothinus is Bishop of Lyons today, and Bishop of Lyons tomorrow, and all the days after that until he dies and goes to God.'

'As I understand it, in your Church, if we may call it such,' Paulina remarked distastefully, 'there are three ranks, headed by the bishop, under him the priests and deacons, and it is this hierarchy of henchmen that makes the evil claim to be the guardian of the only true faith.'

'There is one Church, which must be an orthodox Church, which is a straight-thinking one, and a catholic church, which is a universal one. Outside that Church there can be *no salvation.*'

Paulina shook her head maddeningly.

'We cannot accept your view, and will demonstrate to you that it is we who are the true guardians of knowledge. We are the pneumatics, we are those of the spirit. But you asked how it could be so that I am bishop for a day. In the Church of the Children of Jeshua when we meet, all those of us who are initiated and children of the Father, and of the Mother, and possessed of the charismatic gift of inspiration through the Holy Spirit, we cast lots. One lot decides who shall perform the office of priest that day, another to offer the sacrament, as bishop, a third to read the scriptures for worship and a fourth to address us as prophet and offer spiritual instruction when moved by the spirit.'

'An arcane invention,' sneered Irenaeus. 'Pray tell me what possible function it can serve.'

'It is, not least, so that we shall not become like you,' said the second man, Marcellus, chosen as priest that day. 'Being the instruments of God's will, all have equal access, equal participation and equal knowledge. We make no distinction between those who are newcomers to our Church and those of us who have many years of worship. We distinguish not between women and men, between a professional clergy and those you call the laity. Since our roles change every day, no hierarchy may form, and there can be no fixed orders of clergy.'

Irenaeus's mouth tightened. 'I fail to see any advantage in that.'

'How could you? Do you not crave to be bishop? Will you then not be he who is monarch, sole ruler? As such will you not claim the powers of discipline and judgement over those you see as beneath you? You behave as though you have received your authority direct from God. But we say that such as you are merely waterless canals.'

Irenaeus flushed again with anger.

'I crave nothing except to serve the Lord,' he snapped. 'However, you are correct in that I receive my authority direct from God, for I am of the Church of Rome, that was founded by the apostle Peter, rock of the Church, beneficiary of the keys, appointed by Jesus himself.'

'Not so,' said the black-haired woman, shaking her head. 'We are children of the Father and of the Mother, and trace *our* authority back to Mary, the wife and foremost apostle of Jesus – and to –'

'It is you who are mistaken,' Irenaeus shouted, half rising from his seat. He bumped the table with his bare knees and papyrus fell to the stone floor. 'Mary was a mere harlot upon whom Jesus in his mercy took pity. There can be no place for women within the organisation of the Church, except to worship Jesus as directed by their bishop. Does Genesis not say: "a man is the image and glory of God; but woman is the glory of man. For man was not made from woman, but woman from man. Neither was man created for woman, but woman for man." And from the canon itself, that of Timothy: "Let a woman learn in silence with all submissiveness. I permit no woman to teach or to have authority over men; she is to keep silent".'

'We do not accept the authority of Timothy, or any of the others of your scriptures that you claim to be holy. We do not accept that Mark, Matthew, Luke and John that you call your "canon" were written by those who knew Jesus,' said the red-headed Rufus, the reader for the day. 'No, nor Colossians and Ephesians, which ones like you will quote, saying: "Women shall be subject in everything to their husbands". We say they were written by others, loathing of women as Peter was of Mary, seeking only to enslave them. We *know*, Presbyter, because we know whose servant you really are.'

'And I know who *you* are,' Irenaeus snarled. 'You are those who eat meat defiled at pagan festivals and who violate the strictest warnings regarding sexual abstinence and monogamy. You are black sorcerers, who prepare sinful potions with which to entrap the unwary.'

'We buy our meat from the butcher,' Rufus murmured, 'for its quality. It is unimportant whether the beast has travelled through a pagan temple or the abattoir on its way there.'

'It has become defiled with sin, and is rotten with the stinking blood of Satan.'

'Festivals are festivals. Music, dancing and colourful costumes bring cheer to a hard life,' said Marcellus.

'They lead straight to the gates of Hell.'

'Our faith is proof against contagion, Presbyter.'

'To abstain from sex is not good for you,' said Paulina. 'It produces an excess of bile, and makes men and women wake up in the night with clenched and grinding teeth.'

'Whore,' spat Irenaeus.

'And we are not sorcerers but herb-masters. The divine sparks which fell from Paradise into this world of evil fell both on men and plants. We who serve Jesus, the Children of Jeshua, we have been given true knowledge, we know their properties,' Rufus chimed in again. 'Those who are sick, rich or poor, come to us for relief, to be well.'

'Sickness of mind or body is caused by sin,' Irenaeus snapped. 'There is only one cure, for the sinner to go to a church of the one true faith and there fling themselves to their knees and beg the Lord for forgiveness.'

'And if they do not become well, it is because the Lord does not forgive them?' Paulina suggested dryly. 'No, it is because it is Satan who listens behind the screen and he delights in their suffering.'

There was silence in the room for a moment, broken by the black-haired woman bending to pick up the scrolls from the floor.

'You are a learned man, Presbyter,' she observed, 'you do much writing. What is all this work upon the table?'

'Theological weapons that will smash such as you,' Irenaeus told her with satisfaction. 'See there its title – *Against Heresies!* I cut your pathetic posturings into fragments!'

He snapped his fingers.

'There. You are worth so much dust.'

'And what are these?' she asked, unrolling a scroll and examining it. 'The Gospel of Matthew?'

Irenaeus snatched it from her hand.

'Give it to me before you pollute its very substance.'

'Why Matthew? Here, you have others.'

'You have heard of the Gnostic, Marcion?' Irenaeus enquired, with exaggerated politeness. 'A vile heretic such as yourselves. Many are the pure gospels he has fouled with his own thoughts. It is the task of those in the one true Church such as myself to gather in copies of the gospels to eradicate error, to issue new, clean, pure originals, just as they fell from the lips of God and were written down by the holy apostles.'

'But how do you do that? Were you there?'

'God reveals his will to me in prayer,' Irenaeus said quietly. 'No man may come to God except through his own, one true catholic Church, and it is to his clergy, his servants, that his will is revealed.'

'Whose voice can you be listening to, I wonder?' she said, eyeing the man at his table. She picked up a scroll and held it out. 'For Jesus numbered no Matthew amongst his disciples, no, nor a John either.'

She held up a hand as Irenaeus opened his mouth to shout.

'But we have not come to disturb you in your tinkerings, for as those descended from the living Jesus himself we know just how much truth there is in your gospels.'

Irenaeus glowered at her.

'The scriptures are perfect,' he snarled, 'for they were uttered by the Word of God and his Spirit.'

'Jesus did not even have twelve disciples, let alone one called Matthew,' she said mischievously, unable to resist one last taunt, and he crashed his fist to the table. Then she wiped the smile off her face.

'There is something we would know from you,' she said quietly. 'We have heard that the Church of Rome wants martyrs. It wants people to die for it.'

'For their faith,' whispered Irenaeus, and his eyes burned. 'Jesus Christ died to free men from sin and suffering, so there can be no higher destiny for any Christian than to confess his Name, to travel each step of the road that he took. Martyrdom is the pinnacle of the Christian's earthly life, the reward which all who profess the Name shall earnestly desire. The mighty crown awaits each and every one, whatever his standing in the Church, confessors all, who reaches out to be perfected, to be sealed by death. Through martyrdom does God test faith, separating the divine wheat from the chaff.'

'Blood,' the woman said coldly.

'*Semen est sanguis Christianorum*. The blood of the Christians is the seed of the Church. We shall reach out to the many, and the purity of their deaths shall become the training for fresh generations of martyrs of the Church.'

'There is nothing pure about agony.'

'Suffer do they not! Rather do they delight in the Lord with the flow of their blood, that has quenched the flames and fires of Hell with its glorious gore.'

'You make me want to vomit,' said the woman.

'Embracing death in all its forms, our holy martyrs, valiant champions all, form flowers of every shape and colour as they weave a crown to offer the Father.'

'Not the Father.'

She stood up, staring down at him from her very bright green eyes.

'No, nor the Mother. I am Mary, I am she who is descended from the line of Mary and Jesus. *We* follow the teachings of the true Lord.'

'Heresiarch!' Irenaeus spat out, his face white. 'Blasphemer!'

'We know whom you serve, Presbyter,' she said, ignoring him, and the others rose as well. 'You are the slave of Satan, whose offices on earth are in Rome. God is love, and the one you serve is bloody and brutal, responsible for the evil things in the world. Who but he and his servants would coerce innocent believers in Christ to the executioner, telling them that if they hold fast to the name of a dead man they will become pure.'

'Through suffering of one hour the holy martyrs, the witnesses, purchase for themselves eternal life. They offer their blood to God and he gives in exchange complete forgiveness.'

'God who is love, desires human sacrifice?' Rufus asked coldly. 'If he does, he is a cannibal.'

'They long to follow in the steps of Jesus. The Church in every place, because of the love which she cherishes towards God, sends forth, throughout all time, a multitude of martyrs to the Father. In the intense heat, in the very Dog Star of persecution they are tried by the fire and the sword. Others lie in prison, thirsting for the beasts.'

He glared about the room. *'And all the time, the heretics go about as usual.* And none of those who fear death will be saved; for the kingdom of death belongs to those who put themselves to death.'

'Only the devil wants human sacrifice,' Mary said clearly. They moved towards the door.

'We shall see to you!' Irenaeus screamed, his control lost. Marcellus turned back momentarily.

'You had better beware, Presbyter,' he said coldly. 'We do not turn the other cheek. We follow the teachings of Jesus, we are trained in his school, we can take care of ourselves.'

The door closed behind them and Irenaeus slumped back in his chair, his heart pounding and his chest heaving.

He looked furiously about him. The very air was polluted. He flung back a shutter.

'Sin,' he snarled.

The door creaked open, a young man in a simple tunic stood there, the acolyte, the trainee priest. Irenaeus stared at him.

'Sin,' he whispered. 'Sin has been in this room, it has entered our bodies.'

The youth came into the room, the door closing behind him. He knelt down as he was used to doing, pulling his tunic from his back and resting his head in his arms on the table.

'We must drive it out,' the presbyter said softly. In the corner of the room was a switch of birch twigs, he picked it up in his hand and stood over the boy. The milky-white skin of his back was crisscrossed with faint red scars.

The switch moaned as it cut the air. The body jerked, and fresh marks stood out, livid red.

'Hard training, in the school of Christ.'

He could feel himself swelling with the presence of God.

'Discipline and the renunciation of worldly pleasures.'

A trickle of blood ran down the skin. He was stiff, erect. He dragged back his rough tunic and threw himself against the table.

'Cleanse me,' he commanded.

The switch hung in the youth's hand and he felt the joyous torment of Christ's love.

'Again.'

He had a sudden vision of the heretics, sliced and bleeding.

Once again the Lord Jesus laid his love upon him. The pain stabbed down into his loins and the sin spilled forth from him.

From the kitchen the *triclinium* was filling with the spicy aromas of good food and wine. Clodios Syrus and Irenaeus reclined, their napkins carefully spread, fine Syrian glass goblets ready, the tools of the meal – a knife and a toothpick, a small ladle and a *ligula*, a pointed *cocleare* – in place and waiting. The *ministratores* brought in the *gustatio*, a silver salver of oysters, as another uncorked the *amphorae* and drained the contents into a mixing bowl, where he added the water before serving. These were heavy wines, practically painful to hold in the mouth neat, but bitter and refreshing when diluted. There were just the two of them, the Celt and the Roman, but Clodios saw no reason for the meal to be any the less pleasant for that. He kept a fine table, as befitted his rank.

He speared an oyster from its shell with the point of his *cocleare*. He held it under his magnificent nose to snuff up the scent of the sea and then bit into it, allowing the bouquet of its crushed body to permeate his nasal cavity.

'Live from the rocks,' he grunted approvingly. 'That scoundrel Lupus knows better than to give me something growing by the *cloaca*, for I have *this*.'

He tapped his nose proudly. He adjusted the folds of his loose muslin *synthesis* to ensure his comfort and devoured the fleshy beasts in their shells, draining the liquor and grunting with satisfaction. Hiding his austerity, Irenaeus ate.

'Sorry Pothinus couldn't come,' Syrus said, wiping his mouth. A half-naked slave girl, breasts visible under her light tunic, held out a ewer of warm, scented water and he dabbled his fingers in it.

'The blessed Pothinus is aged. I have taken on much of his responsibility.'

'Ah well. We're all priests together.'

'You come, I believe, from a family of priests?' Irenaeus suggested politely.

The first entrée was brought in, fine scarlet lobsters served with pots of spicy dips – *garum*, the sauce made from rotted fish, a great delicacy; garlic; *assafoetida*, fig and plum sauce – and Clodios drained the remains of his *mulsum* honey wine in anticipation.

'More wine,' he commanded, and the *ministratore* refilled his goblet. Irenaeus had not yet finished his.

Dionysus and Ariadne reclined naked beneath grape vines on the magnificent mosaic on the wall, and quaffed its fermented juice. In a corner of the room stood a painted marble statue of Mithras, the soldiers' god.

'What is more important than wine?' Clodios demanded. 'It is the invigorator of mind and body, the antidote to sleeplessness, sorrow and fatigue, the producer of hunger, happiness and digestion.'

He investigated a cracked claw, pulling out fine white meat.

'And, of course, it is the drink of the gods. Yes, you are right, my ancestors were all priests. They served the old god

Cernunnos, and Esus, the god of war, before the Romans came, but they are little in favour with them, so I perform my duties for Apollo, and for Mars, their god of war.'

'Was this difficult for you?' Irenaeus enquired professionally.

'Why no,' said Clodios, and spat out a fragment of red shell. He looked across at the Christian, lying stiffly by the table. Clodios lay like a fine boar in its sty, fitting the couch perfectly.

'Why should it be?' he demanded reasonably. 'The gods are all much the same in their demands. They require sacrifice. They die, and are reborn. We eat of their flesh and drink of their blood to be as one with them, do we not? The *eucharista* is much the same, whatever god. We drink the wine – the blood of Dionysus – and eat the flesh of sacrifice. Don't you Christians have some ritual like that?'

Irenaeus felt his very skin crawl at the thought of the purity of Christ being tainted by pagan rituals.

'I am interested in the old gods,' he said, skirting the question. The day would come when Clodios and his ilk would bow before the one true God, when they would be forced to exchange their gluttony and lust for the purity of the one way, when they would don rough clothing and practise abstinence.

'Was not human sacrifice involved?' he asked. Clodios splashed a lobster's tail into the *garum* pot and bit off a chunk.

'Quite right,' he said enthusiastically, spraying fish sauce into the air.

'You're referring to Cernunnos, of course,' he said, and Irenaeus nodded. A gleam came into his eyes.

'Yes. How was it done, exactly?'

'Cernunnos the antler-horned, the three-headed was the most powerful of deities,' Clodios said. He was an educated man and enjoyed showing off his knowledge and culture to a fellow priest.

'As such, mere animals were not sufficient for sacrifice.

When, according to the ancient rituals and ancient customs of my tribe, sacrifice to Cernunnos was required, people had to be found, and the custom grew up of keeping children captured in war from neighbouring tribes. They were called *trinqui*. They might be kept for years. When they were needed they were taken to the sacred groves of Cernunnos and there placed upon the altars and ritually carved, while still alive. That is how it was done.'

'Not now.'

'Why no. The Romans, our masters, forbid human sacrifice.'

'*Do* they?' Irenaeus asked, thoughtfully. 'Do they, now?'

'Well, don't they?' Clodios demanded. The lobsters had been taken away and the *ministratore* was carving a fine golden capon stuffed with truffles and mushrooms.

'What is special about Rome?' Irenaeus asked, rhetorically. 'What enables her to defeat her enemies, to impose her will upon the world? Is it not that she thinks in large terms? When your ancestors wanted water, did they not just live near a river? Not the Romans. They summon water from afar, they build mighty aqueducts, they fling bridges to carry it across great gorges, they let it play in fountains, for their very amusement.'

'It is so,' Clodios admitted. 'I have myself seen them.'

The capon was placed upon their plates, steaming and fragrant with costmary and caraway. Clodios took a slice, hissing faintly at its heat, golden juice running over his chin.

'Is it not just that they only like things to be very large?' Irenaeus persisted.

'It may be so. Taste this meat. From my own farm.'

'So if we were looking for human sacrifice, the altar would be huge, the sacrifices many, the entertainment great.'

Clodios peered at him over a drumstick he was dismantling.

'Entertainment?' he said suspiciously.

'The *munera*, Magister, the games! Where men and women

are slaughtered for the delight of others. There it is, the Roman sacrifice!'

'Ah, yes, I see what you mean, now. That's bloodletting on a grand scale all right.'

His face, that had brightened as he had followed Irenaeus's argument, now fell.

'Ah, but don't talk to me of the games,' he said gloomily. 'You are talking to a man about to be ruined, because of the games.'

'How can this be?' Irenaeus enquired.

Clodios sighed and put down a crisp chicken wing he had been thinking of stripping.

'You see me here, one of the leading citizens of Lyons. Yes, a wealthy man. But such a position carries its burdens, its responsibilities, oh yes . . .'

'Tell me,' Irenaeus suggested softly. 'Perhaps I may be of help.'

Clodios gestured with an extravagant hand, spilling fragments of food from his gown.

'These are bad times in the capital of the three Gauls. Only last year we bustled with business. But the wars did not help, and the soldiers no longer buy from the *ferrarium* for their arms, they ship in and beat at their own workshops. Our fine *terra sigilata* pottery suffers from competition. Lezoux and Boucheporn cut our prices. The very trade of the Saône and the Rhône is down, wine, oil, weapons, corn, artefacts, all down. Men borrowed money in the good years, now when the first day of the month comes round and their creditors with it for their interest, they have to reach deep in the chest, and find but little there. But, they say to themselves, the great summer festival is coming. The amphitheatre will be filled with spectators from all over Gaul for the shows. That will at least put a little gold back into the purses of honest Lyons men, they say to themselves . . .'

'This is true,' Irenaeus agreed.

'But who is to pay for the shows?' wailed Clodios. 'No gladiator is cheap, no, not even a fifth-rate hired from the *lanista*, that the people will jeer at. No, no, they want to see cold steel and no quarter, good fighting to the cut-off point, and I, and the few like me, must provide it, *postulante populo*, at the wish of the people, for our very station depends upon it.'

He shook his head dolefully.

'It has been made clear to me that the people expect the best. That they expect the inns and the brothels and the bars to be filled with people from the three Gauls, ready and willing to spend their silver while the finest games of the age take place. Ah . . . it will be week-old bread and hard-rinded cheese for me, all washed down with a cup of water . . .'

'It appears that you have not yet heard of the *Senatus-Consultum* just signed by both Emperor and Senate, that applies to wealthy landowners in your position regarding the furnishing of entertainment for the people,' Irenaeus said smoothly.

Clodios jerked himself up on to one elbow.

'No,' he said eagerly. 'What is it? Tell me.'

'I, who have just come from Rome, have secured a copy. It just so happens I have it with me . . .'

Irenaeus reached inside his tunic and passed over a scroll, Clodios unrolled it and scanned the Latin hungrily. His eyes lit up, shining with joy.

'We may purchase condemned criminals from the imperial procurators, *to use as we see fit!* And for a mere six *aurei* a head! Why that's . . . less than a tenth of the hire of a fifth-rate gladiator . . .'

His eyes ran over the text of the proclamation, ensuring that he had not seen incorrectly. Then he looked up, a slight frown appearing between his eyebrows.

'I wish I had known about this earlier . . .' he muttered, a faint edge of discontent appearing in his voice.

'I am, you may know, also chief magistrate,' he explained, 'and as such, I am aware of the numbers of condemned men in the jails.'

He pursed his lips thoughtfully.

'Very few, I am sad to say. You see, there is no point in keeping them *alive* – not until now, with this most useful, far-sighted and emancipated piece of legislation – they just cost money to keep, so we have them outside, quick as boiled asparagus, and have a knife through their throats. Oh, if only I had known . . .'

He sighed, thinking of all the money he might have saved.

'I was, in fact, aware of your post as chief magistrate,' said Irenaeus, 'which is why I might be able to help you . . .'

'The only way you could help me is by getting a whole load of people to commit capital offences,' Clodios grumbled, still disgruntled.

'They are doing it, right here in Lyons, every day,' Irenaeus said softly. 'As many as you could want. Men of fighting age, and also women . . .'

His eyes had become glazed, as though he had drunk too much, which he had not.

'Many women . . . some young and well-born . . .'

'Where?' Clodios demanded. 'And what are they doing?'

Irenaeus brought himself back from his vision.

'Let me explain. You know that I am Christian, that men like me worship the son of God, that we call Jesus.'

'I know that, yes.'

'I am of the Church of Rome, the one true Church for those who worship Jesus. There can be no other. We have received our authority from Saint Peter, holder of the keys, rock of the Church, founder of the faith, true disciple of Jesus.'

'Yes, yes,' said Clodios impatiently, 'if you say so. One sect is very much like another, is it not. What has this to do with me?'

'We are the one true Church,' Irenaeus said again, his voice steely. 'All others are heretics. They perform foul and sinister rites, contrary to the law.'

'Ahhh . . . *very* foul?'

'Hideous. One such cult is active in Lyons right now . . . they are called the Children of Jeshua.'

'Yes,' Clodios nodded, his pendulous chins wobbling, 'I believe I have heard of them.'

'Did you know that they collect unwanted newborn children from the refuse heaps where they are thrown?'

'Really . . . Why on earth would they do that? Where would we be if all of us kept all the wretched whelps born? Answer me that. You take your pleasure with slaves, they get with child. If it's a strong-looking creature you may choose to keep it, but usually I have them throw it on the heap.'

'They *say* it is to bring up the children in their faith.'

Clodios licked dry lips and reached for his goblet.

'What *do* they do with them?'

'Thyestian feasts,' Irenaeus said chillingly. 'They eat them.'

'No . . .'

'Yes, yes. And there is more . . . they free slaves. They claim – and as a priest of Christ I can tell you it is not so – they claim that Jesus forbade men to enslave others.'

'Ridiculous!'

'Quite. And they practise oedipean intercourse.'

'Hmmmm . . . but will it be easy to prove this?' Clodios asked professionally.

'It will follow on from this,' Irenaeus advised. 'This foul sect shares one peculiarity with the one true Church that I serve. That is, we cannot sacrifice to any other god. We must recognise only Jesus and the creator, the Father, as divine. Jesus himself commanded this of us and we must obey, else when we die, we shall be consigned to eternal torment in the flames of Hell.'

'I have heard of this,' the landowner admitted. 'It seems a very severe prohibition to me. And as for me, I have never pursued the matter rigorously. If people pay their taxes and keep the peace I am not concerned what they do in private.'

'It is a capital offence not to sacrifice to the Emperor, who is – he claims – divine, when required to by a magistrate.' Irenaeus said softly.

Clodios eyed him calculatingly.

'You are on shifting ground here, it seems to me. The same rule applies to *you*.'

'*I* am travelling shortly, with some of the leading members of my flock. We do not expect to be back until the summer games are over.'

'Very wise . . .' Clodios murmured. He glanced up. 'The old man, Pothinus your bishop. He will be going with you?'

'I think not,' Irenaeus said smoothly, 'age forbids it.'

Clodios smiled. 'I see.'

'The Children of Jeshua have two more aspects which may prove attractive to you.'

Clodios signalled to the *ministratore*, who refilled the goblets. 'Yes?'

'Their perverted doctrines are strangely attractive to some who find our own purity too rigorous . . . among their converts are some wealthy men and women. Is it not so that the property of a condemned person passes to the state?'

The fat man's eyes gleamed.

'It is so,' he affirmed.

'Which you represent . . .' murmured Irenaeus. 'And secondly, those of superior status in this cult are required to be proficient in the use of arms. You will find them to make excellent gladiators . . .'

'Splendid . . . Why do they require this?'

Irenaeus shrugged.

'They claim that was the order of Jesus . . . of course it was not. Our Lord was the meekest of men.'

Irenaeus sat up, sliding from the couch.

'May I leave it in your capable hands, Magister?' he asked softly.

'Oh, you may . . . but won't you stay for a peach, for some more wine, a slave girl?'

'I must be away. Although I thank you for your hospitality. I shall make use of your latrine, if I may.'

'Feel free . . .'

He went out. Clodios was the owner of a fine two-hole latrine, complete with channels of flowing water and a small tinkling fountain. Its walls were decorated with an amusing fresco of a bearded, finger-wagging philosopher sternly instructing the occupants in the correct manner of defaecation. Irenaeus did not smile, he had no sense of humour. He bent over the latrine and thrust his fingers into his throat, bringing up the entire meal. Indulgence in the pleasures of the flesh was the most certain route to Hell. A pure life was one in which pain should be felt.

As he went out he glanced through the open entrance to the *triclinium*. Clodios lay on his couch like a fine porker, his gown awry, two practically nude young slave girls cavorting on his gleaming body. They were all laughing immoderately.

Moving out into the dark streets, Irenaeus amused himself by calculating, very precisely, how many thousands of years

Clodios would have to spend in purgatory, in order to cleanse himself of his sin . . .

A shaft of sunlight fell from the high window on to the brilliantly coloured map on the wall behind the head of Marcellus, bishop for the day. It was a map of tragedy, and of salvation. At its centre lay the earth, wrapped about by the *behemoth*. Then came the *ogdoad*, or eight, from the first, the moon, through Mercury and the sun to the outer ring of Saturn. *Leviathan* enclosed all, a vast black snake in the act of devouring its own tail. At the pinnacle of the *decad*, the ten, stood Paradise, ringed by the blue circle of darkness and the yellow circle of light, which joined to create the symbol of life. About all were the circles of the Father, Mother, and Son.

There was evil, controlled by dark forces. The Zodiac and planets were fearful, creations of he who made the world, evil beyond belief, the creator, the *demiurgos*, who was Satan.

But with the evil in the world were divine sparks, that had fallen down from heaven. These divine sparks were imprisoned in matter, in human beings. They longed to return to Paradise, to be with God.

'Only those who are spiritually mature may share the wisdom of God,' said Marcellus. 'For he sent his son Jesus Christ here, to the world that the Devil made, to instruct us. When you have drunk, you will have drunk from the bubbling stream that he has measured out, he who drinks from the mouth of Christ becomes as he is. He shall become us, and the things that are hidden will be revealed to us.'

In the church, in front of the worshippers, were the clergy of the day, led by Marcellus. Standing at the altar, in the glow of the sacrificial brazier and dressed in a robe that shimmered like the sky, that shone like the moon, glittering like the stars, set with tiny singing bells was a young woman. She was Blandina, she had been a slave, but she was now free. She had lived in ignorance, now she was to be of the elect.

'Know, therefore,' called Marcellus, and all listened to him, 'that the one whom those who call themselves Christians worship as creator, God and Father is but a false image. He is the demiurge, the god of the Israelites. His name is Satan and he seeks to overthrow God in our hearts, saying: "I am God, and there is no other". We who know, who achieve gnosis, recognise the true course of divine power, he who sent his son Jesus Christ to guide us through the heavenly gates.'

All, initiated and candidate, were rapt in attention, all focused on the one brightly lit figure standing at the altar of the dark church, his assistants hidden in the shadows beside him.

'Who shall come to know that source of divine power shall at that moment come to know himself and herself, shall discover their spiritual origin, their holy and true Father and Mother. When they know this, then shall they receive the *apolytrosis*, the secret sacrament of release. There is good and there is evil. There is light and there is darkness. There is spirit and there is matter. There is knowledge and there is ignorance. Before we were ignorant, we dwelt in darkness, in our ignorance we worshipped Satan, tricked by his words and mistaking him for the true God. Now we are touched by the spirit, we move into the light, we recognise what is good, we have gnosis. Let us take the sacrament of redemption, and address Satan. Say after me: I am a son, I am a daughter, from the Father and of the Mother.'

The soft crash of voices speaking in unison echoed from the walls of the church.

'*I am a son, I am a daughter from the Father and the Mother.*'
'And I come again to my own place whence I came forth.'

'*And I come again to my own place whence I came forth.*'

'Scorning the one who calls himself God, and rejecting all his works.'

'*Scorning the one who calls himself God, and rejecting all his works.*'

'Whose name is Satan.'

'*Whose name is Satan.*'

'In the love of the Father, the Mother and Jesus Christ.'

'*In the love of the Father, the Mother and Jesus Christ.*'

'Amen.'

'*Amen.*'

They all stood for a moment in silence, in the blissful and certain knowledge that they would, after their earthly pleasures were done, ascend through the heavenly spheres and return their divine spark to Paradise.

Paulina stepped forward into the light. A table was set with a white cloth beside Marcellus and on it she placed some silver dishes. In the first was holy sacrament, magical food, a moist cucumber, symbol of both good and evil, encased in darkness, filled with glistening light.

The worshippers began to come forth from the body of the church, up to the altar. Marcellus held out the cup and they drank the holy infusion of wine and herbs that had been prepared.

Standing next to Blandina, Mary cast blessed herbs into the brazier and pungent, silver-grey smoke began to swirl about them. She had a soft white blindfold in her hand and she tied it about the girl's head. As she did so, Blandina closed her eyes, standing very still. Mary drew in breath to sing and the sharp smell stabbed through her head, penetrating her mind.

I am the first and last.
I am the honoured one and the scorned one.

I am the whore and the holy one.
I am the wife and the virgin.

As each passed Paulina, she gave them a section of the holy cucumber, translucent and glistening, and they ate. Each one, man and woman, passed by Blandina. Each took off one piece of her bridal clothing, gently placing it by the altar. She held out her arms and her robe fell from her body, its bells singing. When she was naked, the worshippers kissed her, on her neck and her belly, they kissed her breasts and her thighs, and Mary sang.

I am the staff of his power in his youth,
And he is the rod of my old age.
And whatever he wills happens to me.

As each left Blandina, the bride, Paulina tied a blindfold about their eyes and they stood about the altar in the rising, scented smoke. Marcellus approached the altar as the last worshippers laid Blandina down upon it.

'Oremus,' he commanded. 'Let us pray.'

Paulina slipped his robes from his shoulders and the worshippers did the same. She anointed him with holy oil and felt the spirit of Jesus rush powerfully into his loins. Then she placed the eucharist of herbal honey between the thighs of Blandina and he bent to receive it. He came to her in the shape of a man, and the Lord was with them.

I am peace,
And war has come because of me.

They broke in the door with a ram, swung between eight sets of strong arms and the soldiers poured into the church. Mary was the only one standing, the only one without a fold about her eyes, for she sang as the others made worship. In the darkness she seized the robe of glory from beside the altar. She took the holy scriptures of the church from where they lay in their alcove, and ran to the room where the robes, the sacraments, the divine unguents were kept. The door slammed behind her, but through it she could hear the bellowed orders, curses and blows.

There was a slab in the stone floor that was made for the purpose. An iron key slid down into the gap. She inserted it, the precious scrolls clasped to her, and heaved. She dropped them all in to the dry, stone-lined space, together with the robe of singing bells, quickly lowering the heavy slab back over the hole. Then she stuffed the iron key back into its hiding place. Outside was uproar. She threw back a shutter, and jumped down to the ground. Blind in the sudden sunlight, she heard the blow that sent her flying, but did not see it.

'You're *hordearii*,' the young man in front of the group said. 'Barley men, that's what you're called.'

They stood in the square outside the gladiatorial barracks. At their backs was the amphitheatre itself, and the cells where they had spent the night were a part of the complex belonging to the arena. In the square fighters were training, novices thrust wooden swords at men of straw and tall *pali* stakes, higher grades fought one on one, but still with blunt weapons. Gladiators were valuable, they could not be damaged before they were used. The air rang with the cries of the professional instructors, men of the first and second grades.

Mary stood with the others of the Children of Jeshua. The fat man, the magistrate, had somehow known who the initiates were, those trained both in the knowledge of God and of the use of arms, he had separated them out and here they were, listening to this sardonic, tough young man with a red scar travelling up his arm to vanish under his tunic. Where the others were, the worshippers, the acolytes like Blandina, she did not know. She stood, paying attention, and felt her bruises throb.

'*Hordearii*. Barley men. That's for the food, to make you strong.'

A thin, starved-looking creature raised a weak cheer.

'Oh, yes, plenty of food, and the best. You look like you need it, Priscus,' he said, and the boy smiled, fearfully. 'We have other names, too . . . Are you all religious? I hope so. You're going to take part in a religious rite. Really. You're not actually going to just hack each other to death, you're doing it for the souls of the dead. *Bustuarii*, that's our other name. Funeral men. Ours or someone else's.'

He smiled ironically.

'It's the *munus*, the service for the dead.'

He glanced across the square, sensing the arrival of importance.

'And here are the priests.'

They turned to look at the two men walking over the red sunlit earth.

'Some of you may know the fat man, he probably sent you here. That's Clodios Syrus, head landowner, chief magistrate and prime shit of these parts. He runs things for his masters, the Romans. The other is Festus. Festering Festus. He owns us, for the time being. He's the *lanista*, our butcher. Let me say now that all of us here do what he says. We have no human rights, we who are here, no *auctorati*. We may be slaves he bought from the block. I see some of you. We may be those he found on the street, starving, like Priscus. We may be criminals sentenced by Clodios, like you Jeshuans. We may be like me, one who is of good family, but ruined. I am Thrasea, and I am like you – unlucky. We are here, where Festus may do with us as he wills.'

The two men of power had come close and Thrasea turned to them.

'The new recruits, sir.'

'I see them.' Festus was short and squat, ugly, his voice like the call of a crow. Clodios looked over them urbanely and the Jeshuans stared malevolently at him.

'See you train hard,' he said. 'The people expect a good show.'

'We know how to fight,' Marcellus, next to Mary, called harshly. Festus stepped forward, the short flail in his hand rising and his face flushing dark, but Clodios motioned him back.

'How interesting of you. Are you soldiers?'

'We are soldiers of the Lord,' shouted Mary. 'We are commanded by him to fight in his name.'

'How can this be?' Clodios asked curiously. 'I understand from one Irenaeus, who worships the same Chrestos as you, that you are commanded to love one another, that the meek shall inherit the earth.'

'We Jeshuans love one another and those who worship the true Jesus. Irenaeus is a servant of Satan.'

'And he says it is *you* who are the devil's slaves!' Clodios chuckled. 'I declare, it is all too complicated for me. How you Chrestians hate each other! But it is all to the good, for here you are, ready to be served up as sacrifice on a far greater altar.'

'You must understand that we Jeshuans will not fight against each other,' said Marcellus. 'We will sooner stand and be slain than do that.'

'Die you shall!' Festus cried, enraged.

'And we must have the chance to live, if you want combat from us,' Mary called, and the others shouted in agreement. 'We have the Lord God to serve, when this is done.'

Clodios stroked a pendulous lip thoughtfully.

'What do you think, Festus? The Jeshuans against the rest? The people might like that. That would stimulate some betting, yes?'

The *lanista* nodded quickly in agreement.

'Loosen some purses,' he grunted.

'I'll have some posters painted up. I'll be away, then.'

He glanced at Thrasea.

'Still alive, young man?' he said, almost genially.

'Still alive,' Thrasea said quietly.

'But not for long, I'll be bound,' Clodios remarked cruelly.

The fat man turned as he walked off, Festus accompanying him a short way.

'Look for me,' he said. 'I'll be up in the *pulvinar*.'

There was a strange, thoughtful look in Thrasea's eyes as he watched the magistrate waddle away. Two slaves were carrying a brazier from the buildings, held between a pair of rods. They put it down nearby and Mary could feel its heat.

'I'm going to train you,' said Thrasea, as Clodios went out of sight through the gate. 'You may know how to fight, but in the *munus* they like it to be special. Some of you will be *retarii*, fishermen, you'll fight with a trident – a tunnyfish harpoon – a dagger and a net, and I'll teach you to do that. No armour except the shoulder-piece. We'll run some races, to see who's fast. You'll have to be, because your usual opponent is the *secutor*, the chaser, and mobility is your asset, as armour is his. You may fight a *myrmillo* as well, the fish-man. I hope you all have good eyesight, which you need if you're to wrap your opponent up properly. Those who can't see well get to fight as *andabatae*, in helmets with no eye holes. They crash about on horseback and have a horrible time while those staining their tunics in the stands laugh themselves sick.'

He glanced across at Festus, who was coming across the sand with a metal rod in his hand.

'Ah, here he is, our lord and master, festering Festus. You'll take the oath now. When it's all done we'll get to work. Very good, form a line then.'

Festus Salvius Capito stood in front of them and spoke in his Sicilian dialect, harsh on the ear.

'The oath is *uri, uinciri, uerberari, ferroque necari*. You will say it now.'

'*Uri*.'

'You shall be burned with fire.'

'*Uinciri*.'

'You shall be shackled with chains.'

'*Uerberari*.'

'You shall be whipped with rods.'

'*Ferroque necari*.'

'You shall be killed with steel.'

The metal rod he had thrust into the brazier. The school doctor had come up, a young Greek, he stood with a pot of ointment. A line of gladiators had formed beyond.

'First,' ordered Festus.

Priscus, starved and trembling with fright, stepped forward. Festus took the rod from the brazier and they could see its entwined F and C brand glow. He took the boy by the arm and pressed it into the flesh of his shoulder. The hiss and his scream were the same.

The doctor slapped salve on to the scarlet sear and Festus looked at him in disgust.

'You won't last long like that,' he said. 'Get through the ranks.'

Sobbing with pain the boy ran through the lane of gladiators and they whipped him with the rods in their hands. He fell at the end and crawled through the sand.

'What do you think, Thrasea?' Festus asked doubtfully. 'I could get a few *aurei* for him from the *aedile*, he needs men for the midday chop.'

'Let me have him,' said Thrasea. 'I'm a good chef, I can make a meal of the strangest ingredients.'

'If you say so.'

Mary ground her teeth together, shutting her mouth tight. The brand was like a blow.

Salve dripped on her arm. The gladiators swung their rods with the grim amusement of the initiated over the novice. She put her head down, as though through driving rain, and ran.

Someone was moaning, out down the corridor, in the darkness. Mary could hear him, above the steady muttering of voices praying. She was shackled to her bunk in the stone dormitory of the gladiatorial *ludus*. All about her in their hard beds were the other Jeshuans, a dozen in all. Her body ached from the weals and bruises of the rods, her shoulder was on fire. Her hands hurt from the hours of handling net and dagger. Out in the darkness, someone moaned in agony.

'One of us, at least, must live,' she commanded, and the others rumbled agreement. 'When the *frumentarii* broke into our church I hid our scriptures in the well of the storeroom. They will still be there. But one of us must walk free when these games are over. It does not matter who, as long as the true word of God still lives in the land of Satan.'

'We shall all be reunited in Paradise,' Paulina called.

'Let us pray to the. Father, the Mother and the Son,' said Rufus.

They had finished their worship when the door was pushed open and Thrasea came in, bearing an oil lamp.

'Get some sleep,' he said. 'We start early here.'

With the door open the noise of torture was loud.

'Who is that?' asked Mary.

'Some Christian,' said Thrasea. 'Clodios spread the word and the mob went on a hunt today. Looking for Chrestians. Not your lot, the others, from Rome. Clodios thought it would be entertaining to have you and them fight each other. He's rather disappointed. They won't do it. So he's having a few tortured to get them to go out in front of the crowd and curse their god.'

The moaning had stopped. A man's voice asked a question.

'*Christianus sum*,' came the reply, weak but clear in the dark. Voices floated down the corridor, the sound of exasperated men wishing to go home. A horrid gurgling came on the air, and the drumming of feet.

Thrasea turned to leave them.

'They aren't having much success with that either,' he commented. 'It's very strange, some of them actually *want* to be tortured.'

'*Christianus sum*,' said the man, gazing steadfastly over the head of the governor. Septicus Severus disliked steadfast gazing, an educated man, he was versed in Aristotle and knew it was mere insolence.

'Very well,' he said, attempting to swallow his irritation. 'Tell me more about this Christ, whose name you don.'

Sanctus, deacon of Bishop Pothinus continued to gaze into the heavens. Blood was oozing from a purple weal across his forehead.

'If you are a fit person, you will know,' he said.

Septicus Severus's patience came to an end, it was late, he wanted *cena*.

'Take him back down,' he said wearily. It was like dealing with an obstinate child. He glared at Sanctus. 'You will tell me what I want to know in time, that I promise you.'

It was all clearly the fault of the wretched Gauls and their fat leader, Clodios Syrus. How he longed to be back in Rome.

'*Christianus sum*,' Sanctus said once again, infuriatingly, and the guards dragged him away, leaving a smear of blood over the marble. There was a roar of rage from the locals waiting in the corridor and the sound of them beating Sanctus as he was hauled to the cells. Septimus Severus paused thoughtfully as he left his *cerule* chair. They needed careful handling. The recent war and the poor trade didn't help. If he, the governor, incurred the expenses of troops to put down a major riot he could end his days somewhere in Phrygia and never see glorious Rome again. He decided to let Clodios Syrus do whatever he wanted.

Blandina awoke in the grey light of dawn. She was cold, even in the summer, damp ran down the walls of the cell. People were crushed up into the stone room, sleeping like cattle, but next to her a man was kneeling, his lips moving in prayer.

'Amen,' he murmured. He was a horrible sight, his face swollen and bruised, trickles of fresh blood rising from purple and black weals, burns and lacerations. The stone floor was sticky where he knelt. As he saw that she was awake he turned to her, smiling. His very teeth were bloody.

'Welcome,' he said. 'Welcome to the ante-chamber of Heaven.'

'Who are you?' she said fearfully.

'I am Sanctus, deacon to the blessed Bishop Pothinus, who lies there in body, but not soul, for he has gone to his reward.'

She glanced at the body of an old man lying on the floor, beaten into offal, and a sob left her mouth.

'I do not want to die,' she whispered.

'Do not want to die?' Sanctus cried in amazement. 'Do not want to be with the Paraclete, Jesus Christ?'

'They said nothing of torture, those who instructed me.'

Sanctus frowned. 'Who? Who instructed you?'

'The Children of Jeshua.'

Sanctus shuddered in horror and placed a swollen, bleeding hand on her head as he chanted a prayer.

'The devil himself has set traps for your soul,' he said passionately. 'How far did it go? Can you be saved?'

'I was to be the bride of Christ,' she said, puzzled. 'When the soldiers broke in, I was consecrated upon the altar.'

'Ahhhh . . . child. Did you not know that all earthly pleasures are but Satan's snares?'

'I have little knowledge of pleasure,' she said. 'I was a slave and the Children of Jeshua set me free.'

'Set you free?' whispered Sanctus. 'They are the devil's agents, they negotiated for your soul. When you were upon the altar, Satan himself came to collect it. Did you feel joy, there?'

'Yes. They did . . . pleasing things to me.'

'Did they take your clothing, did they make you naked?' the deacon asked, looking into her eyes intensely.

'Why yes.'

'Did one of them enter you?' he demanded.

'Yes . . .' she faltered. 'He came as Jesus himself . . .'

'As the devil!' Sanctus thundered, and in the cell someone moaned in pain. 'It was the devil with his black arts, reaching into you to take your soul!'

She began to weep.

'What am I to do?'

Sanctus placed a comforting hand upon her.

'You can be rescued. Join me.'

She looked fearfully through her tears at his wounds.

'I do not want to be tortured. Can we not do as they ask and pay homage to their gods?'

Sanctus cried out and held his scarred hands up in the air.

'See how the devil works in you! Do you not know that Jesus himself warned us that any who denounced him before men, he himself would denounce *before God*?'

Sanctus pointed to the air just above her.

'There sits Jesus himself, waiting to see your faith.'

The simple young girl whirled in terror, peering about.

'You shall not see him until that final moment when you are perfected, when you are sealed in death and collect your crown of immortality.'

His hand ran over the wounds on his body.

'You see hurts of this world, which are in truth the badges of rank, the medals of those who are athletes for Christ.'

'Athletes . . .'

'*The contest is now!* The devil is fighting with all his strength, he is responsible for the mob that beat you, he is moving the magistrate who sentenced you. His demons it is who appear as men, wielding the whip, stretching the rack, heating the iron.'

She whimpered, she could not help it.

'But its heat is as cold as snow compared to the furnaces of Hell where he keeps those whose souls he has captured,' Sanctus said anxiously. 'And whatever slight pain we suffer here will vanish the very moment our confessions are sealed by the mightiest prize of all, when we emulate our Lord, Jesus, and he anoints our wonderful wounds with his holy ointment.'

'I am not made of your metal,' said Blandina. 'I am no martyr.'

'I neither,' Sanctus said quickly. 'I will allow no one to call me martyr, I who have not yet been perfected, who has not yet had my faith sealed by death. I cannot claim that proud title. I am a lowly and humble confessor to the Name, who ardently desires to follow in Christ's footsteps. Oh, how I hunger for the wild beasts to crunch my bones into the pure white bread of God! How I long for them to release my blood, to transform it into the wine of Christ's eucharist!'

From down the corridor there came the noise of the gladiators' dormitories being opened and the sound of their feet going up to their mess hall and on to the practice-ground.

'Put your faith in the Paraclete, our Advocate Jesus,' Sanctus urged. 'For when he comes – he comes soon – he will judge this world as he did the Pharisees. He counts on us now, for we are his soldiers, through us he vindicates his cause. What we suffer here are the moments before the coming of Antichrist, and when he comes, it is but another moment before the Millennium of the Saints.'

Strangely, she found her eyes dry of tears.

'We shall go straight to Heaven?' she asked.

'While we live, we rank higher than any save Christ himself. You, who were a slave, will be higher than the mightiest in the land. When you die, as a combat soldier of Christ, you shall go straight to his bosom.'

From the window came the clash of steel on steel, the grunt and shuffle of trained fighters. Sanctus waved a bloody, dismissive hand.

'We have no need of earthly arms. We are as vessels, filled to the brim with a pure, shining liquid. We are filled with the Holy Spirit, and none can overcome us.'

He looked steadfastly into her eyes.

'Will you not come to the forefront of the battle? Will you not fight for Jesus?'

'Yes!' she cried out.

'I shall!' she said fervently. 'I shall!'

8

Lyons, Gaul, A.D. June 181

The oblong *triclinium* was full, the guests reclined on their couches about the square tables. The *nomenclator* had announced them, one by one as they came in, showing them to their places, and the crowd of people jammed about the walls of the great room had applauded, the gamblers amongst them eyeing them closely. Now they reclined on silk as the *ministratores* brought in the dishes and bowls, steaming and scented, placing them on the woven cloth, and the *amphorae* were opened and strained carefully into the mixing bowls. Clodios Syrus was entertaining, and tonight there was to be a lack of nothing for his guests.

The *ministrator* came round with the goblets charged with the watered wine – good quality local Allobrogica, none of your vinegared *posca* for them – and the beggar boy Priscus raised a cheer, sitting next to the burly Saltus. He raised his Syrian glass high and drained it in a gulp. Laughing, Saltus did the same and the *ministrator* brought more. Lying with the others of the Children of Jeshua, Mary looked at them thoughtfully through ice-green eyes.

The two gladiators pulled lobsters from the bowl, and began tearing the flesh from the pink shells. Rufus and Marcellus, placed together, began to help themselves to food.

'In moderation,' murmured Thrasea, the instructor, and they nodded.

'We know.'

A red-faced young man was walking around the tables, looking carefully at all the gladiators, occasionally making notes on a waxed tablet he held. He glanced contemptuously at Priscus and Saltus, who had emptied their glasses again.

'It's hot, down on the sand,' he commented. He looked at the Jeshuans.

'Well, well,' he chuckled, 'what have we here? Girl gladiators! Come on then, show us your tits, ladies!'

Mary looked up at him, the knife with which she was disembowelling her lobster in her fist.

'I'll show them your guts, if you like,' she said chillingly. He stepped back a pace, but eyed her thoughtfully. He smiled.

'Yes,' he murmured, 'you've got spirit. I think I'll bet on you to last the first day.'

He nodded quite amiably at them, as they ate what would be for many their last meal, and stepped back into the steady swirl of ghouls and gamblers about the tables of the *cena libera*. Clodios Syrus knew how to raise interest in the games of the morrow.

'I shall last more than the first day,' Mary said tersely. 'One of us, at any rate, has to walk out at the end.'

'Lucky for you,' said Thrasea, philosophically, reclining next to her. 'That's something I can be sure I won't be doing.'

'Why not?'

'I'm here until I die.'

'You'll be fighting?'

Thrasea dipped his lobster tail into the *garum* sauce.

'Oh, yes. Clodios will see to that. He put me here, he will want to see me leave – but not through the *Sanavivaria*. Dead meat is what I must be.'

'How did Clodios put you here?' Red-headed Rufus asked curiously.

'Ah, there's many a poor wretch you could ask that of. Me, my fault was to be born of a wealthy father.'

'That can't be much of a fault,' Marcellus called, and Thrasea smiled enigmatically.

'Don't keep us in suspense,' said Paulina.

'My father died and I became a rich man. Not as rich, it is true, as Clodios Syrus, who is wealthier than most.'

Thrasea used his *cocleare* to remove the flesh from a claw.

'And who wishes, always, to become richer.'

He removed the meat deftly, as befitted a professional with weaponry.

'He had me accused of poisoning my father. He heard the case, as is normal. The will was then set aside, the estate, as is also normal, passing to the treasury of the Emperor. Clodios, for providing this useful service to the economy of Rome, received a substantial share, as is normal. And I was placed in the *ludus gladiatorius*, here to fight until I die. But there, that is the way of the world. The powerful prey upon the weak.'

'It is not if you are one of the Children of Jeshua,' Mary said clearly. 'We fight, all of us, all for one, and the one will fight for the all. We have no permanent rank or position, no few rich and many poor. No slaves, no slavemasters.'

'But you are still here, as I am,' Thrasea said sadly.

'When we die we shall go straight to Paradise. For here we fight against the slaves of Satan, who made the world. Jesus, our master, will reward us most richly and we shall be with him.'

Thrasea eyed Rufus thoughtfully.

'Perhaps I should join you,' he said jocularly. 'It is the only way I shall go anywhere pleasant from here.'

On the other side of the room, Priscus and Saltus were beginning to sing.

The early morning was pleasantly crisp. As they collected their weapons and accoutrements from the armourer they could hear the steady thumping of feet as the crowds filled up the stands, the hubbub of their voices, happy and excited. A *secutor* further up the line, sweating with a hangover from the banquet, broke ranks to vomit. *Secutors* and *retarii* were on the programme being so avidly read by those settling themselves on the cushions, placing their bets, looking at those about them for amours.

The man wiping sick off his chin was Saltus. The armourer handed Mary her *fascina* harpoon, dagger, net and *galerus* shoulder-guard, piled on top of her gold and purple cloak. The weapons were heavy and cold in her hand.

In the yard outside there was a clanking and fumbling as the fighters prepared themselves, the lightly clad *retarii* finishing quickly, the heavily armoured *samnites*, *thracians*, *myrmillos* and *secutors* taking longer. A group of *sagittarii* stood to one side, simply carrying their weapons, a short bow and a quiverful of arrows.

Thrasea was not fighting, he and the other instructors were organising the pairing-off. He looked at Mary expressionlessly as she came up to him.

'You're fighting Saltus,' he said.

The herald was calling out, and they went through the gates to the waiting chariots.

The *paegniarii* and *lusorii* were through, they limped off carrying their sticks and whips and wooden swords, bearing the small marks of their combat, a weal here, a few missing teeth there, a handful of lumpy bruises.

The crowd buzzed, its appetite whetted by the illusory

fighting, and they brought out a young man to conduct the
probatio armorum testing ceremony that ensured that all the
weapons now to be used were *arma decretoria*, properly sharp
and dangerous. The young man was the beggar boy Priscus.
Living on scraps all his short life had kept him weak and
uncoordinated, he could not hold a heavy sword, did not have
the technique to draw a bow, was unable to grip a harpoon.
But he was still of use to Festus the *lanista*, the butcher.

So they tied him to a stake and representatives of each
group of gladiators tested their weapons. A *sagittarius* fired an
arrow expertly into him across the arena and the crowd roared
their approval, ready now for blood that ran red. A *thracian*
chopped off a leg with his scimitar, a *myrmillo* an arm with
his *spatha*, cold eyes observing its performance from inside his
visored fish helmet. Rufus thrust his harpoon into his guts, as
a *retarius* was trained to do, and the barbs tore him open. A
second thracian let the round butcher in his left hand drop
low, as he went for a victory stroke and lopped the head off
the writhing, screaming thing at the post with his short sword.
The crowd settled back in their seats, well assured that this
was a properly run affair.

The war-trumpet sounded, the members of the orchestra
settled with their horns and pipes and flutes. The organist
flexed his hands and the slaves took up their positions at the
pump. The choir took sips of water to moisten their vocal
chords and the fighters squared off.

Thrasea had taught Mary how to tie the net-fighter's special
knot. The net was connected to a long gold cord at one corner,
so that it might be drawn back if it failed to ensnare. This was
tied about her left wrist. The knot was such that it would not
come loose in combat except if the net was seized by her
opponent.

Three lay dead on the sand, the officials in the uniforms of

Charun and Hermes Psychopompos were busy. The crowd was tetchy, she could hear the waves of their disapproval beating down from the stands. Yellow bitch. Get on with it. Someone get an iron and get some fire into her.

She ignored them, staying inches beyond Saltus's swordpoint, dancing back every time the big man lunged forward. Sweat was dripping off his body, from under the visor of his helmet his breath rasped.

It was time. The net was still folded in her hand. Stinging sweat would be running into Saltus's eyes by now, making him blink. She had thrown the net a thousand times in the training square, it flew straight, its weighted edges opening it out like the wings of a bat. Following up at speed as it wrapped about the *secutor* she simultaneously jabbed the trident into Saltus's knee and pulled the cord of the net tight, jerking him off balance. He fell on to the sand and she set the points of the harpoon to his throat.

They both looked up to the *pulvinar* where Clodios and his fellow priests and landowners sat with the governor. They saw his face look left and right – whose games were these? Yes, his face seemed to say, for here was where ruled and ruler could communicate, they are yours.

The crowd was in no doubt. Anyone who couldn't chop up a rotten *retarius* – a woman at that – couldn't expect any mercy from them. Ho no. *Pollice verso* for him.

Saltus hadn't been a bad fellow. A warrior of the bedroom, more proud of his exploits with the pork dagger than his acquired skills with the *spatha*, he had entertained his fellows with accounts of the many conquests he had made. *Ars amatoria* was what brought him to a bed of bloody sand, an infuriated, elderly but powerful husband.

'Sorry,' said Mary. 'Go with God.'

The blood gushed, Mary untied the cord of his net and

went over to where the survivors of the five combats were standing, near the wall, as the man dressed as Charun smashed in the dying man's forehead with an iron mallet and the *libitinarii* carried him away. The Jeshuans had done well, but on the sand Marcellus lay dead. A *thracian*, the one who had killed him, was trying to stem the bleeding from a deep gash in his leg.

They began to walk to the far end of the arena. The people of Ludguniensis were not offered the fare of Rome every day, they wanted full value. At the opposite end of the killing-ground a line of five stakes had been set up. Five *sagitarii* were there, and the instructors with them tethered them to the posts.

The *thracian* weaved, leaving a jagged trail of blood, and then fell, face forward, on to the sand. They dragged him off and the four surviving Jeshuans waited, spread out across the far end, each in line with an archer. The stands were buzzing and the bookies' bags ajingle with money. The games were bringing some prosperity back to the city, everyone was suitably grateful to those dying down there, provided they did it in style.

'Gut him, net girl,' a yelling figure bawled, hanging over the balustrade of the podium. 'I've got twenty *denarii* riding on you.'

It was the red-faced young gambler of the night before. All around, similar exhortations flew about them. The substitute arrived. It was Paulina. She joined Mary, Rufus and two brothers, Rutillus and Piso. It was not considered sporting to allow the use of shields and these were left behind. The heavies retained their helmets and greaves, all toted the weapons of their speciality.

From the governor's box a white scarf fluttered down. The brass mouth of the *cornu* sounded and arrows flew through the air. The crowd came to its feet as the five Jeshuans began jogging down the arena towards the archers.

The arrows came like deadly black bees, seeming slow at first, then speeding towards them. As each left the bow Mary paused in her running, standing as it flew, and then going left or right. Her opponent was a fine shot, each missile pierced the air where she had been, smacking deep into the sand behind her path. As she heard each impact she ran forward, waiting for the next dart to leave the short bow.

A roar. *Habet, hoc habet!* One of the *thracians* was down, fingers tearing at the goose-feathers protruding from his chest. It was Piso! In the stands men and women shouted with joy and rage as money changed hands.

She was half way. Now she was in range, the arrows flew fast, this was where the killing was done. She was on the left and as she passed the choir, she heard their trained melody, saw from the corner of her eye the movements of the conductor as he took his singers through their piece.

Habet, hoc habet! No time to stop now, the archer had her in range, an arrow went past her ear and she heard the thrumming of its flight. She dashed forward, darting left and right, the sand spurting up from her bare soles, and the crowd roared with pleasure.

She could see him clearly, a small man, fast and deft in his movements; see the black unwinking eye behind the bow; the string drawn back to the ear; the white teeth bared in a snarl of concentration; the noose tied firm about the waist, holding him to the post.

The thumb was released, the arrow sprang from the bow. She dived and rolled, hitting the sand in a cloud of flying dust. On her knees she hurled the trident like a spear as the bowman pulled back on his still target.

The harpoon transfixed the archer, pinning him to the post

through the stomach, and the arrow flew over Mary's head. She scrambled up, dagger in her hand, and put it through his throat. Then she stood leaning on the post gasping for breath as the life gushed out beside her. The boy's name had been Hylla, he had sat at the next table to her at the banquet. He'd been fond of fish and he'd had two helpings of the mullet.

The crowd nearby was pulsating with laughter. Glancing over she saw where Hylla's arrow had landed. A man in a toga was gargling to death on it, while his neighbours wiped the tears from their eyes and congratulated each other on the narrow escape they'd had.

Rutillus, the second *thracian*, was butchering his opponent nearby. Only one of the Jeshuans lay on the sand, his brother. When they were done, only one archer remained standing. Rutillus went up to him and decapitated him.

'That's for Piso,' he said, and a grumble of disapproval went through the crowd. When you were down *there*, you were supposed to play by the rules. Some instructors came out with bows and began to shoot at him. He staggered as the first arrow hit him, then, angry, began running at his tormentors. They filled him like a porcupine and he fell to the stained sand.

The three survivors walked down the length of the arena to the *Porta Sanavivaria*.

Above the gate the gambler was counting his winnings into his purse.

'Hey, net girl,' he called to Mary, 'you've made me some money today, I'll bet on you again tomorrow.'

She looked up at him.

'Get me some herbs. Root of Achilles, leaves of boragina. Plantago and elder. Hyssopites and henbane. Poppy's tears, mushrooms and minced pepper.'

'I'll try,' he promised, 'if it will help you win.'

She followed the others through the gate. The sun was not yet at its zenith, it was still morning. As she went into the darkness the *cornu* sounded, brass-mouthed, and gladiators marched past her into the arena, their muscled bodies shining with oil, the sunlight glittering and gleaming upon their gold-chased helmets and accoutrements, their savage blades. Thrasea was amongst them, she saw him marching, head high, the plume of his helmet scarlet as blood.

They were the soldiers of Christ, dressed all in white, so that they might be well seen by all in the stands and so that the blood would show up nicely. The Children of Jeshua came out into the sunshine and a roar of approval went up. They were eight strong, with Mary at their head, chosen by lot that morning to be their general. The crowd noted the presence of the three women amongst their number with pleasure, it was always interesting to see females fight, and die. Die they would, the crowd had no doubts, for had their gods not defeated these foolish Christians time after time? A poor and feeble deity, this Christ, that allowed his servants to be roasted alive in the arena without protest.

The swirl of pleasure that had greeted the arrival of the Jeshuans was dwarfed by the bellow of joy that signalled the arrival of their executioners. They came out, a picked combat team, class one gladiators all, announced one by one by the *stentorian nomenclator* standing below the *pulvinar* where Clodios lounged with the Roman legate, Severus.

They were the gods!

Clad all in silver, with his silver bow, Apollo, tall and strong. He glittered in the sunshine.

Thor, all in black, a mighty man like a smith, his muscles knotted, wielding a brutal black hammer.

Zeus, his clothing jagged yellow and black, clutching a handful of silver javelins in one huge hand.

'Mark the big men, Paulina,' said Mary. 'They'll be large targets.'

Paulina looked up from tightening the laces of her leather wrist guard and nodded coldly. Her bow was slung over her shoulder.

A shout of laughter. *Priapus!* He capered forward, his huge phallus swinging. He had another, more effective in his hand, an iron-headed club. They heard him bellow, his members thrusting obscenely, pointing at the women of the Jeshuans, and the crowd roared approval for the refinement of rape as well as murder. In the *pulvinar*, Clodios fell about with laughter. He was dressed in green, vine leaves twined in a wreath about his head, he represented the merry god of wine, the powerful god Bacchus, whose assault upon the senses was more subtle than hammers and clubs.

Below the *pulvinar*, the gladiators in their costumes of gods were massing. As she waited at the head of the Jeshuans, Mary felt the air metallic in her throat, the shaft of her harpoon cold in her hand. She saw the enemy, the troops of Satan, come out one by one, through eyes like crystal.

'They outnumber us,' Rufus remarked. He was holding his long, naked sword. All their weapons were ready.

'Jesus is with us,' said Mary certainly.

There were but eight of them left, only eight who could bring the love of Jesus to the world where the black Lord was king. The crowd was settling back on their seats, a swirl of pleasure in the air as they saw the number of their gods arrayed against the Children, the glory of their raiment. It was not meant to be a fair fight, it was meant to be victory, it was meant to be slaughter.

A scampering dwarf, dressed as Cupid. His arrows were sharp. Gauze wings sprouted from his hunched back.

Pan, fast as a goat in his hairy breeches. The band played the pipes as he ran in. His sword glittered in his hand.

Diana the huntress. Mary heard the deep booming bark of her hounds on the leash. And Diana was no woman, but a young gladiator dressed to suit.

They were nearly done. Mercury the messenger, fleet of foot, a long *spatha* shining from one hand. Sabazios the creator, with a long sinuous whip to symbolise his snake, and a long dagger. Nearby, in the front row Mary saw some of his cult holding up their hands in triumph, making his sign, thumb and two fingers raised. Mithras the bull-slayer in honour of the legate. The goddess Cybele. They yelled in delight as the young man dressed in her silver clothes held up a fearsome, long-handled sickle. They knew what Cybele was good at. Cut off their balls!

And tumult, the crowd standing and cheering, their *mappas* and parasols waving for their great captain, Mars, dressed all in scarlet, a huge double-headed axe shining as he held it up in the sunlight.

She had her long black hair tied up and pinned, a white scarf about her head to keep the blood out of her eyes.

'What's that?' muttered Paulina. She glanced up, as though a shadow had fallen across her. 'Wings. Great wings, can you not hear them?'

'Let us get ready to fight,' said Rufus quietly. 'We can bother about birds when the fighting for God is done.'

'I do not know what creature it is,' said Paulina. 'I hear the beating of its wings . . . I smell it.'

She coughed and gagged suddenly.

'It is horrible,' she said. She shivered all over with an ague. 'Cold,' she said. 'It is so cold.'

'Let us take up our positions,' called Mary, watching the gladiators in their bright robing beginning to deploy. The Jeshuans split into two similarly armed groups of three, each of which went forward and to the side, like mailed fists. Mary stayed in the centre with Scipio, one of the converts from Vienne and a skilled archer, the two ready to reinforce either of the fighting groups. They had a tree in a great wooden pot at their backs, the arena was lush with vegetation.

The brass mouth of the *cornu* sounded, and they saw the gods slipping through the undergrowth. A bow twanged and someone screamed. Paulina nocked another arrow into her string.

The combatants came together in a sudden rush, all of them swirling about the left-hand group, the archers standing out on the wings, firing at their targets.

Wasps flew in the air, snapping with the speed of their flight, next to her Scipio gargled horribly, falling backwards, only the feathers of a Cupid's arrow sticking from his throat, pumping scarlet. Men screamed in the dust, metal clanging together in their fury.

Mary held her net ready, on the edge of the fray. Apollo staggered from the mêlée, blood streaming from a wound in his side and she despatched him with a single thrust of her harpoon. The great barbs stuck in his chest, meant to hold a thrashing tunnyfish, and as she heaved them out she heard the deep bellow of a hound. It came leaping from the dust with the goddess Diana running behind, a bloody sword in his hand. It stood near chest-high, foam and gore coating its muzzle. As it leaped at her she flung minced pepper, given to her by the gambler, into its face, and heard it howl. The harpoon came free and she lunged under the swinging sword of Diana. The gladiator impaled himself upon its points, tumbling thrashing to the bloody sand. She picked up his sword in the fury, hacking at both hound and master, and they lay still.

As she tore at the harpoon, a giant roared in the dust, huge and black. She threw her net with her left hand and it spread like the wings of a butterfly. The giant was Thor, it tangled about him, as he freed himself the harpoon came out of the body, disembowelling it. Mary and Thor drew back their weapons, hurling them at each other. The gigantic hammer was like a thunderbolt, it thrashed whirling at her in the air. Her feet slipped on the trails of intestine as she ran from its path. It slammed into her body, throwing her backwards, and she knew no more.

The crowd. Yelling. But not the blood-heat screaming that had accompanied the killing, the fighting. They were shouting instructions, commanding.

Mary opened her eyes. Her side was on fire, blood was sticky on her face. She had been hurled under some bushes by the impact of the great hammer. It lay nearby on the sand, its gory head coated with feasting flies. Not far away Thor was dead, the savage barbs of the harpoon sticking out of his back.

The dead lay in heaps. She saw Rufus, still gripping Mercury, his sword buried deep in his guts.

The crowd was shouting, their voices ripe with anticipation. Through the foliage she saw Paulina, over by the wall. She had abandoned her bow and held a long *spatha*, her arm bloody to the elbow. Arrayed about her were Priapus with his club, Sabazios with his long whip and dagger, and their captain, Mars, holding a sword.

The shouting of the crowd became clear. The gods had won, the crowd wanted the victory celebrated, they wanted Paulina violated out in public, where everyone could see, held down while they all cheered as they did it to her. They wanted her alive.

Paulina was very visible against the wall as she faced her tormentors, her tunic standing out white. Under the bushes, Mary pulled hers over her head. Her body was brown, like the sand.

Someone was moving, out in the artificial wood. She saw him, the dwarf, Cupid, prowling with his bow drawn. By the wall, Mars and Priapus came at Paulina from one side. As she struck at them with her blade the long whip of Sabazios snaked out, wrapping itself about her ankles. He jerked her feet from under her with a single heave and they were upon her.

They carried her out into the open, thrashing like a fish, and they ripped her tunic from her. The crowd roared, on its feet as they saw her body. Mars held her down and Priapus capered before her with his giant phallus, poking it at her, jabbing between her legs. Then he put it to one side, kneeling down as he pulled up his tunic. In the stands, forearms were raised, thrusting obscenely.

The dwarf was close, he kicked at the dead and looked up, grinning as he heard the tumult. She had a stone in her hand, from inside the bush she tossed it over his head to land amongst the rocks nearby. It clattered as it landed and he swirled to face the danger.

Like a feral cat, Mary sprang out from hiding, landing upon his bowed back with her feet. She had his head in her hands and snapped his neck with one convulsion of her body. She heard it break, like a dry bough. As she pulled his bow and quiver from under him, she heard a man scream.

Priapus was on his feet, clutching at his groin. Blood spurted through his hands, splattering the sand. Something glittered in Paulina's hand, a knife. Mars, at her shoulders, hit her, and her struggles were still.

Mary slipped the quiver over her shoulder and nocked an arrow. She jogged forward and the two men standing over

Paulina saw her coming. As she came through the trees Priapus fell forward on to his face, still clutching the place where his parts had been.

Mars was a big man. She drew back the bow to her ear as he ran at her, and shot him, in the very centre of his chest. The arrow vanished and he tumbled on to his knees, then his face, and blood began to seep out on the sand in a pool.

Sabazios, the god with a whip, was out in the open. As he began to run for cover she drew back the bow, tracking him.

There was a sudden jerk, and the bow flew forward in her hand. The string had snapped. Sabazios saw it and suddenly he was running at her, the whip snaking back in his hand.

It was too late to search for weapons. She stood naked, her arms outstretched, waiting for him. He slowed in his rush, balancing on his feet as he drew the plaited whip back, dark eyes glittering as he measured his distance.

His arm snapped forward and the silence of the crowd was broken with a roar. And then they were silenced again, as Mary ran into the whip, seizing it as it bit into her side. It was bloody in her hands, she whirled, using the momentum of her body and it was torn from his grasp. She had it in her grip, dancing away from him as she drew it back, and then she was moving the other way, the weight on the front foot, the heavy leather slashing like a blade. Blood fountained from the wound, flying scarlet in the sun, and he howled in sudden pain. She cut him into a bloody mass with heavy, measured strokes, and when he fell to the ground, picked up the dagger, cutting his throat.

On the sand Paulina moved feebly. Blood was still pumping from a terrible wound in her neck, she looked up at Mary.

'Leathern wings . . . I hear his wings,' she whispered. 'Satan is coming.'

Mary bent, closing her eyes as she died.

She stood up, the only living creature in the arena. The gods lay dead amongst the Jeshuans. There was a muttering, a grumbling, an anger running through the crowd, it beat through the pain and bruising of her soul. She began to stagger towards the *Sanavivaria*.

'*Bring her back!*'

'Make her fight again!'

'Kill the bitch!'

She turned. She was under the *pulvinar* and could see Clodios and the Roman legate Severus looking down at her.

'*We won,*' she called clearly. 'We fought as we were commanded to, and I am left. I am to live.'

Clodios was on his feet, he beamed down at her.

'For *today,*' he called out to the crowd, and they cheered. 'But the games have one more day to run!'

As the noise died down she called up again.

'Tomorrow I will fight one adversary of your choosing, with the weapons of my choice.'

They liked that, they drummed their feet on the stone and waved their cloths.

'When I win, I am to go free.'

Septimus Severus stood up, tall in his white toga. He was suddenly sickened by all the slaughter.

'Agreed,' he commanded. She stood up straight and walked down the arena to the gate, the sand hot under her feet, looking neither to left nor right.

It was quiet in the long cell, just the steady shuffling of the feet above on the stone as the spectators went home. She heard the creak and squeak of the gates shutting and it was silent, only the sound of her own breath rasping in her throat. She was stretched out on the single bunk where she had lain herself down. The others were all empty, bare boards and palliasses. Her eyes were half open, they looked out at the blue sky that was slowly being washed pale, through the small, high window.

She heard the sound of sandals and the door opened gently. She smelled charcoal and looking up saw Thrasea putting down a small brazier. He smiled silently at her and went out, returning with cloth and a skin of wine. He poured some into a metal pot and set it on the heat.

'Where are the herbs?' he asked.

'Under the bed,' she said. It was almost too much effort to talk. Thrasea reached under the planking and drew out a small sack, opening it.

'Put the root of Achilles, the henbane, the boragina, the plantago and elder into the pot, but not the poppy's tears, nor the dried mushroom.'

She heard the rustling, and a fresh, pungent smell as the herbs united with the hot wine.

'Take it from the heat and let it rest.'

He had a bottle of hyssopites. He dipped a cloth in its fluid and began to clean her wounds, in her side, where the whip had opened her like a knife, up her back and neck into her scalp, where the fearful hammer had lacerated the skin, had raised weals that rose swollen and purple.

'I never saw people fight like you and the Children,' he said quietly. 'They outnumbered you almost two to each one.'

'We fight for Jesus,' she whispered. The hyssopites was soothing, she felt the pain deadening. 'We are descended from him. He was sent here to battle with Satan, whose world it is. He is dead, but we fight in his name.'

'There is but you left,' he observed, 'and you must fight on the morrow.'

'Then I must win,' she said. His fingers were gentle, they

were loosing the knots of her muscles, bound up by the fighting.

'How will you fight?'

'With the *fascina*, the harpoon, and the net. It is the only way. I must use speed to defeat whatever champion Satan sends against me. I must tire him in his armour.'

'You will be stiff from these wounds,' he said knowledgeably. 'You must be supple.'

'Give me some wine now,' she said. 'I shall leave more to infuse overnight, and drink it in the morning, before the battle.'

She heard the sound of the herbal wine pouring into a beaker.

'I wish to be with you,' he said quietly. 'I wish to be one of the Children of Jeshua.'

He held the beaker out to her and she drank, feeling its power. She gave it back to him.

'Then you must drink too.'

He drained it.

'Again,' she said.

He felt the blood roar in his veins, felt its pungent aroma fill his head.

'Our ceremonies are beautiful,' she said sadly. 'With music, and foods, fine clothes and flowers. Our churches are wonderful, the glades of the Great Mother, not cells. But we must make do . . .'

She had a pottery jar like a small *amphora*, the Children had placed herbs in there and covered them with fine nut oil.

'Take the poppy's tears and the dried mushroom, and throw them into the coals,' she commanded.

Outside the blue of the sky was fading to indigo, he cast the herbs into the brazier and silver smoke streamed out. It was sharp and powerful, it stabbed into his mind like a knife.

'Take the oil,' she said.

He spilled some into the palm of his hand, and began to massage it into her skin as she lay stretched out on the bed. He spread it gently over her wounds, but they did not hurt. Her hair was tied up, he massaged it into her neck and over her shoulders, down to her breasts, feeling them smooth and round, slippery under his fingers. He rubbed it over her stomach, she took his hand in hers and put it between her thighs. He was kneeling beside her, as she moved her long legs, feeling the pleasure of his hand. She opened his tunic, taking him in her mouth. They were ready, and she pulled him down to her.

'Jesus is with us,' she said. 'Feel his spirit.'

She awoke in the morning, hearing the creak and squeak of the great gates as they opened, and the eager, scurrying scuffle of the sandals above on the stone steps, running up to take their places. She was covered with a blanket. Nearby on a table were her fighting clothes. She got up, moving freely despite her wounds, and began to dress.

A young slave boy brought her flat bread and goat's cheese on a platter, with some dried olives, and she ate. The infused wine was still in the pot; she poured it into the beaker, but did not drink. From above she heard the roar of the crowd, and from somewhere within it, the sound of people shrieking in agony.

The boy returned.

'It is your time,' he said, and she got up. She drank the beaker of wine and felt her vision tighten, the gloom of the cell becoming brighter, becoming clear, her hearing acute. She was dressed in a white tunic, she had leather sandals on her feet, carefully and firmly tied, she had a forearm guard and shoulder armour. On her belt she wore a slim dagger. Her gold net was tied to her wrist, she gathered it up. Her hair was bound up and in the half light her green eyes glittered. She picked up her long harpoon and went out and up the stairs to the gate.

She stood in the gloom, looking out over the bright, sun-splashed arena. Something was hanging upside down from a pole, its arms spread out in the shape of a cross. She thought it might be Blandina. On a griddle set over coals something else flapped, purple and black and dying.

She waited, while the engines of death were taken away. Then heard the *nomenclator* announce the contest. The arena was clear, they had not decorated it today. From the far end of the arena she saw the champion emerge into the sunlight, his cloak purple, his helmet gold, his weapons shimmering. He was tall and powerful, and fell.

He was Thrasea.

9

'Soldiers of Christ,' Irenaeus cried joyfully, 'forged at high heat, filled like transparent vessels with the pure light of the Holy Spirit!'

From his vantage point in the little house on the sun-drenched hillside, amongst the purple-berried vines, the pres-byter had watched the young priest trudging slowly up the valley path. He had ink, he had a reed, he had papyrus; now he awaited to hear from the young man the word of God, transmitted direct from his lips.

'One step from Jesus!' he crooned. He fiddled impatiently with his tools of learning. 'Tell me what is his will.'

The priest finished draining a beaker of water, and sat wearily down on the bench, wiping his mouth, leaving red dust streaks on the back of his hand.

'I went, as you instructed me, to the amphitheatre in Lyons. I was able to find the cell where they were keeping those who swore the Name.'

'They have put on Christ, the invincible champion!' Irenaeus cried, bouncing on the seat. 'And in bout after bout, they defeat their adversary, the crooked serpent! How found you them, as they trained for the coming contest?'

The young man was rather pale, he found himself unable to meet Irenaeus's searching eyes.

'I found the cell,' he said again. 'I was able to speak to some inside, to tell them who I was, that I had been sent as your emissary, on behalf of the Bishop of Rome, to hear the word of God, to be given the judgement of Jesus on the pressing question of the false prophet, Montanus.'

'Good, good,' Irenaeus grunted approvingly. He fingered the tip of his reed eagerly, ready to dip ink and scribe, forging holy weapons.

'There were some there who were angered when they heard your name,' the priest said hesitantly. 'They cried out that they had been betrayed, they asked why you were not there with them, suffering in the cell, there were those there that I knew, who were of our Church, that had received the wounds of Satan, who had suffered, in the arena.'

'Lucky souls!' shouted Irenaeus. 'How I envy them their badges of rank, their medals of honour. I stand here and like a warhorse that scents the fray from afar off, I hunger to be there with them in the midst of the fight, to taste the arsenal of Satan. But someone has to be outside, to perform the lowly functions of the Church while others go forth to claim their crowns of immortality.'

He looked at the clean papyrus, that awaited the imprint of God's will.

'Ah me,' he said quietly, 'it is harder for those who must deny themselves glory, who but stand aside to serve.'

The table was set in the shade, sunlight dappled its surface as the leaves waved softly in the breeze. He dipped the reed firmly into the small glass vessel of ink that he had prepared while he was waiting.

'But found you Sanctus the deacon?' he demanded. 'He the confessor who stands at the very mouth of Jesus, and transmits his word? You asked for his ruling upon the false prophet Montanus, vile in thought and deed, amongst the whores of Phrygia?'

'I explained, yes, that we wished for a ruling. I explained that Montanus claimed the gift of prophecy, that he claimed to be descended through Isiah, Job and Jesus himself.'

Irenaeus snorted with contempt and anger.

'I explained that in this region of Phrygia the teachings of Montanus had become very popular, that he had converted whole congregations of those who formerly had served with our Church, that these people fasted, saw visions and talked in tongues, that many were the women who flocked to him, many of them well-born, and possessed of riches.'

'What more proof do we need?' Irenaeus shouted out. 'Is it not known that women are gateways of the devil? One that attracts such is clearly one of his agents here on earth.'

'Sanctus cast doubt upon the claim of Montanus to be a prophet simply by fasting.'

The priest swallowed uneasily.

'He said, as best he was able, for he was weak from his wounds, that only those who swore the Name could claim kinship with Christ, that fasting was at best a poor substitute. At least, I believe that to be what he said, for he was sorely troubled by his suffering.'

There was just the sound of Irenaeus's nib scratching upon the paper.

'. . . cast out shall he be, excommunicated from the fellow-ship of Jesus . . .'

'Purple and yellow he was . . .' the boy muttered. 'His body just one great wound.'

'What else?' Irenaeus demanded.

'He spake no more, for they came to take him to the arena.'

The presbyter looked at him thoughtfully, but then began to write again, filling up his page.

'I understand what he meant,' he explained. 'Were you able to speak with any other confessor?'

'There was the slave girl Blandina, that was with the heretics. I was told that she had put on Christ, at the urging of Sanctus.'

'Brave soldier!'

'She was crying, I heard her call out, asking Jesus when he would come . . .'

The pen slashed quick strokes across the page.

'Blessed woman . . .' he muttered. 'Wrestling magnificently, she grew in strength as she proclaimed her faith, and found refreshment, rest and insensibility to her sufferings in uttering the words, *Christiana sum*, I am a Christian.'

'She was weeping . . .' the boy mumbled, but Irenaeus ignored him.

'Now,' he snapped, 'did you see their last hour, as they flung the devil to the ground, triumphant at last?'

'I went in as you bade me,' the priest said reluctantly. 'I was there when Sanctus met his end. They lashed him once again to the rack, and placed red-hot copper plates upon his organs.'

'I can see it!' Irenaeus said softly, looking down over the dusty valley. 'And his body became erect and straight from these new torments, recovering its former appearance, wondrous glory and grace blended upon his face.'

The young man swallowed uneasily.

'Then they took him off to the iron chair, to be roasted . . .'

Irenaeus seemed to squirm with joy on his bench.

'Alive now and braced up, his ordeal sweetened by God . . .'

'He *screamed*,' the priest said suddenly. His face was very white, and shone with sweat. 'They placed him in the red-hot chair and he *screamed*. Smoke gushed from his body, surrounding him with its reek, but you could hear him screaming . . .'

'His face glowed with joy, exulting at his departure as though invited to a wedding supper, and spake he only the Name . . .'

Irenaeus looked up irritably from his work as he heard the

priest vomiting noisily at the side of the house. The boy propped himself weakly against the wall and looked over at him.

'The heathens, those who were torturing him, they laughed and blessed their idols, crying "Where is your God?", and answer came there none.'

'Sons of perdition!' the presbyter roared. 'Know they not of the wedding garment, left outside shall they be, out where there is but the wailing and gnashing of teeth . . .'

'Jesus did not come,' the young man said quietly. Irenaeus assessed him with a certain measure of satisfaction. Dire sin had entered his soul on his trip to Lyons. He felt himself stiffening agreeably as the hand of Jesus touched him. It would have to be driven out.

'Let us pray,' he said.

Through the window of the hospital room Mary heard a short, gasping scream. Festus's new recruits were signing on. There was a rattle of blows like a stick running along a paling fence. She swung her legs out of the bed and got up, the flax stitching of her wounds making her wince. They were scarring over, the *familia* doctor, whose speciality the savage slashes of lethally sharp weaponry was, had declared her sound.

The gate of the gladiatorial barracks opened for her and she went outside. At her back, quiet now, was the fearful amphitheatre, its dark, arched entrances like open mouths.

A certain prosperity had returned to the city, as though the gods of the people approved of their actions in cleansing it of atheists, and the streets were bustling. She began to walk, going out of the city, and soon she was in the countryside. She knew what she was looking for, her trained eyes scanning the foliage about her as she moved up the small, dusty valley in the sunshine. In a shady grove she found what she wanted. She had a small leather sack with her, and she gathered berries, glaucous and purple, some flowers, yellow and white, narrow but scented and some leaves, sword-shaped and shiny, a dark green.

She emerged on the other side of the valley, and found herself on a small path. Intending to return to the city, she followed it and came about a small copse of olive trees. Ahead was a farm cottage, set amidst a patch of vines, the grapes a dark-blue against the red soil. A man was standing near a great pot that was upon a bed of coals. A strange, unpleasant odour drifted on the air and her nose wrinkled.

As she came up the path he looked up. He knew her, and she him. He blanched in terror. It was Irenaeus.

'I am not to be harmed!' he cried. '*Egnatius, Simonides!* Come quickly.'

Two burly slaves burst from the house, bearing clubs.

'What are you doing her?' Irenaeus demanded, recovering some courage now he had assistance.

'I had been enjoying the summer countryside,' she said coldly. 'I planned not to have it spoiled by meeting you. What are *you* doing here?'

A strange, sly expression slipped over Irenaeus's face.

'This is a holy place,' he said. 'You are in the presence of one second only to Christ himself. Can't you feel it?'

'I sense nothing but this foul smell.'

'Go on,' Irenaeus urged, gesturing to the pot. 'You may see . . .'

She took a step forward, looking through the steam. Something horrible was in there, a vile stew. The water roiled, and for a second she was looking into the eyes of Blandina, boiled opaque like a fish. The head rolled in the hideous water, and she jumped backwards.

'*Ossuari sancti*,' Irenaeus crooned, 'holy bones, of the blessed Blandina, Martyr of Lyons.'

'That's revolting,' she spat. 'She was of our Church, as well. Let her be buried in peace, in the cool earth.'

'She fell from grace, never having known the honourable, glorious, life-giving Name of confessor, and was counted among the sons of perdition. And Satan came to make her eternally his own, on the vile altar of sin that you call a Church. She was but a pace from freedom, a pace from Hell. And the spirit of Jesus moved within her. In ringing voice did she cry out: *Christiana sum*. And with what shining visage did she go to collect her immortal crown!'

'She screamed. When they put her in the chair she screamed and screamed until she died. I was there.'

'Wondrous joy, Satan forced to disgorge the living bodies of those he had thought swallowed.'

Irenaeus scuttled over to a table, where something like papyrus lay drying in the sun. He lifted it from under the stones. It was cruelly marked and scorched. He held it reverently in his hands.

'Holy wounds . . .' he murmured. 'The sacred skin itself . . .'

He looked up at her from under dark lids.

'I am bishop, now. The blessed Pothinus is dead . . . They will come in their thousands to see. To pray over the sacred relics. To hear her story. The martyrs bestowed grace upon her, having denied her Master she travelled once more the same road, now moving boldly, conceived and quickened a second time, and learnt to confess Christ. Noble martyr, valiant warrior. And great was the joy of the Virgin Mother, the Church, to receive her still-born children back alive. They will come, in their thousands, bearing their sins, and bend their knees.'

She glanced about the gruesome scene.

'The pagans, I have heard, dislike your Church collecting the parts of those it has had killed and calls martyrs,' Mary said sharply. 'How came you by these?'

Once again, the sly expression came over Irenaeus's face.

'Things can be arranged . . .' he suggested. 'God moves in mysterious ways.'

'And where is your priest? Is he not here, helping to boil up poor Blandina?'

'The road of Christ is too hard for some,' Irenaeus snapped. 'He has returned to perdition, where he belongs.'

'He did not have your taste for flagellation?' she suggested.

'Whore!' he snarled. 'Do you worship upon your back? I do not have to talk to you! Egnatius, Simonides! Beat this impudent servant of the devil!'

There was suddenly a short dagger glittering in her hand, and the two men halted in their tracks.

'Don't you know who I am?' she asked quietly, looking at them. 'But I see you do . . .'

They let her go without hindrance and she turned back to look at Irenaeus, the sheet of skin hanging in his hand.

'You have stolen the body of our disciple, and called it your own,' she called. 'What else will you take, like a thief in the night, before you are through? We shall be watching you and yours, Bishop, we know how Satan dresses up in the clothes of the righteous, to deceive the unwary.'

She walked back down the valley, and into the town set about the great river. The church at which the Children had worshipped was deserted, the altar overthrown, mice running across the floor. She lifted the great slab, and the scriptures were there underneath the shimmering robe. She packed them carefully away in a bag, together with the robe, and when she took it the tiny bells sewn to the fabric made music. Searching amidst the desecrated ruins she found the tools that prepared their holy herbs and lit some coals in the altar brazier, putting wine on to heat. Working skilfully, she squeezed the juice, purple and bitter, from the berries, and sweetened it with the scented flowers. Then she steeped the leaves in the hot wine and when it was cool, she drained the whole into a glazed pottery jug and sealed it. Finally she gathered up her things and went out into the afternoon.

Down by the river she found the boatyard, where they were melting black tar on the side of a vessel. She had *quadras* and *aureii* in her purse, enough to buy a small rowing boat, stoutly made and capacious. She put what she had into it and pushed out into the stream, guiding herself past the heavy-laden barges being pulled upstream by the slave teams.

Near the edge of the city the great river passed by green fields and woods, and not far from the water, a fine country mansion. There she steered her little craft to the shore, feeling it crush into the green reeds. She pulled it up on land, hidden from sight. Then she stripped off her clothes and pulled on the silk dress.

Working carefully, using a *specula*, a polished-silver mirror, she made herself up. She painted her forehead white with chalk and white lead and made her eyes large with antimony on the lids. Lees of wine reddened her cheeks; ochre made her lips scarlet, she dipped a forefinger into a small *gutti* pot and made them glisten. Then she took her small jug of wine and a Syrian goblet, pulled up the cowl of the ceremonial dress and slipped through the trees to the house.

The slave at the door looked questioningly at the exotic woman in front of him, her painted face in shadow, framed by the white cowl and raven hair.

'I have been sent with gifts from Bishop Irenaeus, the Chrestian,' she said.

His face brightened, he knew of whom she spoke.

'He is taking the baths,' he said. 'You will have to wait.'

'I am commanded to be there with him at his bath,' she said, and he saw her smile voluptuously. He chuckled in sudden understanding.

'Come with me, then.'

He let her in, and led the way through the luxurious villa. Steam was issuing from vents high on a wall. He put his head about the door and she heard him speak. He came out.

'You're to go in,' he said, eyeing her form enviously.

Clodios Syrus was a wealthy man. No waddling amongst the scrum in the *thermae* in town for him, he had his own baths, marble-lined and of differing heats. The one he was in was hot, the *sudatoria*, intended to make a man sweat. It was dimly lit, and steam gushed from vents low on the wall. He was sitting naked on a huge towel spread on a marble shelf. As she came in a slave was placing some fresh hot rocks into a grate. Small, pig-like eyes gleamed in folds of flesh as the magistrate saw her enter.

'Who are you?' he asked warmly.

'I come from Bishop Irenaeus, to bid you thanks,' she said in a low, pleasing voice. In the steam the shimmering dress of many colours was clinging to her body and she saw his eyes moving eagerly over her.

'But the gifts I bring are to be enjoyed by you alone,' she said playfully.

Clodios chuckled.

'Cordus! A ladle of water on those rocks, and I'll see you in the *tepidarium*.'

The slave obediently splashed water from the bowl and with a fierce hiss fresh steam billowed across the room. She felt it bite into her skin, and march across her tongue and down her throat. The sweat oozed afresh from Clodios's naked body, as pink and slippery as a porker. He patted the thick towel.

'Sit here with me.'

'All in good time,' she said mysteriously. 'But first . . .'

She took the small jug and the goblet, pulling out the stopper and filling it nearly to the brim. In the heat the scent of the wine was pungent and intoxicating. She handed it to Clodios with both hands, bowing low so that he could see her breasts.

She stood in front of him and slowly undid the silk ribbons that held the front of the dress closed. Keeping the cowl about her face, she began to dance, singing a strange, wordless, mesmerising song. As the dress swayed back and forth, its bells singing, Clodios caught tantalising glimpses of round, swaying breasts, her smooth stomach and long legs, for beneath the dress she was entirely naked. She saw him stiffen, watching her eagerly as he gulped at his wine.

'Ahh . . . that's good,' he grunted. She danced forward, picking up the jug, and refilled his glass. He reached out, his hands slipping inside the dress to feel her, slippery and warm.

'Drink,' she urged, 'Bishop Irenaeus bids you be merry, as he is. He has what he wanted, he wishes you to have what you want.'

Clodios tipped his beaker, watching her as she slid her arms out of the dress, keeping the cowl on, so that she was part naked, part dressed. Red wine ran over his chin; he laughed.

Her clear skin was marred. In the dim, steamy air she saw him peering at her, suddenly puzzled. Her shoulder and arm bore the clear, red slash marks of a sword blade, scored by the white flax stitches that had knitted the lips of the wounds together. The purple scar of a gladiator's brand disfigured her upper arm.

Breath rasped in his throat, the goblet slipped from his hand, and clattered on the marble. It did not break, Syrian glass was light, but strong. He seemed not to notice it, his eyes bulging as he looked at her.

'Thrasea sends you greetings,' she said softly.

'*We have to make this look good.*'

Thrasea had been equipped as a *secutor*, she had danced around him, her net and trident at the ready, his sword high, ready to slash. The roar of the crowd beat on them like heavy waves crashing down on a rocky beach.

She over-reached herself, and felt the sting of the blade slicing her skin, the hot spill of blood down her arm.

'They don't like it if they can't see the gore,' he said laughing. She jabbed with the trident and he caught it on the edge of his shield.

'*Verbera!* Strike the bitch!'

She could hear them howl up above her.

'*Iugula!* Slay! *Iugula!*'

'He slipped . . .' said Clodios. The words were slurring in his mouth. He looked at her, and she could see he knew who she was.

'He slipped, and you had the trident at his throat . . . he asked for mercy . . .'

'*Pollice verso* . . .' she said softly. 'You stood, so that he might see you . . .'

'You killed him!' Clodios protested. He was trying to shout, but the words were whispers in the steam.

'He was one of us, the Children of Jeshua, now he is with Jesus in Paradise.'

'We let you go . . .'

Clodios fell sideways on the wet marble, like a side of pork slapping down on to a butcher's slab.

'We pay our debts,' she said quietly. She gathered up what she had brought, and slipped from the bath. There was no one about, she went over the wall and into the trees, slipping down to the great river. There she pushed her boat out from the reeds and the current took it. Sitting in the back, she conned her craft with a single oar as the waters swept her the long miles to the sea.

Towards nightfall she came across an island in the stream, a long, thin spit of land rising up out of the river, clad with trees and shrubs, and she guided the boat up on to its sloping sand beach, pulling it safe from the drag of the current.

She gathered dry, bleached driftwood all along the beach, putting it into a pile. As night fell she struck spark and tinder licked into flame. She fed it with rustling leaves and twigs, and it grew. The logs and branches took hold and fire blazed, turning the swirling waters about her blood-red. In the darkness she sang the sacred prayers of Jesus, the holy psalms he had taught them in the beginning. She danced, and the tiny gold and silver bells of her robe sang the songs of heaven. She cast upon the fire the divine herbs of the Lord and sudden sparks erupted, red and green and blue and gold, rising fast to the heavens and never coming back down, as the souls of the Children of Jeshua flew straight to Paradise.

Hook Norton

Dusk had stolen over the sky as he was reading, he was holding up the last sheet in the dying rays of the sun. In the grate an embered log crashed softly, scattering pale-grey fragments and exposing its glowing heart. Connell put down the text on his small pile and got up. He put some split larch on the fire, watching as the strands of wood curled in the heat, browning, and then burst into flame.

Juliana looked up from her table, where she was quietly shifting the photographed fragments into coherence.

'That must have been where they learned the value of dissimulation,' he remarked.

'Who?'

'The Children of Jeshua. They'd become a form of Gnostic sect, and the Gnostics were renowned for *not* standing up in public and shouting the name of Jesus. They were quite prepared to pretend to be pagans, in order to survive. A bit like some Muslims, today, living in hostile countries, they kept their heads down. You can see why, the Lyons massacre was particularly terrible. Anyone who'd survived that would work out a strategy to see it didn't happen again.'

The rivulets of flame suddenly joined and the fire licked up, brightening the room. A woodlouse emerged scurrying from under a section of bark. In the heat it backed away, to and fro, and then fell into the flame.

'I can't look at a fire the same way,' Connell remarked. 'I keep seeing that horror Irenaeus crooning over Blandina's scorched skin and charred bones . . .'

'He was horrible,' she said positively. 'They're quite attractive, the Children of Jeshua. Not bleak at all.'

She put down a fragment with a sigh, and glanced at the soft-ticking clock.

'I've done too much,' she sighed. 'In the morning it will fit perfectly, but now I can't see it. Let's be like the Jeshuans and have some wine.'

'I won't say no,' smiled Connell. 'Red or white?'

'Red. Like they would have had.'

'All right,' he said amiably. In a nook of the wall he had assembled a rack and the noses of bottles peeped out into the firelight. He took one out and twirled a cork. As he poured into a pair of bellied glasses, she smelled the rich blackcurrant.

'I can't get over the power of the initiation ritual,' she said, staring into the glass. 'Such impact . . . the herbs burning like incense, filling the church. Would there have been some dope there?'

Connell glanced up.

'Oh, yes. I think it was all designed to have an enormous bonding effect. Very tribal. The use of some kind of hallucinogen in religious ritual occurs again and again, from the druids to the American Indian peyote culture. The Jeshuans against the world . . . Blandina would have felt the bride of Christ, as she was meant to.'

She seemed to shiver, by the fire.

'The music, the girl singing, the wine,' she murmured, 'the smell of the herbs releasing their vapour into the air. Standing blindfold as they slowly take all your clothes off. Kissing you, all over . . . then laying you down as God makes love to you . . .'

'You saw that, did you? The spirit of God was intended to have entered into the one who was chosen as the priest . . .'

She shook all over suddenly, and the wine shivered in the glass. She put it to her mouth and tipped it back, draining it.

'I wish it had been me,' she said, in a low voice.

The coals in the shovel had a fine coating of white ash hiding their glowing centres. Connell tossed on the handful of herbs and pungent silver-grey smoke began to roil up into the room. It stabbed into his nose, piercing his head. She stood very still, tendrils of it drifting about her, and as he tied the soft white blindfold about her head she closed her eyes.

He undid the buttons of her high-necked white blouse one by one, and it slid off her shoulders. She was naked above her skirt, except for a plain gold necklace that gleamed in the firelight. He kissed her breasts and she shivered.

Some small dishes were on the table. Peeled cucumber was in one.

'Here,' he said, and she opened her mouth.

He undid her red skirt and it pooled like blood on the floor. He dipped his finger in a dish, where salt crystals glistened white.

'Here,' he murmured, and she sucked his finger, licking it clean of salt. She reached out with her blind hands, finding him, and undid his clothes. He held out the dish of honey and she dipped her fingers in it, anointing him. She knelt down, licking it away.

When she lay on the soft rug the firelight made her gold. He knelt down, kissing her inside her ankles and knees. He kissed her thighs, her stomach and her breasts; the smoke drifted about them in its power, the blood drumming in their heads.

She cried out, in a tongue he did not know.

The fire was low again, the coals in the shovel were cold. Connell pushed himself up on his knees. The night was chill on his body, he reached out and put some logs in the grate. The bottle was half full, he filled the glasses and smelled the fruit in the air. On the rug she stirred and pulled the white cloth from her eyes.

'That was how it was, when the Lord God came to the Virgin Mary,' she said. 'He came in the form of a man.'

She shivered all over, her eyes unfocused, and he stood looking at her in the dark.

10

Oxfordshire

Abercrombie hung up a length of ivory lamb fat on a string to a hook on the bird-table, his breath puffing white in the air. From the silver-rimed bushes about his garden and the tree branches above came an impatient cheeping. A hundred pairs of liquid eyes observed him. Connell held the jug of warm water.

'It's a rough time of year for the little chaps,' said Abercrombie. 'For the insect-eaters it's migrate or die, of course, so what we have here are the tough eggs who stay. I like to give them a hand. They've made it all the way through, it must be a bastard when they get a late cold snap like this.'

He strung up a mesh bag of peanuts and a halved coconut, and took the jug of water, filling the broad and shallow bird-bath.

'It's a bugger for them,' he said. 'Water everywhere, but most of it frozen. They must feel like avian ancient mariners.'

The cheeping was becoming something of a crowd riot, and little figures hopped from twig to twig.

'They want us to go,' Abercrombie chuckled. 'They say we've done our bit and thanks, but just get out of the way!'

He led the way back to the house.

'Try and stick to the path,' he said. 'If you tread on frosted grass you leave your bloody great footprints there for ages until it grows through again.'

'I know, George,' said Connell, and smiled, 'you said so when we came out.'

'So I'm a repetitive old bore. Just keep off the blasted grass.'

They went inside the white-painted Cotswold farmhouse, and into the sitting room whose stone walls were lined with old books, the items of his trade. Abercrombie shrugged off his Barbour jacket and tossed a couple of logs on to the fire. He glanced at the carriage clock on the mantelpiece.

'Let's have a snifter while we watch the little fellows,' he suggested. 'Sun must be over the yardarm somewhere, that's what I say.'

'I'll have a beer,' said Connell, and Abercrombie opened a can of bitter and poured himself a gin and tonic. He stood by his window looking at the thronging birds, and Connell joined him.

'Cheers.'

'Bottoms up.'

Abercrombie dipped his nose into his glass and inhaled with pleasure before taking a sip.

'My old dad liked a pink gin, but he was in the Navy,' he said. 'I prefer tonic. How are the texts, Frank? Got something to whet the appetite, when we go public? Among our select institutions, that is. We want something that proves the Children of Jeshua to be the real thing, and controversial, but not yet the whole hog. Something to get them hooked, so we can reel them in.'

'I have three that fit the bill. The Jeshuans are at war with the Church of Rome. They suffered terribly at their hands in the massacre of Lyons, but survived as an organisation. It's clear that after that they made penetration of the Church of Rome one of their priorities. We know that the Catholics in the first centuries are constantly complaining of Gnostic infiltration – they see Reds under the bed, if you like – but it's evident that they had real reason to worry. We've found two texts giving intelligence information about the thinking of two Popes – Zephyrinus and Fabian, end of the second century and middle of the third – giving evidence of the hardening official strategy of confrontation with the Roman authorities, the encouragement of martyrdom. *Semen est sanguis Christianorum.* The blood of the Christians is the seed of the Church. Irenaeus said it at Lyons. We have the texts in the Jeshuan's library, they clearly had agents close to the highest office.'

'Sounds like the Cold War,' George grunted, half-amused. On the table, gangs of small birds shoved and pecked and fluttered.

'Nothing new about spies,' said Connell. He sipped his beer, and wiped soft froth from his lip. 'Read Sun Tzu.'

'Tough little buggers, sparrows,' Abercrombie said, almost approvingly. 'Really quite Mafia-like. They operate as a gang and simply terrorise the other small birds. They beat up the blue tits and take their food, their nests, whatever they want. Then they all go off and have a dust-bath and brag about it to each other.'

'No different to the Early Church.' Connell commented. 'Hordes of little sects, all slowly driven out of existence by the Church of Rome.'

Abercrombie glanced at him. Behind them the fire popped, the sweet smell of apple-wood in the air.

'Except the blue tits still survive,' he said, 'despite being bullied.'

'Oh yes,' Connell nodded at the table, 'but that, out there, is a harmonic balance, despite the violence – or perhaps because of it – prey and predator have to exist together. For actual extermination you have to believe in God.'

'Yes . . . I'm an atheist, myself. I suppose if I had to believe in a god I'd choose one of those comfortable deities who like a lot of feasting and drinking, and good-looking women.'

'All gods could be dangerous, even the jollier ones like Bacchus and Pan. The pagans understood that. But it was the Church of Rome's god that proved so lethal, because he wouldn't tolerate any opposition, he wasn't even like your sparrows out there, he was jealous, he was paranoid, a psychopath, and he killed all the others off. The Jeshuans believed he was Satan.'

Abercrombie drank some gin while he thought.

'You said three texts, Frank.'

'Yes. I *think* I have the original of *Revelation to John. The Apocalypse.*' Connell said quietly. Abercrombie looked at him, interest sparking in his eyes.

'How's that, now?'

'When the Church of Rome was putting together its ideological package – over a considerable period – before they froze the design and claimed that it had come direct from the lips of God, they were like magpies or jackdaws, they stole attractive ideas from the other competing ideologies, and soon after claimed they were their own. You can see them at it all the time. When they were putting together their canon of belief they had a lot of scriptures of various sorts to sift through and choose from. Once they liked something they took it, rewrote it from their own vantage point, and presented it as theirs. I happen to think that Revelation is a terrific piece of writing given that it was meant to be read out loud – hence the repetition. It's *effective*. You can see why the Church of Rome included their version in the New Testament. With their commitment to the martyrdom of their own believers – *semen est sanguis Christianorum* – they had to keep the sheep within the fold, had to keep them believing, up to the point of death in the arena. Revelation states most clearly that those who have suffered persecution or who are about to suffer must endure, for Rome is doomed and will shortly receive what she deserves, because the Lord is coming soon and will dish it out hot. It's a most useful piece of writing, from their terms, it kept people going to the lions or the griddle for a good three hundred years.'

'But you say the Children wrote it?'

'No, I don't think that they did. Juliana put it together from fragments and I'm trying to fit it in. I think it fits with the codex I'm working on right now, in Nero's Rome, in fact I'm sure of it.'

'So who is John?'

'It's not John – whoever he might have been, or whoever the Church of Rome meant him to be. No, I think it's Paul.'

'*Paul.*'

'Yes. I'm sure of it.'

'But technically, is it Pauline? Stylistically?'

'No. But was he Paul, or was he Saul?'

'Have you got a copy?'

'Yes. I've been making transcripts of all our translations. But I don't want to use it until I've got it in context. It's the speech of a demagogue, he's inflaming his audience. To do just what, I'm not yet certain.'

He had a folder with him, filled with typed pages.

'You know, we're going to be quite famous, when all this breaks.'

'*You* are,' said George, draining his glass. 'Me, I plan to take my cut and retire to a life of ease.'

'And I don't think it'll go away quickly.' Connell continued. 'It'll get in the way of academic thought. Too many people asking questions.'

Abercrombie looked across from the gin bottle, amused.

'Being given a lot of money always comes with a price,' he observed.

'Oh, I know. But I have to be able to think . . . I bought a cottage in Wales.'

'A retreat?'

'Something like that. Down a little *cwm*, by a stream . . . It's surrounded by an old orchard, and it's a three-mile walk to the pub. I've even used another name.'

He smiled crookedly.

'I think I must be getting like the Children. They went underground. I stocked it up last weekend. Crates of wine and long-life meals, I've even stashed some money down there! I took it all down in the old Morris Minor shooting brake, and left it there. I walked out to the station.'

'You don't mind being on your own?'

'I have the company of the ghosts. They're very real, you know, George. The Children are more real to me than the people walking down Carfax, I live with them . . .'

'They'd be a better lot to be with than the bloody Christians,' George grunted. 'They seem to enjoy life.'

'They still have a lot of their Jewish origins. They haven't become narrow, bleak, acidulated. They *are* fanatics, but that's because they see themselves as soldiers in enemy territory, they're fighting for their side, and it's very dangerous . . . Somewhere in the texts is the reason for it all, why they think this particular, individual way . . . I'll find it.'

There was a sudden, swerving streak outside, an explosion of small birds flying in all directions. The sparrowhawk vanished over the far hedge, her long, swept wings marking the pale-blue sky, and a few brown feathers floated in the breeze.

'I was waiting for her to turn up,' Abercrombie grunted. 'There's the angel of death for you.'

Anno Domini

Lyons, Gaul, July, A.D. 200

The evening sun was going down as the woman came down the street. It stabbed across the open fields with their cattle, bathing the stone tower of the Church of St John with its red rays. The heavy wooden door was still open, and she slipped inside. She wore a peasant skirt of coarsely woven wool under a linen smock, and her head was wrapped in a cloth, in the manner of the local people.

She stood for a few moments as her eyes adapted to the gloom inside. The church was lit by narrow, slitted windows. It smelled of dust, damp and ancient candlegrease. A glow came from the stone steps that led down to the crypt, and she went down.

A man was down there, he turned as she came into the narrow, subterranean stone chamber. Candles were burning on the altar, and in their light he was arranging something underneath. He looked around, and she knelt down before him.

'Are you bishop?'

Her voice was quiet, sibilant against the walls. The man was old, with silver hair, he turned from his work.

'I am Bishop Irenaeus.'

'I have come to pray. To pray to the blessed and saintly Blandina.'

'You are too early,' Irenaeus said. 'Her death-day is not until tomorrow.'

'I know. But I may not be here tomorrow.'

She fumbled in the folds of her clothing and brought out some coins.

'I have brought an offering.'

Irenaeus took the money.

'Very well,' he said, 'I am arranging her blessed bones under the altar. She was a glorious victim, let her take her place where Christ offers himself as victim. He who was put to death for us all is upon the altar, she who was redeemed by his suffering may lie underneath.'

'She too suffered,' the woman said quietly.

'Not so!' Irenaeus cried. 'She was relieved of her burden by the joy of martyrdom, her ordeal sweetened by the anaesthesia of God the moment she put on Christ, the Invincible Champion.'

He went over to the altar and lifted the cloth. On a wide, deep dish lay a collection of yellowed bones.

'They are marked by the whip, slashed by the sword, burned by the red-hot iron, but felt she not these torments, such is the mercy of God.'

'I am comforted,' the woman said quietly. 'And rests she with the Lord?'

'The Son of God sacrificed himself for us,' Irenaeus said intensely, sincerely. 'It is his promise, written in the Gospels, that those who become his colleagues in suffering shall rise like larks through the skies, straight to the bosom of God.'

'Were I eager to quit the company of men to stand among angels, I should also rise up like her?'

Irenaeus looked thoughtfully at the shadowy figure kneeling in front of the altar. He swallowed, like a man just beginning to realise that it was suppertime and he was hungry.

'There are few so prepared to volunteer, to win their heavenly crowns.'

He indicated the pathetic little heap of aged bones.

'That is one reason a martyr's bones are so precious,' he murmured. 'But yes, those who put on Christ, the Great Champion, who defeat the crooked serpent, who shall not shudder at their own blood, streaming forth, those shall rise to be amongst the apostles, shall breathe in the sweet perfume of angels as they cluster about the Lord.'

The woman raised up her face, in the gloom he could see the gleam of her eyes.

'Then let us dress in Christ's robes together! Bishop and sinner, we shall be as one.'

She stood, holding wide her arms.

'Let us become athletes in God, the two of us.'

Irenaeus threw up his palms.

'Alas! So few can take the easy road . . . I must remain here, to do the weary work of God, while others find glory.'

The woman reached out for him, gripping his tunic in the darkness.

'No, no,' she said, her eyes glittering in the last of the light from the thin windows, 'God has told me to come for you.'

There was a sudden pattering of sandalled feet on the stone about them. Hands seized him, he drew in breath to shout out, only to find himself wrapped up in a great rug, his voice silenced by its folds. They bundled him up, carrying him up the steps and outside, where a wagon was waiting. They tossed him in and sat on him, the carter slapped the reins, clucking with his tongue, and drove him out of the town.

They rolled him out on to the earth and he pushed himself up, coughing and spluttering, grit and dust in his nose, coating his teeth. Trees and vines flickered red in the flames of the fires. Figures were about him. One stepped forward, and he saw that it was the woman. By the wall of a small house the horse champed in a bag.

The woman threw back her cowl.

'Greetings, Bishop,' she said quietly. 'It is some twenty-three years since we have been together here. Do you remember me?'

Irenaeus's heart was pounding, he brushed at his gritty teeth with his hand, his mouth dry. The woman pulled down one shoulder of her tunic and there on her arm an old scar gleamed white, a branding mark.

'I am Mary, of the Children of Jeshua.'

She turned about her, one hand outstretched.

'And here we are, the true servants of Jesus. Like our Lord, we live again.'

'Blasphemer!' Irenaeus spat. 'I remember you, whore.'

A man appeared from out of the darkness carrying a box. He held it out to her and in the firelight Irenaeus could see bones. Mary nodded at the man.

'Take them to the graveside,' she instructed. 'She shall be at peace.'

She turned to Irenaeus.

'You killed her. Blandina was taken into the Children, to be with us, to serve the true Lord. You, the disciple of Satan, had her murdered, most horribly. Here, look about you, here are the tools and engines of your work.'

A pit had been dug, and glowing charcoal lain in it. At one end two long iron prongs stood up, attached to wooden handles. Mary pulled one free and at its end a round plate shone dull purple. She held it out at his face and he could feel its heat.

'These they clapped to her breasts as they did to the organs of the deacon Sanctus. Tell me, Bishop, is it hot?'

Irenaeus stayed silent, staring at the fearful disc in front of him.

'You had better answer, Bishop, before we clap them to you,' Mary said sharply.

'It is hot,' Irenaeus whispered, reluctantly. She pushed it

back into the coals. Further along in the centre of the fiery bed a hideous chair sat, its orange rust beginning to glow.

'Here is the seat where they burned her, suffocating in her own reek,' indicated Mary. 'Step closer, feel the warmth.'

Irenaeus felt hands push him close.

'Do you feel the Holy Spirit moving within you?' she enquired. 'Now that you are on trial for your faith, you should be filling up like a crystal goblet, pure and clear for all to see.'

Irenaeus stayed silent again.

'Is that not right?' she asked. 'Is that not what you claim Jesus said? Yes? In Matthew's Gospel?'

'Satan can quote from the scriptures, when it suits him,' the bishop snarled.

'He does indeed,' Mary said quietly, 'for you are his servant. Why did you write that, Bishop? Why did you put that in?'

Irenaeus's mind went back through the years, out in the darkness, amongst those who had come for vengeance in the Gaulish killing-ground he remembered the quiet of the room, of his thoughts, and the scratching of his quill.

'The spirit of God moved within me,' he said sincerely. 'He spoke to me, told me what to write.'

'So that simple people might die for you.'

'Not for me!' Irenaeus cried. 'For Jesus, as He died for them.'

'*Semen est sanguis Christianorum.*'

'You will see,' Irenaeus said stubbornly. 'The blood of the martyrs shall be the seed of the Church. One day, all will serve the true God.'

'You had better know that we are going to send you to be amongst their number,' Mary promised. 'Now, Bishop, we have read your text telling how the Martyrs of Lyons died, our Blandina amongst them, whose bones and skin you stole. Many must have read it, all about the great sea, for scribes have copied it and sent it to all the churches that owe allegiance to your Catholic faith. In fact, I have a copy here.'

One of those who stood about her pulled a scroll from his sleeve and she unrolled it, looking at the flowing black script in the firelight.

'What is its purpose?' she asked softly. 'Why did you write it, why was it sent out to all the churches?'

'It is a memorial to those who have competed,' Irenaeus ground out, 'and a training and a preparation for those who are to follow suit.'

'Did they suffer?'

'Their blood was their key to Paradise! How could they suffer, knowing they were to speed straight to Christ and the Father?'

'*Did they suffer?*'

'Their ordeal was sweetened by God,' Irenaeus whispered.

Mary glanced at the scroll.

'Perfumed with the sweet savour of Christ, according to you,' she commented. 'I was there, Bishop, and all I could smell were the sulphurous fires of Hell, as the agents of Satan went about their work. We know who *you* serve, it is the dark Lord himself.'

She allowed the scroll to roll up again with a snap.

'Strip him!' she shouted. 'Let us see if your Master will sweeten *your* ordeal.'

They led him naked past a great cauldron, where water hissed and roiled. At the edge of the bed of coals they paused.

'*We* serve Jesus, who was sent here to defeat Lucifer, the Lord of Hell, whose domain this world is,' she said quietly. 'He does not ask us to torture anyone to his death, not even Satan's servants. All I wish to know is, can you feel the Holy Spirit moving within you?'

Irenaeus stood in the glare of the furnace. All about him

the Children of Jeshua were silent. He was alone in the night, and he shivered.

'No,' he whispered.

'Shall we place you upon the red hot chair, to see if Jesus will descend from the clouds above us, to snatch you away to Paradise?'

'No,' he said quietly, and bowed his head. Mary nodded, and from behind him they threw a noose about his neck, pulling it tight, snuffing the life from him. Nearby, the huge cauldron seethed.

In the dawn, the pilgrims came into the city, to the church, for it was the death-day of the Martyr Blandina. The sick and the halt came, those who could not walk were carried on litters, for the relics had miraculous powers, it was known. Those possessed by demons were led by relatives, that they might kiss the sacred bones, for malign spirits could not stand the presence of Christ. Pregnant women came to hold the holy skull to their stomachs, that their babies might be born without fault, just like the Redeemer. Many were those who felt that the Goddess Cybele had not favoured them that year, that Zeus and Diana took little interest in that part of Gaul. They had respect for a deity like the Christ, who could order the sacrifice of a live human being, right there in Lyons, where they could keep the magical bones for themselves.

When they went down into the crypt they cried out in wonder, for the dessicated yellow bones had become quickened. They shone a pure white in the candlelight. When the pilgrims touched them, they found that they exuded a faint dampness, as though the spirit of the holy Blandina had only just left them. They gazed at them in wonder, and knew that the Lord God had moved amongst the people.

11

Hook Norton

Daffodils had splashed the edges of the garden with yellow and white, purple crocuses kissed the newly green grass, and Juliana stood by the window looking out, waiting for the kettle to boil on the Aga. She tapped her dark-green HB pencil against her teeth.

'Are you still in Rome, Frank?'

Connell looked up and the nib of his pen stopped its gentle scratching.

'Hmm? Oh, yes.'

'With Maria?'

'Yes, she's with Jeshua, they're living with Saul.'

'What's she doing?'

'From what I can gather, Saul's got her work as a maenad. One of the temple dancers. She's trained, of course.'

'I want to read it, when you can spare it,' she murmured.

'Of course.'

The kettle began to warble faintly.

'It's the same girl, Frank.'

'What?'

'Mary, Ruth, Maria. All through. She is the same. I know she is.'

'Are you suggesting reincarnation?'

Juliana went into the kitchen and took the kettle off the hob.

'Yes,' she said, without turning round.

'So who is she?' Connell asked.

Rome, A.D.61

'Chickens,' said Saul.

Jeshua's eyes adjusted to the light, dim after the bright sunshine outside.

'Cocks, really,' Saul amended himself, 'no hen birds here.'

It was noisy, men crouched over and around the bowl-shaped pit in the ground, yelling encouragement, offering and taking bets, coins jingling and flashing from hand to hand. There were also a lot of birds. They poked their heads out of wicker baskets, wattles and combs aflame with rage at the sight of other birds, and opened their beaks threateningly at each other. They pecked at the air, clasped under their owners' arms, their legs gyrating with the desire to disembowel each other. They flapped and struck into each other's flesh in the pit and the knives attached to their heels turned red. Blood flew in droplets, spattering the flushed, sweating faces above them that watched them die. The dead hung on hooks on the wall, the victors pecked yellow corn from their owners' palms, and suffered their iridescent feathers to be smoothed.

'Chickens,' Saul mused. 'They eat well, they're very tasty. We'll have some for *cena*, they're young, you see. They don't live to be old.'

There was a roar in which triumph and annoyance were equally mixed, from the men about the pit. A cockerel staggered about the earth floor, his glossy feathers matted with blood, one wing trailing. Fluttering about him on merciless angel's wings, his opponent slashed at him with razored heels and pecked at his comb. A scything blade opened his throat and he fell forward, dark blood pooling on the sticky earth. His killer perched on his body as he died, and crowed in unashamed joy, his comb and wattles bright-red with passion. Jeshua looked up at Saul and saw him observing the bird with a strange calculation.

Nearby was a bigger pit, almost as deep as a man, round, with wooden sides. The planks were splashed with dark gouts and streaks, the hole gave off a rank smell.

'What do they use that for?' Jeshua asked.

'Dogs,' Saul explained. 'They also fight dogs. Timothy has a champion dog, Wolf. I'm going to buy one of his puppies. If it has the right stuff inside it.'

Bending over from the cockpit, a man reached down and scooped the victor up. Deft fingers untied the leather thongs of the fighting blades; he held out his hand for his winnings.

'Hoy there, Timothy,' Saul called. 'That your champion?'

The man looked up. Jeshua recognised the Greek bookie from the horse race in the Forum. His seamed, sun-tanned face creased in a smile.

'Saul,' he said. 'You said you'd come.'

'Thought I'd show the boy the chickens. He's not been before.'

'Didn't he have a sister? She's not with you. Doesn't she like the sight of blood?'

Saul laughed. 'She'd better not mind it. She's a maenad. One of the Corybantes, I should say. I got her a place with the temple of Attis and Cybele.'

Timothy frowned, thinking, as his quick brown fingers tucked away his coins. He scratched the bird's neck and its comb began to droop in pleasure, red lids sinking over its yellow eyes.

'I thought they shut them down, after the last time.'

'They're back. The Emperor likes the more exotic cults.'

The Greek gave a hoarse chuckle. He fished in his pocket and scooped out a handful of grains, cupping them for his cockerel to peck at.

'They'll be well suited, then.'

'She's over there now,' Saul commented. 'They're inaugurating a new priest.'

The street that led to the temple was lined with coffins, and as the chariot passed it was filled with the wailing of the women, mourning he who was dead. The chariot was drawn by men in lion-skins, in it stood the widow who had lost her lover. Cybele was her name, and behind her came her priests and Corybantes, her worshippers and initiates. At the wheel of the chariot, Maria danced, singing the death-song of the god.

There behind her, among the initiates was Scorpus, his wife and two sons, just in their teens. All men knew that one could not have too much protection from the gods in this world, and some recent setbacks in trade had caused him to look for some deity who could more successfully protect his cargoes from ill-weather and mishap. One Maximus whom he knew was in the service of the gods Attis and his consort Cybele, on examination he wondered why he had not sought the protection of them before. No mere fowl or goat did they sacrifice, but bulls. There was a lot of blood in a bull, they had an entire day devoted to blood; today, at the end of three days of fasting. He was light-headed, images flickered behind his eyes, all about him he saw the crazed faces of the half-mad and he knew that the gods were among them, for humans were driven insane by the aura of deities.

The howling of the women deafened him, the cobbles beneath his feet were slick with the crushed petals of the violets that had sprung up from the earth when it was stained by the blood of Attis, as the boar ripped his flesh. The wild beast had killed the god, who now lay cold in his tomb within the temple.

The goddess Cybele, the great mother of all gods, stood tall in her chariot, the sunlight flashing from her gleaming silver body, her face jagged black stone. The lion men brought her to the wide marble central altar, where she was to preside over the acts of worship. The fires were burning, the priests had cakes of frankincense and bundles of dried herbs, the altars were wreathed in pungent smoke and Scorpus smelled it as it drifted across the throng. The goddess reached up into his brain through it, he knew that he was in her presence.

Music there was, the sound of trumpet and cymbal and drum, the first bull bellowed in anger and fear as it was led into the sacred arena in front of the temple, sweat dripping from its black hide, steam rising from its body. The initiates knelt in a group, in their white shifts, to receive their baptism.

The priest Musaeus came down the temple steps with the others, and with them Tisiphone, priestess of Cybele, in her scarlet robes. Behind her came Maria, carrying the glittering bronze knife of office.

As he reached the altar Musaeus held up his arms, chanting prayers for Cybele and her dead lover. The attendant of the fires threw on more herbs and incense, the music became louder, the women were shrieking as they drew his robes over his head and laid him on the altar, fastening him there with red silken cords, hands and feet one to each corner.

Kneeling, Scorpus saw Maximus in the crowd. His head was thrown back as he chanted the prayer of blood with the others again and again, spittle flecking the corners of his mouth.

The legs of the bull were tethered, his eyes rolled and he bellowed in protest, for he knew where he was. The priestess of Cybele sprinkled cold water over him from a silver bowl, and it made him shiver. The animal's assent had thus been given for what was about to happen to him. Howling the song of blood, the sacrificial priest approached, ceremonial axe raised high, glittering in the sun as it swung. The air was filled with the piercing cry of the female Corybantes giving the sacrificial shout of the Greeks since time immemorial.

The blow that was meant to stun the beast while they opened its throat to collect the gallons of hot red blood inside, went awry, the axe-handle slipping in the priest's hands, slippery with sweat.

Enraged, blood spurting from its superficial wound, the bull jerked forward. The bonds on its hind legs snapped, it caught the priest through the guts with one shining black horn, flinging him high through the air, shrieking as he went. It lashed out as the others attacked it, a hoof went through the head of the man kneeling next to Scorpus.

Its mighty body crashed to the ground, knocking him and others flat among the violet petals. He crawled out from under the pile of animal and men, helping his wife and sons. They had opened its throat, and rich red blood splashed rhythmically into golden ewers.

Out in the *ager* were the fields and the market gardens, the farms and smallholdings. Out in Veii and Ficulea, Tibur and Gabii they could see the great *urbs* of Rome and there the *lupinarii* and *fructuarii* grew their flowers and fruit, there the *olitores* grew vegetables and herbs, there among the olive groves and postrows of purple grapes the farmers kept their chickens and pigs, goats and cattle. They took all their produce in to Rome, which consumed it, and paid them with the money that flowed in from its Empire.

Up on the hill they could see the city wall and the great plain of the Campus Martius. Soldiers were exercising in units down there, the sunshine flickered and flashed on pinpoints of glinting metal.

'Fighters,' said Timothy approvingly. 'Fighters every one.'

Saul and Jeshua watched the half-grown puppies tumbling and chasing in mock combat.

'Fighters like their father,' the Greek continued. He glanced at Saul with a smile and jingled his winnings in his leather purse.

'Fighters like Wolf. Winners like Wolf.'

The victorious animal lay stretched out in the late sunshine, his long muzzle resting on his paws. One of his sons leaped up on his muscled shoulder, his paws lost in the heavy grey fur, and used the height to launch an attack on one of his brothers. The father barely twitched, lost in dreams of victory, his stomach full.

'I like him,' said Saul. The dog had bowled his brother over and was practising tearing his throat out with little milky teeth.

'He's the one,' Timothy agreed.

The door of the house behind them was open, through it Jeshua could see into the room. On the wall Timothy had placed a rack of smoothed, squared planks, in its holes were the scrolls of a library. On a desk were placed the tools of a scribe's trade, jars of sand and ink, papyrus, wax, a candle, a small jar filled with long goose quills sprouting like blooms, a small knife for cutting the pens. From inside came the orderly clatter of a housewife at work. Timothy looked up from where he squatted by the dogs.

'What about a drink?' he suggested. He put back his head and called out in a cheerful voice. 'Julia? There are thirsty people out here.'

Jeshua heard the clatter change tone and the scrape of sandals on the sandy floor. A smiling, black-haired young woman appeared with a jug and three light glass beakers.

'Some of us are busy enough to work up a thirst,' she said. She turned to Jeshua.

'A little wine?' she asked. 'It is good for the stomach, though our water here is pure.'

Saul took a beaker from Timothy's wife and laughed.

'We have drunk some sour stuff in our time, haven't we?'

He passed a glass to Jeshua.

'You may go on the road one day, spreading the word of God like we. Take this advice. Carry the best, the spiciest, the sweetest *conditum* you can buy, it is sometimes the only way to make the local wine palatable.'

'This I know,' said Jeshua, and sipped his watered wine solemnly, 'for my mother made it for my father, on his journeys.'

'Yes, your father . . .' Saul said quietly.

A frown had passed over Julia's pretty face.

'And why would he need to go on the road, risking dangers?' she objected. 'Timothy is not travelling any more. There is no need for that now. God will soon be here.'

'So he will!' Saul cried out. 'The *parousia* is nigh. But still, so few know of the true Jesus, so few have come to the faith.'

Julia waved a slim hand at the room behind her.

'Then let us spread the word with Timothy's pen! Does he not write down all that the Lord and his apostles have done?'

Timothy smiled reassuringly at his young wife.

'I shall not be going on the road again,' he said.

'You will soon have children to keep you at home,' she promised, and went back inside, where the clattering resumed.

Saul turned his attention back to the puppies playing in the dust.

'I'll take the little one.'

Timothy looked at the runt of the litter, panting about after his bigger, faster brethren.

'You want *him?*' he asked in surprise. 'I almost put his head in a bucket when he was born. I would have, if he hadn't been Wolf's cub. Always last, that one.'

Saul watched the puppy closely. Bright eyes gleamed in the ash-coloured fur, flecked with white.

'He is small, yes, but what of his spirit?' he murmured. The little dog launched a surprise attack on one of his passing brothers from the shadows of his father's flanks, and succeeded in knocking him over. His throat filled with a small, triumphant growl.

Jeshua chuckled, and Saul smiled at him.

'That's right,' he said, 'size is not everything. What of belief?'

He turned to Jeshua.

'What do you think? Has the little one inherited his father's mettle? Will he fight? When he is in the arena with death will he fight to the end?'

Saul looked at him intently.

'Will he win?' he demanded.

'He is smaller. How can he win, if he is weaker than the others?' the boy asked.

'What is winning?' Saul asked mysteriously. 'Here, Timothy, how much for the runt?'

The scribe-turned-bookie shrugged, mystified.

'I wanted you to have his big brother. The gamblers all

know me. I want you to fight him, and I'll make the book,' he explained. 'We'll clean up.'

'And so we shall,' Saul said patiently, 'if he really is a winner. Faith is not an easy thing to measure.'

Timothy turned to Jeshua with a smile. 'Are you a priest in the making, is this what you are doing with this man? Watch out, he'll break your ears with all his talk of the gods.'

'My father is a *hasid*.' Jeshua said proudly. 'I too understand God.'

Saul glanced at him suddenly, from under his brows.

'So what about this runt, Timothy?' he said, turning away, and rubbing his scarred ear stump.

'Why, take him. But come back for his brother. He's a champion, I'm telling you.'

'Jeshua, take the little pup.'

As the boy went forward, reaching out to scratch the animal by his ears, making friends before taking him, Saul sniffed the air.

'Is that cooking I can smell?'

'Food for the dogs. I cook up the liver and heart of an ox with barley and wine. They thrive, it makes them quick and strong.'

Saul went into the hut alongside the house. A big black pot was hanging from its chains in the fireplace. He emerged with a brand of wood from the grate, glowing and smoking. Timothy frowned.

'What do you want that for?'

'It's cold,' Saul said without expression. 'I want to light a fire. Here, we'll not be long. Are you ready, Jeshua?'

The boy was playing with the puppy in the dust, laughing as it charged at his flapping hands.

'Yes, I'm ready,' he said, without looking up.

'Come on then.'

They set off on the path through the vines. The breeze sent some dry leaves tumbling over the dirt and the puppy chased after them.

The smoke was dense over the altar. The priest Musaeus howled the prayer of blood, the priestess Tisiphone bent over him, raising up his genitals from the marble. Maria held up the purple cushion with its terrible ceremonial knife and the priestess took it in her hand. The glittering point entered his scrotum and blood ran over the altar.

The cymbals crashed and the blast of the trumpets drowned the gurgling shriek that abruptly replaced the chant of prayer, the bronze knife slicing within him at the command of the bloody fingers of the woman priest.

White spittle foamed the mouth of Maximus as the priests splashed blood over the head of Scorpus, hot and pungent, gushing down over his face and neck. Maximus had an iron razor in his hand, his tunic was torn off, he hacked at himself, blood spouting from the wounds.

At the altar, Tisiphone held up the parts for all to see, and the women shrieked piercingly once again. Her eyes were glazed, saliva ran down one corner of her chin, she stood amidst the powerful smoke from the fires.

Cybele, mother of all gods, had fallen in love with Attis. So that no one else might have him, she had caused him to castrate himself, and she required the same of his priests.

In the pungent smoke, Maximus hacked his organs clear of his body, holding them high as his life-blood spattered his thighs and feet. The razor fell from his hand, his eyes were glazed and he fell slowly to the ground. Blood ran out from his body, mingling with the pools already formed on the holy marble of the temple floor.

Two more bulls were brought in to die. The priests, expert butchers in addition to their skills in the service of their god, were cutting up the animal already dead into joints and parts, working quickly and surely with axe and knife. Three days had they all fasted for the dead Attis, the morrow was Hilaria, a day of feasting and rejoicing, and the bulls would be roasted and boiled, carved and served. The Roman gods allowed their devotees to eat unsacrificed meat, those of the Greeks were more severe, and the flesh had to be offered up to them before consumption by those who worshipped them.

The testicles of Musaeus were rising as smoke to Cybele from the altar, they had bound up his fearful wound that he might continue in the service of his god, it was time to enter the temple.

The initiates rose from the welter of blood in which they had been kneeling; they were coated in it, sticky from head to foot, its stench enveloped them. The priestess Tisiphone led the procession. Blood squelched under their feet. Maximus's dead eyes stared sightlessly at Scorpus, his gory genitals still in his hand like so much offal. Inside was the tomb of Attis, cold stone amidst the drifting smoke. There they had laid the cold body, dead by the boar. The floor was stained with violet petals.

The music ceased, the Corybantes were silent. Only the crackle of the altar fires and the moaning of an apostate holding his partly slashed testicles could be heard as Tisiphone and Musaeus, supported by two other priests, approached the sarcophagus.

The heavy stone lid was drawn back, stone scraping on stone. Smoke curled in. A roar went up, the trumpets sounded, the cymbals clashed. The Corybantes shrieked with joy.

The tomb was empty. The god had died, had been killed and was buried. On the third day he had risen again from the grave. His followers were promised life eternal in Heaven after death. Tomorrow was Hilaria, they would celebrate the feast of the resurrection.

Saul put his still-glowing brand down on the dirt. He gathered some bone-dry leaves and some vine twigs. He held a leaf to the heat, blowing on it, and a finger of flame leaped up. He fed his small blaze until he had a little fire. The dog sat on its haunches, his head on one side, quizzically watching the dancing flames.

'The puppy is to die,' Saul said quietly. He glanced up at Jeshua. 'But that must happen to all living things.'

The boy stayed silent, watching Saul.

'Why are we here, do you know that? Why do we live here, beneath these clouds, above which is Heaven?'

'We are here to serve God,' Jeshua said certainly.

'Yes,' Saul said softly. 'I'm glad you said that. We are here to serve God. If we serve him faithfully, will he reward us?'

'If we serve him according to the Law, he will take us with him to Heaven. He shall raise us from our graves, and lead us back to the soil of Israel. He is Yahweh, though we be in our graves he shall put his spirit in us, and we shall live.'

Saul still squatted by his little fire, appraising the youth.

'Of those who lie sleeping in the dust many will awake, some to everlasting life, some to shame and everlasting disgrace,' he murmured.

'God will judge,' said Jeshua. 'He is coming.'

'Yes, he is coming soon. The *parousia* is nigh, he shall come amidst clouds and angels, to raise up those who believe in him.'

'Those who are zealous for the Law,' said Jeshua.

'What of the gentiles, who have no law?'

'The gentiles are dogs,' Jeshua said dismissively. 'The one true God is *our* God, the God of Israel.'

Saul opened his mouth as if to dispute with the boy, but then stayed silent. The puppy had wearied of watching the flames and lay down, resting his muzzle on his paws in imitation of his fighting father.

'It is easy to say: "I believe in the Lord our God, he is my master." Easy to say. But what test of faith is that?'

Saul noted that Jeshua was familiar with his reasoning, his eyes were attentive, following what he said.

'Faith must be proved,' said Jeshua. 'Did not the seven brothers of the Maccabees die under torment rather than transgress against the Law? "It is for his laws that we die, to live again for ever," said the one, and his brother said to his torturers: "Ours is the better choice, to meet death at men's hands, yet relying on God's promise that we shall be raised up by him." And he said to those that were killing him: "Whereas for you, there can be no resurrection, no new life."'

'Yes . . . only for those who believe . . . for the Maccabees, those zealous for the Law . . .'

Saul's eyes were unfocused for a moment.

'Faith . . .' he murmured.

In front of him, his little fire crackled as it consumed a dry twig. He brought his vision back from where it had been, and looked at the puppy.

'To the little dog, we must appear as gods,' he said. 'We can reach down upon him, as if from the skies . . .'

He pointed to the dog.

'He has his faith. He is a fighting dog. We saw his father, a champion. Does his son have the same belief? Is he zealous for the Law? *Will he fight, whatever the suffering?*'

The puppy seemed to know he was the subject of conversation, he looked up, and wagged his bushy tail.

'That we must know . . .' he murmured.

'For the dog?'

'Not just for the dog, no . . .'

Saul looked up. 'But right now, yes, for the dog. Have we a champion? Shall we buy his brother if he, the weakest of them, has faith? The answer must be yes. For if the weakest keeps faith to the end, what shall the strong not do?'

Saul reached inside his tunic, bringing out a knife, its blade set in a riveted leather sheath.

'As I said, faith may only be measured through suffering. You do not have to watch.'

'I have faith,' the boy said stonily. 'I will die for the Law, if I am asked to. I will not deny it to others, not even the dog. That is what he is, if he dies for it then on the day of mercy the Lord God will raise him up, shall give him back his limbs, shall quicken him again.'

'So he shall,' said Saul, and slashed the puppy's furry face open with his hooked blade.

The animal gave a sudden yowl of shock, pain and rage. Droplets of bright red blood sprayed into the air as he snapped at Saul's hand.

'He knows the Law,' Jeshua cried.

'He has faith,' Saul said softly, and cut the puppy again.

The soft fur was soon splashed with gore. The little dog was backed against a twisted vine stump. He snarled defiance at his tormentors, and his small white teeth ran with his own blood.

' "The earth is given into the hands of the wicked," ' said Saul to the puppy. ' "He covereth the faces of the judges thereof, If it be not he, then who is it?" '

Saul took a brand from the fire and thrust it at him. The fur that was dry caught alight in its flame and the animal twisted and tumbled in the dust, howling and snapping at itself. Smears and splashes of blood decorated the ground in its path. Mercilessly, the flaming branch in Saul's hands followed it, relighting the fire whenever it went out.

' "Yea, though he slay me, yet will I trust in him." '

The body of the dog finally lay still, charred, muddied in blood, swollen and oozing, a faint flickering of breath in the mess the only sign of remaining life.

'He was wounded for our transgressions,' said Saul. 'He was bruised for our iniquities.

He tossed the smoking branch to one side and bent down. Reaching out he put his fingers on the bleeding, half-cooked muzzle and one eye amidst the horror gleamed with a sudden slit of light. The puppy snapped, a snarl of triumph in its little throat, and its teeth buried themselves in Saul's flesh.

He gasped in sudden pain, but smiled down on the dog.

'The chastisement of our peace was upon him,' he intoned. 'With his stripes, we are healed.'

With the knife in his free hand he opened the dog's throat, and its living blood spilled over the blade. He raised up his wound which bled from the punctures of the teeth.

'He dies so we may live,' he said.

Jeshua was watching him carefully.

'He obeyed the Law,' he said.

On the terrace the two children sat quietly. Below the great Tiber flowed, the torches of those making their way on the far bank flickering liquid red and orange on its surface.

'He killed a little dog,' Jeshua said, his voice whispering in the darkness.

'Why?' said Maria.

'It was to know if they would fight to the end, the puppy

and its brothers. He killed it slowly, and as it died it still bit him. He was pleased.'

'Wherever he goes, his thoughts are on a god,' Maria observed. 'Whatever he does, it is not as it seems.'

'He said the dog had faith.'

'What did you say?'

'I said it obeyed the Law. I spoke as I have been taught to as one of the *zelotai*, that they should not know me for what I am, and what we are.'

'That was right,' said his sister, 'for did not they murder our mother?'

They sat quiet for a little while longer, holding hands.

'How was it, in the temple?' Jeshua asked.

'Satan rules in this land,' she said. 'Like you, I did as I have been taught, I sang his songs, I danced his dances, so that he might not see my face.'

As they were sitting, the sharp white sickle of the waxing moon had risen over the jumbled rooftops opposite. Jeshua squeezed his sister's hand.

'I see her face,' he said. 'May we not pray?'

'Not out loud,' she warned. 'Those who serve the evil one have ears.'

They sat in silence, staring up into the sky, comforted by the pale, pure light.

Behind them a door opened, and an orange glow raced across the terrace from the oil lamp in Saul's hand.

'Looking at the moon?' he said quizzically.

'Just looking at the moon,' replied Maria.

Saul came over and sat by them.

'How was it, in the temple of Cybele?' he enquired.

'Very bloody.'

'They are known for it. But the gods have a taste for blood.

Perhaps the rites of Dionysus would be more to your taste. The Romans know him as Bacchus.'

'I know of Dionysus.'

'The Emperor himself is interested in the cult,' he explained. 'His prefect, Tigillinus, plans to hold a party for him and Bacchus must play a part. I have promised some help . . .'

He smiled amiably at her in the darkness, the pale, clean light of the moon on his teeth.

'A maenad?' he asked.

'Yes, of course,' she said.

'Good. You must be tired, both of you, after your day.'

He got up to go back inside.

'You must come to *my* church,' he said. 'We spill no blood there. Only the blood of the Lord Jesus, that he commanded we drink.'

'*Real* blood?' Jeshua asked quickly.

'No,' Saul said gently. 'Wine. And bread, that is his body.'

'A *eucharista*,' Maria said in understanding.

'There all is *agape*,' Saul promised. 'There is love.'

Tigillinus slipped inside the leather curtain that closed the door to the plain, white-painted room. He held it open as he stood there, so that the air from the atrium flowed about him.

'It is not catching,' the man lying on the bed said, 'as far as I know.'

He opened his eyes and looked bleakly at the Praetorian prefect, the man who now held his job. The lump on his throat seemed to have gathered all the flesh about it into itself, the wasted muscles stood out like cords under the thinning skin. The eyes, however, were still bright. Hands from which the flesh was falling held clasped an old scroll. More scrolls lay neatly piled on a low table at his bedside.

'I attribute it to much breathing of the smoke from the midnight lamps, working on the papers of state. I have served four emperors in such a way, beginning with Tiberius, and now ending with Nero. Now it is your turn, but I do not feel you will run the risk of catching it in the same manner as I.'

Tigillinus smiled faintly, he was semi-literate.

'You may, should you cease to give satisfaction, be required to *open* your own throat,' Burrus suggested acidly, 'but that is a different matter.'

'It is a pleasure to see your mind is unaffected,' Tigillinus said pleasantly, 'and also your tongue. How *are* you, anyway?'

'The Emperor came to see me yesterday and asked the same question, to which I give the same reply. *I* am doing all right.'

'You are dying,' Tigillinus objected.

'Exactly,' Burrus replied sharply.

He glanced out of the window. The waters of the Tiber glittered in the sunshine, in the distance the hills were taking on their autumnal coat. Between the two, great buildings of painted stone stood high.

'The greatest city on earth,' Burrus said quietly, 'head of the mightiest empire the world has ever seen. We are members of one great body. Nature has made us relatives, we are members of a vast and truly common state, embracing alike gods and men. We should all live for one another, live for our neighbours if we would live for ourselves, for do we not all possess a share of the divine spark? Are we not all of us, whether aristocrats or slaves, are we not brothers? Should our laws not be the laws of reason and nature? And should the highest natural laws be those of human compassion and cooperation, of love for one's fellow human beings?'

He sighed.

'Of course, these are ideals, and reality is different. But they are still the ideals that we should aspire to. They are the ideals in which I and my companion, Seneca the stoic, have instructed the Emperor since we were given him into our charge as a young child.'

Burrus brought his gaze back from the hills and into the room, where Tigillinus still stood by the door.

'Yes, as a young child,' Burrus murmured. 'The Emperor has been steeped in the highest and most noble values of life since before he can remember. And now he is a man. And the most powerful man in the world, chosen from out of the host of mortal beings to do the work of gods on earth. We should, should we not, all of us, all we brothers in this great, and truly common state we call the Empire, be about to enter a new golden age? How could it be different?'

He eyed the man who had inherited his office of state with distaste.

'Ah, me. I shall not, thankfully, be here to see how different it will all be. I have to take some blame. I tried not to add to his power for evil. I attempted to simply keep in check his destructive forces. I thought to keep him amused, and was willing to become his pimp, sending him comedians and women, and other such delights to temper his brutality. So. Doubtless there will be those ready to desecrate my grave in years to come. Now. I have but little time left, and resent its expenditure on things of unimportance. I am reading Zeno once again.'

The skeletal hands gripped the scroll on the multicoloured damask quilt that covered the bed.

'I'll be quick, then,' said Tigillinus. 'A little Jewboy called Saul. Infected with religion. Claims to know all about what goes on over there where the Hebes live.'

'Oh, yes,' sharp eyes looked up at Tigillinus, 'he knows about that, all right.'

'He says the Hebes can make trouble for us.'

Tigillinus's thickening features grimaced in contemptuous disbelief.

'They are as doves before their Lord, so they say. But as ravening wolves to the heathens.'

'*Hebes?* Prick-slicing, pig-worshipping Hebes?'

'It has been our policy to divide and rule them ever since we acquired that part of the world. They worship, in one form or another, a strange and brutal single god that is forever inciting them to throw off our rule and establish his. They yearn constantly for a leader, a Messiah descended from their past glory who will put us to the sword, at which point this god of theirs will descend from the skies and give them rule over the world.'

Burrus paused to clear his throat painfully. He drank a little water from a glass beaker by his side.

'Fortunately they are as split as this glass would be, should I throw it upon the floor. While they are disunited, they are no threat. However, we constantly look for potential leaders, these Messiahs.'

'And this Saul is useful to us.'

'Of course! He is one of them. He understands the intricacies as we outsiders cannot. And yet he works for us. But why are you here, tiring out what is left of my voice. Go talk to Flavius Sutorius, he is the one who controlled this Saul for many years, since he was but a tribune in Jerusalem.'

'The senator?'

'The same. He lives not far from here.'

'I know where he lives. And this Saul is useful to us? He seems just a religious maniac of some description.'

'You have just described half the Hebrew people. Which is

why you neglect him at your peril,' Burrus said shortly, and opened his scroll.

Tigillinus went out and down the steep street, built on the side of the valley. Garrets hung over his head and his burly *cursores* cleared a path for him through a swirling crowd. He passed the entrance to a park, an old shrine that a Jew was using as a bank, saw a brothel doing good trade under the colonnades of the court, turned the corner where a lodging house had fallen in through the weight of the people living in it, setting its neighbours ablaze and roasting the survivors.

The mingled scent of incense and purple dye stewed in stale urine striking his nose told him that he was crossing the street of the Tuscans with its beautiful papyrus books and high-class prostitutes. He caught a brief glimpse of them, men and women for hire, and went up a steep alleyway. There he dived through what had once been someone's door and into a sun-drenched courtyard. An old god looked down from one end and a giant fig tree ripened its fruit at the other. Syrian ragmen had set up home in one corner, their children, in long, coloured robes, were clambering about in the branches, like strange, brightly feathered birds, their cries of laughter filling the square. He kicked the door of the old, genteel villa on the shade side, built in the time of Augustus. You had to know your way about Rome, and even then, overnight, someone might close your right of way and build a house through it.

A slave came out and soon he was seated in the atrium, the noise of the streets shut out, just the tinkling of an ancient fountain in his ears.

He saw Flavius Sutorius emerge from a doorway. You didn't see that many of his sort about, he mused, as the middle-aged aristocrat negotiated his urns and fountains in full toga. Caligula hadn't done their class any good, and Nero seemed to be taking up where his uncle had left off.

Some slaves came out with him carrying cloths and jugs of water, he paused, setting them to work washing down the marble floors and walls. Then he came over to Tigillinus.

'Burrus suggested I see you.'

The aristocrat sat down on the smooth edge of the fountain.

'In what way may I help you and Sextus Afranius?' he enquired politely.

'Saul, who calls himself Paul. A little Jewboy.'

'Oh, yes. Saul of Tarsus. I know him well.'

'He's an agent of ours.'

Flavius Sutorius nodded.

'Goes on and on. Talks about some god of his called Jesus, who turns out to be some wretched criminal we nailed up about twenty years ago!'

'That's correct.'

'We nail 'em up all the time,' Tigillinus said brutally. 'It sends a message to anyone else thinking of stepping out of line. So what's special about this Jesus?'

'Jesus . . . Jeshua . . .' Flavius said thoughtfully, casting his mind back. 'I was there, you know, in Jerusalem, a broad-stripe tribune I was back then. Do you know much about the situation out in Palestine?'

'I understand that the Hebes are troublemakers. I'm told they could rise against us.'

'That's right. While we have the resources to put down an uprising, even smash a major revolt, it is not something we wish to do. The consequences for other parts of the Empire have to be considered. Our policy is to take out the potential leaders, the ones with the message, whatever it may be.'

'And this Jesus was one.'

'That's right. We'd heard a bit about him. Then he came into Jerusalem about the time of the Jewish passover, one of their festivals. Suddenly there was a real swirl of activity, people cheering him in the streets, and lots of the wrong sort, rabble and slaves and women, all very excited. It caught us by surprise, and we didn't have a heavy troop detachment. I was in charge of "knowing", if you understand what I mean. I think you do, I have heard that you have run spies in your time.'

Tigillinus grunted.

'I had to know,' said Flavius, 'but I am, and I was, a Roman.' He gestured at himself, his height, his aristocratic mien.

'I am not, and I was not, a Jew. If I wanted to know what was happening amongst the Jews. I required Jewish informants. One of the best I had was a young aristocrat from Tarsus, one Saul. When this new Messiah Jesus suddenly appeared in Jerusalem I put him on to it. What he reported back to me I didn't like. This man was some kind of rabbi – their holy man – who'd been out in the desert without food and water, as they do, and who'd concocted some strange brew of ideas that appealed to the very worst types. Rabble, I tell you. Slaves and criminals. Servants and beggars. Women, even. Yes, even women were baying his name.'

Flavius's blue eyes bulged out at Tigillinus and the two men found themselves with at least something in common. The Sicilian nodded in shared disgust.

'I tell you, Prefect, I couldn't have cared less what nasty notions this unwashed fellow had come up with, I just had to look at the sort that liked them! I decided then and there to nail him up as quick as I could where his nasty followers could see him, soon cure them of any funny ideas.'

Tigillinus nodded in agreement.

'Very wise,' he said.

'My problem was finding the swine before he could whip up his rabble into a full-blown riot. Jerusalem positively seeths with Jews at that time of the year, it's like trying to find one particular maggot on a corpse, I can tell you. Actually disposing of him wasn't a problem, we had the Jewish priests in our pocket, and they didn't like troublemakers any more than we did, all I had to do was give him to them and they'd fix it with the governor. Pilate, it was, back then. But as I say, I had to get the little bastard, so I went back to my Jew, Saul, and he went out into the seething mass to find him for me.'

Flavius looked over his shoulder at his slaves, two of whom were talking together, and shouted a command, at which they resumed their cleaning.

'Blasted slaves. Sometimes I buy a new lot and sell the old, but they're all idle.'

'I find a good whipping keeps them on their toes.'

'You're probably right. Though they have thicker skins than people,' Flavius sighed. 'But where was I? Oh, yes. We had to find this Jesus before he could really make trouble for us, and I sent out my Jew, Saul. Well, he didn't come up with Jesus, not immediately, but he did get one of his followers, a terrorist called Peter. Savage fellow he was, I remember. Now, it turned out that this Jesus was a part of a whole boiling of these maniacs. They all had different ideas about how this god of theirs could be induced to come to Israel and release his people. Whatever it was this Jesus was preaching didn't fit with what the others thought – not even his own family. He had a brother who was strongly into it all – now, what was his name, I forget . . .'

'James,' said Tigillinus, 'that they call the Just.'

'Why yes,' Flavius said in surprise, 'that's right. How do you know?'

'Saul told me. He doesn't like him. He thinks he'd be better off dead.'

'Oh, yes,' Flavius nodded his head sagely. 'That sounds like my Saul. A bloodthirsty little bastard he was. I'm out of touch with things there now, not that it's changed much, I'm sure. So James the Just is still making trouble, is he? It doesn't surprise me. Now, where was I? Oh, yes. This Jesus, it turned out, was a bit of an enigma. Was he the Messiah or wasn't he? James and Peter had thought he was, but he'd got some funny ideas. Married some woman they didn't approve of, some Mary. Peter the terrorist, the zealot, he hated her, I remember that. And young Saul, he was very smart, you know. He knew how to manipulate the people. And don't forget, he was one of them.

'You should have seen him and Peter. Jabbering away at each other, they were, jabbering away in Aramaic. I spoke it at the time, though I can't now, and I could follow what they were saying. And Saul was chipping away at Peter. Was Jesus – Jeshua, they called him – the Messiah or wasn't he? *Was he or wasn't he?* If he wasn't, then he'd betrayed his people, he didn't deserve to live anyway. Hadn't he married this bitch Peter hated? But if he was the Messiah, then if he died for his people they'd rise up for him under a new, living leader, see if they wouldn't. One of his followers, yes? What did Saul say? Oh, yes, one of his disciples. Why not you, Saul says to Peter. You. They'd call you the rock of his Church, they would. You'd inherit his people, set them on the true path.'

Flavius stared at a purple-flowering plant climbing up his wall, lost in the past.

'And he got him, Saul did. This Peter told us where he was going to be. He'd gathered with a bunch of his rabble in a garden, we sent Saul along there with some soldiers and nabbed him. This Peter, he was a cunning sort, right as our lot were grabbing Jesus he hit out at Saul with a sword and chopped his ear off. Made him look good with the others, y'see. I don't suppose Saul liked it much.'

'So what happened?'

'Oh, it all went through,' Flavius said casually. 'We nailed the bugger up and that was it. Or it should have been, at any rate.'

He sighed.

'They're a very trying lot, you know. No sooner was this Jesus dead than rumours started up amongst all these Hebrews of his that he was dead and reborn! That he'd come to life again! After that the bastard was more trouble than he'd been when he was alive. It made 'em more fanatical than ever, and of course, they all claimed he'd been one of them all along, even his own brother, who'd hated him when he was alive. So there I was, back where I'd started, you might say, and still having to deal with him. That's when young Saul came in useful once more. He was known, you see, as the high priest's man. So we arranged for him to be given warrants and an armed gang and to be sent to arrest some of the leaders, over near the Dead Sea – nasty salty place it is, very hot, probably accounts for the strange views those people cook up out there. And on the way he falls down in a fit, claiming that this Jesus has come to him in a vision. His mob take him to the leaders of the Jesusers, and he joins them! Of course, they're a bit suspicious, but he plays along and eventually he gets accepted, up to a point. Very valuable to us, he was, oh yes. They nearly nabbed him in the end, I heard. Jerusalem, it was.'

'I've spoken to him,' said Tigillinus. 'I can see he was useful to us. Perhaps he still is. He seems to believe this god of his has chosen him for some special purpose.'

'That wouldn't surprise me. Give a man strong wine every day, he can't give it up. The gods were what did it, for young Saul.'

'What of the Hebes, then?'

'They'll make trouble one day, mark my word. I'm glad it's nothing to do with me any more.'

'It's to do with me,' Tigillinus said shortly.

'Yes, Prefect, it is,' Flavius said genially. 'Use young Saul, if you can. I always found him able to deliver.'

'Yes,' Tigillinus said slowly, 'I think I will.'

Flavius's face lit up with pleasure, looking behind the Sicilian. Tigillinus turned to see a handsome youth coming in from the street. He wore an expensively woven tunic and gold gleamed at his throat.

'Calenus, dear boy,' Flavius cooed. He patted the flat side of the fountain next to him.

'Come and sit down and say hello to Prefect Tigillinus.'

The youth sat down next to him and looked wide-eyed at Tigillinus.

'What an honour,' he murmured, and Tigillinus understood exactly what and who Calenus was. He had, when young, lissom and handsome, looked wide-eyed himself at other powerful men with the tastes of Flavius Sutorius. A sore arse was a small price to pay to get where you wanted.

He got up. He had business to attend to, as, he suspected from the way they were looking, did Flavius and Calenus. In the atrium the slaves were really polishing the place up.

'Having a party?' he asked casually.

'I'm getting married,' Flavius said precisely. Tigillinus saw a flash of pure hatred pass through Calenus's face, and then the boy smiled sweetly.

'He requires an heir,' he murmured, 'for the family honour. Don't you, Uncle?'

'Yes,' said Flavius. 'I require an heir.'

Tigillinus chuckled. It was the kind of thing that appealed to his sense of humour.

'Well, do have fun trying,' he said.

'Oh, we will,' said Calenus. 'We will.'

'Offended with her husband.' The phrase drifted into Gaia's head like a scent from the street, an echo she was not meant to have heard, the complaint of a bride in the light of the morning. She thought of asking Plecusa, carefully arranging the six pads of artificial black *capilli Indici* hair that supported her coiffure and dismissed it. The mating of slaves was no different than the breeding of livestock. She, Gaia, was marrying an aristocrat.

Her hair had been arranged the previous day by the *ornatrix*, and imprisoned intact overnight in a crimson net. She wore the clothes that custom decreed for a bride on her wedding day: the hemless tunic, secured at the waist by the woolen *cingulum herculeum*, tied in a double knot of virtue; a bright, saffron-yellow silk cloak from the mysterious Seres, far, far away over the seas, cunningly dyed with reseda, iridescent in the sunlight. Yellow was the colour of her three bridesmaids – two cousins and her aunt Livia – who would attend her at the ceremony and sit with her at the banquet. Around her neck was a light metal *monile* collar, colourful with lustrous enamel and small jewels, on her feet soft doeskin sandals the very shade of her cloak. Like all aristocratic women she knew from Ovid the importance of harmonising one's complexion to the colour of one's clothes, even if his other counsels remained annoyingly obscure to her, and the *ornatrix* had made up her daytime face from her *alabastrotheca*, the carefully constructed box of jars, pots, little flagons and vases filled with liniments, pomades and colours without which a lady of quality would be entirely unable to leave the nuptial room for the outside world at all. Her brow and smooth young arms were tastefully whitened with a mixture of chalk and white lead; her full lips made as desirable as ripe, bursting figs with ochre; her carefully and painfully plucked eyebrows jet with powdered antimony;

her eyes, purple as a wine-dark sea, enlargened with dark grey ash over the lids.

She stood sideways, checking her figure in the polished bronze mirror. Her new breasts were not that large, but certainly shapely. She was past the stage where they vanished if she lay down on her back, much to her chagrin. Suitably wrapped and supported by the linen *mamillare* they made pleasing dents in the folds of her tunic.

Over her coiffure she wore a *flammeum* veil of the brightest, most flaming orange, that modestly concealed the upper part of her face, held to her head with a woven bridal wreath of myrtle and sweet-smelling orange blossom. On the *anularius* of her left hand she wore the plain gold ring that her future husband Flavius had given to her on the day of their betrothal. It was known that if you did as the Egyptians and cut open a body after death, delicate dissection revealed a slim nerve that travelled all the way from the *anularius* to the heart, and this was why the ring was worn on that finger.

She tried to remember what Flavius Sutorius looked like. She had a vague picture of a tall old man in a purple-edged toga, a memory of her mother's hand in the small of her back, pushing her forward.

Through the unshuttered window she could see groups of gamblers and idlers and vulgar folk from Suburra heading towards the circus for the horse races.

'Offended with her husband.' It was still no use asking Plecusa, nor her mother. A cry of pain came from the *cubiculum* as her mother relieved her tensions by lashing the breast of her *ornatrix* with the bull's hide thong she kept for the purpose. The pursuit of beauty, especially when it involved the merciless removal of greying hairs, brought suffering to both parties. No, not her mother.

She glanced out at the sundial, where the *gnomon* was casting its shadow on the curve of the *polos*. He would be here soon, and then she would know for herself.

The ewe bleated plaintively. On the altar lay the parchment scroll of the marriage contract, colourful with irregular stamps of scarlet wax impressed by the seals of the ten witnesses gathered for the ceremony. The *auspex* handed it to Julia, the bride's mother, and she tucked it into the folds of the bleached white wool tunic into which she was beginning to sweat under the effect of the fire burning at the altar. A smile finally fixed upon her face, the deal had been struck, the bag of money that Flavius's slave had brought had changed hands. She reached up, adjusting the set of her wig, dyed a fashionable blonde with goat's fat and beech ash, and mentally withdrew all the nasty things she had ever said about her new son-in-law, the man standing by her daughter, some six years older than she was herself.

The ewe bleated plaintively again, recognising the *auspex* for what he was, and the augur thrust his hooked blade skilfully through the unfortunate beast's throat. The slave that had held her steady pulled the head back and the fresh red blood gushed rythmically into the waiting bowl as the terrified eyes slowly dulled. Its smell filled the atrium where they were gathered, it was bright and had pumped forth vigorously, they glanced one to another in approval. In front of the altar the couple stood up straight and tall in their finery.

The *auspex*, both augur and priest, able to interpret the opinion of the gods who lurked about them, opened the ewe's abdomen expertly, slitting the muscle without spilling the guts. A warm, pungent smell mixed with the smoke of the fire and metallic tang of the blood as the *auspex* solemnly examined the entrails steaming in his hands. Then he stood up straight and held his bloody hand high.

'The auspices are good. The gods approve of this union.'

Strips of the tender meat crackled on the altar, feeding the gods with their smoke as the *auspex* ceremonially mixed the ewe's blood with wine in a special silver bowl.

'The *eucharista*,' he said, taking two strips of the cooked meat. He was a Greek, and cultured, for cultured things, he used his own language. He placed the meat in Flavius's mouth and he ate it. The *auspex* held up a shining chased silver cup and Flavius sipped the wine and blood. When he had done Gaia ate and then drank, and after her all the witnesses, so that all shared the communal meal with the gods. When the eucharist was finished the couple exchanged their mutual vows and bound themselves to each other.

'*Ubi tu Gaia, ego Flavius.*'

'*Ubi tu Flavius, ego Gaia.*'

As her voice died away, solemnity vanished and the air was filled with congratulations. *Feliciter*! May happiness wait upon you! *Feliciter*!

Flavius ceremonially handed her the spear of Diodorus the gladiator and she ritually parted her hair with it. Now the good luck of the couple was meant to be certain. Diodorus was dead, the blood spattering the handle under a day old; his bad fortune the guarantee that theirs would be good.

The blood on the spear was musty, its smell reminding her of its origin. She thought of her brother, Speculus, who had sent it to her in lieu of his presence. He was required elsewhere, in the arena, it was he who had killed Diodorus. Her house was not a lucky one, they had all been sold, one way or the other.

In the *triclinium* she reclined upon her couch as the *ministratores* poured the *muslum* wine. Nearby she saw her mother loosen the striped *zona* about her waist and lean forward to guzzle her first goblet.

She wondered, suddenly, where the *cubiculum* of her husband was, the bedroom of this serious old man she did not know. A stab of apprehension went through her stomach. She was sixteen. She reached out, and drank from her goblet, smiling all the while.

She could hear the drunken singing going down the street, the bawdy songs and guffaws. She could imagine the flexing forearms, the jerking hips, the shining lips and teeth. It was rightful, even a duty, on behalf of the guests, to celebrate what was now legitimate.

She was a married woman. She nervously fingered the *nodus herculeus*, the double knot of her girdle. Somewhere down the street two slaves were supporting her mother home. Standing outside the curtain of the cubicle Gaia smoothed the muslin of her clothes over her slender body. The thought suddenly occurred to her that sold by weight, she must be quite valuable. She wondered if her mother would live long enough to enjoy the money.

It was quiet, the noise of revelry had vanished. Bravely, she pushed the curtain aside and went in.

'Oh!'

Somebody was in the room. A young man in a gold-edged tunic, lounging at the end of the bed. He smiled insolently at her.

'Who are you?' she demanded.

'Who shall I be, mistress?' he replied mockingly.

A picture was on the wall behind him. A bride sat veiled upon a bed, with figures about her.

'Shall I be Persuasion?' he asked.

Her eyes flicked to the bride, and to the goddess seated beside her in encouragement. The groom was not in the picture, the deities were preparing her.

The youth was grinning at her.

'You won't be familiar with it all,' he said. 'Uncle Flavius picked you for that.'

His eyes glittered.

'Not right, you see. *Honestum*. Uncle would never do anything that was not honourable. You'll be untouched.'

Her neck stiffened, she looked down her nose at him.

'I wish to have nothing to do with you, whoever you may be.'

'Calenus,' the young man said, 'and I'm afraid you will have to. Uncle likes me, you see. But where was I? Yes, Persuasion. Let me give you a tip or two. He's very old, is Uncle.'

Calenus reached down obscenely and grabbed his groin. He jerked it at her.

'It doesn't get up very easily,' he said. 'You have to work at it. And it takes a long time to finish, too. It's because he's old. Now me, I'm like an iron bar. You'll have to try me, you will.'

'I'll have nothing to do with you,' she spat, 'and I'll have you out of this house.'

'You won't,' Calenus said confidently. 'Uncle needs me. I know how to make him happy.'

His eyes widened in mock concern.

'Which is why I'm passing on these helpful hints to you. It'll save you getting sore while Uncle gets in a nasty sweat all over you trying to make it.'

His lips puckered up into a perfect O.

'The mouth,' he said. 'Very helpful all round. Gets Uncle started very well. And then you go ooh, and aah, and it helps a treat.'

Calenus glanced round at the picture, to where the god sat

confident and relaxed at the end of the bed, waiting for the moment when Persuasion and Venus had done their work. He giggled.

'Just like Hymen, is old Uncle, when you do your stuff.'

He cocked an ear, as alert as a wild beast.

'Here he comes,' he whispered, his eyes gleaming maliciously in the yellow lamplight. He was past her and outside the curtain before she could stop him.

'Enjoy yourself,' he said mockingly.

The heavy woven cloth that covered the door went back with a scrape of rings and Flavius came in. He stood before her as she sat nervously on the edge of the bed. Calenus had somehow left a vile taste in her mouth and she tried to swallow, but her lips were dry.

'I haven't had a chance to talk to you,' Flavius said heavily. He rubbed a hand over his face, which was sweating from the heat and the wine of the banquet.

'*Auctoritas* and *virtus*,' he said seriously. 'I have lived my life by the codes of honour. I have not married, because . . . I have not until now felt the need to. I had an older brother who married and had a son to commemorate the glory of our father. But my brother is dead, and his son too. Only I am now left to carry the glory of our family, and I must have a son. Not to do so would bring *turpe*, evil and shame upon us, and with that I could not live.'

He paused, drawing breath and gathering his thoughts.

'You, too, have the chance now to bring *honestum* to your family, to clear their name, sullied by your father. Your brother Speculus is a ruined man, he is reduced to fighting as a gladiator and has become degenerate, without a soul. It is up to you to restore your family name by providing me with a son.'

'I understand that,' she said, speaking for the first time.

'Very well,' he said. 'Duty and honour. We shall begin tomorrow.'

She was puzzled, surprised.

'It is the wedding night,' she said, 'don't we . . .'

'It is not honourable,' he said patiently. 'Equally it is not honourable not to.'

His large hands undid the knot of her girdle, he turned her over, *a tergo* and completely bemused, on to her stomach. She felt the air cool on her legs and buttocks as he pulled up her clothes.

She cried out in sudden pain. As was honourable, and customary, Flavius proceeded to bugger his bride.

From somewhere in the house, she heard Calenus laugh.

12

Jerusalem

They came for the Righteous One when he was in the Holy Place, he who alone was permitted there, for his garments were not of wool but of linen. He who was called the Righteous, and the Bulwark of the People, they broke in when he was praying on his knees for forgiveness for his people, he who drank no wine, ate no animal food and who smeared himself not with oil, nor allowed a razor near his head; they came for him and took him out.

The high priest Ananas was nearby, but he said not a word as they took the Righteous One up on to the Parapet of the temple. From the height they threw him down, but the Righteous One, that they called the Just, was not dead in spite of his fall. So they said, one to another, 'Let us stone the Righteous One,' and they took stones in their hands and pelted him. When they were done one took a fuller's club that he carried, for the beating of clothes, and he brought it down on the head of the Just. And from above, Ananas the high priest watched, and did not stop them as they ran away.

Hook Norton

Connell sat staring at the short block of black script, looking puzzled. Juliana glanced up from what she was doing.

'What is it?' she asked.

'I've got a fragment here describing the murder of James, the brother of Jesus, leader of the Early Church in Jerusalem.'

She frowned.

'Haven't we already got a passage dealing with that? I seem to remember reading it early on.'

'That's right. But there's no doubt at all that this is James. Ananas is the Sadducee high priest – the Roman puppet, those zealous for the Law like James would consider him a Quisling or even worse – he makes no attempt to stop the murderers. That places it at about 62 A.D., which is when we traditionally think James was murdered – there's a description of it in Josephus's *Bellum Judaicum* that matches pretty well with this one. Ananas was himself murdered shortly afterwards, once the revolt began, as a collaborator with the Roman occupying power, and also, presumably, for having some kind of hand in the death of James. Certainly, he seems to do nothing to stop the gang that drags James off from the Holy of Holies and slaughters him.'

'Would he be responsible?'

'Not off his own bat. He's a stooge, he does what he's told.'

'So who *did* do it? Who's the man with the fuller's club?' she asked interestedly.

'I think we've already seen who's responsible,' he said slowly. 'Saul who is also Paul has convinced Tigillinus of his usefulness by this time. Tigillinus is a very powerful man, his reach easily extends to Jerusalem.'

She looked worried.

'I still can't come to terms with this image of Paul as some kind of ruthless, devious political operator, capable of organising assassination and murder. Paul was a man who breathed love.'

'What did Tacitus say?' Connell asked laconically. ' "Behind every great fortune lies a great crime"?'

'What great fortune?' she cried. 'The early Christians were poor, they gave their money to the needy.'

'The Church went on to gather the greatest fortune on earth,' he pointed out. 'They blackmailed people into leaving them all their money, for fear of Hell's fire. But that isn't the point. What is the benefit to Paul of having James the Just murdered, what kind of fortune will *he* inherit from this great crime? That's what we have to ask ourselves.'

'So?' she asked shortly, twisting a strand of her black hair.

'*One* benefit is easy to see. James is a powerful man, acknowledged leader of those zealous for the Law within Israel. He leads the early Christian Church in Jerusalem, from which Paul has sprung, but with whom he has seriously fallen out following his own invention and promulgation of *his* version of Christianity. If you're a Mafia man from Palermo selling bootleg liquor in Prohibition America, in competition with another Mafia man from Corleone, then if you can, you take that man out and enjoy a pleasant monopoly. If you're peddling new brands of religion to the devoutly thirsty in the first century, then if you can, you do the same.

'Don't forget, whatever one may think of him, Paul is without doubt, historically, a religious genius, in a class of his own. He knows the techniques of religious propaganda, he knows what is required to turn a man into a god. He knows that in the end, one thing above all is necessary.'

'You're a cleverclogs, Connell,' she said acidly. 'You're so certain you're right all the time. So what is necessary?'

'To win. It's in Corinthians: "So though I am not a slave of any man I have made myself the slave of everyone so as to win as many as I could. I made myself a Jew to the Jews, to win the Jews . . . To those who have no Law, I was free of the Law myself . . . to win those who have no Law . . . All the runners at the stadium are trying to win, but only one of them gets the prize. You must run in the same way, meaning to win." '

'So Paul has James bumped off, just like some Mafia hoodlum.'

'Oh, there's more to it than that. Tigillinus didn't see it, he thought that Paul was advising him for his – Tigillinus's – own good, that this was the way to avoid a Jewish uprising. But Eusebius, with hindsight, saw what had happened. *He* described the martyrdom of James, and the added cryptic moment: "Immediately after this Vespasian began to besiege them." Vespasian being the Roman commander sent to put down the great *bellum Judaicum*, the great Jewish Revolt. Eusebius implies that the death of James and the revolt are directly linked, that the latter happened because of the former. *As Paul knew it would.*'

'But hold on, what year is this, it's 62, and the revolt didn't get going until 66. Four years.'

'It isn't necessarily as long as you might think. Simeon bar Kochba worked in secret for that long before launching the great second revolt in the 130s. The Jews had a network of underground tunnels they dug as arms dumps, lines of communication, ambush sites, forming up points and all the rest of it, just like the Vietcong in the Vietnam War. That's the other thing Paul understood – being one of them – that once they'd done it once, they wouldn't stop until they either won or were massacred and scattered throughout the world. Which of course is what happened.'

'But why would he want that?'

'Same reason he murdered James the Just, leader of the Jerusalem Christians. In the first century the Jews were aggressively evangelical for Judaism, they were a militant religion, seeking converts. They were formidable competitors to Paul's brand of Christianity. Not so after the Diaspora. After that, Jewry was so damaged that it turned in on itself, Judaism became a glue to hold the identity of the Jews to themselves. They never went out for converts again. It all left the field clear for the Orthodox Church.'

'You can't be serious.'

'It worked, didn't it?'

'I suppose so,' she admitted, 'but what about the earlier version of James's death? That one doesn't quite fit.'

Connell got up and went to the window, looking out, reaching for his packet of cheroots.

'I got some new ones,' he said, lighting a long black one.

'Tar must coat your lungs,' she said, and opened a window. '*You* smoke.'

'That's different. And only occasionally.'

'We're going to have such fun with all this,' he said gleefully. 'We're going to sound out the big universities soon. See who'll come up with enough for a really prestigious foundation. God, I can't wait, I've been in the wilderness too long. I think I might grow a beard.'

'A beard? Why? You'll set it on fire with one of your cheroots.'

'I read the other day that ideological prejudice exists against men with beards. Politicians with beards do not gain high office, men with beards do not get the best jobs.'

'Which is why Frank Connell wants one. Just to be difficult. Do you like annoying people, Frank?'

'I've never liked being told what to do, how to think. The minute I sense it I want to do just what they don't want me to do.'

'Frank, doing what they didn't want you to do lost you your career, last time. You can't beat really powerful vested interests.'

Juliana was leafing through a file of photographs, she took one out and began looking at it.

'Can't fight city hall? I can this time. With the texts I can do anything I bloody want. I suppose we want to think where we'd like to live,' Connell continued, 'choose somewhere salubrious. The Japs have the money, but I don't want to go to Tokyo. Perhaps Boston. Plenty of Hoirish there, I'll fit in.'

'Frank,' Juliana said, interrupting him. 'Put that foul thing down and look at this. This is the other version of the attack in the temple.'

Connell obligingly rested his cheroot on an ashtray.

'It just isn't the same,' she said. '*This* man, Zaddik appears to be questioning the very basis of zeal for the Law. And there are women there. And "the woman that came with Zaddik", who pursues Paul – if it is he – after the attack. How do you reconcile that?'

'I don't know,' he said thoughtfully.

'I do,' she said. 'Different men.'

'But if Zaddik isn't James, then who is he?'

13

Rome, A.D. 62

Jeshua sat in the warm sun. It was well known that its light aided the recovery from illness. Were not soldiers tanned and strong? It was peaceful in the little *peristyle*, just the voices of those fishing, the boatmen and women, washing down on the Tiber bank.

Occasionally he shivered with a sudden ague, and then he drank from a beaker set next to him, that Maria had prepared from the herbs she had gathered. Soon the tremors left him and the pain of his wound troubled him less.

He heard the voice of the slave at the door and footsteps coming across the marble. He looked up to see Timothy. The Greek smiled.

'I came in with Julia to sell. We have snails, dormice, thrushes and asparagus. Not to mention tomatoes and lettuce. She's in the market. Is Paul not here?'

'He is gone to the villa of Tigillinus. The prefect is entertaining the Emperor there.'

Timothy rubbed a hand over his face. He seemed momentarily worried.

'Oh, yes. I'd forgotten. Paul moves in high circles, he always has done.'

He smiled wryly.

'Put him down anywhere and you find him dining with the high priest, engaged in cultured conversation with the governor, exchanging views with the general. While poor peasants like me chew rinds and hard crust with the guards and door-keepers!'

Jeshua smiled, he liked the scribe-turned-bookmaker, who tended his garden up in the hills.

'Maria has gone with him, they have priests there, she is to dance for Bacchus.'

'The bacchantes, eh? I have seen them in their masks, in the great theatre in Crete. A show for the Emperor, no doubt. Well, look, tell Paul I came by. I must get back to the market, we are expecting a good price today, all are plump and good, and freshly washed.'

'They will be back before nightfall.'

Timothy left, and Jeshua was once more with the cries of the people and the seabirds down on the river. He had woken in the night, his tunic heavy with sweat from his fever, he was tired. He put his large white *mappa* over his face and within minutes he dozed.

'*My name is Peter. Mark me well and tell your master.*'

Terror seized him, he cried out under his handkerchief.

It was not a nightmare.

The sun shone white through the cloth, he was awake. He heard nailed soles moving in the atrium, the protest of the slave at the door.

'So this is where the Liar lives.'

It was the Fisherman, he would never forget the harsh voice howling in triumph; the knife slicing through his mother's throat; blood; the gargling death-cry.

He dropped down on the far side of the couch, his cloth in his hand.

'These riches belong to the Way.'

Peering fearfully through the legs of the table he could see the savage form of the Fisherman, staring about him in anger.

Holding back the slave with one powerful arm was his hench-man. Jeshua felt a sudden pain of remembrance in his side, it was the one who had thrown the spear. Mark.

The jug of water that his sister had given him was on the table. He took it and the big cloth, and shuffled forward, bent as a cleaner would be, wiping the marble.

The Fisherman was close to him, he kept his head down, moving towards the inner rooms.

'Leads he more astray in this city?' growled Peter. 'Is it here he preaches to the unfaithful of the New Covenant?'

Jeshua could see the heavy sandals, the thick toes, the nails like shards of carved candle. The rough voice brought the hairs on his head up on end. Frantically, he scrubbed at the stone.

'Tell him the Bishop of Antioch is here,' Peter said, lowering his tone. 'Tell him, the one pregnant with deceit, that those who believe in the Covenant of God and who do not profane his holy name have come.'

The strain of controlling the rage that swirled in his body gave way. Only inches from Jeshua his foot lashed out savagely, catching the boy in the ribs and throwing him across the patterned marble.

'*Love the word*!' he screamed. Jeshua felt himself sprayed with spittle. '*Caress his holy name*!'

The blow had thrown Jeshua towards the atrium, he scuttled on hands and knees away from the men. In the gloom near the threshold he was out of sight. The bar of light by the door beckoned and he slipped through. The hubbub of the street enveloped him, and he ran.

The priest Cadmus rode down the narrow way in a small chariot drawn by maenads in panther-skins. Running by the side of the chariot, tethered to it, was a white goat, bleating plaintively, sober and worried. About Cadmus and his car bacchantes of varying grades capered to the music of flutes, castanets and tambourines, their hair in disorder and their doeskin tunics awry. Satyrs danced among them wearing brightly painted theatre masks, sporting flapping phalluses and long tails, and the senior maenads fended them off with the cone-tipped *thyrsos* they carried, symbols of their gods. All appeared drunk, and with their heads thrown back, approaching a state of possession.

Citizens who saw the parade of the priest and his accompanying *thiasos* entourage passing by on the city street watched them go with a wary eye. Attractive, half-naked and uninhibited though the bacchantes and maenads might seem, most were aware that in the mythology that was being played out maenads traditionally tore apart any living thing that, crossing their path, displeased them in the state they were by then in. The white-painted, stylised and staring masks they wore were not those of comedy, as were those of the satyrs, but of tragedy.

But they were not on the streets, they were in the park of the prefect, they performed their rites for the Emperor, his master and guest. Rich tents stood pitched about the glittering lake, scented smoke rose up from pyres of gods, and barbecues, sometimes one and the same. On the green grass Maria danced among the other maenads, wearing like them, only the skin of a fawn, and an ivy wreath in her hair.

In the chariot the Greek priest Cadmus stood up tall, a tiger skin falling down over his back, his head framed by its jaws, crowned with vine leaves. The chariot was decorated with vines and bunches of grapes.

They emerged from the tree-lined way into the Garden which was bright with fresh green shoots, dappled with the shade of the trees. There an altar was set up, they could smell the dry twisted vine branches burning. Cadmus descended from the chariot, surrounded by his panther-skinned maenads. At the altar he conducted the rites of the god, mixing the wine and heating it, adding the sacred herbs to both the holy drink and the fire that warmed it, so that the air was filled with intoxication and music. He chanted in Greek as he performed the satisfying rituals, promising mystical union with their deity.

Cadmus told how the previous autumn the god had died and his body had been crushed. His blood had come out. Now the green shoots about them told of the miracle of his resurrection and rebirth. His blood was wine, by drinking it he entered them, and god and worshipper were as one in communion.

As the flutes piped and the tambourines and castanets clashed and clattered rythmically, the maenads and satyrs gathered about the altar. They tipped back their white, open-mouthed masks to drink. The wine was hot, spicy with fermented resin, and burned most pleasurably as it travelled down. They left a swallow in the bottom of the cup which Cadmus drank, symbolising the union between deity and worshipper.

They untied the goat from the chariot and brought it to the priest. He touched it ritually on its head, its shoulder and its feet, just as the god Dionysus had touched Pentheus, King of Thebes, before sending him up into the tree to spy upon the maenads. They were clustered around, their eyes wild behind their masks, the breath panting in their throats.

'I offer up to you the one who laughs at you,' Cadmus intoned ritually, 'at me, and my secret rites.'

The goat bleated plaintively.

'Avenge yourselves on him.'

They fell on the goat and tore it into pieces, stuffing bloody fragments into their mouths. Gods punish men for disbelief. Dionysus had driven the women of Thebes mad. For disbelieving in him he had them tear Pentheus apart with their bare hands in frenzy.

All gods had two sides. Dionysus was merry, the friend of the worried, the support of the fearful, the soother of pain and the giver of exaltation. There was but one thing he would not permit, which was disbelief. To those who disbelieved in his existence he provided bloody, final proof.

The bacchantes were dancing among the flowers, the music loud, insistent, their heads thrown back in abandon, half-clad, their breasts bouncing. One ran over the green, and through the bushes, she tripped and fell in the long grass, the satyrs about her, pulling the fawn tunic from her body, their hands on her breasts, feeling her thighs, between her legs. The powerful wine roared in her head, the music beat in her ears as they mounted her, one after the other.

The worshippers began to scatter. A pot-bellied satyr waddled towards a silk-walled, purple-striped tent, accompanied by an entourage of others. He pulled his mask from his head, revealing yellow, crimped hair above a sweating face dominated by protuberant blue eyes and fleshy lips. He cast himself down upon a cushion-strewn couch and a slave began to fan him.

'Quite splendid,' he cried, and Tigillinus, who had come to recline next to him smiled.

'I *like* those,' the Emperor Nero said approvingly. 'Where did you get them?'

The prefect glanced across the tent, to where the lesser fry were arranging themselves about the walls.

'Saul got them for me,' he said generously, and a one-eared man bowed in response to Nero's regal wave.

Refreshing drinks were brought and served.

'Ah, me,' said Nero, 'what entertainments have we now?'

Tigillinus gave a short clap of his hands and a waiting servant hurried away. Upon the lake, only feet away, an ensemble of players struck up a sweet melody.

'Later, music and songs. We are hoping that you, *Imperator*, will favour us with a performance,' Tigillinus said unctuously, and Nero flushed with pleasure.

'Of course, of course,' he said.

'But first, an active show. A contest of skill between very different opponents.'

He nodded to his servant and two men came forward to stand in front of them. They were, as Tigillinus had promised, a complete contrast. One was strongly muscled, with black curly hair, his hands like powerful shovels. He was dressed in heavy armour that encased his calves and his torso. Mail glittered upon his arms. He carried a shining helmet, a round shield and a long sword.

'Flamma,' announced Tigillinus. 'Winner of the Palm, Champion of Champions.'

The fighter grinned sardonically, and bowed.

'His opponent. Faster than a snake, his bite death, Speculus.'

The second gladiator, lounging upon his trident, smiled benevolently, and twirled the golden net he carried. He was quite naked except for a scarlet loincloth.

Nero eyed them for a few moments without speaking, and a trace of anxiety entered Tigillinus's expression. Then he relaxed, as he saw that Nero's face had taken on a set of slightly malevolent mischief. He turned on his couch, to include those he had brought with him.

'Who will win?' he cried amiably. 'Let us take opinions.'

He cast his eyes towards the back, where he could see some soberly clad, middle-aged men.

'Senator Paulus!' he called. 'Come give us your learned view.'

A dour, leathery creature in toga, contrasting greatly with Nero's silken, feminine fripperies, came out.

'It is a warm day, Emperor,' he said, 'and the netman looks fast of foot. If he can keep his distance for long enough, he may be able to tire the *samnite* out. However, I shall side with the armoured man.'

He was a senator, an aristocrat, and gladiators to him were simply barbarians, degenerates without name. He did not use them. Speculus, the broken nobleman whom his views condemned to death, looked at him with the expression of a man assessing meat in the butcher's window.

Nero smiled, and looked back again.

'Flavius Sutorius! What about you? And is that your young wife? Bring her forward so that we may see her.'

Flavius came through the throng, Gaia with him.

'Doubtless you favour the net man,' said Nero, and Flavius bowed in agreement. It was not wise to publicly flout the Emperor. Tigillinus, who thought he sensed what Nero had in mind, leaned forward, murmuring in his ear. Nero beamed.

'And what of you, wife of Flavius? Gaia, is it?'

Gaia looked at the tall *retarius* with a steady gaze, and he at her.

'I too will take the man with the net,' she said quietly.

'You look remarkably similar,' Nero said, smiling. 'Can you be related?'

'He is my brother,' she said, turning to face Nero.

'Your brother! Tigillinus, how can you do this?' he said in mock disapproval. 'We cannot have this young man killed in front of his sister, how could you?'

'So sorry,' said Tigillinus, grinning.

Nero turned to the two senators, uneasy in their togas amongst the degenerates of the Emperor's court.

'No. Paulus, you approve of armour? Very well. Flavius, you like the net man. So be it. Prepare yourselves!'

The blood ran from their faces, but the Emperor's servants were at hand, stripping them of their garments, his soldiers of the guard stood by, cold-eyed and ready to carry out his commands. These were evil times for men of their rank, you survived as you could, and in a grim silence the pair of middle-aged aristocrats suffered themselves to be equipped with the accoutrements of the two gladiators.

'On the raft?' Tigillinus suggested, and Nero slapped his palm on his thigh in approval. The platform of musicians was hauled to shore and they disembarked; Paulus and Flavius climbed aboard, to be pulled out on to the waters.

'Gaia,' Nero commanded, 'you may watch with me.'

Very pale, Gaia came to recline next to the Emperor.

'Let the contest begin!' Tigillinus bellowed, and there was a crash of cymbal and drum from the ensemble. On the raft, the two strangely matched men began to shuffle about each other. The pimps, whores, gamblers, charioteers, clowns and murderers in the tent began to cackle with laughter and shout out obscene encouragement.

On the couch, Nero put his hand up Gaia's tunic.

Flavius stabbed at his opponent and sword and trident clashed. Blood spattered over the wood from a gash on his arm.

Gaia was stiff, she sought to push Nero's investigating hand out of her thighs, her face taut with horror. The Emperor laughed, Tigillinus gave Gaia's tunic a hefty pull and it tore away from her struggling body. Looking on, those about them bayed in approval, calling out to Flavius to see what was happening to his wife.

Tigillinus held her down with one brawny arm as she tried to rise. He squeezed her breasts cruelly and she screamed, to the delight of the Emperor's cronies gathering round the couch. On the raft Flavius lurched in alarm, looking across at the spectacle, and Paulus lunged at him. He barely caught the sword on the trident, and the raft rocked dangerously, water splashing over the sides as the two men manoeuvred for position, Paulus in his heavy armour panting for breath.

Nero heaved his bulk on top of Gaia, straddling her. His sychophants held her arms and legs, their faces alight with cruel pleasure, children tormenting a captive cat, and she closed her eyes tight.

His face purple, streaming with sweat, Paulus hurled himself at Flavius, charging like a rhino in his armour. Flavius went flying, his trident turning over and over in the air before hitting the water with a splash. He tumbled off the side. His net was wound about his opponent's ankles, and with a hoarse scream the armoured man lost his balance, falling into the water.

His passion gone for the time being, the Emperor pushed himself up on to one elbow, looking good-humouredly out at the empty, bobbing raft. As no one appeared, he clambered off Gaia and led the way towards the water.

The raft rocked, and very slowly, very wearily, Flavius crawled on to the slippery surface. He was naked and blood streamed over his soaking body from his wounds.

Tigillinus, peering into the clear depths of his lake, let out a roar of laughter, pointing, and all were soon guffawing and laughing until the tears ran free. There on the bottom, something like a great crab crawled about. It was Paulus, pinned down by the weight of his armour. After a while he stopped moving, and wiping their faces, the guests made their way back to the tent.

The Emperor was in fine humour. Tigillinus, his host,

escorted him back to his couch. By the lake shore, Gaia and Flavius were staggering away. In the crowd, Saul caught the eye of Tigillinus, and they smiled, one to the other. The prefect nodded his head, and Saul reclined, closer to the Emperor than he had been before.

The thick hedge of pines, cypresses and laurels that cast shade upon the path, told Jeshua that he was walking alongside the estate of a wealthy man. The mesh of branches and twigs that barred him from passing through allowed the passage of smoke and scent, he breathed the smells of sacrifice and of banqueting, it was the private park of the prefect, Tigillinus.

Coming round the dusty corner he saw a stone god staring at him with one of its two faces, and where Janus set guard, there was a gate. Two slaves stood there, in front of a stone gatehouse.

'I am come to see Saul, friend of Prefect Ofonius,' he said boldly, using the proper title of Tigillinus. The slaves seemed not to think his statement out of order.

'You're late,' one grunted. 'The others are here.'

Jeshua moved to go through, but the slave motioned for him to wait.

'Your mask,' he said.

He went into the gatehouse and came out with a strange, vividly marked mask with staring eyes and a red mouth carved into a smile. Jeshua took it and found it to be very light. It fitted right over the head like a helmet.

Again, he moved to go through.

'Where are you from?' the slave demanded. 'Clothes off first, you know that. I'll give them back when you return the mask.'

The boy pulled off his tunic and gave it to the gatekeeper.

He fitted the mask over his head and advanced into the park. The sun was strangely warm on his body. A lake glittered, brightly coloured tents ringed its edge, flags waved in the breeze. He could see people down there, but not what they were doing.

He felt exposed, out on the grass, and made for a small copse of trees close to the lake. Hiding there he peered out. The wreckage of a banquet littered the grass. Men and women lay strewn about in various states of disarray. Some drank, some were drunk, some unconscious. About an altar some maenads sat, in their distinctive doeskins, watching the groping, quaffing and coupling forms with impassive faces. Music was playing, from a band that was sober.

He heard a rustle of leaves as someone moved through the shrubs. He turned, and a man was on him, masked as he was. As he ran the man caught him by the arm, flinging him to the ground. He was up again on one knee but the man was there with him, his breath rasping inside the mask, forcing him down on to his face.

He felt a terrible pain as the man entered him, and he screamed. His mask was knocked awry, and a harsh hand clamped down over his face. A finger entered his mouth and with all the strength of his jaws he bit down into it.

His assailant let out a hoarse yell and he felt a great blow on the back of his head. He was dazed, yet he shouted out.

'*Maria! Maria!*'

The man hit him again, and he was half-conscious, lying crushed in the long grass. On top of him, his tunic hitched up about his waist, the man gripped him by the shoulders and resumed his pleasure.

Only a few seconds later the grunts of growing satisfaction turned into a howl of pain. A tremendous blow caught him across his shoulders, knocking him bodily from the body of the boy. A maenad stood over Jeshua, her eyes blazing, a heavy branch readied in her hands like a club.

Abruptly, and without a word, the man turned and ran off through the shrubs. The maenad helped Jeshua sit up.

'Maria,' he gasped gratefully, 'I called out for you.'

'I heard you. I was by the altar. What are you doing here?'

'The Fisherman,' he said fearfully. 'The Fisherman came to Saul's house. With him was the one that threw the spear.'

'Mark.'

'Yes. I managed to slip away.'

Maria looked about her.

'We had better not stay longer here, it is becoming dangerous. Within these grounds those with the Emperor may do as they please. I have already seen a man murdered, and a woman attacked. Now you . . .'

She looked about her, as they kneeled together in the wood.

'And yet the house will not be safe if the Fisherman is still there.'

'Timothy,' he said quickly. 'Timothy came to see Saul, before the Fisherman arrived. He is with Julia in the market, selling food.'

'Let us find him, then. They are good people, and kind. We can hide with them.'

Swiftly and quietly, the two slipped out of the wood and across the lawns to the gate.

Cadmus, priest of Dionysus, strode through the park. Wine and powerful herbs, magnificent ritual and dancing women roared in his blood and filled his mind.

He saw her there, with but one servant, gorgeous in black hair and shimmering *palla*, he let out a roar of lust and approval. The women screamed in terror, as they should. They ran, and he pursued them. He caught them both and they clung to each other. He tore the clothes from their bodies, flinging them joyously to the turf. The one with the black hair lay, her body like cream, and he fell upon her, consummating the worship of the god. He looked for her servant, to finish the rites, but she was gone.

He was still in communion when she returned, with others. They hit him over the head and carried him away.

When Cadmus awoke, it was to awful pain. There was the crashing pain of the day after, of the seventh bowl, of the rites. That he knew. But when he opened his eyes the dim light was not that of his tiny garret, stuck up the top stair of the swaying tenement building he lived in, firetrap and home of every bug that lived in Rome.

He was in a cell. Dirty stone walls and a low ceiling, a small barred window that let in a little light and some air. He moved to get up and cried out in fresh pain. He was manacled to the wall.

There was someone out there that was listening, for shortly afterwards the door clanked as the lock turned, and it opened. Two men came in, the first burly, gold at his throat, a man of power, and he stared at Cadmus with a terrible rage.

'Why do you keep me here?' the priest asked feebly. 'I am Cadmus, priest of Dionysus, I have done you no harm.'

'You do no harm?' the man snarled. 'You call attacking women doing no harm?'

The memory came sweeping back. The pursuit, ripping her clothes, the feel of her body hot under him.

'It is a part of the ritual!' Cadmus protested. 'It is understood by all who worship at the shrine of Dionysus. They do not come, any who do not wish to commune with the god.'

'And where is your shrine, priest?' the man whispered viciously. 'For you were in the park of Ajax, within the city walls.'

Realisation came over him.

'I had been holding ceremonies at the villa of the prefect,' he said weakly. 'I must have been drunk.'

'I do not doubt either of those things,' his captor said acidly. He clapped his hands in summons and two more slaves came shuffling through the door, bearing a brazier, freshly ignited, beginning to glow within itself. They put it down and one of them handed the man a pair of iron tongs, and a bronze knife that a priest might use. He inspected them and thrust the tongs into the heating coals.

'I'll be back later,' he said. 'We'll see to it you never touch a woman again. You won't even have anything to piss through. Lucipor, stay and watch him.'

'Yes, master.'

He swept out, leaving Cadmus with the slave.

'In the name of Hector,' Cadmus protested, 'why does he hate me so?'

'The woman you enjoyed,' Lucipor said precisely, 'she is his wife.'

'Oh, no,' He put his manacled hands over his eyes.

The memory of the woman came back to him, beautiful, voluptuous and . . .

'But she was willing!' he said suddenly. 'I know I pursued her, but I meant her no harm, I thought she was an acolyte, for I was drunk. I did not use her harshly.'

The slave smiled sardonically.

'This the master knows. For he is a jealous man. All the more reason to make you into a little girl.'

Cadmus blanched.

'Who is he?' he muttered.

'Lucius Licinius. Merchant, slavemaster, keeper of brothels. This is his private prison you are in.'

Lucipor took the handle of the tongs and gave the brazier a poke. The coals crackled and glowed.

'Getting nice and hot now,' the slave said conversationally.

On the hillside they could see the city below, spread out over her hills and the valleys in between. Timothy loaded the last basket of produce on to the side of the donkey, standing patiently outside the little farmhouse, with Julia at its head.

'Now, we'll be gone for the day,' he said to Maria and Jeshua.

He smiled reassuringly.

'But you're not to worry. Nobody knows that you're here. The Fisherman won't find you up here and we'll let Saul know. What's more, Wolf there won't let anybody near that he doesn't know. And there's no one who can take on Wolf.'

At the mention of his name, the fearsome dog looked up from where he was resting and yawned, showing his long jaws of savagely sharp white teeth.

'We shall be safe here,' Maria told him. 'Won't we, Jeshua?'

Her brother smiled and nodded, and together they watched the couple leading the little beast of burden down the hill towards the market in Rome.

Then it was quiet, except for the crickets creaking amongst the olives and the snuffle and clop of Wolf's jaws as he sought out an escaping flea.

'We must leave this city,' said Maria, watching Timothy and his wife get smaller, going away down the farm track.

'It is not safe for us here,' he agreed.

'We must find our father,' she said. 'We know the places on the shores of the Great Sea, the places he will go to be with the people of the Goddess and her consort. When we are with him we shall be safe from the Fisherman.'

'We will need money.'

'Saul will give us some. But first we must pray to the Father and to the Great Mother, we must give thanks for our safety and ask them to protect us, and to protect our father, in the time we are apart, before we find him.'

Jeshua took a basket from Julia's kitchen and the two wandered knowledgeably about the wild hillside, selecting and gathering the herbs that grew there – ones that were green in the rock crannies, others tough of root that gripped the hillside like the olive trees, those that were lush by the stream and those that liked the cool damp of the wood. When they were done and the basket filled, they made a small fireplace in an open glade from flat stones that they found by the brook.

They gathered dry twigs and pieces of vine root, dessicated and brown; they made a fire and Maria ignited it with her tinderbox. Jeshua took a wooden pipe, a panpipe of several hollow tubes, carefully cut and joined, and he began to play.

'We are here,' Maria called. 'We are here, far from the works of man, amidst the works of the Great Mother of All.'

She cast the first bunch of herbs upon the little blaze and sweet silver smoke drifted upon the air.

'I am the first and the last,' Maria sung, her voice shining in the wood, and the notes of Jeshua's pipe danced about her.

> I am the honoured one and the scorned one.
> I am the whore, and the holy one.
> I am the wife and the virgin.
> I am the mother and the daughter.

A man was coming quietly up the hill, a staff in his hand, helping him along on the steep slope. When he heard the playing and singing, he stiffened in recognition. He moved carefully amidst the lush vegetation of the wood, making no sound. Going from tree to tree, he went forward until he could see the two young people engaged in worship, could smell the fragrant smoke, hear Maria's silver voice in the glade.

> I am the silence that is incomprehensible
> and the idea whose remembrance is frequent.
> I am the voice whose sound is manifold
> and the word whose appearance is multiple.
> I am the uttrance of my name.

The man was very still, there behind his tree. Maria's voice lifted, high and pure, he recognised her song.

> Why have you hated me in your counsels?
> For I shall be silent among those who are silent,
> and I shall appear and speak.
> I am the one whom they call Life,
> and you have called Death.

Maria cast on the last of the herbs, and the heat of the coals burst them into magnificent, spiced smoke, rising towards the clouds. She raised her voice for the last time and her silver poetry rang through the glade.

> I was sent forth from the power,
> and I have come to those who reflect upon me,
> and I have been found among those who seek after
> me.
> Look upon me, you who reflect upon me,
> and you hearers, hear me.
> You are waiting for me, take me to yourselves.

Crouched behind the tree, the man ground his teeth with rage, the muscles bunching in front of the puckered stump where his ear had been. The music of the pipes continued, and behind him, as he slipped away back down the hill, Maria danced the dance of love upon the soft green grass, on the skin of the great Mother of All.

The grimed door, slimy with damp, ground open on its rusty hinges, and Cadmus lurched into the wakefulness of terror, his manacles clanking as he sought to cover his groin, his legs clamping together in a reflex of fear. In the dim light he saw a small man enter and stand looking thoughtfully at him. He was by the brazier, now glowing a deep and purposeful red.

'Who are you?' he cried.

'I shall tell you, in my own time,' the man said. He was speaking Greek, as Cadmus did. He sounded an educated man, unlike Lucius. The slave, Lucipor, came in, and silently placed a stool by the man, and he sat.

'But you are Cadmus, priest of Dionysus, are you not?'

'I am.'

'Tell me something about this god of yours.'

Cadmus glanced at the hideous brazier, with its jutting implement of torture.

'I will tell you anything you want, if it means keeping the parts I was born with.'

'Your god,' the man said, without response, 'who has brought you to this place, has he not? Where you lie, fearing for the future of your loins.'

Cadmus shuddered, unable to help himself.

'The gods punish men for disbelief, but also sometimes for believing too much. Three bowls is what Eubulus recommends – one for health, one for love and pleasure, one for sleep. The bowls after that belong to violence, uproar, drunken revel and hurling the furniture.'

'Attacking women you do not know.'

'I thought she was one of our worshippers,' Cadmus protested. 'I had gone far beyond the third bowl. Drunk temperately, wine distils into one's lungs like sweetest morning dew, in excess, commits rape upon reason. But then, one is keeping company with a god.'

'This Dionysus that the Romans call Bacchus, one sees his image abroad, in bars, restaurants, about the very necks of amphorae. Is there any more to him other than that his followers make themselves ill by an excessive belief in his works?'

'If you wish to know about Dionysus, the god of wine, you could not have chanced upon a better person, for not only am I his priest, I am a travelled man, who has seen and heard much, for many are the legends that surrounded his name.'

Talking had made Cadmus recover some of his confidence, he sat up by the wall, crossing his legs.

'Now, let me show you this, for Dionysus is oldest among gods, he comes from the very earth itself, unlike the later gods, who live up in the air and are cold. Dionysus is warm, the god of ordinary people, folk such as you or I.'

He looked hopefully up at the man, but still saw no fellow feeling. He scratched in the dirt that coated the floor of the cell.

'This I saw with my own eyes in shrines of enormous antiquity, so old that those who made them and worshipped there are not even a memory. But this representation they left in their shrines. It is the earth mother herself, here, see her seated with the shawl about her head, and she is holding her infant in her arms, the baby Dionysus.'

The man leaned forward to look at the representation in the dirt. Cadmus was a skilled artist, the drawing of mother and child was clear. He quickly sketched in vines and leaves with his fingernail, and the grapes synonymous with the god of wine.

'That is the oldest representation of Dionysus that I know of. Dionysus reigned where I come from, in the island of Crete. There the sun shone on fertile fields, on Athena's olives and Dionysus's vines. There men and women were equal, and the towns needed no walls to keep out enemies. Go today, there are paintings of those times, you will see birds and flowers, dancing maidens and flying fish, fruit and wine. But no spears, nor swords.

'Those came in the hands of men from the north, who invaded the land of Dionysus at the command of their gods, who lived in the sky. The ordinary people, folk like you and I, rejected the cold, hard gods in the sky, and took comfort and courage from their god of the earth, Dionysus. From his blood that he gave to them through his vines they found the courage to band together, to gather together in harmony, to cast off the chill influence of Apollo and his kind.'

Cadmus swallowed, licking dry lips. The atmosphere was smoky, his eyes were watering, but his mouth was parched. The man still sat watching him impassively, as though awaiting some proof that had not yet arrived.

'The struggle between good and evil is eternal,' Cadmus went on. 'Years passed, and those who believed in Dionysus came into the grim orbit of new men with spears and swords, and different gods.'

He waved a hand all around him.

'The Romans came, seeking to have dominion over all. There was no far hidden gulf, no unknown continent which if it exported gold did not become an enemy, and the Fates prepared for it murderous wars for the conquest of new treasure. Thus it was we Greeks fell under their sway, they saw the power of our god Dionysus whom they called Bacchus and were afraid. So they invented lies about us, they said that we indulged in every vice, that men and women indulged in the basest debauchery, that we were poisoners and murderers, that we ate the bodies of our victims and drank their blood.

'We were persecuted and had to follow our religion secretly. Persecution gave us strength and more and more flocked to take comfort in our rites, to live a good life and reject evil, to be rewarded in the afterlife, when one will live in Arcadia with our saviour, the god Dionysus. Those who believe in him and follow good and reject evil, when they die, he will supervise the journey of their spirit to the Isles of the Blest, which lie beyond the furthest waters of the ocean. At this command the souls of the dead are carried there by merry, gambolling creatures of the deep. There they will find Paradise. The taste of the pleasures they will find in Paradise they know from imbibing wine and celebrating with their god in the Bachanalia. Thus is was that Dionysus, the power of good triumphed again, and the Emperor Caesar lifted the persecutions. The great and powerful now numbered themselves among his followers, like the mighty Mark Anthony, as well as the humble folk like you and I. Now you may see his image on walls everywhere, his statue reigns in temple and street.'

'Does he reign here in this cell?' the man asked, his voice sharp. 'Will he save your loins from the red hot tongs that rest in the brazier here next to me?'

'I do not know,' Cadmus whispered.

'Is he more powerful than a mere mortal, this Lucius that hungers to clamp them, glowing red with heat, upon your parts, until they are but so much char?'

Cadmus was silent, unable to speak.

'Answer me.'

Cadmus looked about him, at the grim walls that encased him, as they had imprisoned others.

'No,' he muttered.

'What?'

'No, I said. He will get me drunk, but he will not get me from here.'

'No. He will get you here, where you would lose all, for the one you have served, have worshipped, this Dionysus, is but one of the Devil's playthings.'

The man stood up and although small, he seemed suddenly tall, filling the tiny room.

'There is only one with the power to release you, to save you from torment.'

'Tell me who he is,' Cadmus begged.

'His name is Jesus, he is the son of the one, the only god. He has come to save you not from the mere torture of the tongs that you fear, and which is but as the bite of a gnat compared to the fires of Hell where you would burn into eternity had you not known his holy Name.'

'Let me know him!' Cadmus shouted. Tears suddenly poured down his cheeks. 'Let me sit at your feet while you instruct me in his works.'

The man stood up, and indicated the manacles about the wrists. The slave Lucipor stepped forward and silently undid them.

'All that you have known before are but the twisted teachings of Satan,' the man said sternly. 'The crooked serpent who takes the pure word of God and bends it to his own ends. Our Lord Jesus too knew of wine, he called himself "the true vine". "Every bunch in me that bears not fruit he takes away, and every branch that bears fruit he purges it, that it may bring forth more fruit." But nowhere does he say we should drink until we become mad.'

'It is said that he broke bread and poured wine with his disciples, and said that those who ate the bread are his flesh, and those who drank the wine drank his blood. There were those who did not understand him, and said: this is a hard saying, who can understand it? And they walked no more with him.'

Cadmus thought quickly, with his priest's training.

'For by eating the god's flesh, and by drinking his blood, he dwells in you, and you in him.'

'That is what he meant. You must know, the teachings of Jesus are not always easy to understand at first hearing, for he was the Son of God.'

The man led the way out of the cell and up a narrow and winding brick stair. They emerged into the sunshine and Cadmus stood blinking in the bright light, breathing in the sweet air.

'Who are you?' he asked. 'Now that I am your servant, you must tell me who you are.'

'You are not my servant,' the small man said admonishingly. 'We are both the servants of Jesus. I am one who had been given the power to know his Name, to bring him to those who dwell in darkness. I am Paul.'

'We're sorry to be leaving,' said Maria, and Jeshua, standing beside her, nodded in agreement.

'It isn't safe,' he said. 'If we stay, the Fisherman will find us.'

'We cannot wait until the end of the sailing season. We will do better to go out on the shores of the great sea and find our father.'

Julia came forward and kissed them both on the cheeks.

'We shall miss you,' she said with a smile, 'Timothy and I,

we have grown fond of you this short time we have been together.'

Timothy gave Maria a leather flask.

'*Conditum*,' he said proudly. 'My own recipe. It will make any wine on your road palatable. In it there is pepper, saffron, mint, absinthe, resin and malobathre.'

'Thank you.'

'Get along down to the villa,' Saul said, smiling. 'It is safe now. I will meet you there with money and take you to the port in the morning. But now I have work to do for the Lord, people flock to his very name.'

'I hope you finish your histories,' Maria said to Timothy.

The two set off down the hill. A little way down they turned to wave.

'Thank you, Julia and Timothy, for all that you have done for us. Thank you, Saul.'

He beamed down at them.

'Saul's not here today,' he said, almost to himself, 'Paul is.'

He went over to the stream as the children went away down the path, and unwrapped the bandage that was about his hand. In his forefinger the marks of teeth showed, still red where the skin had been broken. The finger was swollen. He washed it in the stream and left it exposed to the sun and air.

They came down the bank of the Tiber, pausing to watch the fishermen down on the muddy sides and those in their little round boats. Then they turned off through the marketplace and up the narrow *angiportus* that led to Saul's villa, overlooking the river. At the strong, wooden door Maria knocked, kicking with her foot. There was no reply.

'Phidias is asleep,' Jeshua said, smiling, and his sister joined him. The slave catnapped at the slightest opportunity. She twisted the iron ring to raise the latch, and the door swung in smoothly.

'Phidias!' she called. 'It's us.'

'Here,' a voice sounded from somewhere inside. They went in, closing the door behind them. The atrium was suddenly lush with greenery after the dirt, plaster and brick of the city street. A fountain played, the noise of the pressing people was shut out.

'I'm parched,' said Jeshua as he headed across the open space for the kitchen, 'let's squeeze some lemons and have a drink.'

He passed through the arch, and as he did so, a huge figure swept him from his feet, pinning him to the wall.

A knife was at his throat.

'You shall not thirst long,' said the Fisherman.

Before she could move, a blow sent Maria flying, a heavy weight landed on her back, powerful hands bound her arms behind her. She was hauled to her feet and Peter's henchman, Mark, brought her forward.

'Who are you?' Maria cried bravely, pretending not to know them. 'What do you want with us?'

'You know who we are,' Peter snarled, 'and what we want from you.'

With a jerk of his powerful hand he tore Jeshua's tunic aside. Still livid on his back was the scar of the spear.

'I see my sign,' Mark said.

With a strange dignity Jeshua pulled his clothes back around him. He stared Peter full in the face.

'What of it?' he asked. 'I am Jeshua, son of Mary. This is my slave, who waits upon me. What is it to you?'

Maria opened her mouth to protest and then shut it again. It was, somehow, her younger brother who was in charge of the situation. She stood in Mark's grasp and waited. The

Fisherman rammed Jeshua against the wall, the fury that seethed within him boiling over.

'I am sworn to wipe the stain of that woman and her blood
from the earth, in the name of God,' he hissed, 'and I shall
fulfil my vow.'

Jeshua was still staring impassively at the terrifying figure
towering above him.

'I see there is no reasoning with you,' he said calmly. 'But
let my slave girl go. You have no quarrel with her, you or your
god.'

'Blood,' Peter muttered, 'I shall have your blood to show.
As a sacrificial lamb you shall be.'

'But not hers,' Jeshua insisted.

Then Mark spoke out, as the insane light was gathering in
Peter's eyes, and his knuckles grew white about the hilt of his
dagger.

'Why not sell the girl?' he suggested, and the thought took
hold in Peter's mind.

'Sell her?' he murmured. He seemed to find the idea
attractive.

'A slave is a slave. This one is young and attractive, people
would pay for her body.'

'True.'

Suspicious, crazed eyes, certain of treachery, dropped on to
Maria.

'But she is a witness . . .' he said.

Then he smiled.

'I have it. You are a slave, you say . . . Then you shall do
my bidding.'

He held out his dagger, hilt foremost.

'You shall kill this boy for me.'

Maria stood completely still in Mark's grasp.

'Obey my command,' Peter whispered, the thin sound of his voice sharp with menace. 'Obey me or die yourself.'

'I shall – '

Jeshua's voice cut across her.

'I shall go straight to Paradise,' he said clearly and strongly, his eyes burning as he stared at her. 'There shall my mother be, next to the Father, and the Great Mother. I shall join them as I have been promised. You but hasten me on my way. You shall do this last service for me.'

Mark pushed her forward, and she felt the icy steel of his own knife at the side of her throat.

'Do it now,' commanded Jeshua.

The silence was broken by the sudden creak of the door, the darkness vanished in the crackling orange light of a torch. Paul stepped into the vestibule, kicking the door shut behind him, and thrust the twisted bunch of tarred twigs into an iron holder on the wall.

There was movement in the dark and Mark came forward into the flickering light.

'Is the Bishop of Antioch content?' Paul demanded. 'Did he receive what he came for?'

'See for yourself,' Mark said grimly. He turned to indicate a small bundle of rags by the wall. Paul retrieved the torch and brought it forward. Jeshua lay curled up, as though asleep, but a long pool of blood ran from his throat to the drain in the marble floor. In the sudden light, cockroaches broke off from their feasting, running for the darkness. Paul's eyes flashed in the orange glow as he looked up at Mark.

'And the girl?'

'She is sold, as you wished.'

'Good. Then it shall be as we agreed. The Fisherman Peter

has what he desired, which is the death of the boy. You will spread the word amongst the churches of the Great Sea. These two, the boy and the girl, they worshipped in the manner of the Cowled Man. You will get the word to him that his son is dead and his daughter enslaved here. I shall keep a watch for him.'

'Why do you care so about the Cowled Man?' Mark asked curiously.

'We all have things to oppress us,' Paul snapped. 'Ask Peter if he sleeps well at night.'

'I have never met the Cowled Man,' said Mark. 'I have only heard of his name. But I shall do as you ask, and it may be that word will get to him.'

'It will, it will.'

Paul prodded the corpse with his foot.

'Now what of this?' he muttered.

Mark moved towards the door.

'I shall leave that to you,' he said.

When he was gone Paul went inside and emerged with a strong sack, that had held grain. He stuffed the boy's body inside. It had long ceased to bleed. He tied its neck, swinging it easily over his back; it was only light.

He carried it outside loping down the *angiportus*, pushing his way through the carts grinding and cursing, braying and creaking their way through the marketplace, bringing fresh goods into the city by night, as Caesar had decreed. He stood briefly on the high wall where the mighty Tiber swirled below, and threw his burden in.

The chalk was white on her feet. The light of day broke through the small barred window, she could hear the sound of the Romans as they emerged from their houses and on to the streets. The iron-bound door was pushed back and the harsh voice of the slavemaster summoned her.

Maria rose from the rough plank bed and went out, up the stone stairs into the day. The market was waiting, she stood naked on the block, ready to be sold.

In his room, sitting at his table, separated from her by hundreds of years and thousands of miles, Connell put down his last sheet of text. He rubbed his hands over his eyes, and found his cheeks damp with her tears.

14

Connell let him in and he went through into the room over-looking the garden, where they worked. Connell had put the tables away, hidden the boxes of photographs, the piles of hand-written notes and translations in the next room. Only one set of texts, photographed originals and Connell's own transcription, rested on his desk.

'Sit down, Jack,' he said amiably. 'I'll get you a drink.'

'Just a coffee,' the man said defensively. He spoke with a rounded American accent. He adjusted his glasses nervously.

'I shouldn't really be here,' he said, as though joking, which he was not.

'Keeping the company of sinners?' Connell said jocularly. He went into the kitchen and put a kettle on to boil. 'Don't worry, Jack, I shall soon be as pure as driven snow. I'm about to rehabilitate myself. I've got a text I want you to look at.'

Jack Halloran held up his hands.

'Frank . . .'

'Don't worry. Though I am going to offer it for sale.'

'Frank, I am not in the underground antiquities market.' Halloran said firmly. 'I am a professor at Yale, I am in Oxford for a conference. Now . . .'

'It's not for sale to *you*,' Connell said smoothly. 'You couldn't afford it.'

His rival academic eyed him carefully.

'So why do you want me to look at it? Don't tell me the great Frank Connell needs a second opinion on something.'

'I don't,' Connell said cheerfully. 'I don't want your mind, I don't want your body, Jack, I want your money. Yale's money. What I've got is worth a fortune. A whole foundation's worth. And I'm going to let you see just a little of it, to whet your appetite.'

'You showing it to anyone else?' Halloran asked calculatingly.

'Not yet.'

'Why Yale?'

'I like Yale. I'd like to have a foundation there.'

'And if we don't come up with it?'

'Then I'll learn bloody Japanese and sell it to Todai,' Connell said brutally. 'It's worth it.'

'Then I'd better see it,' the American said mildly. 'What is it?'

'It's a conversation between Zephyrinus, Bishop of Rome, and Tertullian. It's very illuminating.'

He went to his desk, and gave Halloran the texts, both original and in translation.

'It's in Coptic,' the American said quickly. 'Frank, what have you been up to?'

'Just read it, Jack.'

Rome, A.D. July 203

From his window Zephyrinus could see the men hammering the elder-wood stakes into the ground, lining the way up the Capitonline Hill. On the air came the thud of the mallets and the mournful baying of the dogs in the pen.

He had the shutters open wide. The summer air of Rome tended not to be fragrant, but it was better than that within the room. The young man seated opposite him was barefoot and clad in what clearly was his only coat. He was also possessor of a fine and fast theological mind, the continuous use of which prevented him from finding time to bathe.

He was from Carthage, where a different, African Church was springing up. Zephyrinus, Pope of Rome, needed to know more about it. His nose urged him to ask whether the fine Roman institution of the public bath had arrived in Carthage, but he repressed the notion, for he was familiar with men like Tertullian, he knew them to have no sense of humour.

There were many leather-bound books in his room, among those on the table lay the five massive volumes of Irenaeus, *Adversus Haereses*, Against the Heresies, with which the battle against the Gnostic heresiarchs had been won. Tertullian had nodded in approval when he had seen it, for it had been his own weapon in smashing the heresies in Carthage.

'A most thorough investigator of all doctrines,' he said warmly. He handed over to the middle-aged Zephyrinus a far smaller volume.

'*The Acts of Perpetua and Felicitas*. The diary of the martyr Perpetua, which I have edited.'

'I shall read it. The martyrs of Lyons have new comrades, murdered in the old fashion. Is it easy to whip up hatred against us, in Carthage?'

'Many hold us in contempt. But they fear us too. You hear on the streets snatches of conversation: "How could that wise man Lucius Titius become a Christian?" "Christ was some man the Jews condemned." "The fast set – they have become Christians." "The Jews say they worship donkeys." We embrace martyrdom and they call us "faggot-fellows", and "half-axle men".'

'Clearly you are winning converts, if they talk about us so much.'

'Day by day the pagans groan over the ever-increasing number of Christians. Their constant cry is that the state is beset by us, that we are in their fields, their camps, their *insulas*. They grieve over it as a calamity that every age, every rank is passing over to us. They talk about us as *latebrosa et lucifuga natio*, a vast and invisible state. It is simple, the world is awakening from error. What have we not seen in the name of their religions! Pitiable and ridiculous! And what of Jove's brother, hauling out the corpses of the gladiators, hammer in hand. If they overturn the honour of deity, it means sheer contempt felt by those that do these things, and by those for whom they do them. It is no surprise to me that men and women are turning to Christ. In Carthage, we embrace him, we are the *militia Christi*, we are ever ready for death in his name. Our storm-troops lead the fight against Satan.'

It was the second mention of the Carthaginian viewpoint of what made up a true believer.

'You mention Jews,' murmured Zephyrinus.

'*Synagogae Judaeorum fontes persecutionum.*' Tertullian spat. 'Ever they seek to use us as scapegoats for public hate. Where in the past the Jews were held responsible for everything from earthquake to a cloudless sky, now they direct the venom of the ignorant to us.'

'Here too. We have had the burnings, the beatings and beheadings, and the Jews busy behind it all, the moment they saw that the edict of the Emperor gave them a chance. Still, it is over now. We are able to ransom our women converts from the *lupanariae*, soon if I am not wrong, we shall enjoy again the peace we had following the martyrdoms in Lyons, so many years ago. The emperor Severus is a hard man, but there are those about him of the highest rank who are Christians. Julia Domna, his wife, and also her daughter Julia Mammaea are sympathetic towards us, as was the mistress of the Emperor Commandus, Maria, who helped us greatly. Many have been the conversions we have secured among aristocratic women. For the first time the Church in Rome is able to legally purchase and hold property. Our cemeteries along the Appian Way increase. News came to me that the Governor of Syria was about to send troops to hunt down Christians who had gone into the desert in anticipation of the *parousia*, but was dissuaded by his *wife*, who was one of us. While I think we may have to wait awhile for God's coming, the day when we have a Christian Emperor may be upon the horizon.'

Tertullian's eyes flashed.

'God is coming, be sure of it. And there can be no Christian Caesar, for Caesars are necessary to the world. We are Christians, and for us what greater pleasure can there be than contempt for pleasure, than scorn for the activities of the world. Our business lies against these things, against the institutions of our elders, against the authority of traditions, the laws of the masters of this world, the arguments of lawyers, against the past, against custom and necessity, against the examples, prodigies and miracles that have fortified this bastard divinity. All that the Romans hold, occupy and possess is the spoil of outrage; their temples are all of loot drawn from the ruin of cities, the plunder of gods and the slaughter of priests. What could we want with that?'

'We could make it Christian.'

Down on the hill, men were leading a procession of dogs towards the elder stakes.

Tertillian held back from comment, reigning in his natural propensity to tell everyone, from the Bishop of Rome downwards how the universe was constructed and his place in it. He recognised that while Zephyrinus was interested in finding out in which direction the Church of Carthage – and by implication, the great province known as Africa – was moving, it was possibly even more important for Tertullian to find out whether the Church of Rome was headed in the same direction. If the Carthaginian Christians were aboard a small, rigorous craft, made for speed in one direction, and armed with fire and steel, the Church of Rome was a grain-carrier, already a leviathan and growing all the time, her lead-plated hull able to roll over and sink the impudent sailing in her way.

Zephyrinus picked up a few other small volumes on his desk.

'Clement of Alexandria gave me some of *his* works,' he commented artlessly. 'He came to see me recently.'

'Ah,' said Tertullian, recognising the books for what they were, a stalking horse. 'And has the bishop returned to his see?'

'Not to my knowledge.'

'He fears to die for the glory of God.'

'Is it not written in Matthew: "When they persecute you in this city, flee you into another"?'

Tertullian remained uncharacteristically silent, refusing for the moment to be drawn.

'He has been vigorous in the service of the Lord in Alexandria, and is, as we are, deeply concerned with the problems that face our Church. Clement has faced the difficult task of bringing Orthodox Christianity to a people hitherto dominated by the Gnostics and Jewish-Christian sects. He faces very real practical problems doing this. Many among his congregation attracted to Christianity, are both educated and wealthy. Such would-be converts tend to be treated with insolence by those who take the scriptures literally.'

'Is there any other way?' Tertullian asked dangerously.

'This problem he has addressed in his work, *The Rich Man's*

Salvation,' Zephyrinus continued smoothly. 'Taking, obviously, the parable of the rich young man told by our Lord Jesus to sell all he has as his theme. He states as a general proposition that it is not in the nature of God the giver of all good gifts to exclude from salvation those who enjoy them. The words of the parable – he says – are susceptible to meanings other than the obvious. Seen this way, can wealth not be a good thing? Is it not foolish to fling away the riches that are of benefit to our neighbours as well as ourselves? Here he brings the issue to one of conduct. Outward things are a matter of indifference, what counts is their use. Wealth rightly used to do some noble or divine deed, used in trust for others, makes the possessor blessed.'

Tertullian did not reply for a moment, but looked about the room, at its fittings and furniture, gifts to the premier representative of God in Rome from wealthy converts, the richly-bound books and fine religious pictures on the walls. He looked at Zephyrinus himself, well-clad and well-fed, clean from the baths.

'Wealth belongs to the world,' he said clearly, 'and the things of the world belong to Satan. It is not permitted to those who will attain salvation that they take up employment, for possession of money is prohibited by the Gospels and connected with idolatry. I would not even take up a tailor's job, for is he not the one who transforms God's sheep into costly raiment?'

'But if as you say Satan moves here on earth, is it not with money that we fight him? Do we not support our Churches in parts of the world where they are hard-pressed, do we not ransom our fine men and women from the mines with money? Is it not with money that we spread the word of God in the land?'

'There is another, a better weapon,' Tertullian said indifferently.

'It is perhaps not as simple as we all wish it was. Are we not really dealing with the questions of the function and status of the clergy, the organisation of our Church, and its relations with the state? These are weighty matters that affect us all, and the future of our Church.'

From the hill came a growing mournful yowling of dogs. Men were crucifying them to the stakes of elder, nailing them to the wood.

'We come to the all-important question of sin,' said Zephyrinus. 'Baptism, we all agree, involves the complete remission of sin by the power of the spirit.'

'Certainly,' Tertullian said warmly. 'The baptismal water is the abode of the Holy Spirit, poured upon the convert it separates him from the world, and saves him from its destruction.'

'Of course,' agreed the bishop. 'But what of *after*? You and I perhaps disagree slightly as to the closeness of the *parousia*. For the early Christians it was clear-cut, there was but a short period between baptism and the arrival of God on earth. For his own divine reasons he has not yet appeared, and it may be for us as for them, that he will come when we are gone. In this case the problems of sin committed after baptism, perhaps through a whole lifetime, becomes acute.'

'We should also address the problem of those catechumens preparing for baptism, who spend the years of preparation wallowing in sin in order to store up enough for the time they shall – they think – be pure,' Tertullian said sourly. 'But the question of forgiveness of sin after baptism is a far greater one. In Carthage those who have sinned spend the day sorrowing and the night in vigils and tears, lying on the ground among clinging ashes, tossing in rough sackcloth, fasting and praying. I have seem adulterers led forth amongst the brethren and prostrated in sackcloth and ashes, a compound of disgrace and horror before the widows and elders, suing for everyone's tears, licking their footprints and grovelling for forgiveness. It is generally thought that a Christian has one, and only one chance for forgiveness. I would advise them to read Romans. For me, the commitment of the sin after baptism proves them never to have had election in the first place.'

'Clement argues that salvation is achieved through long and hard schooling in self-mastery, through prayer and contemplation inspired by love of God.'

'Clement has invented a God that does not take offence, who neither grows angry, nor takes vengeance, a God in a Hell wherein no flames bubble forth, and which has no outer darkness, no terrors to make you tremble, no gnashings of teeth. In Africa, we know of these things.'

'Then is not the question of how those who sin may be cleansed and saved from the terrible fate that awaits them an important one? Since baptism by the Church enables the complete remission of sin, may not the Church have the power to remit sin afterwards, for penance? When Matthew's text reads of "binding and loosing" is this not exactly what he means?'

'And where will this lead? I see clearly why it might be attractive to sinner and to bishops. The one is spared his just and eternal torment, the other gains power. The power to remit sin is conducive to the universal mission, and conducive too to the emergence and consolidation of a clerical caste. With it, the day would come when the very Emperor himself will tremble before the power of a bishop, who can, by allowing him within the Church or no, decide his future forever.'

'As I said,' murmured Zephyrinus, 'we could make the Empire Christian.'

'It is all irrelevant, for there is but one mighty weapon the Christian needs, but one certain route by which he may enter Paradise. When the martyr Saturus was on the way to the amphitheatre – "Tertullian leaned forward to tap the book he had given" – he turned upon the unrepentant and exultant mob of pagans all about him. "Today friends, tomorrow enemies. However, note our faces well, so that you may recognise us in that day." Shall I tell you of that day?

'What a spectacle is at hand! The return of the Lord, now no object of doubt, now exalted, now triumphant! And still to come other spectacles – the last, that eternal Day of Judgement! How vast the spectacle that day, and how wide! What sight shall wake my wonder, what my laughter, my joy and exultation as I see all those kings, those great kings, welcomed – we were told – in Heaven, along with Jove, groaning in the depths of darkness! And the magistrates who persecuted the name of Jesus, liquefying in fiercer flames than they kindled in their rage against the Christians! Those sages too, the philosophers blushing before their disciples as they blaze together! And then there will be the players to be seen, lither of limb by far in the fire, and then the charioteers to watch, red all over in the wheel of flame . . . And then shall I turn an insatiable gaze upon the torment of those who vented their rage and fury upon the Lord . . .'

Tertullian wiped his mouth clean of spittle with the back of his hand.

'*Ad tubam angeli erigere, ad martyrum palmas gloriare,*' he said, his eyes burning. 'A Christian is filled with the Holy Spirit from the moment it enters him through baptism of water until he is baptised in blood. The reward of martyrdom – longed-for, provoked – is full remission of sins. Only God can do it, and only the martyr receives it.'

With the Carthaginian gone Zephyrinus had his slaves open

the doors to get rid of the smell. Well he now understood the saying: avoid an African at the baths. Down on the hill the rows of crucified dogs were howling in a chorus out of Hell, as men solemnly carried geese past them in litters on purple and gold silken cushions.

Six hundred years before, the celtic king, Brennos, had attacked Rome. During the long-drawn-out siege the sacred geese in the temple had given warning of a Celtic attack. The guard dogs had failed to do so, and judgement had been passed on both. The sentence and reward were still being carried out.

The Pope stared down from his window. The Roman Empire would not surrender to God easily. Tertullian would have his martyrs, as many of them as he wanted.

Halloran put the texts carefully down at his side, and picked up his cold coffee.

'Who got that, Frank? Who was close enough to Zephyrinus to hear that, to record it, and, one assumes, much later to translate it into Coptic?'

'That's right.'

Connell sat on the arm of a chair, a glass of beer in one hand.

'It's an early sect,' he said.

'Why are they so close to the Catholics? Close enough for what really is intelligence information.'

'Well done, Jack,' Connell said warmly. 'They hate them, that's why.'

A flash of what was almost anger went across Halloran's face.

'Hate?'

'Of course. In the eyes of the Catholic Church, they're

heretics of the worst kind. So, in the end, was Tertullian, I would point out.'

'The Catholic Church was and is all-embracing. Its victory was because it disseminated the word of God.'

Connell was slightly taken aback.

'Are you a Catholic, Jack?'

'I am.'

'I didn't know that. Anyhow, it isn't really important. What is is getting this off the ground. Is Yale interested?'

'There is more, you say.'

'Much, much more,' Connell promised.

'Don't tell anyone else,' Halloran demanded, 'not yet. I want to talk to some people.'

15

Rome, A.D. 204

Her coffin was made of stone, they had brought her to it in the darkness, with just the shuffling of their feet in her ears, they had lain her in it and dragged the heavy cover shut. The coffin had been cold then, now it was hot. The smell of the roasting pine cones pierced the lid and all about her the stone grew hotter and hotter. She could hear the incantations of the priests as they fed the fire; sweat streamed from her naked body, she squeezed her arm up and bit on a finger to stop from screaming.

The herbal draught she had drunk roared in her veins. The heat was gone, like a distant memory of summer, the coffin was a tomb, the stone as chill as ice. Water dripped down the sides, unable to move in its constraints she shivered uncontrollably in the darkness.

She would have drunk the water, licked it up with her tongue, as dry as bone.

Wine. In her tomb her body was drying up, her mouth dry, her whole stomach racked by hunger cramps. She needed wine, to wash lovingly over her, to caress her brain.

She banged her head from side to side in the coffin.

There was a noise, a scraping. An intense smell of pine filled her head. Hands pulled her upright in the darkness, and she stood.

Pine charcoal burned cherry-red on the altar. The light

slowly grew and in front of her she could see the Lord Jesus, flanked by his two torch bearers, the one with his torch high, signifying light and life, and the other with his lowered, for death and darkness.

The priest in his robes stood before her. She knelt and was blessed.

'Heat have you suffered, and cold,' he said. 'Through darkness have you come. And you have travelled into light.'

Above him. Jesus stood tall in a white robe, a young man with long curly locks, his hand raised in blessing. Behind his head was the sun, its rays blazed about his head in a halo.

'He who will not eat of my body and drink of my blood, so that he will not be made one with me and I with him, the same shall not know salvation.'

The priest's robes were white, edged with red.

'Thirst has tormented you, quench your thirst in me.'

The priest held forward a chased silver goblet, and she bent her head and drained it.

'Hunger has wracked your body. Eat of me and be comforted.'

The priest held out the strip of flesh from the sanctified bull, charred on the altar, and she ate.

She stood naked and they anointed her body with holy oil until she gleamed in the red light of the altar fire.

'The Lord Jesus is within you. Now you must travel through darkness to find him.'

The altar fire was low, she turned to face the blackness in front of her. The herbs in the wine sang through her fingertips, she could hear the sound of life, of people, her nostrils flared as she smelled the scent of perfume.

There was a sudden rush of air in the pitch, a man's hands were on her, she felt the hard strength of his muscles. He was behind her, his hand squeezing her breasts, he was naked, she felt his heat as he pressed into her. She twisted, her whole body slippery with the holy, scented oil; she gripped his wrist and arm, throwing him off balance; he tumbled over her outstretched leg and she hurled him into the night.

She moved forward, as she must. The sudden pungent smell of herbs on incandescent coals stabbed through her head. Her outstretched fingertips brushed against the cold and she padded along a wall of stone.

Sudden warmth. A hand, an arm tied to a shackle. Sweet breath. Her hand ran along a slender arm and shoulder, brushing long hair, soft lips. She felt a woman's breasts, caressed them, ran her hand down over her stomach and between her thighs, and heard her gasp in the night.

She undid the ribbons that imprisoned her and felt a mouth on her breast, a hand moving between her own thighs. The mouth slid down, licking her stomach, she stood still as it came to her groin, and she gasped in her own turn.

She moved again, in the darkness. There was a dim light. As she came towards it it was white, the robes of the Lord Jesus. His arms were outstretched, as though on the Cross. She reached out for him, and he was living flesh. She drew his robes aside, kneeling before him, and felt him grow in her mouth. Then she stood, impaling herself upon the Lord in communion.

In the darkness only the pool of light from the green-shaded lamp showed, and Connell put the sheet of text down by it. He got up, and put some logs on to the fire. His mouth was dry from reading. The flames licked up, flickering yellow and gold in Juliana's eyes. He had a bottle, and splashed wine, ruby-red in the firelight, filling the glasses.

'Their rites are changing,' she said.

'They're evolving,' he agreed. 'So did the Catholics, of course. Neither side has won yet, they're still able to experiment, to take on board the most powerful elements of competing religions. The Jeshuans have clearly borrowed from the cult of Mithras. The entombment of the acolyte passing through rigorous initiation to a higher form of knowing is obviously Mithraic. But they have their own stamp to it, they have a fabulous sense of theatre.'

Her hand shook slightly as she lifted the glass to her lips.

'Makes you wonder why the Jeshuans didn't win.'

'Too advanced,' he suggested, 'too capital-intensive, if you like. Requires too much input, compared to the command exerted by a Catholic bishop over his worshippers by fear. Too enjoyable.'

'Oh, yes,' she murmured.

'Did you notice something? Once the woman has passed through the extremes of heat and cold, has been suitably starved, has a fearful thirst, has suffered extreme sensory deprivation, once she is resurrected, brought back into the living world, all her faculties now hypersensitive – helped by the powerful rituals of the priest and the cocktail of herbs in the wine – she has dangers to face. Not animal ones, nor, actually, ones of the gods. It's other people. She demonstrates her fighting skills by throwing the man into darkness. The woman is shackled to the wall, she does not release her until she is certain she is an ally. The woman then helps her commune with Jesus, who makes love to her whilst on the Cross.'

He drank some wine.

'The Jeshuans are most aware that they live in a very dangerous world. They believe it to be that created by Satan, that they are the only forces there of the true God – the Mother and the Father who sent Jesus, as a kind of commando leader into enemy territory. They trust no one but themselves, and they bond together with very powerful rites.'

Juliana sat staring into the growing fire, and in the flames her face shone gilt, like a statue.

The coals broke in the grate and their glowing centres cast a red light into the darkness. They crashed inside Connell's head, the sharp smell of burning herbs seemed to fill his mind.

The room stretched into infinity, in the black something moved, glistening, shining red in the glow. He saw Juliana, as lithe and quiet as a cat, the firelight on her naked body; he smelled the scent of the oil that anointed her, saw the flowers of the herbs in her hair.

A fragment of wood caught in the renewed heat, in the light it cast he saw a woman by the wall, her arms outstretched, yellow ribbon pinning them. She was naked. The flame shone on her white teeth, lit her body. Juliana was stopped in the darkness, as a cat, then she padded forward.

On the stone wall Connell could see them. Their mouths met, and he could see Juliana's hands moving upon her, slippery with the holy oil, saw her travel down over her body to kneel between her thighs.

The yellow ribbons fell away from the wall and she stood still as the woman's mouth moved over her.

The eucharist roared in his veins, its power filled his skull. On the wall he stood pinned, his arms in the shape of a cross. He felt the soft hands of the women as they pulled aside his white silken robes. They knelt, either side of him, accepting communion, and then they stood, one and then the next, to become one with God.

The sunlight pierced his eyelids and he woke on the rug. He sat up, stiff and chill. In the grate the ash was cold and grey. He was naked, he pulled a dressing gown from its hook on the door to cover himself. In the air hung the faint tang of forgotten herbs. He reached out to open the window, and clean and cold air flowed into the room. He turned, going towards the kitchen to make coffee. On the floor lay strands of yellow ribbon, like the fallen petals of a flower, it shone from the iron hooks on the wall.

Connell pulled the folds of his dressing gown about him and stood by his Aga as he waited for it to boil the water for his coffee. As he stood in the warmth radiating out from his oven he peered out of the window. Yellow daffodils were showing in his garden. He wondered if they were wild, or if they had been planted there by previous owners.

The red kettle began a wavering note that strengthened into a full-throated howl. A round-bellied coffee pot sat waiting, and he poured the water over the grounds, sniffing the vapour before he put on the lid. He left it to brew next to the Sunday paper, sitting fat and folded on the table. He liked his coffee strong. Through the glass he could hear the pealing of the church bells, calling people to prayer. The glass vibrated softly, as if to a car engine. He poured milk into his mug.

His own house bell jangled, hanging on its metal strap by the front door. He hesitated, looking longingly at his coffee. He wasn't expecting anyone. Then he shrugged, and went to the door.

A lean, middle-aged man was standing there. He wore a grey herringbone coat that he had buttoned up against the cold. Dark, intense eyes looked at Connell from out of a seamed face. A Rover hire car stood parked in the lane behind him.

'Dr Connell?'

He was American.

'That's me.'

'My name's Fox.' He put out his hand to be shaken, smiling in an American manner. His teeth were very white, and square.

'Stanton T. Fox,' he said. 'I believe you are in possession of some religious scrolls of great antiquity.'

Connell put his hands in his dressing gown pockets.

'I am surrounded by ancient documents, Mr Fox,' he said. 'That's what I do.'

'I am referring to specific documents,' Fox said, smiling relentlessly. 'Liturgy and gospels, history and war plans, of an early Christian cult, all part of a new hoard, unseen by almost any except yourself? Am I right?'

'Are you a journalist, Mr Fox?'

'I? No, of course not.'

He sounded slightly shocked.

'I am talking to some carefully selected institutions of great academic standing about some ancient documents, yes,' Connell conceded.

'I know,' said Fox, 'and I want to look at them too.'

'My world is a fairly small one,' Connell said mildly, 'I know most people in it. I don't know you. What are your qualifications for looking at ancient Coptic documents, Mr Fox?'

Fox reached into his coat and drew out a leather wallet. He opened it and took a small slab of new one hundred dollar bills. He sectioned out some like a thick ice-cream wafer and held them out.

'Will that do for a start?' he enquired.

Connell stared at him and the money non-plussed, and Fox smiled disarmingly.

'Look, Dr Connell, this is yours to keep whether you let me see any documents or not. Will it get me across your doorstep so we can talk in the warm? And is that coffee I smell? I've driven quite a ways to see you this morning.'

'Of course,' said Connell, stepping back, his natural courtesy taking over. Fox held out the money, still smiling, and only when Connell had taken it did he step inside. He rubbed his hands together.

'This sure is a nice house you have,' he said politely. Connell took down another mug from his dresser, stuffing the money in his pocket.

'Milk and sugar?'

'Just milk,' said Fox.

Connell poured the coffee and they sat down at his wooden kitchen table.

'How did you get to hear about these documents, Mr Fox?' he enquired.

'A friend of mine at Yale told me the news,' the American said promptly.

'Jack Halloran? Why should he do that?'

'He knows I'm interested in that kind of thing,' Fox replied enigmatically.

'Who are you, that you're interested?'

'It isn't that way about,' said Fox. 'Just take it that I'm interested. Who am I? I'm a businessman. I'm very rich. I've made a fortune in the oil and gas business. I have interests in Alaska and the Gulf, I own rigs in Kazakhstan and in the sea off Texas.'

Connell nodded politely.

'Do you believe in God, Dr Connell?' Fox said suddenly.

'I don't think so, no,' Connell said carefully.

'I do,' Fox said intensely. 'I believe that around two thousand years ago God revealed himself to various peoples in what we now call the Middle East in ways that he has not done since. The documents that are now surfacing from such parts of it as the Dead Sea are of quite unique value in helping us understand his wishes.'

'They thought that too,' Connell commented absently, sipping his tea.

'Who did?' Fox demanded.

'Lots of them,' said Connell, 'all you really needed then to found your own cult was a belief that you had a direct line to the Almighty.'

'You're talking about someone specific,' Fox said acutely, staring intently at the academic. 'Someone in these scrolls you have.'

Connell shrugged.

'I might be.'

Fox sat back, making himself relax. He brought out his professional smile.

'Does my money get me a look at anything?' he asked.

'Do you read Coptic?'

'I can read Coptic,' Fox said quietly. Connell felt a sudden stab of unease. Fox was looking at him with dark shining eyes.

'All right then,' said Connell. 'How about a most interesting discussion between Pope Fabian and the greatest Christian religious thinker of the day, Origen? About A.D. 236 by my reckoning.'

'That would be very interesting indeed,' Fox said quietly.

'They're deciding what's to be allowed in the Bible,' said Connell and Fox's eyes glinted strangely.

'Shall I fill you in on the background?'

'Please,' said Fox. He smiled sincerely. 'I always enjoy listening to an expert, on any subject.'

'All right, then,' said Connell. He poured more coffee and sat back down.

'236 Anno Domini, the year of our Lord. Zaphyrinus is dead. His successor Callistus was one tough egg. He survived slavery, the Sardinian mines and the vicious political infighting of his rival, Hippolytus to take his place. Sin was at the bottom of it. Hippolytus and Tertullian had both agreed that the Church was the Bride of Christ, having neither spot nor wringle, and was the dwelling place of the Holy Spirit and the representative of the martyrs. It could not therefore by definition sustain the presence of the impure, the adulterer and all other demon-inspired sinners – *non communicandum operibus tenebrarum*, it was as simple as that.

'Doubtless through a better understanding of the true nature of sin, the former convict and future Pope Callistus disagreed with them, putting forward the notion that spiritual gifts were to be canalised through the ordered ministry of the Church, which was held together by a sacramental communion stronger than the defects of individual members. Through the workings of the representatives of God on earth, his bishops, it was therefore possible for sinners to be cleansed through penitence, and be readmitted to the body of the Church. Even the ark of Noah, he pointed out, contained both clean and unclean beasts. While certain of which variety Callistus belonged to, Hippolytus and Tertullian lost the day. They survived into old age, Tertullian the leader of his own minute band of followers, far, far out in the sectarian wilderness, holding discussions with God, and Hippolytus on Sardinia, banished together with his enemy Pontianus, the previous Pope, by the Emperor Maximin to have interesting theological discussions with each other as they coughed to death in its horrid and unhealthy climate. Although a barbarian, Maximin had a sense of humour.

'Callistus died in a riot, and the man in the Papal chair in 236 was Fabian. It was held that if a rich man or a lawyer or an official was offered a bishopric he should not be ordained unless he had previously acted as reader deacon or priest, and had risen to the highest rank by progressive promotion.

Ordination was to be conferred on those whose whole life had been under review for a long period, and whose worth had been proved.

'This was especially the view of Hippolytus and Tertullian, who recognised that the more powerful and rich the Church became, the more unscrupulous men might wish to get their hands upon Christ's bride and her dowry. The news that Pope Fabian had been a layman before his election to the see presumably came as no surprise to them in their different exiles. Fabian is an early example of the appalling Popes of the middle ages, the Borgias and so on. It didn't take long for the Church of Rome to become corrupt.'

Fox's eyes glinted from under his brows, but he said nothing, and Connell continued.

'Fabian is smart, however. In his position, it was essential he acquired a thorough working knowledge of the strong issues confronting his Church, which was why, in the text we have, we find him sitting surrounded by the odour of ancient sweat, with the man who had invented a new science, biblical theology.

'Origen's whole life was religion. Its rigours he appreciated when his father was taken out and roasted in the persecution of Severus, its demands he obeyed; reading in the Gospel of Matthew that there are some who have made themselves eunuchs for the Kingdom of Heaven's sake, he promptly fetched a razor and performed the necessary surgery. He slept on the floor, ate no meat, drank no wine and believed it unnecessary to own any shoes or more than one coat, which was the one he had on as he sat in Pope Fabian's room. He was also the greatest theologian of his age.'

Connell got up and went to the dresser, opening one of its drawers. He took out some photographic sheets, and a typescript, passing them to Fox.

'The photos are the original Coptic. The typescript is my translation.'

Fox took them, passing the script back to him.

'I prefer to read the original.' he said politely, if pointedly.

'By all means,' said Connell. 'I'll go and get dressed, while you get on with it then.'

He went out of the kitchen, and Fox began to read.

From his window the Pope could see the wedding party, hear the music play gaily. The bride was seated at the table with her new husband, yellow and red and green streamers blew in the breeze. When she got up to dance his eyes followed her appreciatively, she was young and well-formed. He became aware of a bleak and chill gaze upon him and brought his attention back to the matter at hand.

'The Eastern bishops will be here,' he said. 'We shall have another wrangle as to the true nature of the canon.'

'Paul has been damaged' said Origen, 'because of Marcion's championship. It appears likely that he can be restored by attributing to him the epistles they call "pastoral". The letters to Timothy and Titus are clearly not Pauline, but the issues they confront are so relevant to the needs of the church today they will almost certainly be included. They were written to counter the false teaching of those who peddle "myth and endless genealogies" – which you will find useful in suppressing any Gnostic attempts to foist their scripture upon us, as you will Timothy's injunction against godless chatter and contradictions of what is falsely called knowledge. You may like to use the condemnation of ungodly practices such as the love of money and argument.'

They were laughing, down there in the garden, Fabian could hear the clapping of their hands as the bride and groom

danced for their guests, he risked a glance out to appreciate
the celebration. From where he was he could see the breasts
of the bride in her low-cut wedding dress. He found it a
pleasing sight. Origen frowned at him.

'The epistle to the Hebrews is not Pauline, but even so is a
great work, one written by a learned man. It is popular with
those in the east, not least because it offers those about to
suffer persecution and martyrdom confidence in the certainty
of salvation through Jesus. The easterners will want you to
accept it, but that will probably be the work of one of your
successors. Equally, you will want them to accept Revelation,
which they are uncertain about to say the least. It may be
possible to get it in by attributing it to one of the four Apostles.
We need to, for it is a most powerful and stirring exhortation
to all Christians to withstand persecution and embrace martyrdom in the certain knowledge of the Lord's revenge upon
one's oppressors. We live in wondrous times – so great is
the harvest of the people gathered in and collected into the
threshing floors of God, which are the churches, that there
are not the labourers to reap in the harvest. But let us not
forget that such a harvest is coming to the notice of those who
rule on earth.'

A shudder ran through his emaciated frame.

'Bring wild beasts, bring crosses, bring fire, bring tortures.
I know that as soon as I die, I come forth from the body, I
rest with Christ. Therefore let us struggle, therefore let us
wrestle, let us groan at being in the body. Bring beasts, and
let us be set free from it, and change our body to one more
spiritual.'

The wedding feast was in full swing. The bride and groom
were together again, they linked their arms and drank a toast
to their happiness, and fed each other tasty morsels from their
plates. Watching them Fabian felt the urge to celebrate with

his mistress. But first the business at hand. He waited as Origen returned from his vision. What they were discussing was more than theoretical theology. Philosophy and martyrdom had to exist in the same soul, where they fought each other.

Origen returned to his subject as though the martyr within him had not momentarily slipped the grasp of its wrestling partner.

'John is the Gospel you may still have trouble with, but it is also the most important. There are still some uncertain whether it should be included in the canon. The problem with John is firstly that it is so different to Mark, Matthew and Luke, and secondly that it has been much used and favoured by heretics such as the Montanists and Valentinians. The Gnostics use John, and claim him for themselves. However, he is ours.'

'Who wrote John?' asked Fabian.

'We don't know. Someone, or possibly a group of scholars. They had some sources independent of the other three Gospels – two of the disciples had previously been disciples of John the Baptist, and the early ministry of Jesus overlapped that of the Baptist.'

Origen paused, and ran a hand through the grey stubble of his hair.

'How I wish we knew!' he exclaimed. 'So much hidden in the mist of time.'

'You were talking of the authors.'

'Yes. He or they display some Hellenistic ingredients – they interpret their Jesus in the form of a redeeming and revealing figure who descends and ascends, which is one of the reasons the Gnostics find the Gospel attractive – the Valentinians and the Children of God, for example. It fits with their own concept of divine sparks of light falling to earth, a demonic world of darkness. To redeem and restore these lost sparks to

Paradise their God sent knowledge, in the form of a redeemer, that they call Jesus. Having shown them the way home, the redeemer ascends to Paradise, leaving the sparks of light to follow. It is not dissimilar to John. However, John puts forward the view that the world is not evil but divinely created and redeemable, and that redemption is open to all in the world, only provided they believe in Jesus.

'More than Hellenistic, it is strongly Jewish. Paul deals with the gentiles, John does not mention them, apart from Pilate and the Romans. And Greeks, fleetingly. John is complex, it is both Jewish and anti-Jewish, contains Gnosticism and anti-Gnosticism, apocalyptic and non-apocalyptic material. Written in Greek, and for Greeks. I can't tell you who wrote it. But it must be included in the canon.'

'Why John, and not any of the Gnostic books – the *Gospel of Truth*, *Gospels of Thomas and Philip* and so forth. Are they not authentic?'

Origen paused. The day was hot, below the wedding guests were in the shade. In the room the smell of sweat was wrinkling Fabian's nose, but the theologian seemed unaware. He would be, thought the Pope. He has lived in his own reek for decades.

'Some of the Gnostic books are ridiculous. Some are not. The ones you mention are all written by people who have come across sources that knew Jesus. But this is not the point at issue. The Gnostics claim themselves to be a "spiritual" Church, and one furthermore that is an élite. We do not. We are creating a *universal* Church, which is why we call it catholic. It is open to all, no matter what class, race or culture; rich or poor, educated or illiterate. Our only demand is that those who enter must submit to our system of organisation. This is made up of three elements – doctrine, ritual and the clerical hierarchy – and anyone who challenges even one of those elements may not remain within the Church. The Gnostics challenge all three, which is why we rigorously suppress any of their attempts to bring any of their scriptures within the canon.'

'So why John?' Fabian said softly.

'Let me quote: Thomas said to him, "Lord, we do not know where you are going; how can we know the way?" Jesus said to him, "I am the way, the truth and the life; no one comes to the Father but by me." Only through Jesus may one find God. Only through the Catholic Church may one find Jesus. Only through the bishop may you enter the church.

'I do not, as you probably know, have a high opinion of many bishops and clergy as individuals. A bishop should be blameless, meek and chaste, merciful and adept at making peace. He should be learned and lettered, and a man of keen discernment. His powers are awesome, for while kings reign only over their subjects' bodies, bishops, who rule in the place of God, reign both over the subjects' bodies and souls. They may both bind and loose, they have the power to invoke the wrath to come and the very fires of Hell.'

Origen's face pursed in disapproval of all those who fell below his divine standards, of which, it was clear, there were many.

'Few attain this ideal,' he said disapprovingly. 'Do not most terrify people and make themselves inaccessible, especially to the poor. To those who come and ask them to do something for them they behave as no tyrant even would.'

He looked directly at the man who was closest to God in Rome.

'Have you read Numbers? I often give offence to certain people in discussing this text.'

'Bishops such as myself?' Fabian said wryly.

' "And the Lord said to Moses, Take all the chiefs of the people and expose them to the Lord over against the sun, and the anger of the Lord shall be turned from Israel." '

The band struck up a lusty tune, Fabian could hear the cheering as bride and groom were encouraged on their way. He really must see Marcella, he thought. Just as soon as he had attended to business.'

'Christians are commanded to love their bishop as a father: fear him as a king: honour him as God. In his turn, the bishop would do very well to remember that he shall, on that day, be accountable to God for both his own sins and those of his Church.'

'I shall bear that most earnestly in mind. The personalities of certain bishops aside, the order itself is different.'

'Exalted in its dignity and power!'

'In the days of the saintly Paul, did not the Holy Spirit move among all? "If you are led by the Spirit you are not under the law.".'

'The Holy Spirit still moves among us, and may be seen in those who witness. However, all are under the law of the Church.'

'Which is interpreted by the bishops.'

'Through the bishops all ecclesiastical measures whatsoever must be carried out.'

'May I quote? "And God has appointed in the Church first Apostles, the prophets, third teachers, then workers of miracles, then healers, helpers, administrators speakers in various kinds of tongues." That was what Paul said.'

'Precisely. He meant bishops. Without the office of bishop there is no Church; without the Church, there is no salvation, only error and darkness. He who decides who may enter the Church is the bishop, for a man may not be saved by individual contact with God, only through the office of the bishop.'

'It is possible to read Paul and believe him to be preaching individual freedom, based on the power of Christian truth.'

'The great champion of Paul was the heretic Marcion, whom

the martyred Polycarp, mentor of the great Irenaeus, met but once. Marcion asked him if he knew him, and Polycarp affirmed he did. "I see the first-born of Satan," he replied. The division of Christians into laity and clergy was established by Jesus Christ and the apostles. With the exception of those who bear witness and are sealed, the Holy Spirit moves only within the bishops, who are designated by God to rule over the members of their Church. Has not God prepared the way? Did he not allow Augustus to unify the Empire in order that a framework might be set up for the spread of the Gospel? God prepared the nations for his teaching that they might be under one Roman Emperor, undisturbed by wars caused by the large number of kingdoms. Polyarchy has given way to monarchy, the babel of tongues to a single language. In consequence, has not the teaching of Jesus reached the ends of the earth? We are close to a world united in the service of Christ.'

'One Emperor, one Empire,' said Origen, 'one God, one Church, one Bishop.'

In the garden, the wedding party were gathering to see the bride and her husband on their way. The bunting and flags flew gaily in the sun, the band was playing. Merry laughter came on the breeze. The bride bent in the carriage to throw her bouquet, and Fabian caught a glimpse of her breasts, round and smooth. He felt pleasure at the sight, his fingers twitched in anticipation.

'*Idolators*,' Origen spat, rising and staring down. 'We shall put an end to their blasphemy, on that glorious day.'

Connell came in, dressed in jeans and a woollen plaid shirt. Fox was looking out of the window in thought, the photographs of the text still in his hand. Connell had counted the money, Fox had paid just over two thousand dollars simply to read it.

'Interesting?' Connell enquired.

'Extremely,' said Fox 'in many ways. Not the least of which is: Why was such a piece in the hands of an alternative cult?'

'Very good,' Connell looked at the other man in admiration. 'It's an intelligence report, isn't it, gathered by one of their spies.'

Fox stared steadily at Connell with his unblinking black eyes.

'Are they at war with the Catholic Church?'

'They see it that way,' Connell said defensively. He was aware of sudden electricity. The American made him nervous.

'Were they wrong?' he blurted. 'Where are they now? Where are all the alternative cults? Gone, Mr Fox. The Catholics saw to that, once they had the enforcement agencies of the Empire at their disposal. It was a nasty business.'

Fox was staring back at the texts.

'Great men,' he murmured.

'Origen got what he wanted,' Connell said, rather callously. 'The Emperor Decius brought wild beasts, crosses, fire and tortures for him, all right. Fabian too, though I expect he was less enthusiastic about it. They made a spectacle of him so that the others would get the message, and they did. The Christians sacrificed to the pagan gods in droves. Mass apostasy. Decius got what he wanted, which was public loyalty, but it didn't halt the slide in the Empire's fortunes. His neither, he died the next year. The Church was in a hell of a state about it, of course. They needed martyrs, not their people queuing up at the pagan altars, downing sacrificial meat like wolves.'

Fox gathered up the photographic sheets like giant playing cards, tapping them into a neat pile before placing them in front of him on the table.

'I'm interested in reading some more,' he said.

'You'd better tell me why,' Connell said carefully. 'You paid me money to read that, and maybe I shouldn't have taken it without asking you more questions than I did. This hoard of ancient texts is the most exciting to appear in my lifetime. If you've been told of its existence by someone at Yale then you must know that too. What *I* need to know is why you are interested.'

'I believe in God,' Fox said flatly, his voice brooking no contradiction. 'I believe that God puts men on earth for his own purpose. He had given me the gifts that have made me a wealthy man. He expects me to use that money to further his will. I believe what you say, that this hoard is the most valuable to appear – perhaps *ever*, let alone in your or my lifetime. You are looking for a foundation to house the collection. You seek an appointment to be the man who collates, translates, interprets and edits these texts. You are seeking a wealthy institution to fund you. Very well. I will provide all of these things for you.'

'You?' Connell found his eyes bulging slightly.

'I told you. I am a wealthy man.'

'You do understand, I do not own or have possession of the texts. They are in the hands of another party. They are, it is true, for sale, and I come with them as the man, as you so rightly say, who will produce the definitive edition and commentary. But are you aware of the kind of value such texts would have? A simple letter ascribed to Simeon bar Kochba, who claimed to be the Star of Israel, but who wasn't, can fetch a hundred thousand dollars or more. These texts are incredibly valuable.'

Fox gave a wintry smile.

'Do you know how much you are worth, Dr Connell?'

'Roughly speaking, yes.'

'I don't. When you're quite rich, you use the money as a

means of keeping score. When you're very rich, you lose count. I lost count some time ago.'

Fox reached out and drank some lukewarm coffee.

'When you're very rich you do things like buy an entire American Football team. Or in my case, you listen to God, and you ask him what he wants you to do. And God wants me to set up a foundation for these texts.'

Connell found the hair rising on the back of his neck. He could feel it, stiff against his collar.

'If they are what you claim,' Fox added.

'They are,' said Connell. 'They are.'

'I'd like to read some more,' Fox repeated. 'So that I can be sure before I put anything in motion.'

He reached inside his coat, that he had now undone, and took out the rest of his slab of money, placing it near Connell on the table.

'That's ten thousand dollars in all,' he said unemotionally. 'Let me see something to do with the sect themselves. What are they called, do they have a name?'

'Yes. The Children. The Children of Jeshua.'

'Jeshua. As in Jesus.'

'Yes,' Connell said levelly. 'They believe themselves to be descended from Jesus.'

He was rewarded by the sight of eyebrows rising in Fox's impassive face.

'And Mary of Magdala,' he added, for good measure.

'Well,' said Fox softly, 'I think I should enjoy this.'

Connell went out, and came back with a thick pad of photographs.

'These are the pages of a particular codex,' he said. 'They are in order. As you noticed from the first text, the Children see themselves as at war with the Catholic Church. This is from almost the same time, 237 A.D.'

He handed Fox the photographs, picking up the wad of dollars, and Fox began to read.

16

Smyrna, A.D. March 237

Goats moved on the hillside. Dry root, rough bark, curled leaf had been their lot through the winter, now they foraged at ease on rocky slopes that were brushed with the green of returning life. By the little stream that tumbled tinkling and icy from the snow-capped mountain, Aristides the shepherd sat watchfully. Others than goats were hungry come springtime in that part of the world, predators four-footed and two-hungered for the taste of meat.

The two dogs squatting nearby were protection against that. Rough-haired and sharp-toothed, tall at the shoulder and fleet, they were capable of driving away the worst, whether wolf or brigand. As the shepherd sat in the new sunshine he heard a low rumble deep in the chest of one of the dogs, looked quickly up and saw it lift one lip, showing his long jaw of white teeth. Aristides followed his gaze and saw the running man.

He was following the line of the river in the valley below. As Aristides watched he darted up the hill where a patch of dry scrub was burgeoning green. He bent swiftly, as though thrusting something in amongst the thorns, and then leapt back down to the path.

Almost no sooner had he done so than the hackles on the dogs beside Aristides rose, and they growled anew. The reason for the running man's flight became clear. Two more men were pursuing him. Metal flashed in the sun from their hands.

Cypress and olive extended long bony roots towards the water down there, the rock was cracked, the surface rough. Aristides saw the man tumble headlong. He was up again, nimble as one of the goats, but moving unevenly, one leg halt. He turned as his enemies came up, bending to fling a rock, but then they were on him in a flurry. A man screamed, Aristides lost sight of them as they pulled him under the trees.

The dogs were up, alert eyes questioning him. He reached in his leather sack with its goats' cheese and hard bread, and took out his sling and smooth, heavy pebbles from the river bed, that would fly true. Very quietly, the shepherd and his two hounds slipped down the slope.

The dogs cast anxious glances at their master, hearing the cries of violence and distress. Aristides moved very cautiously through the scrub, these were dangerous times.

They had stripped him of his clothes; his blood spattered the ground. One held him down, the other raised a rock high before slamming it into the man's groin. He screamed, a dreadful, gargling scream, and the one that held him shrieked a question that the shepherd could not make out.

The dogs were trained to know who was good and who was bad, who would steal sheep and who were friends. Without a sound, they suddenly bounded forward. The one that was working on the man saw them coming, he got up and tried to run. The dogs were upon him, they dragged him down and his terrified howl was cut short as they ripped his throat out. The second attacker leaped for the safety of a tree and crouched in its branches like an animal as they bayed beneath him, gore foaming about their muzzles.

Aristides looked down at the twisted figure of the tortured man on the ground, swollen and bloody, moaning and semi-conscious. He walked over to the dead one. Something gleamed in amidst the blood, he bent down and drew a chain from about his neck and stood looking at it, before turning to the tree.

'Get your dogs off!' the man yelled. 'Get them away.'

Aristides held up the bloody chain, with its silver emblem.

'You are men of the fish,' he said. 'What does this man have that you do this to him?'

'He had things we want. Things he should not have,' the man snarled.

'Things that men of the fish hate cannot be wholly wrong,' said Aristides. 'Men of the fish hate the gods of the air and water, of the green places and the flowers of spring. So this man you have hurt must like good things.'

Very carefully he fitted a stone into his sling as the man looked balefully down at him. The whistle and the thud of the stone landing on target were almost as one. The man fell to the ground and the dogs tore him apart.

They were close to the river. Aristides pulled the bodies over, throwing them into the thundering, grey melt water. Briefly they bobbed and tumbled, and were out of sight.

Nearby was the bush. He went up to it and reaching under, found a leather sack. Inside he found parchment scrolls and books. Shrugging, he slung the bag over his shoulder and returned to the man. His blood was pooled about him, his breath rasped in his throat, he was not conscious, only moaning in pain as Aristides picked him up. Gripped in his hand were flowers and green stems, he had been gathering herbs.

The shepherd put him over his shoulder as he would a sheep, and carried him away to his nearby stone bothy. He lay him down on his simple bed, dressing his wounds as well he might. Then he went back to guarding his sheep, for these were dangerous times.

At nightfall, he and the dogs drove them into the pen. Inside the little hut he lit his fire and the man stirred.

'Who are you?' he whispered.

'I am Aristides the shepherd. I have rescued you from those who wished you harm, those of the fish.'

'Servants of Satan . . .' the man said weakly. He pawed about him, suddenly fearful, and Aristides brought the sack from under the bed.

'Is this what you desire? I was on the hill, I saw you hide it.'

The man's hand closed gratefully on it and then he stiffened again in alarm.

'My wife . . . Ruth is ill with the fever, my daughter Mary is with her . . . I came to gather herbs . . .'

'Where is she?'

'She lies in the town, where we were waiting for a ship. I must go to her . . .'

He attempted to move, and sank back with a cry of pain.

'You will not be able to walk, not for some days,' said Aristides, 'and the nights are not safe. Tomorrow I will go to the town for you.'

Before he went into the basilica, Melito the bishop stood for some moments outside in the chill morning light, solemn and authoritative in his robes, his deacon, Felix, at his side. His eyes flicked down the long street, but saw not what he waited for.

'You had better get on,' he said shortly, and the deacon nodded in agreement, hurrying away into the town.

The worshippers were going in. As they came up the path there was one there awaiting them, all clad in rough sackcloth and clinging ashes, lying in the dirt, holding up grimed hands in supplication, clasping at their knees as they went by, his voice wailing for forgiveness, licking the very ground they trod upon in self-abasement.

A lovely young woman came up the path to enter and the howling and grovelling increased, the tears cutting lines in the filthy ash, the voice sobbing for her prayers. She skirted him, looking ahead of her, and Melito saw the gleam of the youth's eyes as his gaze followed her, knew the unappeased lust still in his heart, and he himself went forward.

'There is but one way,' he said, knowing that the boy Colluthus heard him, though he forced his head down in the dirt and ash at the presence of his bishop.

'Embrace Jesus the Lord,' he commanded, 'and all the rewards of earth and Heaven will be yours. No longer will you be low amongst the low, despised by all. No longer will Thymele draw her skirts from you. You shall rise up amongst the angels, shall you only embrace Jesus.'

Then he went in, leaving the sinner in his filth outside. The basilica was chill, despite the braziers scattered under the stuccoed vaults and arches. The baptismal water flew like chips of ice over the heads of the two kneeling at the altar, but they did not shiver. They were filled with the heat of the Holy Spirit, and by the words of the bishop.

'You are virgins,' said Melito, 'and your purity brings you sixty times the benefit of an ordinary Christian. Not for you the long delays after death, the millennia in which you cool and are refreshed, yet submit to correction and discipline in the bosom of Abraham. No, pure as you are with the water of the Holy Spirit upon you, were you to die today you would speed straight to Christ and the Father.'

Melito, in his fine robes of office, smiled wisely over his congregation, gathered together for the baptism of Cassian and his sister in Christ, Felicita.

'Would that we could all retain that purity till we die! Yet

Satan is all about us, working with his wiles to tempt the believer into sin. Skilful are his arts, his wares shine like the apple of Eve. Few are those that can remain clean of sin. Sackcloth and ashes must we don, on our bellies must we go, grovelling in the dirt as did the serpent, begging our brothers and sisters for forgiveness, kissing their feet, licking the dirt from their boots.'

The congregation listened glumly, fully aware of the power of the devil's temptations all about them, and the desires that swirled within. Payment by penance was both painful and degrading. Few wished to join Colluthus in his dismal misery outside. They were men and women of some substance and standing, their skins more used to sweet rosewater and silk than clinker and hemp.

'Only one Christian exceeds the power and virtue of the virgin. That is he or she who bears witness to Christ. From the moment of their confession they glow with the Holy Spirit. As they await in prison their bonds are but spiritual pearls. Higher than all they stand, higher than the mightiest bishop in their powers. Bind they may, and loose, and all are subject to their word. When the glorious moment comes and they are led out, ready for the fray, their faces gaze steadfastly towards Jesus. When Satan plies them with his torch they feel not the flame. In a wonderful analgesic state they are not harmed; they feel no pain, nor does their flesh scorch. It is as the baking of bread, as the Holy Spirit rises up within them. Martyrs become breathing, heavenly things, who delight the Lord with the sublime, the great, the acceptable spectacle. When the claws of the beasts rip open their flesh their flowing blood quenches the furnaces of Hell with its glorious gore. God collects it in his golden bowl for his wine. When the savage jaws of the animals crush their bones they do but grind that temporal flesh into the pure bread of Christ, and he takes it to be his eucharist.

'The Holy Spirit moving within them like the finest wine, as they depart this life they see the world ahead of them, the road to Paradise lying through a country of lovely meadows, clothed in the lush foliage of green woods, shaded by tall cypresses and pine trees.'

The eyes of Felicita sparkled as she knelt at prayer, her hands clasped, her pure white gown clothing her young body. The fine muslin over her breast tapped with excitement as she listened to the great holy man, and her lips were parted.

'Within the grove is a hollow beneath a pure blue sky and there abounding are the teeming veins of a crystal clear fountain. There the stream drinks the martyrs' blessed blood, there Christ awaits to take them to Paradise.'

Felicita sighed.

'That is the route followed by the blessed few, those who have trained hard in the school of Christ and fear not to take up his burden and follow him. Few, it must be said, are they, for that schooling is rigorous and long.'

'True, true,' they murmured.

'For most, tainted with sin as we are, we fear the sword's bitter edge, the torch's fiery tongue.'

They did, Melito knew it.

'For us, the long years of waiting with Abraham.'

Not a bad fellow, they felt.

'But we must all aspire to that divine state of witness, hope and pray that one day we too will find that strength to join the holy martyrs as they sit, serried rank upon serried rank, with Jesus, their blood proven the sure key to Paradise.'

They prayed that they would.

The light coming through the little window lit up her mother's skin, as dry as parchment, dragged taut over the bones. The fever that had so reduced her was still hot, Mary felt it in her fingertips as she reached out to close her eyes. She put down the damp cloth that she had been using to cool her, she would not need it any longer.

Her father had taken the sack of scrolls and codexes and the robe of glory with him, as was his warrant. The last priest of the Children, his was the task to keep them safe until the Church of Jeshua could be built anew. She glanced up at the light and felt a renewed stab of fear, he should have been back the previous day.

The rites had to be done. Her mother's soul had to be helped on its way to Paradise. She opened the sacred pouch and put the dried herbs on a dish. There was tinder, she lit a little blaze in the brick cooking grate that stood under the window. Softly chanting the prayers that released the soul of her mother, held down in the world Satan had made, she cast the herbs on to the hot coals and sudden, vivid sparks shot through the silver smoke.

It was like a knife of perfume, it thrust its fabulous fingers up into her head, and the sparks, red, green, purple and gold, flew from the smoke, blazing in the sunlight as they rose higher and higher into the sky, taking the soul of her mother to the arms of the Father, to the bosom of the Great Mother of all, her fighting done, her part in the eternal war finished.

The shining smoke wrapped itself around her, she was alone, it released her tears and they flowed down her cheeks like jewels.

Somebody was at her elbow. A man, a small man in a grey tunic.

'Your father,' he said, 'he says to come.'

She was dazed now, now that it was over. But the rites were

done, the thin body on the bed was no more her mother, simply the husk of the soul, and the soul was safe from Satan, guarded from his icy grasp. She could leave now, she suffered herself to be led outside.

'In the square,' the man insisted. 'That is where he will meet you.'

She went as he directed, walking as one asleep, and stood where he said, by the great colonnades, her eyes glazed. Soon she would have to put on the mantle of the priestess, as her mother had done, soon she would inherit the offices of all who had passed before her. The rites would have to be done, her father would help her as the souls of the ones who had gone before came into hers. Now the herbs of departing helped her as she prepared to make the transition. Unaware of who or where she was, she stood waiting for him. The small man, Deacon Felix, stood close by her, watching with rodent eyes down the street, to where the basilica stood.

Melito stood at the door of the basilica and watched the two flying white figures running down the paved street to the great colonnaded city square, shaking his head in wonder.

'They are touched by the Holy Spirit,' he said, marvelling at the presence of God moving among them, and all in the congregation cried out for joy, for the miracle had happened again, as it had the year before. Then they all followed cautiously after, to the courthouse where Lucius had been denounced by Jacob the merchant, to whom he owed money.

They were in time to see Lucius being brought out and led towards the temple of the two goddesses Nemesis, where the *neokoros* senior warden was waiting and the altar fire lit, for he had denied any connection with the atheists known as Christians. Pointing to the known avarice and stone heart of

Jacob the Jew, and the piffling sum of money owed, which he would repay once the good weather brought the harvest, he in turn accused his accuser of wishing to appropriate all his goods, having falsely accused him of this crime.

Seeing Lucius ready to partake of the consecrated meat the crowd which craned about the *kibotia* booths of the shop-keepers and peered down from the *bathra* steps, agreed that it was too bad, for were not their own stomachs only half-filled, with the grain store almost empty and the harvest not yet due?

A slim figure in white, a circlet of spring flowers about her head, slipped through the crowd to the public altar, followed by her young male companion.

Lucius knelt at the altar where fresh goat meat sizzled upon the griddle, its fragrant smoke making the mouths of the hungry crowd water. Let Jacob accuse us, and we too can sacrifice, they joked. The great statues of the goddesses looked down, wreathed in the smoke and incense curling about in the fresh sea air.

'*Demons sit upon that meat!*'

The clear young voice rang throughout the square. Lucius turned in alarm. Felicita pointed her finger in dire warning.

'Do you not see them Lucius? About you they swarm, within the very smoke, seeking to gain entrance to your body and take up abode in your soul.'

The magistrate turned in annoyance at having his cere-monies disrupted, and the crowd buzzed, sensing something interesting and exciting about to happen.

'Who are you?' he demanded.

'I am a Christian,' she said proudly.

'And I,' shouted Cassian at her side.

There was a sudden explosion through the crowd and a filthy creature, encrusted with dirt and ash, clad in rotting sacking, threw people aside as he ran towards the altar.

'Yes!' yelled Colluthus. 'I too am a Christian.'

The fear in the eyes of Jacob the Jew vanished, and he smiled.

Lucius bowed his head in shame, then stood up.

'It is true,' he said, 'I am a Christian.'

Standing behind Mary, Felix gave her a sudden vicious shove, sending the dazed young girl tumbling amongst them.

'She too!' he shouted, and without thinking, Felicita and the others took a hold of her, claiming her for their own.

Standing back among the pillars of the great colonnades, Melito heard the roar of excitement burst from the crowd, the soldiers running at the magistrate's command, the four figures, two in shining white, heads high, marching proudly away to the jail, and with them, staggering in their midst, a girl, moving as one who was asleep, and he smiled.

The crowd buzzing with interest, began to break up, taking the news about the town. Deacon Felix, standing satisfied by the colannade, saw a lean man staring down the street where they had gone. He recognised him.

'Hoy, you, shepherd,' he called, abruptly.

Aristides turned to look at him with cold eyes.

'Yes?'

'Two of our Church were out on your hills yesterday. I would have word of them. Saw you with them when you were out with your sheep?'

'I saw them.'

'Well?' he said impatiently.

'I saw them kill a man.'

'Ahhh . . .'

Aristides regarded his pleasure.

'You are pleased?'

319

'A disciple of the devil,' he said shortly. 'A stealer of men's souls. They were out on the work of Jesus. Where are they now?'

'The man they threw into the river, with a sack he had.'

Felix's eyes shone.

'The man had a purse of silver. And they said, one to the other, "let us go and spend this money we have taken." They went away along the paths, and I saw them no more.'

Felix pursed his lips in understanding. He knew the men Melito had sent for what they were. He turned abruptly, leaving Aristides, and the shepherd hurried away out of the town, back into the hills where David lay waiting for him.

'Daughter, have pity upon me.'

Leonides held his child's hands and kissed them as he spoke.

'Have pity on your father, if I have loved you more than all your brothers, do not abandon me.'

He was kneeling by her as she stood beneath the dais.

'Think of your brothers, your mother and your aunts, your little nieces and nephews. Think of little Sulpicia, who loves you. Give up your pride!'

He cast a fearful look up at Rufinus, the procurator looking coldly down upon them from his curule chair.

'You will destroy all of us,' he whispered desperately.

'Do as your father urges,' said Rufinus. 'He is wise and you are but a child. Have pity upon his grey head and make sacrifice for the *salus* of the Emperors.'

'I shall not,' Felicita said clearly.

'Why?'

'Because I am a Christian,' she sang out, pride ringing in every syllable, and her father winced, as though in pain.

'So? It is very little to ask,' Rufinus said patiently. He had children of his own, he understood childish obstinacy. 'A mere token act of loyalty.'

'I cannot,' she said certainly, 'for we Christians have discovered an ancient and terrible secret. You ask me to sacrifice to your gods, they that stand behind the powers that you and your Emperor wield. But these are not gods, but demons.'

'Demons?' Rufinus sighed. 'And how did you stumble upon this secret, hidden from us all for so long?'

'It is in the book of Genesis. The patron gods of Rome are none other than the fallen angels, cast out of Heaven at the very beginning of time.'

The procurator's eyes narrowed, and he paid attention to what the young girl was saying. It smacked of more than mere childlike foolishness.

'The sons of God were the angels, they saw that the daughters of men were fair and they took to wife such of them as they chose. They came into the daughters of men, and they bore children to them. These children were demons. When God discovered that the angels he had entrusted to administer the universe had so betrayed their trust he expelled them from Heaven, and they fell to earth. There, still possessed of their divine powers, they joined with their offspring the demons, and enslaved the human race.

'The truth must be told,' said Felicita. 'Since of old these evil demons, effecting apparitions of themselves, both polluted women and corrupted boys, and showed such terrifying visions to people that those who did not use their reason were struck by terror; being carried away by fear, and not knowing that these were demons, they called them gods. Taking as their ally the desire for evil in everyone, the demons became the patrons of powerful and ruthless men, and instituted private and public rites in honour of those who are most powerful.'

Rufinus was an educated man, trained in philosophy and

the law, he did not need to be told who the powerful and ruthless men were, nor what the public and private rites were in aid of.

'And who has pointed this out to you?'

'Jesus Christ,' Felicita said proudly, 'who was sent by God the Father to release his people from the tyranny of the fallen angels and their demons.'

Leonides moaned and bit upon a knuckle to muffle his anguish.

'Arrogant, brutal and licentious are the demons who masquerade as your gods,' she said. 'In the amphitheatre do not the gladiators dress up as Attis and Hercules? Do not Mercury and Pluto, gods of the dead, poke the bodies of the dying with red-hot irons? In the theatre is not lust on public display? Venus couples with Mars, Juno performs unnatural acts with Jupiter, Zeus rapes the young boy, Ganymede. Is Jupiter good? Is he the protector of supplicants, the avenger of wrongs? No, he is unjust, the violator of right and law, the impious, the inhuman, the violent, the seducer, the adulterer, the incestuous.'

Felicita gazed steadfastly above Rufinus's head.

'It is Jesus who is good, Jesus who protects and saves, he who is the avenger of wrongs.'

Refinus had little time for steadfast gazing. Of necessity an interested observer of phsyiognomy he knew that a man could be told by his face, and steadfast gazes simply revealed impudence. And what was more, subversive impudence.

The procurator realised that the child could not have worked out this elaborate framework of justification for herself. However the fact that she was able to produce it at will proved it to be easily digested, attractive, and thus ultimately lethal to the entire Roman Empire. Official propaganda portrayed the Emperors as universal rulers by divine right. These Christians were exposing them as puppet-tyrants, enslaved to demons. Official Rome saw in its persecution of Christians simply the disposal of a few bloody-minded dissidents. The Christians painted them as the unthinking agents of fallen angels, contending against a people allied with the one true god. It was a message easily transmitted and readily received among the hordes of the underprivileged and the have-nots the Empire ruled, and one redolent with menace.

Leonides watched Rufinus fearfully as he made up his mind.

'Sacrifice to the gods,' he urged.

'I am a Christian and will not sacrifice to idols.'

'*Save us all*,' he begged.

Gazing towards the skies, he turned from his daughter, whom had he not been in the grip of such urgent terror he would have smacked, and scrambled up on to the dais, flinging himself at Rufinus's feet.

'She is but a foolish child,' he entreated. 'One who has got into bad company.'

The procurator stared down at him with contempt and loathing.

'And whose child?' he asked. 'Yours.'

He kicked the old man back down the steps.

'Beat him,' he ordered.

The *lictors* stepped forward and the courtroom echoed to the smack of their rods and the gasps of pain.

Rufinus looked down at the young girl who now did not acknowledge his presence.

'*Ad bestias*,' he said curtly, and the watching crowd cheered to see justice done.

The Holy Spirit filled her like a pure wine. She sat in prayer in the dim cell with her hands outspread and felt them catch the radiance of God.

People were gathering outside, in queues in the darkness of the prison tunnels, for God himself had visited the city, there were three there possessed of the Spirit; as Jesus had promised, it accompanied them from the moment of their witness on trial. Death was to seal them, but while they lived they enjoyed miraculous powers.

Raised high above all other Christians, they were brought gifts by their fellows; soft pillows to lie on, fine clothes to wear, wine and the best of food. Felicita abstained; Colluthus and Cassian gladly exchanged their rough prison tunics for silk and accepted the food and wine that was pressed upon them.

'Enjoy yourself,' they urged Felicita.

'Did our Lord enjoy such comforts as these when he awaited his destiny?' she asked.

'We are forgiven all our sins,' said Colluthus, 'for we have confessed, and shall go straight to Paradise.'

Bright-eyed with wine, Cassian smiled beside him, grinning in agreement.

Among those who brought comforts and honours was Thymele, whose aristocratic beauty Colluthus had previously admired but from afar, from half-lowered lids. He drew her down on the cushions with him, pulling at her clothes, and saw her naked.

Witnesses were filled with the Holy Spirit, they enacted God's will.

His fingers felt her body, his mouth tasted her breasts and he mounted her as Felicita prayed, kneeling on the hard cold stone.

When he had finished Thymele got up, drawing her gown about her, and stumbled out through the waiting Christians.

In the darkness she felt other, eager hands upon her, pulling her clothes from her, hands upon her breasts, between her thighs. She felt herself forced down; opening her mouth in protest she found it filled with hard flesh.

They came out of the dark, the four of them, doing up their clothes, and knelt before Colluthus.

'We have sinned,' they said. 'We are adulterers.'

He smiled drunkenly and sprinkled them with wine from his goblet.

'Now you are pure,' he said.

Confessors could bind and loose, they could forgive sin.

A vision came to Felicita, as she had been promised it would. The sun blazed down into the arena. A mighty wrestler awaited her, shiny with oil, his muscles rippling. Casting off her robe she found herself a man, and understood that she and Jesus had become one. Together they threw the wrestler to the ground, and standing with their feet on his neck she knew they had defeated Satan.

The blaze of the arena faded and she returned to the dim cell. Colluthus and Cassian lay on their piled silken cushions amid the remains of a banquet, snoring drunkenly.

A man was kneeling in front of her, bending to kiss her martyr's chains. It was Melito, her bishop.

'Forgive me,' he said softly, 'for I have sinned.'

She placed her hand upon his head.

'Tell the Lord of your sins and they shall be forgiven you.'

'I have broken the commandments that God gave to Moses.'

'Which?'

'You shall not kill.'

He went down the corridor away from the congregation awaiting confession and forgiveness. A feeble light was leaking from the barred window of a little cell. He peered in. It was coming from a simple oil lamp with a single wick. In its glow he could see a young woman. She looked up and he saw savage, glittering eyes. He was startled, Felix had told him she had been dazed.

'Who are you?' she demanded.

'I am Melito, I am Bishop.'

'I am no longer asleep,' she said in a low voice. 'My forebears have come to me. I know you for who you are.'

Despite the door, a *frisson* ran down his spine and he shivered. But then he smiled, for he was Bishop.

'Who am I?' he asked mockingly.

'Satan's slave, leader of the men of fish. And I know who those are, the poor young ones that I hear.'

'Be joyful,' said the bishop, 'they shall receive their crowns. *Semen est sanguis Christianorum.*'

'You told them did you not, how glorious it will be?' she said savagely. 'How in the midst of the fire their faces will glow, how Jesus will join them in their perfect, analgesic state? How they shall but fall gently asleep in the arms of God?'

'God wants them,' Melito said stonily.

'No, *you* want them. You offer them to the heathens here as your yearly sacrifice. Always children, always the little ones who do not know you are Satan's servant.'

'The Holy Spirit often burns brightest in the young.'

'The young will believe what they are told, they are not old enough to know that things are not as they seem, that their bishop hungers for their flesh and bones.'

Melito smiled. 'My sins are forgiven me.'

He allowed the mirth to die away from his face.

'And I know who you are. Scum, spawn of heretics.'

He regarded her closely.

'Your father is dead,' he said suddenly, and savagely, laughing horribly to see the pain stab into her face. 'Yes, we slaughtered him down by the river, we destroyed all the filthy writings he had with him in his sack. Your heresy is no more.'

She looked him bravely in the eyes through the rusty bars.

'There is yet me,' she said. 'I am priestess of the Children, they live in me. We have been but one before, and recovered to do the work of the Father, and the Great Mother, in the land of the devil.'

'No more,' he promised gleefully. 'For tomorrow those in the cells shall win their crowns, they shall fly to the arms of Jesus.'

He felt the stirrings of joy within him, and bent forward to the little window so that she could hear him.

'And you, heresiarch, you shall be with them.'

Aristides looked at David in the light of the fire, saw how his swollen body was stiff and racked with pain.

'You cannot do it,' he said.

'I am a soldier of Jesus,' David said. 'We have ways that we have been taught.'

'And the men of the fish, are they not followers of this Jesus? That is what I have heard.'

'It is what they claim.'

David dragged himself upright on the plank pallet, his face taut with pain.

'They serve Satan,' he said grimly. 'Our God the Father, and our Goddess the Great Mother know this world we live in. We are a part of it, we do not rule it. We gather what we need, we put back what others need. In the sack there, you will find a leather bag.'

Aristides opened it, inside were a multitude of dried seeds, flowers, roots and leaves.

'Take a handful,' David instructed, 'place them in water in

an iron pot upon the fire, and when they have boiled, leave them to cool.'

Aristides smelled the fragrance as it rose from the pot, it felt like clean, icy mountain water in his mind. When it was cool he poured it into a beaker and gave it to the wounded priest.

David sang a song, in a language the shepherd did not know, and drained the beaker. He lay still upon the bed for some minutes longer and then, as though his wounds had never been, he lifted himself up. The herbs that had infused into his drink lined the bottom of the pot, with a flick of his wrist he sent them into the red coals of the fire, and stood, as smoke swirled about him. He took the iron rod that Aristides used when he roasted mutton.

'I am ready,' he said. The smoke stung Aristides's mouth and nose, his eyes watered.

'I shall come with you,' he said.

People came down from the hills and through the streets, filling them like river beds following the spring rains, they collected in pools in the squares, and moved on, to settle all about the curving serried rows of the city amphitheatre. It was a holiday and the gods were pleased, the sun shone down out of a clear blue sky.

Two soldiers came for Melito at the basilica, they brought the bishop out and hurried him down the street to the jail. He caught a glimpse of Felicita deep in prayer, of Colluthus snoring in drunken slumber. At the end of the corridor, where the small cell was, he saw Rufinus.

The procurator was angry. He pointed in silence into the cell, and fearfully Melito looked inside. It was empty. Where the barred window had been, a gaping hole of torn masonry opened into the filthy alley beyond.

'But how . . .' he faltered.

'How indeed?' Rufinus said icily. 'What giant has ripped my jail apart?'

He came forward and thrust his reddening face close to the bishop's.

'And where is my show? At least two young women you have promised me.'

'You still have the others,' Melito said weakly.

'*Two.*'

He jerked his head upwards, where the steady tramp of feet vibrated on the stone.

'Young women,' Rufinus said grittily, 'it is what they like.'

His voice dropped to a whisper.

'But if you cannot deliver on your promise, then they can have *you*!'

He motioned to the soldiers.

'Take him away. I'll be in the *pulvinar*, Bishop.'

Melito hurried out into the sunshine, his face chalk-white, his hands trembling. Looking down the hill, he could see the white sails of a ship suddenly fill with wind. In a flash of insight, he knew where Mary was. But it was too late. With the soldiers jogging beside him, he started to run for the basilica.

The beast shows and the gladiators warmed their spirits, they were in fine mood when the Christians were led out, they leaned forward and bayed with approval. In their midst was Felix the deacon, for the sight of the witnesses being perfected, their holy confession sealed in blood, was one that had to be sent by swift letter to all the other churches, the wondrous spectacle to be read out loud as an inspection to all believers; one which, who knew, might provide an example and a training to others to follow in their glorious footsteps.

The savage roar of twenty thousand voices hit the small figures below like a blow and they stumbled to a halt, looking fearfully about them. Their guards dragged them forward, towards the hideous engines that had been prepared for them.

Eagerly strode they forth, Felix scribbled on his pad of papyrus, *ready for the fray, in the strength of a clear conscience, for they had trained hard in the school of Christ and had been among our most constant witnesses to the truth.*

They had a cross prepared for Colluthus. They laid him down on it and nailed him to it through his wrists, and he screamed.

First on his way to Paradise was the blessed Colluthus. A cross had been prepared for him and as he was fastened to it he cried out in ecstasy to follow in the very manner of his Lord.

They got him to his feet and made him drag the heavy beam around the arena as they whipped him on, and the crowd roared with laughter to see the tears running down his face. Then they laid him flat again, by the big smoking pot.

With magnificent, superhuman courage did the heroic Colluthus face his ordeal, nobly withstanding the entire range of human cruelty. Wicked people hoped that the persistance and severity of his tortures would force him to utter something improper, but with such determination did he stand up to their onslaughts that he would not tell them his own name, race, or birthplace. To every question he replied: I am a Christian.

'Jesus is with you, Colluthus,' Felicita mothered. 'Feel him within you.'

The thing on the cross squealed with agony.

'*Stop, stop*,' he begged, and those that did it to him guffawed with laughter.

'Too late now,' they said, and dripped more boiling pitch on to him.

When he was well coated they stood the cross up straight and the thing in a shirt of tar screamed afresh as the nails tore at his flesh. Then they put the torch to it and his death agony filled the arena.

Suffer did he not amongst the fierce flames, but stood like a noble ram presented from a great flock as a whole burnt offering acceptable to God Almighty. As the great flame shot up the fire took the shape of a vaulted room, making a wall round the martyr's body, which was in the middle not like burning flesh but like gold and silver refined in a furnace. The air became filled with a wonderful fragrance, like a breath of frankincense or some other costly spice. As the fire burned only his pure voice could be heard, in steadfast prayer to God. As the final Amen sounded a wondrous sight was seen, as his earthly body released his soul, winging like a fabulous silver bird straight to Heaven.

Standing in the reeking smoke Felicita sobbed in terror, and urine ran down her legs.

Then was it the turn of Cassian to claim his crown. Wilt did he not, an athlete in his prime, but filled was he with courage and joy, and his features full of grace. The wicked vied with each other calling for ever greater torments with which to wrack his body, but he remained serene. Having strained every nerve to make him deny Christ his torturers could think of nothing else to do to him than press red-hot copper plates to the most sensitive parts of his body. His ordeal sweetened by God, he finally found glorious fulfilment as they tore his living body apart with tongs heated in the fire.

Melito found Thymele the beautiful in prayer, her lips moving silently as she knelt in front of the gilded cross over the altar.

He forced himself to stand quiet at the back of the church, to regain his breath. The soldiers stood outside, brutal and callous. When he was ready, he stepped forward solemnly and knelt beside her.

'Soon they shall be with Jesus,' he murmured, and she nodded, her eyes closed.

'I pray for them,' she whispered. 'That they shall not suffer.'

'They long for their crowns,' he assured her. 'Felicita has sent me. She asks you to come, so that she may give you her blessing.'

'To come? I went last night.'

'Can one refuse the elect?' he said, and desperation edged his voice. 'They are next to Jesus himself.'

He took her by the elbow.

'Come,' he urged. 'She is waiting.'

Cassian stopped screaming, in the end, and they brought Felicita forward.

'*Help me, Jesus*,' she begged, and those all around her laughed, for in the bloody, sandy arena were only those who would do with her as they wished.

Last of all, like a noble mother who had encouraged her children and sent them before her in triumph to the King, blessed Felicita herself passed through all the ordeals of her children and hastened to rejoin them, rejoicing and exulting at her departure as if invited to a wedding supper. The blessed woman, wrestling magnificently, grew in strength as she proclaimed her faith, and found refreshment, rest and insensibility to her sufferings. Those who tortured her became exhausted by their efforts and confessed themselves beaten. After the whips, after the rack and griddle they brought on the wild beast.

Blood was running down into her eyes, she shuffled over

the sand on scorched feet, impelled by a hot iron behind her. She heard the coughing roar, smelled its feral breath. The blow knocked her across the arena ripping her skin.

Blood sprayed high in the air, spattering the delighted spectators nearby with gore, and passing on to them much good luck from the gods.

'*Well washed, well washed,*' they roared happily.

It was empty. There was only the beast loping towards her. There was no God.

'Daddy,' she screamed. '*Daddy.*'

Indifferent now to all that happened to her because of her hope and sure hold on all that her faith meant, communing with Christ, she became sealed with perfection, and grasped her joyous crown.

It was her birthday. She was fifteen years old.

The cell was empty. Thymele looked about her in bewilderment. From close above came the savage roar of the crowd.

'Where is she?' she asked.

'She is coming,' Melito assured her. 'Have faith. Let us pray while we wait.'

Disturbed, the young woman allowed herself to kneel, while Melito's shaking voice was raised in prayer. Then she heard the door clang. Turning, she found herself alone, and heard only Melito's feet running away down the corridor.

The door in the far wall burst open and the guards dragged her into the sunlight, over the bloody, char-stained sand. The bellow of the crowd burst about her.

Melito stood at the window. Behind him Felix the deacon was polishing his text. It was a proud thing, to have sent four fine young witnesses to God, something to boast of to all the other churches. The sailing season had just opened, the letters would be travelling to all four corners of the sea in days, telling all of the fresh jewels studding the Church's crown.

A pitiful procession was hurrying along the street, heading out of the city. A grey-haired man carrying a little child, his wife, three boys. The crowds cursed them and pelted them with ordure. In the distance the mob was looting the house they had driven them from.

'There goes Leonides,' said Melito in satisfaction. 'Maybe he is having second thoughts about being so righteous. Perhaps others in his position will think again before denying our glorious Church favour.'

Felix smiled, working on his rough draft.

So later we took up their bones, more precious than stones of great price, more splendid than gold, and laid them where it seemed right. When we assemble there the Lord allows us to celebrate with joy and gladness their martyrdom, both in the memory of those who have contended in the past, and for the training and preparation of those whose time is yet to come.

Rufinus gave them the bodies, as he had promised, and they cut them into pieces. They had the fires lit and the pots boiling, the bones were free of flesh and drying by the morning. There was not much of Colluthus left that was worth having, unfortunately, but the other three furnished a rich haul. The skulls and long bones they placed with the others in the ossuary of the church. The small bones were distributed among the congregation. Melito took a fine finger bone from Thymele to mount in the amulet he wore about his neck. The one he had taken the previous year had lost some of its potency.

He could hear the catechumens coming in for their instruction. They would be ready for baptism this time next year.

Anno Domini

Smyrna, A.D. July 260

'Stride forth with joy!' Melito proclaimed, in ringing tones. 'For the gates of Heaven lie open. The great serpent has arisen once more. Wrestling magnificently, let we Christians pin him to the ground, and drown him in the glorious flow of our blood. Fear not! Pass by the millennia of waiting, in one single bound let us reach Jesus. St Peter stands waiting. Let us pick up our martyrs' chains and wear them like the finest pearls, let them bring fire and steel . . .'

He paused.

'Felix, you're not writing,' he said irritably.

The deacon, aged and grey as was Melito himself, sat slumped on the rude bench in the hovel.

'What is the point?' he said acidly. 'Our congregation was all rich, for a start, they've dashed down to the magistrates the minute they saw this coming, and have a *libellus* to wave at any inquiring procurator. And what is the point of sending out letter exhorting them to grasp their martyrs' crowns. Where's the bishop, they'll say. Let him get munched by the beasts first, then we'll think about it.'

Melito sagged on to the bench in his grubby, torn tunic and chewed on a piece of stale bread.

'Woe, woe, woe,' he muttered. 'The world must indeed be coming to an end. The forces of the Emperor face defeat everywhere. The plague kills more than his enemies. The seas are infested with their ships. His money is worthless, and he persecutes us.'

He scratched where the fleas were biting.

'Shall you be dunked in quicklime and eaten up alive like the three hundred, they crow, shall you taste the fire or

335

satisfy the beasts' hunger? Shall you not instead join the synagogue; for we are *religio licta*, these thing do not happen to us.

'Oh, Lord Jesus, why have you forsaken us? The Jews, whom we despised . . .'

His stomach rumbled in protest at its emptiness.

'Money we had, banquets, wine, fine clothes and women ready to find favour with God through the good offices of the bishop. Now we sit with flapping bellies in miserable fear of our lives, and yet only a few years ago life seemed but a foretaste of Paradise. Now we who were great hide lest we share the fate of Fabian or Sixtus, chopped up like common criminals, lest we be beaten to death in the cells like Origen.'

He captured a flea on a dampened forefinger and nipped it viciously between his nails.

'Do you remember how good it was, Felix?'

The deacon had no time to reply. The door crashed in and soldiers stood there. They were the *frumentarii*, the flying squad.

'Are you the bishop?' the centurion demanded.

'He is,' said one of the legionaries, 'I recognise him.'

'He was,' said the centurion shortly, and they dragged him away.

From the harbour Aristides could see islands of the archipelago standing up out of the sea; to land, the smoke rising from the temple of Nemeseis in the market square, as it had done steadily for days, a charred scar in the cloudless blue sky. In the distance he could see holidaying Smyrnian men queuing up outside the *lupanaria*, coins jingling in their purses, to the evident delight of the madam. In a rare rush of faith one of the aristocratic families had refused to sacrifice. Having enjoyed the spectacle of the high and mighty being reduced to ash and lion-meat in the arena, the stimulated spectators were now taking their turn to enjoy the womenfolk of the dead in the city whorehouse. The Emperor Valerian was making the Church *vastata*.

The crew had got the *ponto* freighter almost turned around. The *baiuli* and *geruli* were carrying the last amphorae of oil aboard, the crew were fixing them in place against the motion of the sea. By the goose's head of Isis in the stern, the helmsman was lowering the quarter-rudders, working next to the deity that protected seafarers. Blood was running on the prow, in the kitchen below the appeased goddess the cook was preparing the slain lamb for supper.

Now the crewmen were standing by the bollards, ready to cast off. As the gaily coloured square sail rolled down, Aristides stepped from the quay on to the thick protective wale running about the ship and went on board. The mainsail and the *artemon* above the prow bellied, and the *pontus* began to move, water rustling about its hull, bones of foam forming where the quarter-rudders bit the sea.

Alexandria, A.D. August 260

There was something wrong. As he went down the gangplank and into the port of the great, teeming city, his legs rubbery from the voyage, he felt uneasy. David and his daughter Mary were waiting for him, smiling.

'Where are the soldiers?' Aristides murmured. 'Where the mobs? In Smyrna they were running riot as I left. Where are the constables at the gates, and the men working their way down the tax lists to find the Christians? Have they killed them all?'

'Far from it,' said David.

They led him down a narrow alley, filled with shops and tradesmen, and emerged into a little square where a fountain played. On one corner a basilica stood. People were streaming out and a priest stood at the door.

'He is a Christian?' Aristides asked, amazed.

'All of them,' affirmed David.

'Do they not fear?'

'The Emperor Valerian is the captive of the Persians and rules no more. His son Gallienus is in his seat in Rome. The persecution is off.'

'Why?'

'He needs the Christians. The imperial coinage is worthless trash, the bankers will not accept it. The imperial armies are hard-pressed, the Empire staggers under the blows of the barbarians. Is not the Church, prosperous and stable, the sure refuge for people and for wealth in a world falling apart? They have a new bishop here, they elected him the moment they heard Valerian was gone. He is Dionysus, and the Emperor Gallienus wrote to him personally, granting the Church status, calling off the persecution and asking for his help. Macrianus here proclaimed himself Emperor, but Dionysus has backed Gallienus. It has arrived, the Emperor in Rome cannot formulate policy without them.'

David's face was now grim.

'But tell me, while the persecution was on, how went it for their Church in Smyrna?'

'I saw Melito bringing the scriptures out and burning them in the square. They had him bent on his knees at the altar devouring sacrificial lamb like a wolf and hollering out the praises of Jupiter, Juno and Minerva at the top of his voice.

'Then he's finished,' David said with satisfaction. 'He'll not send any more of the little ones to suffer torment. He is in deadly sin, from which no member of their clergy may be cleansed. Cyprian made that clear. To the penitent layman remission of sin is possible. To the descendant of the Levite it is not; no sackcloth can rub it away, no coating of ashes obscure the pollution of his soul.'

David was silent for a moment, watching the Christians leaving their place of worship.

'The Emperor did not write to me, nor you, requesting *our* help,' he said quietly. 'We have no power, our Church is small when that of Dionysus is large. Does not the Church of Rome operate in the same manner as the Empire, and in the same places? Does it not seek to impose order, uniformity and central control, just as the rulers of the Empire do? Gallienus has realised that there is a uniformity of interest.'

Mary smiled bitterly.

'Can this be why Bishop Dionysus of Alexandria asks to see us, as Bishop Irenaeus of Lyons once did?'

Aristides looked at them in surprise.

'We are to talk with him?'

'Yes,' said David quietly, 'let us go in.'

Bishop Dionysus was a small, alert man, his office lined with holy scrolls and codices in both his native language, Greek, and in Latin.

'Aristides of my Church has just returned from Smyrna,' David announced. 'He was not aware that the persecution was over.'

'It has happened before,' said Dionysus, 'and we return, stronger every time. In the end, the Emperor always has to realise that he cannot do without us, for are we not the most loyal of citizens? Do we not respect the laws and pay our taxes, as Jesus commanded us to do? We give to God what is his, but we also give to Caesar what is due to Caesar. In persecuting us, he persecutes his own.'

'It is not over yet,' said Mary, and Dionysus seemed not to hear her.

'Aristides has interesting news of your bishop in Smyrna, Melito,' David said blandly. 'You know him, the one who sacrifices young men and women to Jesus every year.'

'I'm sure we haven't met here to argue,' Dionysus said smoothly. 'Great shall be the rewards of those with the greatest faith.'

'Which cannot include Melito!' Mary cried. 'For he has abandoned his, publicly.'

Dionysus's eyes flicked slyly at her and away again.

'Yes, I know,' he murmured. He looked up at David. 'That is one reason I have invited you here. It is clear that we need a new bishop in Smyrna.'

'Appoint one, then.'

'I wish to.'

He smiled pleasantly, reassuringly at him.

'You see, David, fellow-Christian, I wish to appoint *you*.'

'*Me*?'

'You worship Jesus, as we do,' Dionysus said persuasively. 'And yet your Church is but small, and without power. Our Church is a catholic one, able to embrace those of differing views.'

He spread his arms wide, to show the volumes of scripture lining his walls.

'See the books and scrolls the others have brought to us. Here I have them on my shelves. Bring your own. Join us.'

'Does not the Church of Rome seek to bring all Christians under its command?' Mary enquired acidly. 'It alters its bible to capture those it considers heretics, and when they are safely caged within, selects and canonises their documents as it sees fit. How many have seen their gospels excluded and vanish?'

'I am speaking to your father, child,' Dionysus said mildly, without looking at her.

'If we join you will you not take our holy works reverently into this library of yours, promising to bring them out for approval at some great ecclesiastical conference. Shall we not be given a see, and appropriate and grand robes of office. Our poor and oppressed shall be delivered up into the hands of a man who does not preach the gospel, and our scriptures will be quietly condemned as heretical and burned. *Vade retro me, Satana.* For you mind not the things of God, but the things of men. We minister to the people of Jesus, his people who suffered under the mighty and the great. We are powerful, because we preach his word.'

Dionysus's face had become flushed with an anger he managed to contain. Aristides gazed at Mary with frank admiration and love in his eyes.

'David,' Dionysus said, making himself agreeable, 'what do you say?'

'It is a very attractive offer,' David said, and Aristides looked at him in horror.

'However,' he went on, 'I myself must stay and work amongst the poor and oppressed, here in Alexandria.'

Dionysus nodded warily.

'Would not another from our Church, the Children of Jeshua, be acceptable in my place?'

Dionysus smiled eagerly. 'Why not?'

'Very good,' said David, 'so it is agreed. My daughter Mary shall be the next Bishop of Smyrna.'

There was dead silence in the room, and Dionysus stared grimly at the three in turn, who were all smiling.

'It is as I have heard,' he spat. 'The Children of Jeshua are the vilest of heretics, with whom there is no dealing.'

'You object to women, Bishop?' Mary asked pleasantly.

'*Women must keep silence in the churches: for it is not permitted unto them to speak.*'

'The words of Paul the Liar, Paul the murderer,' David said quietly, and his words hung in the air.

'God,' Dionysus said clearly, and slowly, 'is a man.'

'So,' said Mary, 'is Satan.'

17

Hook Norton

Connell was in the kitchen when he heard the doorbell ring. When he opened it a tall man with olive skin and black, curly hair stood there. He was unsmiling.

'Dr Connell?'

'Yes?'

'My name is al-Masih,' the man announced. 'I am attached to the Egyptian Embassy in London. I work for the Coptic Museum in Cairo.'

'I'm familiar with it,' Connell said blandly.

'Indeed you are,' al-Masih said, heat entering his voice. 'Many are the documents that have passed through your hands which belong to us.'

'If you care to put that in writing I'll be happy to sue you,' Connell replied stonily.

'You have a collection as we speak,' al-Masih accused. He moved as though to come into the house, and Connell planted himself firmly on his doorstep, folding his arms.

'I have nothing, repeat nothing, that belongs to you,' he said clearly. The Egyptian eyed him in a hostile manner, then turned away.

'Then you shall be hearing from us, you may count upon it,' he promised. Connell shut the door, and shortly afterwards heard a car driving away up the lane. He picked up the telephone and dialled.

'Hello, George, it's Frank.'

'Frank, I wanted to talk to you.'

'I've just had somebody from the Coptic Museum, courtesy of the Egyptian Embassy, sniffing round. They've got word of the texts.'

'All the more reason to get on with the sale, then,' Abercrombie said crisply. 'They're so explosive, so unique, that no real buyer will let a little problem of provenance get in the way of their acquisition. A major institution can fight off the Coptic Museum.'

'What about this man Fox? He says money is no object.'

'But who *is* Fox?' George said acutely. '*I've* never heard of him. If he's really as interested in ancient texts as he claims to be then his path and mine would have to have crossed at some time in the past ten years. They haven't. I made a few calls, asking about a Stanton T. Fox of the petrochemical industry, a big wheel with interests everywhere. Nobody's heard of him, Frank.'

Connell stared at the floor, a frown creasing his forehead.

'So who *is* he, then? He had a great wad of money. He knew what he was talking about. He could read Coptic – he read the texts in the original – which is a fairly rare ability.'

'I don't know and I don't *want* to know,' Abercrombie said crisply. 'He has a smell about him, and it isn't perfume. He's after the texts all right, but probably so he can steal them. Well he isn't going to. Let's go the right route, Frank, especially if these bloody Egyptians are poking about. We'll broaden it up, let a select group of scholars see some of the texts. From the major universities. We'll let them prove their authenticity. Once they're happy we'll hold an auction. There'll be plenty of money for both of us, and a top job for you for the rest of your life. Let's not risk anything dealing with someone we don't know.

'OK, George. You're probably right.'

'I *know* I am,' Abercrombie said briskly. 'In fact, give Mr Fox a call and tell him to bugger off. We don't need anyone with a bad odour screwing up our auction. *Genuine*, wealthy *academic* establishments only, thank you.'

'OK, George.' Connell repeated. 'I'll get on to it.'

He put down the telephone and he went outside to his car. As he opened the door of the Jaguar the scent of warm leather and walnut enveloped him. In the glove compartment he had a mobile telephone and a collection of numbers. He found Fox's on the small white card he had given him and dialled it, sitting with his legs out in the sun on his gravel. Someone answered.

'Hello,' It was a quiet, intense, disembodied voice.

'Stanton Fox, please.'

'Who is speaking?'

'Dr Frank Connell. He knows who I am.'

'I'll put you through.'

There was the sound of shoes walking on a tiled surface. A very quiet room. Connell frowned. Suddenly he thought that Abercrombie was right, there was something badly awry.

'Dr Connell.' It was Fox.

His sense of unease pushed Connell on.

'Mr Fox, I just wanted to tell you that the texts are not on offer.'

'Not at all?' Fox said quietly.

'Only to a major academic institution, of unimpeachable repute.'

'I cannot change your mind?'

'No.'

There was a silence on the line for a few moments.

'Then I must thank you for calling me,' said Fox. There was a click as he put down the receiver.

Connell sat in his old car with his feet in the sunshine. Then he shrugged, switched off his telephone and put it away. He went back inside and sitting down at his table, began to read.

The black ink was jumping on the page, the superlinear strokes seemed to pull one line down into another; the lack of punctuation turned the whole into a blur. Connell sat back in his chair and rubbed his hands wearily over his eyes. He switched off the green-shaded lamp and went to his small kitchen. It was evening, he had been working for hours. He opened a bottle of Australian Shiraz and his nose was filled with the scent of blackberries and blackcurrant as he poured it into two glass tumblers.

Back in the workroom Juliana was still bent over her table. Her hand went out, retrieving a photograph of a fragment of papyrus, cut into the original shape, from the ones spread out in front of her, and pressed it down on to the sticky card. The page was complete. She stared at it triumphantly and opened her bag, fumbling inside until she found an irregularly rolled cigarette. Connell held out a glass.

'Thanks.'

She took a gulp and put the cigarette between her lips, setting light to it and inhaling with a certain joy.

'What have you got?'

'Mark and Maria,' she said. 'The *Bellum Judaicum*. They're fighting in Galilee.'

'Mark, secretary to Peter? In the Jewish War?' he asked, immediately interested. She nodded.

'It's 67, I think. They've escaped from Jotapata – during a massacre, it appears.'

Connell nodded.

'There was a hell of a slaughter there. Josephus the commander escaped under very dubious circumstances.'

'They think he betrayed them.'

'I think it's certain that he did. And Peter, he must be dead by then. How did Mark end up with Maria, Peter's enemy?'

Connell glanced over at the piles of photographed papyrus.

'It'll be there somewhere,' he murmured. The tobacco and herbs hissed as Juliana pulled air into her lungs through the cigarette. She leaned back, still staring at the sheet she had put together.

'Mark is interesting. The gospels attributed to Matthew and Luke are both based on his,' Connell said, almost to himself. 'And yet we know he didn't believe what he wrote – or came not to believe it. There is his later work which he called his secret gospel. We know of it, but don't have a copy – the Catholics did their burning of other people's beliefs too well; it got consumed. Did he write it because he became one of the Jeshuans afterwards? If he is with Maria in the Jewish War he must have done. Maybe the Jeshuans have a copy of his secret gospel. Perhaps we'll find it?'

He turned to Juliana, but she was staring at the page of text, her eyes moving along the lines. He went outside through the French windows, his heart thumping slightly at the thought of uncovering the lost gospel and he took a large swig of wine in the darkness. He was sticky and tired, his neck and shoulders stiff from the hours of poring over the ancient texts. He decided to go in and have a shower.

Juliana was still deciphering the tightly packed script. The stub of the joint lay in the ashtray, a small pool of red lay in the bottom of her glass. In the light, her eyes had a sheen.

Connell stood under the shower for a while, letting the heat work on him, his mind more in the past than the present. He came out into the bedroom still drying himself with a towel.

The room was lit only by the soft gold of a candle burning by the bed. Juliana leaned forward in the dim light. Her eyes closed like moth's wings as she blew out the flame. She was dressed only in a white shirt, like a religious shift, open at the front.

'No lights,' she whispered, 'the Romans may have left guards in the town.'

'Juliana . . .'

'I saw them going down the valley,' she insisted, 'but some may be left . . .'

He felt her hands on him, taking away the towel, smelled the sharp smoke of the herbs of the Jeshuans. His thighs prickled with sudden excitement. She slid a hand under her shirt, running her palm over her breasts, gently plucking her nipples. He saw them pushing against the cloth.

'I have the gospel safe,' she said. 'We must try to get through to Caesarea in the morning . . .'

The faint white light of the moon illuminated the room; she pushed him down, he could see her kneeling beside the bed. He felt her hands on him, cool where he was hot from the shower.

Her tongue was slippery and smooth, and he filled her mouth. The shirt was open, she was squeezing her breasts. She opened her legs and reached down between her thighs, feeling herself. He gasped faintly and she lifted her head. He could see her hand moving between her legs.

'We have to be quiet,' she said softly. 'The ungodly are all about.'

She bent over him again, her teeth scraping him gently. He could smell the herbs, he was on a pallet in a cave, almost two thousand years in the past. His name was Mark, he carried the Word of God with him in the land of the devil.

She was beginning to shiver under the strokes of her hand

and as she lifted her head, he could see her eyes shine in the moonlight.

'Are you ready?'

The breath rasped in her throat as she started to shudder.

'Yes,' he gasped, and she plunged her mouth down on him to muffle her cries.

Connell woke. In the moments between sleep and wakefulness he was confused. The girl sleeping next to him was Maria, they had the gospel, they had to take it out over the hills to the coast. The Romans were everywhere.

What had woken him? A tread, a scrape of a sandal. A soldier nearby.

Then he was fully awake, faint moonlight still illuminated the bedroom of his house. Juliana lay curled up asleep under the bedclothes beside him.

He shut his eyes to rest again, and then he heard it. A floorboard creaked very faintly, out in the room overlooking the garden, where they worked at the tables. He lifted his head, he could hear the faint riffle of paper.

Under his bed he kept a bayonet, eighteen inches of shining steel viciously serrated along its top edge, a memento of a youthful enthusiasm for military history. Burglars from the city had taken to coming out into the countryside. Very quietly, he slipped his legs out from under the duvet, his heart thumping in his chest. He reached down and took the old metal-and-wood grip in his hand. It was cold and dry.

He was silent in his bare feet as he edged carefully into the room. By the table, a light was moving, a small flashlight focused down on his work. A shadowy figure of a man stood there. At the wall, Connell reached out his hand and switched on the overhead spot that shone down on the table.

A man was there, a man in dark trousers and jersey. He stood very still as the light went on, then slowly turned to face him. He was middle-aged, lean and fit. His hair was dark and short, his eyes sharp, intelligent and hostile. It was Stanton T. Fox. Connell stepped forward from the wall, the half-yard of steel held out in front of him.

'Where are the texts, Dr Connell?' Fox asked quietly. 'Where are the originals?'

'What the hell do you think you're doing, you bastard?' Connell said angrily.

Fox held out his empty hands.

'Where are the texts?' he said again. His eyes flicked over Connell's shoulder. Connell felt a sudden breath of wind, he whirled about, his short sword in his hand, and a club crashed down on his temple.

He fell to the floor, the bayonet clattering on the boards. Fox bent down swiftly, roughly turning Connell's head. He was unconscious, a livid bruise already rising on the side of his face, blood spilling from the wound. Fox looked up sharply at his companion.

'You've hit him too hard, Giulio.'

'Sorry, but he could have gutted us both with that thing,' said the other. He was similarly dressed, a Latin, lean, perhaps thirty. They both turned as they heard a sound from the bedroom.

'Frank?' Juliana called. 'Frank, are you all right?'

She came to the door of the bedroom, naked and half asleep. As she saw the two men, and Connell slumped on the floor, her hand flew to her mouth in alarm. The younger man, Giulio, slipped behind her, shutting the door.

'Who are you?' she cried fearfully.

A dressing gown lay folded over a chair, and Fox threw it to her.

'Cover your nakedness,' he said coldly. 'We are men who want something. We want the original texts. Do you understand what I am talking about?'

Juliana pulled the gown about her, clutching to its thin cloth like armour.

'We don't have them,' she said desperately. 'We only have copies.'

'Ah, but you know of what I speak,' Fox said with satisfaction. 'Who are you? Not only a slut steeped in sin and fornication. Do you work with Dr Connell?'

'Yes, I help him . . .'

Fox stepped forward.

'Open your mouth,' he ordered, and the terrified woman did as she was told. Fox stuffed in a gag of white cloth. He nodded at his underling.

'Go ahead,' he said, and the man bent swiftly down, his weighted club in his hand, smashing it across the arch of her foot. Juliana fell with a strangled, muted shriek, clutching at her injury, thrashing on the floor in agony. Fox bent down and pulled out the gag.

'Hail Mary, Mother of Grace . . .' Juliana sobbed, her eyes tightly closed, only tears leaking through. 'Hail Mary, Mother of Grace . . .'

Fox paused for a moment, his attention caught, and then he very deliberately stepped on her wrist where she held her foot.

'Where are the originals?' he said, very precisely. 'Where are the texts? Tell me now, before we smash your kneecaps, and then your face.'

'I don't have them!' she cried. 'George gave them to Frank.'

'And who is George?' Fox enquired silkily. 'Where may we find George and his texts?'

'George Abercrombie . . . he's an antiquarian bookseller. He lives not far from here. He and Frank work together.'

'You must show us the way,' Fox said softly. 'Where does he live?'

'He has a farmhouse, outside the village . . . oh, oh . . .'

'Down a lane? Isolated?' Fox demanded, ignoring her pain.

'Yes . . .'

'The old car outside. Is that his?'

Fox indicated Connell, still unconscious on the floor.

'Yes . . . Frank likes old Jaguars. He restored it.'

'It is the middle of the night,' Fox said thoughtfully. 'You shall knock on the door for us. Giulio! Fetch the woman's clothes. I want you dressed.'

Juliana clutched the dressing gown in fear, but Fox reached down, taking hold of the garment and ripping it from her with one powerful heave.

'We are not interested in your body,' he snapped. 'It is but mortal carrion. We are about the Lord's work.'

The younger man dropped her clothes by her side and she began to struggle into them, whimpering with pain from her swelling, discoloured foot. Fox looked about him and his eyes settled on a strong crook, five feet of straight ash with a heavy brass head that Connell used when out walking. He took it and put it by her.

'You can support yourself with that,' he said coldly. 'Where are the keys of the car?'

'On the dresser there. By the jug.'

Fox found them and tossed them to his companion.

'Open it up and put Dr Connell into the trunk. I'll drive. You follow.'

Displaying great strength, the younger man picked Connell up in a fireman's lift and carried him out. Juliana did up her bra and pulled on a jersey before struggling to her feet. She dragged on her skirt, standing on one foot, looking fearfully at Fox.

'You don't have to look primped like a whore,' he said viciously. 'It's an emergency, we want him to open the door to you. Now let's get outside.'

Lights obliterated the pale moonlight and painted the big old Jaguar in its true racing green. Hope sprang up in her heart, and died as Giulio wound down the window of a Citroën saloon.

'Ready,' he said, 'Connell's in the boot of the Jag.'

'Then I'll drive,' Fox said evenly, 'and this woman will show me where to go. You follow on.'

Juliana struggled into the passenger seat and Fox slid into the driving seat next to her. He put the key into the ignition and thumbed the starter button. The straight six engine came to life and in the dim lighting the needles began to swing across the dials.

'Tell me where to go,' Fox ordered.

He shifted the lever into first with a clunk from the gearbox, twisted the chrome light switch and in front of them the yellow mortared stone of the wall lit up. As they drove out the lights of the Citroën swung across the interior.

'Turn left,' Juliana said submissively.

Fox twirled the big steering wheel and the Jaguar heeled on its suspension. From the boot there was a soft thud as Connell rolled against the side.

In the distance the velvet sky glowed orange from the streetlights of Oxford. Trees thrust out their arms above them in the darkness as they went down the lane and the side of the old limousine brushed against sprouting elderflower. There was a house, solid and square, showing through the garden undergrowth.

'That's his,' said Juliana. Her breath was short, coming in

gasps as the pain of her broken foot took hold. Fox glanced in chill satisfaction at her.

'You will do,' he said. 'It's an *emergency*. Dr Connell has had an accident, you need help.'

The lights of the car swept the walls of the house, clad in creeper and rose, as Fox turned in. Behind them the Citroën stopped out of sight in the lane, its lamps extinguished. Fox was out of the car, her door suddenly opened and he was there, pulling her out, thrusting the staff into her hand. She was by the door with its heavy brass knocker, the two men standing by the jamb in the darkness. Fox reached out and lifted the knocker, the violent clatter disturbing the still night. Somewhere in the bushes an animal ran.

'Now,' Fox hissed. There was a sudden gleam in the faint moonlight and she felt a sharp pain as he cut her side. She shouted in terror.

'What is it?'

They heard Abercrombie's voice from inside, a curtained window glowed.

'George, it's me!' Juliana called, her voice high with fear. 'Come quickly.'

'*Connell*,' she heard Fox whisper savagely. She saw the glitter of his knife again.

'It's *Frank*,' she shrieked.

There was a rattling from inside as Abercrombie drew back the bolts and undid the latch. The door opened, a sudden bar of light in the night, and she saw him there, in blue dressing gown and pyjamas, his hair awry from sleep.

'Now what's – ' he began comfortingly.

Then they rushed him. She found herself hurled on the wooden floor, screaming as the broken bones of her foot grated together. They hit Abercrombie with sudden blows; she heard him cry out in pain. The door slammed shut, they dragged him down his own corridor and out of sight.

She could taste blood in her mouth where she had bitten into her lip. There was a polished round yew table under the window, it had a telephone resting on it. Abercrombie liked to look out over his garden while talking. She stifled her crying and began to crawl towards it.

There was a thud of metal on metal, of a hammer, and the shocked bellow of sudden agony from inside.

She was at the table. She reached up for the receiver, pressing the ninth button three times.

Again, fast hard blows like a man putting up planking, Abercrombie's voice shouting wordlessly in hideous pain.

'Emergency services.'

The voice of salvation.

'*Get me the police.*'

'Where are you speaking from, caller?'

She drew in breath and suddenly her world disintegrated in a burst of violent noise. The table and telephone flew in fragments about her, she held a useless receiver. Fox looked down at her, his face contorted with anger, a heavy, clawed hammer in his hand.

'Stupid bitch,' he snarled. He kicked her savagely in the groin and dragged her into the room by her hair. Brutal fingers lashed her wrists together and she found herself lying tied to the iron about Abercrombie's hearth. Fox had thrown wood on to the embers, she could feel its crackling heat. A man groaned. She looked up through her own tears of pain and saw Abercrombie against the wall. His arms were outstretched. He seemed to be gripping two flat pieces of wood in his palms. Blood was running down the plaster, round nailheads projected from the wood. They had nailed him to a beam.

Fox thrust his face close to Abercrombie's.

'Where are the texts? Where is the filth of the Children of Jeshua?'

'I don't know,' Abercrombie gasped. Fox's hand thrust inside the crotch of the pyjamas and the crucified man bent in agony. He vomited as Fox pulled a brand from the fire. Flame brushed against Juliana's face, she smelled the sudden singeing of burning hair, and thrashed in terror, trying to put it out. Fox rammed the flaming branch into the antiquities dealer's groin and he shrieked.

'Where are the texts?' Fox howled.

'*In my shop!*' Abercrombie screamed. 'In the safe in my shop.'

Fox let the wood drop, tossing it back on the fire.

'And where is your shop?' he said quietly.

'In Oxford. Turl Street. Just off the Broad,' Abercrombie said, half-sobbing in pain.

'And how do we get in? And how do we open your safe?'

Abercrombie told him, and Giulio noted it all down in a pad.

'Go and get Connell,' Fox ordered. A few moments later the younger man came in, carrying Connell over his shoulder. He was still unconscious.

'Put him on top of that,' said Fox pointing to Juliana. Connell's body thudded down, knocking the breath from her. Fox looked at her with loathing.

'Women are but gateways of the devil,' he said, 'receptacles of corruption and evil.'

It was an old house, its wood aged and dry. The two men took burning branches from the fire, moving quickly about the room. Tongues of flame licked up from chairs and desk, from the bookshelf and the hangings. Suddenly, they were gone, and flaming sheets of paper fluttered about the room, burning ash rising to the ceiling.

Connell moaned, lying on top of her. Frantically, she seized his ear in her mouth, biting him as hard as she could. Hot salt blood squirted between her teeth and Connell suddenly screamed, thrashing to get away.

'*Frank*!' she shrieked. '*Wake up*!'

He was on his hands and knees in the smoke, shaking his head.

'*Frank, cut us loose.*'

He was awake, conscious, able to use his brain. On the burning desk lay a pair of scissors, he was on his feet, she felt him hacking at the bonds about her wrists.

Then she was free. She rolled on to her stomach and began to crawl for the door, trailing her damaged foot. Smoke was roiling about the room, the crackle of the flames turning into a roar in her ears.

Connell attacked the nails that held Abercrombie to the wall, attempting to use the scissors as a pry. But the nails were huge, zinc-coated and six inches in length, designed to provide structural strength. The wood in his palms acted as giant washers, driven through into the beam the nails pinned him as securely as steel bolts. As he heaved in the middle of the smoke, his bloody hands slipping on the metal, a tiny, academic portion of Connell's brain noted that it was how crucifixion was done, to hold and immobilise a man until he died.

Fiery breath swirled about them, the scissors snapped in his hand.

'*It's no good, Frank*,' George screamed in his ear.

Connell hesitated. Behind him part of the ceiling crashed in with a roar. The flames leaped up through the hole, licking eagerly into the next floor, and blazing fragments enveloped the two men.

'*Get out! Get out*!' shouted George. 'But don't leave me to burn, Frank.'

Connell realised that he was holding one blade of the scissors like a dagger.

'Don't let me burn!' Abercrombie pleaded.

Fire licked his neck. Connell pushed the scissor blade against the middle of Abercrombie's chest.

'*Sorry, George* –'

'*Just get the bastards, Frank.*'

'*Sorry* –' Connell sobbed. He rammed the blade home and blood cascaded from Abercrombie's mouth. His legs gave way, he hung from his hands. His face was slack, his eyes closed, and Connell ran from the room as the rest of the ceiling came down.

He found himself outside, in the clean, cold air. Juliana was by the Jaguar, bent over its wing. He was holding the scissor blade, bloody to the handle. He threw it down on the gravel. The fire was sucking in air greedily, he could feel its wind.

He grabbed Juliana, pushing her into the car, and ran around to the driver's seat. The key was still in the ignition, the big engine fired up and the limousine shot out of the gate in a swirl of flying stones. Before he turned into the road he stopped in the lane. Juliana was staring through the windscreen in shock, her face chalk-white. Connell got out, and opened the boot where he had been imprisoned. Inside was a red toolbox and some work clothes. He pulled on a blue coverall and a pair of boots. From the toolbox he took a heavy pipe wrench and got back into the car. The fire had come through the windows, its flames lit up the lane with a lurid light. Connell put the car into first and drove away.

Juliana was shivering, shaking all over. She cradled herself in her arms.

'Where are you going?' she whimpered.

'To Oxford,' Connell said calmly. She looked across at him fearfully. In the fading light of the fire his face was intent.

'Isn't that where Fox is going? To George's shop?'

'How did you know?'

'Fox wants the texts. Fox is a fanatic.'

'Let him have them.'

'No.'

Connell held up a bloody hand.

'I had to kill him.'

'Still let him have the texts.'

'No.'

'But *why*?' she wailed.

'Because they're the truth. About what happened. The world's been living a lie all this time. I have to know what *happened*.'

She was quiet then. The old car hissed through the night towards the faint orange glow that was the city.

'Are you hurt?' Connell asked.

'They broke my foot with a club,' she said, so softly he almost could not hear her. 'Don't take me into Oxford with you, Frank.'

'No,' he said, 'I won't do that. The hospital is on the way, I'll drop you there.'

The signs for accident and emergency glowed fluorescent red and white in the lights. Through the windows he could see a nurse at the reception desk.

'I have to get to them before they take the texts,' he said as she got out and began to hobble inside. Behind her she heard the whine of the gears as Connell drove away.

He came down the empty Banbury Road into the city. It was long past midnight, almost nobody about but the inebriated making for home. He turned left at the base of St Giles, into the Broad, where the pavement was lined with parked cars. He spotted a gap at the corner of Turl Street, close to the great and ancient college, and pulled in.

He got out, slipping the pipe wrench inside his coverall. As he walked down the narrow street he looked for the Citroën, but could not see it.

Here was the shop, its window filled with elderly volumes, leather-clad, gold-blocked. *George Abercrombie, Antiquarian Bookseller* in copperplate upon the glass. George, who would never be coming in again.

The shop was dark. Connell glanced both ways down the street, but all was quiet. He pressed down upon the handle and the door opened smoothly on oiled hinges. He slipped inside, closing it silently behind him.

There was a smell in the air, something alien to the scent of old leather and fine paper. A harsh modern stench drifting in the interior of the shop. Petrol.

The safe was in the back of the building, a small room with a huge fireproof door. The room was kept to an even temperature and humidity, for inside George kept his most valuable and ancient scrolls, books and artefacts.

Connell crept towards the rear, quite silent in his rubber-soled boots. He took out the pipe wrench. In the darkness, his teeth gleamed white, his lips drawn back.

A faint glow illuminated the back of the shop. Peeping through the doorway Connell saw a small battery lamp upon the floor. Giulio was standing by the door of the safe, carefully turning the circular combination lock. In the quiet, Connell could hear its clicking. At the feet of the man in his dark clothing was a square, red can of petrol. Fox was nowhere to be seen.

Connell heard Giulio grunt in satisfaction. He slipped his notebook into his pocket and pulled on the shiny lever. The great steel door began to open. He bent down to pick up the can of petrol and Connell sprang forward on to him, his heavy pipe wrench swinging.

The metal went home with a hideous thud and the man sprawled on the carpet, blood beginning to flow from his head. Connell ignored him and pulled the door open, carrying the little lamp inside with him.

The safe room was lined with shelves. Connell saw what he wanted almost immediately, two large stiff cardboard boxes. They were marked *Jeshuans*, and when he carefully raised one lid he could see ancient papyrus scrolls and fragments suspended from silk in the racks within. He fitted the lid back on and picked them up by their handles. As he passed, Giulio lay still on the floor, a dark and sodden pool spread about his head on the carpet. He was breathing stertorously through his mouth, like an old man snoring.

Connell paused in the doorway to the street. Nobody was about, so he went outside, walking quickly past the college walls towards the Broad. The Jaguar still stood parked on the corner, he set down one of the boxes and opened a rear door. As he put the boxes on the wide bench seat there came from behind him the sudden roar of an engine at full throttle, and a screech of tyres. He looked up to see the Citroën swerve out from the kerb where it had been parked. He saw Fox's face, contorted with fury. Then the wide lights of the car blazed, and held him in them like a rabbit in the farmer's searchlight.

He scrambled into the driver's seat, slamming the door as the Citroën crashed into the side of the car, its wheels locked. He turned the key and thumbed the button, the old engine catching smoothly. The Citroën was partly across his nose, blocking his way. Fox was out of the car, running around, the heavy clawed hammer in his hand. Connell rammed the lever into first, floored the throttle and let out the clutch. The power of the engine pushed the Citroën aside in a howl of rubber and a grinding of plastic and alloy. Fox's hammer blow bounced off the roof like a shell glancing from a tank and the Jaguar shot out into the Broad. A late reveller ran in horror as Connell shot down the road. He caught the lights, swinging right and making for the wide thoroughfare of St Giles. He took the left fork on to the Whitney Road, and as he changed up into fourth gear he remembered to switch on his headlamps.

The Jaguar was built as a limousine, for people to ride in comfort. Fast for its day, it had never been meant as a racing car, and as Connell negotiated the bends and roundabouts he saw in his mirror lights coming up fast behind. There was no blue flashing lamp, it was not the police.

As the Citroën came up behind, Connell slammed on the brake as hard as he could, thrusting down with both feet on the pedal. The yowl of tortured rubber was doubled as Fox reacted. There was bang and a blow from behind. As the Jaguar stopped in a reek of rubber, the Citroën lay stopped behind him.

For any day, the Jaguar was a very strongly constructed car, with a huge girder chassis and mighty pressed-steel bumpers. Connell slapped the lever into reverse and banged in the clutch. Fox was scrambling out of the Citroën as Connell smashed into it. The door sent him flying across the road. Connell selected first and pulled out of the wrecked French car. The light bodywork was completely destroyed, steam fountained from the engine, the front wheels splayed out at angles.

Connell accelerated up the road, his car practically unmarked. In the mirror he saw Fox push himself up on to his hands and knees on the tarmac. Then he vanished into the gloom.

Free from pursuit, Connell slowed his pace. He was bathed in sweat, he wound down the handle of his window and the cool night air flowed over him. He became aware that the side of his head felt as though it were on fire where he had been hit. He coughed and black mucus spilled into his handkerchief.

The signs for the ring road came up in his lights and instead of following his usual track home he swung south. The road was clear, he stopped in a layby to check his car, but it was hardly scraped. A plastic bottle of mineral water was in the boot, he drank, and washed his hands and face before driving on.

Near Swindon the great orange ribbon of the motorway lit up the sky. He took the slip road heading west, and vanished into the late night traffic. It was still pitch dark as he crossed the Severn into Wales. Dawn was brushing the sky behind him like powder as he crept up the stony track of the *cwm*. His stone cottage lay in front of him, set about with its gnarled apple trees. A fox jumped lightly up on to one of his spilled stone walls, a furry body in its jaws, eyeing him disdainfully before vanishing for its lair. He put the car inside the old stone barn and switched off the engine.

In the kitchen he put a kettle on, laying his precious boxes on the table. The larder was filled with long-life food and cans, jars and boxes of supplies. He made himself a huge mug of sweet coffee and poured brandy into it. When he had drunk it a shattering weariness came over him, he dragged himself upstairs and crawled into bed. ·

He slept for most of the day. Finally waking in the late afternoon he got up and ran a large hot bath, washing away the blood, the smoke and the grime. The side of his head was still swollen. He made himself a meal and drank most of a bottle of red wine. The two boxes sat on the table in front of him but he did not open them; he was unable to think about what had happened the day before, unable to make any decision or do anything more than finish the bottle of wine and go back to bed.

In the morning he felt better. He ate some cereal, drank some tea. The air was fresh, it was sunny. He decided to walk down the *cwm* to the village and buy some fresh provisions, have a half in the pub, try to decide what to do.

Dressed in jeans and wellingtons, an old green Barbour jacket and a floppy-brimmed fisherman's hat, he went out and down the old cart track. After a while a church steeple rose through the trees in the distance, and he stepped down on to the tarmac road that led into the village.

There was a shop next to one of the pubs, he went in and made up a small basket of extra supplies. Seeing a selection of newspapers, he took one and added it to his shopping. The woman behind the counter was busy dealing with customers and with the affairs of one of her neighbours, into which she was delving in some detail with a crony; she added up what he had bought and gave him his change as he packed it away without comment.

Connell went back outside. He pulled the folded newspaper from his shopping and opened it out. As he looked at the front page he found that he was staring at himself. The gutted ruin of the burned-out house. Satanic ritual. A scissor blade found at the scene of the crime. Dr Frank Connell. His fingerprints. Wanted on suspicion of murder.

He looked wildly up and down the little village street. Murder.

18

Connell opened the passenger door of his Jaguar and slid on to the seat. He opened the walnut-fronted glove compartment and took out his mobile telephone. Tucked inside its case, was a small oblong card marked Stanton T. Fox. Underneath, in jet black ink, was a telephone number.

Connell activated the equipment and a small red light glowed. He pressed the buttons and put it to his ear. There was a click and then a steady plain howl.

He stared at the phone for a moment, then dialled the operator. A woman answered.

'Operator services, how can I help you?'

'I'm calling a number,' said Connell. 'It doesn't seem to connect.'

'I'll try it for you. What is the number you are calling?'

Connell gave it to her and heard the clicking as she dialled. There was the same plain wail.

'That number has been disconnected, caller.'

Connell thought quickly.

'Oh, dear,' he said. 'It's the only number I have for that person. Is there any way I can get through to them?'

'Let me see . . .' the operator said sympathetically. 'They asked for it to be disconnected only two days ago. Oh, now wait a minute. I have another number for that organisation. Would that help?'

'Oh, yes. Very much. Thank you.'

Connell quickly wrote down the number on the card. Once again he pressed the buttons, and this time his call connected. He listened to the ringing tone for a few seconds and then a man answered.

'The Order of Jesus. May I help you?'

Connell sat silent in his car. His entire body prickled.

'This is the Order of Jesus,' the man said again. 'Who is calling?'

'Let me speak to Fox.'

'Fox? Who is –' There was a silence of several seconds before the man spoke again.

'Hold the line, please.'

Connell heard the switchboard click and then the voice of Fox.

'Yes?' he said quietly.

'This is Connell.'

'Good morning, Dr Connell. Do you still have what we want?'

'I have them.'

'What do you want for them? You may have whatever is in my power to give.'

'Is that a lot?' Connell enquired.

'I am the agent of the Church of Rome,' Fox whispered. 'We have the power, Dr Connell. Quickly now, let us make an exchange of worldly goods, before we make you give us the texts as an *auto-da-fé*.'

'An act of faith? I know what that means. And I know who says it. You are the Order of Jesus. Directly descended from the Inquisition.'

'The Pope is God's Vicar here on earth, Dr Connell. We are his soldiers. One God, one Bishop, one Church.'

'You had a can of petrol in the shop. You were going to burn the texts.'

'Our memory is long in Rome. We are zealous in our defence of God. We remember the Children of Jeshua in the Vatican, though long centuries it is since their kind were free to pollute the minds of men. We thought ourselves the only ones to hold their infamous memory, until your texts emerged.'

'Your Church murdered the last of them, some time in the fourth century. Wouldn't that be right?'

'We are the soldiers of God, we protect the minds of men from the devil's works.'

'They had a devotional library. Back so long ago, when you destroyed them – I haven't read what happened yet, but I know it will be there – you can't have found their library.'

There was a silence on the line.

'Can you?' Connell insisted.

'It was never found,' Fox said slowly.

'Until now. The texts are genuine, Fox.'

'*They are the genuine texts of Satan*,' Fox hissed malevolently. 'Give them to us, Dr Connell, before we come for you.'

It was Connell's turn to be silent. Fox spoke again, this time with honey in his voice.

'Come now. Why are we arguing like this? We both have what the other wants. You like money, Dr Connell. There is nothing wrong in that. We have it. More than you could dream of. Let us give you some. As much as you will ever need. Just for a few old scrolls.'

'You seem to be forgetting that I am wanted for a murder I did not commit.'

'Exactly,' Fox said pleasantly. 'One you did not commit. We can sort that out for you. Just say the word, arrange for us to have the texts, and I will see that you face no charges.'

'How?' Connell demanded sceptically.

'Shall I have Giulio confess to the murder? That should do it.'

'Why would he do that?'

'Giulio, like myself, will do anything God asks,' Fox said chillingly. 'If God wishes him to confess, he will do so.'

Connell was quiet again, trying to digest what he had heard.

'Shall we come to terms, then?' said Fox, seeming friendly. 'I will arrange for the money to be paid wherever you wish. I will have Giulio confess to Mr Abercrombie's murder. You will see it on television, read it in the papers. You will have confirmation of your money. And then all you have to do is arrange for us to have the texts. We need not even meet. You can leave them for us to collect.'

'And burn.'

'Cleansing fire,' Fox said softly, 'consuming evil, creating purity.'

'The Children of Jeshua were descended from Jesus. They believed they carried his word. They fought for him against the forces of Satan.'

'They are all dead. We killed the last of them a very long time ago.'

'Their message lives,' Connell said quietly, so softly Fox could hardly hear him. 'They left it in the hope that someone would find it and spread it again. They found me.'

'We will kill you, Dr Connell,' Fox said warningly.

'You will have to find me first.'

'Steep yourself in sin then!' Fox cried. 'Bow down at the altar of the devil! You will not serve the dark lord long.'

Connell said nothing.

'We will find you,' promised Fox.

She sat in the corner of the room. Dimly through the windows of the flat she could hear the sound of Oxford traffic, of people in the street. She sat with her head in her hands, as though to keep out the light that had made its way to the darkest corner of the room. She seemed afraid of the light, the curtains were partly drawn. In what light there was, the clean plaster about her foot and ankle shone white.

The telephone on the nearby table rang. Her face peeped out from her hands like a frightened rabbit at its hole, fearing the weasel. She reached out a cautious hand and picked up the receiver, holding it an inch or two away from her head.

'Hello?'

'Juliana, it's me.'

She heard Connell's voice.

'Are you all right, Juliana? Are you safe?'

'I'm in the flat,' she said slowly, like someone in shock, the survivor of an accident. 'I suppose I'm safe. My mortal body, I mean . . . oh, Frank, I fear for my soul . . .'

But he had begun talking again, he had not heard her. She looked despairingly at the receiver.

'Listen,' Connell said, intent, concentrating on what he had to say. 'Have you been to the police?'

'What?' she asked vaguely.

'The police. They want me because they think I killed George. We're going to have to talk to them, give them the true facts.'

'I want to talk to God,' she said indistinctly. Tears were beginning to roll down her cheeks. 'I need God, I wish he would come to me . . .'

'This is all about God,' Connell said angrily. 'I'm on the run because of someone else's god. I can't talk to the police myself, I can't give myself up, because I have the texts. Fox would get the texts, Juliana. *They* have the story of God. I'm beginning to work it out. I know who they were, and I know who Fox is.'

Juliana had the receiver in her lap, the tears streamed silently down her face.

'Fox is of the Order of Jesus,' Connell continued. 'Do you know them? More Jesuit than the Jesuits. Catholic soldiers of God. They are a military order, under the command of their general in the Vatican. At the forefront of the Inquisition. They've never left. They want to burn the texts of the Children. That's what they had with them, Juliana, in George's shop. Petrol. So I can't give myself up, I have to guard the texts. That's why I need you to get in touch with the police. And we'd better meet, to work out some way of putting the texts away safe. Juliana? Are you listening to me?'

Juliana heard the silence on the phone, and held it up with a wobbling hand.

'It's the sin . . .' she cried, her voice almost incoherent. 'I'm afraid for our souls . . . I'm afraid of Hell, Frank . . .'

'What's the matter? Is your foot all right? Did you have it seen to? What's the matter, Juliana?'

'I'm all right,' she choked. 'They set my foot . . .'

'OK. I have to read the texts, Juliana. I have to know why Fox hates them so. They're counting on me.'

'Who are?' she said. She was confused.

'The Children. It was their last hope, that someone would find the texts in their jar, would keep their gospel alive. They've found me. I'm that hope.'

'But you don't believe in God, Frank,' she said unhappily.

'I'm starting to believe in theirs,' he said quietly.

The line was silent for a moment, and then he spoke again.

'I'm going to read,' he said. 'I must find out what happened. Then I'll get back to you, and we'll sort it out.'

The telephone went dead, she sat with it in her lap. Outside, the light was fading. She put the phone back, and sat in the gathering darkness.

A tapping.

A tapping on the door.

Not loud, but firm. Calling her. Demanding she came.

She got up, hobbling across the floor.

It was calling her.

She opened the door. Outside there was a priest, tall and strong in faith, just as he had been when she was a little girl. Tall in his black robes. The way to God. The only way to God.

'You need help, my child,' he said softly.

She fell on to her knees and buried her face in the black cloth.

'Forgive me father,' she sobbed, 'for I have sinned.'

'The Lord forgives all those who come to him in true penitence and an open heart,' said the man. 'Let me come in, and I will hear your confession.'

19

Alexandria, A.D. March 309

Dim dawn lit the room and Simon awoke. The wicks of the oil lamps that had lit their party were cold charred stubs, on the tables lay dreg-filled goblets, the remains of a magnificent supper. In the great bed Eupolemus had built lay his wife, two young female slaves and Simon.

The room was filled with the scent of rose oil. The mistress, Paxaea, had had the two girls massage them both with it. Then, because she enjoyed the sight, she had had them massage each other, rubbing the oil over their smooth skin, on their breasts and thighs, between their legs, their breath coming ever quicker, lips parted and eyes sparkling, and she and Peter had fallen on to the great bed as the two girls stood locked together in oiled embrace, tongues in each others' mouths, fingers squeezing, feeling, rubbing.

They had shone in the soft gold light of the lamps. Reliving the spectacle excited him again, he reached across the bed and caressed the smooth, oily breast of Eupolemus's young wife and she murmured with pleasure, still asleep. He reached down between her thighs and she moaned in approval. One of the slave girls awoke and watched him.

They were all together, in one ecstatic, writhing, gasping oily heap when Eupolemus came through the door. A roar of rage escaped him and he lashed into the throng with his whip. It was one thing for a man's wife to amuse herself with a young slave girl while her husband was gone. Trips in the service of the government could be long and time hung on a girl's hands, but the presence of Simon placed the sport on an entirely different level.

The bull-whip hissed through the air and slashed Simon across the buttocks as he leaped like a salmon from the mound of slippery girls. It caught him again as he jumped over the table. It got him square as he frantically unbarred the shutter, it missed him as he jumped through.

Naked as a baby he sprinted up the road. There were no sounds of pursuit and by the trees he looked back. The two girls had Paxaea stretched face down across the bed. Eupolemus glared furiously after him from the window.

'I know you,' he bellowed. 'I'll see to you.'

The man turned and an anguished howl came on the morning breeze as he began to flog his wife. Simon's wounds burned in sympathy. He slipped through the trees, towards the city.

'*What, in the name of our ancestors is the matter with you?*'

Ruth, his sister stared furiously at him.

'We live in times beyond compare,' she snarled. 'The Emperors, in one guise or another, have been harrying anyone courting the name of Jesus for the past five years. This includes us, you numbskull, greatly though we struggle against the Church of Rome.'

'I know, I know,' Simon mumbled humbly.

'They cannot tell the difference between us, nor care to try, so persecution breaks over us like waves as they seek to eradicate Christianity from their Empire. It would not matter if they simply eradicated the Church of Rome, but it *does* matter that they wish to slaughter us too. I don't have to remind you that we are, as always, few in number, our task enormous.

Now we have *four* emperors, all snarling at each other like angry dogs, all commanding different parts of the Empire. Men cannot travel for fear that they may be racked and torn as they arrive in port, on the chance that they come from an enemy of an opposed section of the Empire. Everywhere shields, breastplates and spears are being readied. And my brother emerges from under a pile of naked and scented women. And tells me that chief amongst these harlots is the wife of Eupolemus.'

Ruth stared furiously at her brother, momentarily unable to speak.

'Eupolemus!' she cried. 'The very man in charge of the persecution in these parts!'

Peter bowed his head. 'It has ever been so with me, with the women, as you know. But I am not as I should be.'

'Why the wife of Eupolemus?'

'He is often gone long on business. I saw her at the baths . . . she murmured certain words to me.'

Ruth sighed.

'Perhaps it would be better for all if they placed your values on their lives. Pursuing women, it is harmless – except when it is the wife of Eupolemus! – compared to what is happening to the minds of men. The Church of Rome has got what it wanted. A madness sweeps over some when they see what they are doing to the ones who stand up and confess. Tarquin of their Church, a man who survived all, hiding his beliefs, was about his business yesterday. The soldiers had brought forth a young woman of the Roman Church they had found, they stripped her and hung her up by her ankles over a slow fire to die. Seeing her choking to death in the smoke he protested. They took him to Eupolemus who demanded of him if he too was a Christian, and the madness took hold of him and he shouted out aloud that he was. Now he floats in the sea, sewn up like a parricide inside a bloody ox's hide, with a mad dog and a poisonous snake for company. You too will float out there if he finds you.'

'I'll leave the city,' said Simon.

'You'll have to, Simon, it is dangerous enough for us. If you come back while this persecution still rages, you will not find the Children of Jeshua. You will have to look for us in the temple of Mithras, or the Thrice-Great Hermes. The Children are going into hiding. Where will you run to?'

'I don't know.'

'You'd better go into the desert, like the strange ones,' she said thoughtfully. 'No, better still, you had better *be* one of them. A hermit. Enough go out there to cure themselves of the lusts of the flesh, do they not, and chew upon raw vegetables out in the sun. Perhaps it will cure you of this obsession of yours.'

'Perhaps,' said Simon doubtfully.

A table was spread with cloth of pure white linen. He reclined at his ease, freshly bathed and massaged, his body scented with rose-water. From the open windows a cool breeze ruffled the flower petals perfuming the chamber, from outside came the pleasing sounds of water, splashing in the fountains. The plastered walls of the room were covered with yellow- and red-framed frescoes, where nubile and naked young women disported themselves in Arcadia with similarly minded youths. Fresh green vines ran over the walls, bearing grapes as lush and purple as the lips of the maidens.

Simon sighed with pleasure. All about on the couches were friends, the air sparkled with fun and jollity and good conversation.

Wine was served, fine and clear, in glittering goblets, its

aroma filled the head with intoxicating joy. Food was being brought, scarlet lobsters served on a bed of snow as white as their flesh, long, slim green asparagus, oysters still twitching in their silvered shells. More wine, honeyed *colyphae* bread rolls in the shape of phalluses; a pretty girl looking at him and licking one, giggling. The stirring of desire in his loins.

He moaned in pleasure. More wine, and roast boar, the taste of blood in the mouth, hot and spicy, sweet cakes like vulvae and phalluses. He ate one, and the girl ate the other, staring into each other's eyes.

He groaned. She came across the marbled floor and the gown slipped from her shoulders. Her breasts were like wheat heaped up, her mouth purple as she bent to him. He felt her, he buried his whole self within her.

In the blazing sun Simon cried out with anguish. He was clad in rough sacking, his limbs like sticks, his skin black and cracked like an Ethiopian's, and he was consumed by lust. His mouth was dry and his belly flapping.

He rose from the parched patch of ground where on occasion he had found and captured locusts to eat, and stumbled down the hill. There, among the rocks, in the shade of some trees was a spring arising from the bare hills that rose behind him; a small but real spring of cold, clear water. He flung off his garment of sack at the edge of the pool and went into the wonderful, soothing water, sitting in it up to his neck. He cupped his hands and drank from it, as clear as crystal and sweeter than wine, and slowly the women in his mind drew back to the edges of the room, where they watched him, smiling there in the dim light. They changed and adjusted their clothing, he could hear its rustle. They smoothed their long legs with scented oil, they rubbed it into their breasts, pink-tipped as sea shells, its perfume drifted into his nostrils as he knelt on the hard marble, bowed in prayer.

They had long hair, black and lustrous, which they brushed until it gleamed, he could hear its swish. Jewels hung about their slim necks.

They were dressing in full, all the better to take it all off in front of him as he stared with eyes that would not shut, with a body that would not obey his command.

Someone was there. At the edge of the pool, looking at him as he prayed. A boy in a white gown and headdress, staring with dark eyes.

'My name is Valerian,' he said in a soft voice. 'I have come to know Jesus. I am looking for a holy man. Are you one such?'

'I am Simon,' he replied, suddenly nervous at the presence of another human being out in the wilderness. 'But there are others, more powerful in the service of God than I.'

'I will stay with you a while, if I may.'

Simon got up in the cool pool and splashed his way to the edge. The boy looked at him, at his gaunt frame.

'I have become lean pursuing Christ,' said Simon. 'For the way is long, and the path uphill.'

'I know, I know!' the youth cried. 'Already I have been with holy ones, much have I learned.'

The sun was past its zenith, Simon led the way to the cave that had become his home.

'You must tell me of your instruction,' Simon said.

'I am at the end of a course of knowledge,' said Valerian. 'Tonight shall we eat, then tomorrow we may assault Satan together.'

They sat down in the cool shade for which his body longed every time he forced himself out into the arid heat.

Cold beans were all there was to eat, just enough to keep a man on this world while he tried to find his route to the next. He longed to go back to the city. Perhaps the persecution was over. Maybe this strange young man could tell him.

'We are members of the Body of Christ,' said Valerian, 'and that Body is deathless and uncorrupted. When we are baptised we become betrothed to the Holy Spirit. We are within the Church, the Virgin Bride of Christ, a virgin as our Lord was, and his own mother, uncorrupted, pure and unblemished. We have married Christ, to him we give over our flesh.'

'Yes, yes, a virgin bride,' murmured Simon, chewing on a tough bean.

'We are superior to other Christians, for we are athletes for God, our life is that of *ascesis*, of spiritual exercise. Every day we wrestle with the devil on our Lord's behalf. Those who pursue wealth, distinction, public office and the power over others are slaves of futility, they but chase illusions. We who have liberated ourselves from the chains of ordinary life exile ourselves entirely from that life. We abstain from marriage, we gain control of both mind and body, and the lustful desires that afflicted us become but faint echoes on the wind. Through virginity, we become pure, and find Jesus.'

It simply had not worked that way. Simon stared dismally at the animated youth, whose eyes were sparkling.

'Only the Lord opens virgins. He will come to you as you sleep, he will thrust his hand through the opening and caress your thighs, you will start up, trembling all over, and you will cry, "I am wounded with love".'

'How does it begin, this journey to him?' Simon muttered.

'We fast, in the fierce heat of Satan. For four days do we do this, while we chant and pray. Little do we drink, and for the fifth and sixth days we drink no liquid at all, nor do we sleep. On those days the battle with Satan is at its hottest, then does he marshal his most artful demons to challenge us. Then is the fight at its most fierce.'

Valerian stared out into the harsh brass rays of the blazing sun as it fell into the desert.

'I am ready for the fray,' he whispered.

They came singly, then two and three at a time. He passed them on the road as he travelled through the lovely meadows, amid the lush foliage of the green woods. The grass all about was as soft as the pillows of a bed, as they went by him they glanced at him from eyes like sloes, they wetted their purple lips with their pink tongues. He watched them walk, their long legs swishing under their silken garments, their glossy hair bouncing.

Ahead was the crown of the hill, set amid green groves. A crystal-clear fountain was playing there in a crystal pool amongst tall cypresses and pines. The perfume of flowers filled his nostrils.

Someone was barring the way. She stood dressed all in white. She took his hand. It was difficult to see, the sun was blazing into his eyes. The ground underfoot was suddenly rocky and bumpy, he was staggering, his limbs not under his command.

They hit the water together, and Valerian held Simon up, scooping water to his mouth. The boy's white gown clung to his body and he had breasts, and hips. Long dark hair was falling down from the headdress.

Mad, consumed by desire, Simon grasped him, tearing aside the gown, feeling the young body smooth and slippery under his hands in the ice water.

'I am Valeria,' she said. 'A woman cannot travel by herself in this land, so I became a man, on my search to find Jesus. I thought you near to death, you cried out in strange tongues. That was why I got you to the pool.'

Simon was silent, at the edge of the cave.

'Did you find him?' she asked.

'No,' said Simon. 'He did not come.'

'Does he often? He did not come to me either.'

'I have never seen him.'

'Then what is it all for? Such toil and pain, such vigil and fasting. Worth all that and more, if it leads to Jesus, but if not . . .'

She clasped her arms about her knees.

'You do not know how I long to be with him. I have been in church, but he is not there, only ordinary people! People thinking about their supper, or a new dress . . . indulging in furtive little sins . . . Oh, I yearn to be filled with the Holy Spirit, like a powerful wine that rushes through one's head! I knew he was not at church, which is why I came here, to be his warrior, to struggle and wrestle, to overcome the devil, to undergo the seven great struggles of chastity, and possess the seven crowns. I thought here to become pure for my bridegroom Jesus. Holding a torch, I would go to him.'

She got up. 'But it will not happen here, in this barren desert. I shall have to search elsewhere.'

Simon looked about the ghastly, soulless desert.

'Yes,' he said in relief, 'I shall have to too.'

They picked them up at the city gates, for all without a *libellus* signed by the commission were to be taken to the altars set up in the square, there to sacrifice, or be sacrificed. The machinery for both was in place. Fires, for both, knives, for both, meat, of both kinds, animal and human.

They had to stand in a queue with many others, while those ready to affirm their lack of atheism ate the meat and proclaimed their vows, and stood waiting to have their certificate duly named, dated and signed by the clerk. There was a priestess at the altar, with smears of soot on her face where she had wiped away the sweat with the back of her hand. She looked along the line and caught his eye. He recognised his sister, Ruth.

As they stood, a man came hurrying through the square, black-bearded, his eyes flashing.

'Phileas!' he called to the clerk. 'I heard word that Theonas the Christian priest is here, is it so?'

'He was here,' the little man said quietly. 'He would not sacrifice, however much I tried to persuade him of it.'

'These are good words,' the man said savagely. 'He is the one who persuaded my wife Helena of his foul religion and when she believed in this Christ she would not drink wine or feast or sport as we had done before, and no words of mine could change her. So where is the man Theonas?'

'He is with the others,' said Phileas, and pointed to the other side of the square, where men and women were being murdered by other men and women. 'They have him lashed to the pillar.'

'And one may do as one wishes? It is permitted, is it not?'

'It is the governor's desire that all who wish may do to them as they wish,' Phileas said wearily. The man dashed jubilantly across the square and he shook his head.

'It is not right,' he murmured.

In front of Simon and Valeria was a man with a wife and two small children, and he trembled with fear as he looked across the square at the terrible scenes where men and women travelled slowly to their death.

A group of small boys were clustered about the Christian priest, who was lashed face against the pillar with his feet off the ground, the bonds cutting through his skin into his flesh. They were torturing him with the ingenuity of those who had practised on insects and small animals in the past. The man's boot scattered them, but they regathered a few feet away in interested anticipation.

'It is I, Theonas,' the man said, his mouth close to the priest's ear. 'I, Gallus, whose wife you stole.'

'She found Jesus,' Theonas gasped. 'Which is all anyone can ask for.'

'We'll see,' Gallus snarled. 'We'll see what you ask for in a moment.'

All the necessary tools and instruments were provided, cudgels and whips, knives and braziers. Gallus took up an iron and put it into the coals.

The man in front of Simon and Valeria shook, and his wife pulled her children close to her as the awful shrieks came across the square.

'Now, you lisen to me,' Ruth said to them in a clear voice. 'For there is no need for any here to have to go over there. This is the temple of the god of the sun, Sol Invictus, the undefeated sun. Pay sacrifice here, receive your *libellus* from the scribe, and go free. That is not the point at issue, it is the sacrifice here, and the possession of the *libellus*. Your Christ will not be angered by you sacrificing here, for are you not sacrificing to him? Yes? Does he not ride in the sky, with the sun as his chariot? Have you not seen pictures of him, with the sun shining from behind his head?'

The woman and the man looked eagerly at each other. They nodded, and grasped each other's hands.

'It is true,' said the man. 'Let us sacrifice.'

'Well done,' said Ruth. 'Come, I'll have the meat ready in a second and you can be on your way.'

Strips of chicken sizzled upon the altar. On the other side of the square they fed a man slowly into a great brazier, with superhuman courage he called out loud, praising God through the smoke of his cremation. At Simon's side, Valeria watched, wild-eyed.

A small group, their arms about each other for support, limped and hobbled towards a block that had been set up, spattering the flagstones with bloody footprints. Their faces were held high, they shouted aloud, sang snatches of hymns praising God. A man waited for them, wearily leaning on an axe.

'*Yes!*' Valeria shrieked. '*It is the way, I see the Lord Jesus!*'

She broke from the queue, and ran across the square. Halfway across she paused looking back at Simon.

'Come!' she shouted. 'He is here!'

Ruth grabbed Simon by the arm. The group saw Valeria coming, they opened their ranks and took her in.

'The madness has not infected you?' Ruth asked urgently.

'No,' Simon said quietly.

'Phileas, get Simon here a *libellus*, he's one of us.'

Across the square the group had gathered about the block. Valeria bent her neck and held her hair free. The axe swung in the sunlight, and they shouted for joy.

Ruth watched them with a sadness that went through to her bones.

'The bishops have got what they wanted,' she said bitterly. 'They have made the people mad.'

Nicomedia, Asia Minor, A.D. April 311

A man was about to die. A bloated body lay on a pallet, incapable of movement. What did move were the maggots that seethed in the rotting flesh between his thighs. A slime made up of blood, ordure and pus seeped over the coverings that could not be changed. The windows were open, the stench oozed out into the street and made passing men gag.

The man who was about to die stared at the Emperor's rotting body.

'I can do nothing,' he said steadfastly.

'Take him out,' Galerius gasped. 'Execute him like the others.'

The doctor shouted over his shoulder as the guards dragged him away.

'Woe to the man through whom the stumbling block comes.'

'Wait,' whispered Galerius. 'Bring him back. What did you mean by that?'

'It were better for you that a millstone were hung about your neck and you be cast into the sea, than you should offend one of these little ones.'

'Who have I offended?'

'You persecute those who love Jesus.'

'He is clearly a powerful god,' the Emperor admitted. 'The one day I was well and lusty, the next I found myself on this pallet, where I lie now.'

'You should pray to him for forgiveness.'

'Will he make me well?'

'There is nothing he cannot do. Passing through Samaria and Galilee when he was upon this earth, he encountered ten lepers, who called to him, saying: "Jesus, Master, *misere nobis*, have mercy upon us". And he made them clean.'

'I shall ask him for mercy,' Galerius muttered.

'Only one of the lepers gave him thanks and it was he whose faith made him whole.'

'Thanks. Yes . . .'

Galerius sent the Christian away and called for his scribe.

Trier, Gaul, A.D. August 311

There was a mighty arch, forty feet high, opening the way into the amphitheatre. As he passed under it Constantine ducked his head, and the assembled throng sighed with pleasure to see their ruler so great. Surrounded by his guards in gilt armour the Emperor ignored them, which pleased them even more.

In the imperial *pulvinar* he rested a purple-shod foot on the circle of porphyry, the purple stone in front of him that only he might touch. The crash of adulation from the crowd smashed over him; he seemed not to have heard it, he sat, bulging eyes staring straight ahead at some distant source of power, his huge nose jutting, jaw like a battering ram, and concentrated on looking even bigger than he actually was.

'*Imperator* Constantine! The gods preserve you for us! Your salvation is our salvation!'

Reassured by the mighty presence of the Emperor with them, the people settled down to enjoy the show.

'Now we are three,' said Constantine to the man who sat at his left hand. 'Much good did his palinode do Galerius. The Christians are freed, and Galerius is still dead.'

'There are three levels of Hell,' said the bishop, Ossius. 'God in his infinite mercy will not place him in the worst, for his action.'

'I think he had hoped for a little more than that,' Constantine said dryly.

'Nothing is greater than the favour of God,' said the Spaniard austerely.

Down in the arena the *venatores* were bringing out the wild beasts.

'He is powerful, this god of yours.'

At the side of the *pulvinar* stood the statue of the sun god, who had acquired the attributes of Zeus, Helios, Sarapis, Mars and Mithras in one all-encompassing, unconquered deity of power, for it was the age of *religiosissimus*. They were terrible times, barbarians threatened all, they came in waves smashing over the walls of the Empire, no man could take anything for granted any more, the rich man not his country villa, the poor not the free baths and free shows at the amphitheatre. To travel was to risk one's life, to stay at home the same.

In such times, it was agreed, there was but one god, in whatever way he manifested himself. He was at his most visible as the sun, the orb of light and fire in the sky, and Constantine was his agent on earth, for was he not also *invictus*, the unconquered? Imperial power had long since required more than the right bloodline, the men who sat on the purple were thick-necked, bullet-headed, heavy jawed. Their bulging, alert eyes sought out danger and opportunity. They were generals, and Constantine was the best of all. The citizens of Gaul sat gratefully in his amphitheatre as he proved it to them.

'Does your god have his agents in Rome?' he asked.

'He does,' said Ossius. 'The agents of our Church are everywhere. The Christian Church that you see is like an image of the Empire, seen in a mirror. It is catholic, universal, ecumenical and orderly. It encompasses all nations, all peoples and is based upon the law of God, as is the Empire based on the law of the Emperor.'

'But there is not yet one Emperor,' murmured Constantine. 'Is there one Church?'

'There are heretics.'

'One Emperor, one Church,' he mused. Below, the first groups of the more than three hundred Frankish barbarians were being driven into the arena, and he sat forward in relish.

'Next spring I shall march south,' he murmured, watching the first men ripped apart by the claws and teeth of the starving predators.

'Maxentius rules in Rome,' he said to Ossius. 'With more troops than I can command without weakening the frontier. But he is an indifferent general, and I am not. I have no desire to besiege the city in winter. It will be a different matter if he can be persuaded to come forth and give battle outside the city walls. The proof of a god is found in his aid.'

'God will provide,' Ossius promised.

The crowd roared its approval as men scampered about on the hot sand, seeking escape. Ordinary men offered up condemned criminals for the entertainment of their public. Constantine was the representative of the one true god on earth, and he offered up defeated kings.

Alexandria, A.D. November 312

They came limping into the city from the harsh desert, hobbling from their one ankle that would not move, its joints welded together by the hot brand, squinting against the dust through the one eye left free from the sword-point and iron. They were Christians, their marks said so.

They left behind the harsh light of the quarries, the wedges and hammers, the rude shacks they had constructed as churches, carefully set apart from each other, for imprisoned in the same cells as the followers of Meletius Peter, the Orthodox Bishop of Alexandria had austerely divided the space up with a cloak, a blanket and a shirt and announced, through a deacon so as not to be contaminated by heresy, that the Meletians were to stay on their side of the curtain, and both sides had vigorously followed his example in the quarries.

Simon stood with them all, a man with two eyes. His wounds were hidden, Eupolemus had found him. Lust tormented him no longer.

The herald came out and stood on the platform to read the edict, as he had done for three previous days. He spoke in the name of the Augustus, Constantine, and his junior, Licinius.

' "We saw that freedom of worship should not be denied, but that to each man's judgement and will the right should be given to care for sacred things according to each man's free choice." ' As the herald spoke, another man held up a grisly object by the hair, his nostrils wrinkling in the smell. It was rotting, maggots crawled where its eyes had been.

'What's that?' muttered Simon.

'The Emperor Maxentius,' a man said next to him, with satisfaction. 'That was. His head.'

God had shown his disfavour of the Emperor by the way in which his city had become too unruly for him to count upon it over a winter's siege. He had been forced out to face battle, and on the Milvian Bridge had lost his army, his claim to be Emperor and his head; all to the man going the other way, Constantine, who had kept the army, had himself proclaimed Augustus and sent the head south as proof.

The herald finished his address.

' "Further, when you see that this indulgence has been granted by us to the aforesaid Christians, you will understand that to others also a similiar free and unhindered liberty of religion and cult has been granted, for such a grant is befitting to the peace of our times, so that it may be open to every man to worship as he will. This has been done by us so that we should not seem to have done dishonour to any religion." '

The man next to Simon frowned in disapproval, his terrible scar twisting his face.

'That's not right,' he growled. 'There is only one God, and Jesus Christ was his son. Anyone who thinks differently should be persecuted.'

Alexandria, A.D. 25 December, 326

It was the day when God had sent his son to be in the world, they wanted to mark it with special acts of devotion. Their garb marked them out as holy men, they wore the black robes of monks. They celebrated the birthday of Christ with a feast in their newly built basilica, obeying the Lord's injunction to eat bread and drink wine. When they felt sufficiently filled with his will, they surged out on to the street about his work.

Wonderful times they were for those who believed in God. New buildings for his worship were sprouting up – like their own – all over the Empire, with the Emperor himself taking the lead. All had heard of the wonderful Church of the Apostles he was building in his new capital, Constantinople. Fabulously endowed and furnished to the glory of God, it contained his future tomb, placed at the centre, with monuments to six apostles at each side, flanking their chief.

News had come in not long before that he had had his wife and eldest son put to death, doubtless for lack of belief, or perhaps even worse, for contamination by paganism. They were proud to be led by such a man.

They knew that saintly men such as they had seized a prophet of Apollo in Antioch and had him rigorously tortured, much to the joy of devout folk who had gathered to watch. The pagan temple was nearby and they headed that way.

It was closed, much to their disappointment, so they broke in with crowbars and axes. They found no one there, although there were some amphorae of wine in a storeroom. These they broke open and drank. After a while they felt the need to make water, and urinated over the altar and hangings.

The wine stimulated their thinking and they recalled that those who worshipped the god of the sun would be busy today, for in a foul and blasphemous imitation of the holy rites of Christians the sun-worshippers held a ceremony to celebrate what they referred to as the birthday of the sun.

On their way to the temple they came across a Jew hurrying along. The sight of him made them shudder, a member of the deadly sect; parricides, those who murdered God's own son. They knew the Emperor's views on such men, and it was with a will that they set to beating him into a bloody pulp.

When they were done they threw him into a cesspit and hurried along to the temple of the sun, the Holy Spirit working powerfully within them.

At the temple they were pleased to find the doors open and they pushed their way inside. Turnus, who was the most educated among them, had told them that the cult of the sun god was an earthly creation of Satan, set up by him in mockery of all that was pure about Christianity, and the moment their shocked gaze fell upon the interior of the temple they could see that it was so.

Behind the altar stood a statue of a handsome young man, his head surrounded by a halo of sunrays in a vile caricature of Jesus.

Turnus could read, he knew the works of Tertullian and he had told them that the worshippers who came there held a sacred meal in which they ate bread and drank wine in a Satanic eucharist, celebrating the body of the devil and his blood, and that having done so he promised his followers rebirth and life in eternal light. They could see that this was so. Not only was there a large mural depicting a hellish imitation of the Last Supper, with demons portrayed as men mixing wine and holding platters of loaves, but behind the altar was a priest, clearing up the very evidence of Satanic ritual.

He stopped as they crowded through the door and surged into the body of the temple.

'You have missed the service of worship,' he said politely. 'But can I be of help?'

'Who are you, idolator?' Turnus demanded. They crowded, sweating and breathing wine fumes, about the man. He was balding and dressed in his devilish robes of office.

'I am Simon, priest of this temple.'

'And here you worship Satan.'

Simon shook his head. 'Of course we do not. You are Christians, I can see that. We worship the one true God, just as you do. We believe that the god Mithras, Sol Invictus, put on flesh in this earth as a bull. By offering himself as a sacrifice, he takes upon himself the sins of the world and he gives to his followers the assurance of salvation in the life to come. Jesus Christ put on flesh in this world as a man, and became a voluntary sacrifice to free his followers from sin and give them salvation. We both see our gods every day, for the sun is in the sky, that you know as the chariot of Jesus. It is my belief that Christianity and the worship of the sun are but two sides of the same coin.'

They would have laid hands upon him there and then, but Turnus held up his hand to stop them.

'Two sides are opposites, dark and light, evil and good,' he said grimly. 'You seem to know too much of our worship, priest, which confirms you as a servant of Satan, for the devil spends many hours in the depths of his infernal kingdom, there studying the copy of the scriptures he has stolen and instructing his demons, of which you are one.'

Simon looked about them, he thought that they would probably kill him.

'I am willing to pray to your Jesus, if you wish,' he said.

'Please do,' Turnus said menacingly.

'I believe in the Father, the Mother and the Son – '

With a roar of righteous fury they fell upon him, hitting, tearing, kicking and stamping until his blood ran over the temple floor as red as the fires of Hell from which he had come. For that was how the devil's servants always gave themselves away. Through their lack of divinity, they could only construct imitations, they could never approach the purity of God. In their attempts to mimic him, they always made mistakes.

They rolled the body up in a rug. The Satanic filth decorating the walls they slashed with their axes. There was some decent silver there on the altar, so they took it. Melted down, the furnace would purify it of its devilish contamination, and they could recast it in the service of the Lord.

They threw the corpse into the river as they crossed the bridge on their way back to their basilica. They were proud, filled with the Holy Spirit and the knowledge that they had served God. Only one thing they regretted: they all agreed it had been a great shame that before they sent the servant of Satan back to his master they had not tortured him in the name of Jesus to find out the names of his devil-worshippers. They would have liked to have found them, and made them pure.

Constantinople, A.D. March 331

'See how the snares of Satan are turned upon himself,' said Bishop Ossius, opening the forum, and the formidable team of theological scholars he had brought together smiled grimly in agreement.

'The Emperor Diocletian, vile, corrupt and as stinking of the fires of Hell and corruption as any of his predessors, thought to bring us low a quarter of a century ago. The old arsenal, the fires, the axes, the wild beasts were deployed against us, but he only sent willing confessors to their wonderful reward, and the sight of them brought others, formerly pagan, to the service and love of Jesus. He thought to destroy all our documents, all our gospels, our prayers, our scriptures. And, yea, he succeeded. Rare indeed it is to find writings that would have been familiar to those who came before us.'

Ossius looked about him nodding solemnly.

'Yes, he succeeded. But only in the destruction of papyrus and parchment. Not in the message of God. No.'

Ossius thumped his chest with a fist.

'For the words of God live in our hearts. We *know* the words that fell from his lips, we know the message of the blessed prophets. We have now an Emperor, the Emperor Constantine, who shall sit at the right hand of Jesus, for he has given his power, he has issued the order that all other teachings that challenge our own are heretical. With his left hand, he has ordered the confiscation and destruction of all works, all documents by pagans, and most especially by those heretics who call themselves Christian, but who are, as we the Orthodox Church know, only agents of the devil. This work is to go on through perpetuity, until none are left within the world. Only the true, pure word of God is to remain. For with his right hand, the Emperor Constantine has ordered us – who know what the prophets wrote – to produce a new, a perfect text to replace the ones that Diocletian burned. For even they were not perfect. When our task is done, the Emperor will pay for our Bible to be copied by the scribes in its thousands.'

The theologians drew in their breath in awe at the scale of the Emperor's commitment, and took fresh determination to make their work perfect.

'Our word will reach to the four corners of the earth. What we write will thunder in men's ears, will be the law by which they shall live out their days, until the end of time. None shall withstand the word of God that we shall write here.'

Ossius looked fiercely about the room.

'The time has finally come. None shall withstand this holy weapon we forge here. It shall stand as a shining measure, blazing in its intensity. When it is done, we shall know who is loved by God, and who serves Satan, for deviation from its law there may not be.'

Ossius paused to drink some water from the beaker and jug that had been set out for him.

'You all have your tasks,' he continued, in a calmer voice. 'If you are in doubt, come to me. When you have forged each passage, bring it to me. And most importantly, listen to God as he works within you. Listen to him, as he speaks softly in your ear. Be guided by him. The words we know, that the Emperor Diocletian, may he burn in Hell, destroyed, were often not clear as to the divinity of Jesus. Here was the son of God, a God himself, who walked upon the earth amongst men, and yet those early writings did not make that clear. He was God in person, he performed miracles. We must know of them. Listen to God as he tells you of them.

'Our Lord Jesus was divine, he wrestled with Satan himself

and won. He died upon the Cross, he descended into Hell to redeem us all, he defeated Satan once more to return resurrected. Listen to him, as he talks in your ear and tells you of his travail and his triumph.'

Ossius looked about the room, and smiled at his team.

'The Lord God is with us. He blessed what we do here today.'

They settled down to their work. It was on the fourth day of a long task that the young Lucian, chosen for his command of Greek, came to Ossius.

'I am troubled,' he said. 'Our Lord Jesus, who is a god, is known as Christos.'

'*The* God, and one with the Father,' Ossius corrected him sharply. 'It was decided so, by vote, at the Council of Nicaea, which you are too young to have attended. No mortal prophet, no vile heresy as that, but God.'

'The God. I am sorry. If he is the God, he cannot be called Christos, or Christ.'

'He has always been known as Christ.'

'Yes, but Christos or Christ is the Greek for Messiah. The term, whether in Greek or Hebrew means "anointed one", and refers to a king. David, anointed King of Israel became "Messiah", or "Christ". Every subsequent Jewish king of the house of David was known by this term. Before the fall of Jerusalem, what was it the Jews were awaiting? The lost king, the Messiah, the anointed one who would deliver them from tyranny. The one we know of as Jesus wasn't Jesus Christ, he was Jesus, the Christ, the liberator king. But not, according to the meaning of Greek, God.'

'Well then, Greek will have to change its meaning,' Ossius said pleasantly, but firmly. 'For no one, and no thing, may stand in the way of the word God.'

But Lucius had betrayed himself. For whatever reason, the

wholly pure love of God did not burn in his heart. He was not listening to him, not opening his ears to his loving word as he should. Ossius knew of a town in Phrygia that required a new priest. The Phrygians were well-known for their idiosyncratic interpretations of the Gospel of the Lord. He removed Lucius from his team and despatched him there. Some months later he heard that his congregation had torn Lucius limb from limb. Doubtless, thought Ossius, during a particularly interesting theological discussion. He was unsurprised. By then the scribes were busy copying out the Bible that they had prepared, under the instruction of the Lord, and he sent one to the Phrygians, along with a new priest.

20

Didyma, Meletus, Asia Minor, A.D. March 362

'It is all Uncle's fault,' the Emperor said bitterly. 'He let them in and now they are everywhere, like a plague, infesting and diseased. As vermin do they seeth.'

All about them stood the mighty, thick columns and vaulted staircases of the vast oracular temple. They were in the inner shrine, in the enormous, unroofed area where the sacred spring bubbled next to the cylindrical block of the *axon* upon which the prophetess sat, the prophet standing at her side, when she communed with Apollo. The stone still bore the dark scars of fire; Christians had invaded the temple, held the prophet down on the *axon* and tortured him with a will.

From the *paradeisos* of the fore-temple came the sound of trained choristers in song, and Libanius sighed in appreciation of the fitting majesty of site and function.

'He wanted unity to begin with, unity between Mithras, Sol Invictus and Christ, which meant unity for the Empire. The old bastard thought he was a god himself, you know, and all those creeping Galileans like Ossius and Eusebius were glad enough to encourage him. They told him he was the envoy of God on earth and he spent like it. On them. He was never a Christian, you know, they baptised him on his deathbed, when he was too weak to protest, but they've been telling everyone that he was ever since. They will say anything to advance their cause, they have no regard for truth.'

He waved a hand about them.

'Let a man come to the oracle to question, he receives an answer, he receives it in hexameter verse. Prophet and prophetess are educated in the great philosophers. They know theology, they are people of *logismos*, of reasoned conviction; poetry springs readily to their lips, for it is the language of the gods. Go to a Galilean for *logismos* and all you receive is the one word: Believe! – croaked out in bad Latin at best. It is simply *pistis*, blind faith, the very lowest grade of cognition; the state of mind of the uneducated, ready to believe things on hearsay without being able to give reasons for their belief. And yet that is what their Paul of Tarsus laid down as the foundation of Christian life! *Pistis*! It doesn't surprise me at all, he was a common sort of fellow, spoke Aramaic.'

The Emperor looked sharply at his educated friend, an aesthete like himself.

'I know my Galilean, Libanius. Uncle saw to that. I was brought up by a grim succession of the bastards. Which is why I am the best man to bring about their defeat. Should I persecute them? No. It's been tried, the filthy charnel houses they call their churches are filled with hideous scraps of skin and bone from those of their followers they encourage to go out and be murdered. Should I let them do it to each other? They're in the position they are now because of imperial discrimination in their favour. Well, that can come to an end. And I can withdraw military support, which will save quite a few lives. How they hate each other! In the past their Orthodox Church has had the support of troops, thanks to Uncle, and Constantius. Just see what they did with them! Entire communities of so-called heretics butchered. I can give you the names – Samosata, Cyzicus, Bithynia and Galatia. Men and women and children all put to the sword on the orders of the local Catholic bishop, for believing in a Christ minutely different to his. We have never done that, the Empire has always been tolerant to all religions – provided they were willing to swear allegiance to the gods of the Emperor.'

'No wild beasts are as hostile to men as Christians are to each other,' Libanius observed, 'and yet among their own group, how they love one another!'

'It's so. They increase their atheism by their benevolence to strangers, in their care for the graves of the dead and the apparent holiness of their lives. These are the ordinary ones, the ones who would have worshipped at the shrines of wood and stream in the old days, now they bring some modest coin every month to feed the poor and bury them; for boys and girls who lack property and parents; for slaves grown old and shipwrecked mariners; those in the mines, on the penal islands, in prison; in all these ways they seek to propagate their faith.

'Shall we fight them with their own weapons? We must provide aid to the weak and needy. But our priests must be upright, honest priests, we must revive the old festivals, prayers and hymns. And we shall have to discriminate against them. Against the clerics, especially. Many are those who have made their way into the service of the Galileans for their own advancement. Was not Bishop George of Alexandria supplier of bacon to the imperial armies before he suddenly acquired a detailed knowledge of Arianism, which he displayed to Constantius, thus being appointed bishop of that city, displacing Athanasius? There to acquire the monopolies of oil and salt, if not the docks, which had been the property of his predecessor?'

'George they turned into meat for the stray dogs,' Libanius observed.

'I know. Most forward of them. He had a fine library, they say; I've asked them to send me some of his books. It is the bishops we must hit. There are the corrupt, like George, and there are those who seek power. Sometimes they are both, like Athanasius, who had his finger in everyone's pie, who flogged, imprisoned or killed those who disagreed with him and who claims to be a theologian. It won't be easy, for they are rich, very rich indeed. Bishops extort from their followers; wealthy men and widows leave one third of their property to the Church, the ordinary members are taught to treat what they call Christ's Bride as an additional child in their wills, under the promise of entry to Heaven and the threat of descent into Hell. Clerics sit as judges and draw up men's wills, assigning all to themselves. I shall put a stop to that. The walls of their palaces glitter with gold, and gold gleams upon their ceilings and the capitals of their pillars, yet the poor, naked and hungry die outside, despite honest works of charity that the humble folk perform for them.'

By his feet the sacred spring bubbled, fresh and clear. On the air there came the final verses of song. Julian dipped a piece of cloth into the holy water and rubbed at the marks scorched on to the *axon* stone.

'I fear them, for I know them. They lust for power, the power over men's minds, the power to make them live in fear. Of them and their god. I do not wish to live in such a world, nor to have our people live in it. They would create a universe in which men feel shame to have intercourse, are forbidden to discuss philosophy or recite poetry, drink wine only at the altar of their god. Oh, yes, Libanius, I know my Galilean, I know what they yearn for, to make men slaves to their god. It is not like that. I sit here with you and I feel the very presence of the gods about me. Their presence is manifest, master-founders of philosophy. They do not bid me crawl on my belly, croaking a single harsh word in my ear, over and over again: Believe! Believe! Our gods bear witness to their pious servants, they keep their swift eye upon me. I shall reward them.'

He polished the stone with his cloth and it was clean. The sun was dipping below the hill, bathing all in a soft red light. The temple was quiet, the choirboys had gone.

'You had better leave me now,' Julian said.

'You're staying here alone.'

'Yes.'

The great temple was quiet and empty, the shadows stretched across it, and darkness gathered about the young Emperor, as he sat in contemplation by the holy stream.

Smoke drifted about him, it penetrated his mind, both sharp and sweet, he could smell the herbs. He looked up, and it was all about him, silver in the pure white light of the waxing moon. By the stream a figure stood silently, a woman in a horned headdress. Her arms were folded, in her right hand she held a *caduceus* of entwined serpents, in her left a double-headed axe. Her breasts were white, silver-grey smoke drifted about her. From somewhere near her he heard the soft clap of the lunar-bird's wings, heard the dove coo. Swallows flitted against the radiance of the moon.

Something rustled smooth and dry against his foot, he looked down and a viper stared at him. Dew from the luminous moon coated his skin, in the light he saw something skitter on the stone *axon* next to him. By his hand a jet-black scorpion stood, gleaming as polished ebony, its terrible tail curved high over its back.

The woman moved, and moonlight shone on the curved edges of her sharpened axe, there was the soft music of tiny bells shimmering from her dress.

He was unafraid.

'Who are you?' he asked.

'Who am I?' she replied softly. 'Who am I not? I came from the mouths of the highest, so that I might cover the earth as a cloud. I dwell in high places, my throne is in a pillar of cloud. I alone encompass the circuit of Heaven, and walk on the floor of the deeps. I have power over the waves of the sea, and over the earth, and all that is in it. My fruit is better than fine gold, my revenue more valuable than choice silver.'

'You are beautiful,' he said. 'More beautiful than the sun, and above all the order of stars.'

'I am exalted as a cedar and a cypress, I am exalted as a palm tree and a rose plant. I grow as a fair olive in a pleasant field, and as a plane tree by the water. For I came out as a brook from a river, and as a conduit into a garden. My song shines as the morning, my light is seen from far off. I labour not for myself, but for all that seek wisdom.'

'You pass and go through all things, for you are pure. You shall be my spouse, I shall love your beauty,' he promised. 'I choose to have you instead of light, for the light that comes from you shall never go out.'

She unfolded her arms, and held up high her twined serpents and her axe. The tiny bells of her dress suddenly crashed in menace.

'Those come to teach ignorance, ignorance of me. They shall teach the simple ones to love ignorance, they shall make them dwell in the dark places and never know my light.'

'The Galileans . . .'

'Shall you turn at my reproof, then behold, I will pour out my spirit to you, I will make known my words unto you. Shall I stretch out my hand and you regard me not, shall you set at nought all my counsel, and have none of my reproof, I also will laugh at your calamity; I will mock when your fear comes unto you. When your fear comes as desolation, and when your destruction comes as a whirlwind, when distress and anguish comes upon you, then shall all call upon me, but I will not answer, they shall seek me early, but they shall not find me.'

'Let me make you my spouse, and you shall tell me all such things that are secret and manifest.'

'Hearken unto me, and you shall dwell safely, and shall be quiet from fear of evil. Take my light to the corners of the world, let it banish the darkness that is coming. Shine it in the eyes of the evil ones, that they become blind, and leave go the simple ones, who may come to me.'

The sun rose behind him, and when he looked up, the goddess had gone. Only smoke drifted in the bright yellow light, which vanished as he gazed at it. From somewhere he heard the shimmering of tiny bells, but as he turned the music faded, leaving only the quiet song of the sparkling stream at his feet.

Nisibis, Persia, A.D. 26 June 363

Legionaries stood guard about the leather tent of the Emperor. Close by his horses stamped their feet and sent their breath snorting through their muzzles into the cool night air as they heard a man coming. A soldier barred the way with a drawn sword, he put it up and stepped aside as he saw the deputy commander of the guard coming, in the lazily swirling light of the lit torch.

Jovian pushed aside the hide curtain, Julian was at his desk, writing by the light of oil lamps, one of his secretaries there, working on his correspondence, of which, even in the field, out on the fringes of the Empire, a powerful enemy somewhere in the darkness that surrounded them, there was always a plentiful supply.

'What is it?' he asked. Jovian was holding something, some kind of garment crushed in one powerful paw.

'Imperator, I apologise for interrupting you.'

'Well, you have, so what is it?' the young Emperor demanded.

'Our campaign is suffering. After initial victories under your leadership, we have suffered losses.'

Julian frowned.

'I know that. But the Persian is always a hard opponent to beat.'

'You are Alexander,' the guard commander said softly. 'You are the Great, brought back to us. The greatest general of your time.'

Julian was silent, prepared to see where Jovian was leading. His guard gestured at the correspondence.

'How goes your other affairs? You have given religious tolerance to the Empire once more, do the Galileans respond?'

Julian sighed.

'The Galileans want only rule by themselves. I have issued orders for the accounting to be done, that we know what they are worth. If they cannot live with us, it may be we shall have to live without them. Neither fire nor steel can eradicate the erroneous opinions of the mind, but let us see what confiscation of their money will do.'

'Setbacks,' said Jovian. 'Imperator, I believe I may have discovered a cause and a plot against you.'

Julian watched him warily.

'As deputy commander of your guard it is my duty to seek out those who would harm you.'

He nodded.

'Even though they be ones close to you. It came to my notice, on this campaign, that David, commander of the guard, my own superior, was meeting with a young man, a part of his staff, in his tent secretly at night.'

Julian shrugged.

'So he has the Greek vice. He is an efficient commander, that is good enough for me.'

'The young man is not a man. She is a woman.'

Julian smiled faintly.

'I am personally celibate. Others find it more difficult to do without the desires of the flesh.'

'While he and she communed together, I investigated her own tent. There I found devices and accoutrements of dark arts. Of witchcraft. I found this.'

He held up his hand in which soft folds of fabric hung. He tossed it upon the field desk and it sang softly as it flew in the air, with the noise of innumerable tiny silver bells. It fell in front of Julian, and all the blood drained from his face.

'I know what this dress is,' said Jovian. 'I know what the devices and substances of witchcraft are, that I found. They belong to a small but dangerous sect of the Galileans, that call themselves the Children of Jeshua, after this Jeshua, or Jesus that the Galileans worship.'

Julian was very pale.

'Galileans . . .'

'David, commander of the guard, is in his tent with this woman now,' said Jovian.

They slipped silently down a dark lane of tents.

'Here,' whispered Jovian. 'Let us be very quiet.'

A faint light illuminated the thongs that stitched the sections of hide together. With his ear close to the gap, Julian heard the soft voice of a woman singing, and he recognised it. His nose suddenly prickled to the sharp and sweet smell of the herbs that had surrounded the goddess. He put his eye to the tiny gap and saw her, kneeling in prayer with David, commander of his guard.

He stepped back into the darkness.

'You have done well,' he said to Jovian.

'They are planning to kill you, out here in the field.'

'Yes. That is what they would want to do.'

'The Galileans hate you,' said Jovian.

'Put them under arrest. I shall deal with them in the morning,' said Julian, and swept away through the dark, towards the light that was outside his tent.

It was dawn. He came awake on his cot at the sound of voices outside. He was dressed except for his armour, he pulled on his boots and went outside. Jovian was there, with one of the scout commanders that probed on their fast horses, out where the enemy was. Mist had come down, it drifted by them.

'Severianus reports movements of the enemy, Imperator,' said Jovian, turning.

'In this?'

'It was clear as dawn was rising. Up on the hill one may see.'

'We'll go and look.'

His horses stood waiting with their grooms, he ran over and swung himself up into the saddle, with Jovian and the scout following. A small detachment of Jovian's guards were waiting. With a clopping of hooves, they vanished into the mist.

He lay on the cot. He would not rise from it now, they had carried him in, they had lain him upon it, on his side, for the spear went into his back, and it came out of his front. He could see the point projecting through the purpled skin.

Anno Domini

He had asked the physician if he intended to take it out, and the Greek had whispered the answer, no, so the Emperor Julian had known. He had sent the man away and he lay on the cot with only his personal slaves for company. With a single devastating thrust of a spear his power had gone from him, it was elsewhere in the camp that the decisions were being made.

He was the greatest general of his age. He examined the spearhead that projected from his body, dark blood oozing in intermittent gushes from its wound. On the desk was the dress of bells, he commanded them to bring it to him and held it up for some time in his hands, the tiniest motion setting it singing sweetly. He brought it to his nose and smelled the perfume of herbs.

'David, that was commander of my guard is under arrest,' he told them. 'With him is a woman. Bring them to me.'

When they brought them in the woman cried out, and fell to her knees beside him, examining the wound. Then she shook her head, and looked up at him. Tears like her silver bells stood in her eyes.

'I can do nothing,' she said.

'Jovian has sent emissaries to the Persian King to sue for peace,' said David, tall and dark, still in his armour. 'Now I see why. I failed you, my Emperor.'

'Who is Jovian, that he treats with the King of Persia?' Julian demanded angrily.

'They have made him Emperor,' David said quietly. 'He is one of them, a Galilean, a Christian.'

'I have been fooled,' Julian whispered bitterly. 'Come here. You are a soldier as I am. Look at this spear point.'

David bent over him.

'It is a Roman spear,' he said quietly.

'We were in the mist, I could hear no enemy. Only a sudden, terrible blow.'

'Jovian said a skirmish, a sudden rush of Persian soldiers.'

'He is a Galilean. He has killed me. But are you not likewise? I saw you in prayer, I smelled your incense. Who are you?'

He reached down with a still strong hand, and gripped the young woman by the arm.

'Who are you?' he demanded.

'My name is Maria, I am of the Children of Jeshua,' she said steadily.

'As he said!'

'We are not Galileans,' said David. 'We are sworn to fight them unto the end. We are commanded by him who made us, by Jeshua, never to rest until they are defeated.'

'You are of my gods after all?'

Maria knelt at the side of the dying lord.

'We are of the sap that rises in the trees, as does the blood that goes about our bodies. The flowers of the field that perfume the air are our sisters. The hawk in the sky, the deer we hunt, the fish of the river that we eat, these are our brothers. We are a part of the world and it is a part of us. The shining water that moves in the streams and lakes is not only water, but the blood of those that went before us. The sweet air shares its spirit with us. The wind that gave me my first breath will receive my last sigh.

'The earth is our Mother, what befalls her befalls all the sons and daughters of the earth. The earth does not belong to us, we have no lordship over its creatures, we are one with them, we belong to the earth, our Mother.'

'Darkness is coming,' Julian said quietly. 'I know you now, I know who you are. You say you are commanded to fight the Galileans? A dark, dark cloud rides over them, buzzards and crows circle over their heads, they march to one single, dreadful drum, and the world grows dark about them.'

He looked down at the hideous wound, at the Roman spear transfixing him.

'I was your best hope,' he whispered. 'You will find it hard now I am gone.'

He put the last of his breath into his voice, and spoke to his slaves.

'Fetch my horses. Give these two money from the chest, food and drink, for they have to travel far.'

He looked up from his deathbed at them.

'You are commanded to fight,' he repeated. 'Then go, before the black cloud overtakes you, as it has me.'

Rome, A.D. June 366

The spirit of St Peter was moving powerfully in the city. From his tomb in the *aedicula* of the basilica that bore his name he transmitted his instructions to his vicar, the Pope. God had struck down the apostate Julian, servant of the Antichrist; now was the time to complete the business and wipe the pagan gods from the world as though they had never been.

God was glorious, in Heaven his kingdom shone with fine, glittering hangings and jewels, his angels were glad in glorious raiment and played upon golden harps, he entertained the host of martyrs with the finest food and wine. So as it was in Heaven, so should it be on earth.

Peter reminded his servants that he was *Kepha*, the Rock appointed by Jesus upon which his Church on earth should be built. From his tomb his presence radiated out into the city;

all who called themselves Christian should make the pilgrimage there to be bathed in its holy aura.

The man who listened most closely to the wishes of St Peter was Damasus. The message of the saint came at an opportune time, for Pope Liberius was dead, and his successor to be elected. Another there was, a candidate of the devil known as Ursinus, whose demon-led supporters proclaimed him Bishop of Rome. Appalled at the invasion of the holy city by Satan, St Peter sent his troops under the command of Damasus to drive him out.

Sumptuously clad in scarlet, his fingers adrip with fine rings, Damasus arose from his dining table to lead the soldiers of Christ. Directing operations from his gorgeous litter he drove the soldiers of Satan back through the streets. They and their leader barricaded themselves up inside a great and holy church, defiling it most hideously by their presence.

Holding high the cross of Jesus Damasus's men scaled the sides of the church, as though ascending to Heaven, to do his will. On the roof they tore out the massive tiles, and saw them crawling about below, like maggots twitching in hellfire. Praising God, they hurled the tiles down on them in divine judgement.

When it was all over the wounded crawled out. The dead, near seven score, they had to carry. Pope Damasus was carried, live and triumphant, into his palace.

21

Oxford

The phone rang in the bright, sunny flat. The curtains were back, the light of the day was flooding in. Juliana swung herself off her chair. She moved easily, despite the plaster still on her foot. It was a walking cast, a sock guarded her toes.

'It's me.'

'Hullo, Frank,' she said clearly. 'I've been waiting for you to call.'

'I've been with the Children,' he said. 'They had the Emperor, Juliana. They had Julian. They nearly did it, they nearly finished the Orthodox Church off.'

'Yes . . .' she said softly. 'It would have been them . . .'

'They risked everything on that last throw of the dice and nearly did it. Imagine that. A world without what we call Christianity . . .'

In the flat her eyes were very cold.

'You sound like you approve, Frank.'

'Don't you? When you look at all the horror organised religion has been responsible for through the centuries. All the slaughter, all the mental agony people were put through, all the guilt that was forced on them, all the women with their birthright taken from them . . . No Orthodox Christianity, then maybe no Islam and at a stroke you remove two of the great evils afflicting the world for centuries. Oh yes, I approve. But they didn't win. A Christian got Julian, stabbed him in the back . . .'

On the line she could hear the fluting of a bird.

'Where are you, Frank?'

'I'm sitting outside. I've been reading all night.'

'Sitting outside where?'

'Somewhere Fox can't find me,' Connell said, and gave a short laugh. 'So I'm not even going to tell you. What you don't know you can't say. Listen, I need you to help me.'

'Yes?'

'I need to make a deal with al-Masih.'

'Who?'

'Mr al-Masih. He came to see me, he'd heard about the texts from some leaky academic we showed some to. He's associated with the Coptic Museum in Cairo. When he spoke to me he was attached in some way to the Egyptian Embassy. I didn't pay all that much attention because I was giving him the brush-off. He quite correctly said that the texts must have come from Egypt, given their form and that this being so, under the UNESCO-inspired international law they, like all other antiquities smuggled out, must be returned to their point of origin. Since George and I were trying to get rich out of them I wasn't about to give him anything more than the time of day. So I got rid of him. But now I want to deal.'

'Why, Frank?'

'I want to protect the texts, and I want to save my neck. I'm offering to give the Egyptians all the texts back. The Coptic Museum can have them under its auspices. Once they're in the hands of a great institution they'll be safe from Fox. And in return I want the Egyptians to give me asylum while I sort things out over this murder charge. I'll work on the texts while I'm doing it. My problem is I can't find al-Masih. I gave the Embassy a call. I got some underling who started off by saying they didn't know who I was asking for, and then wanted to know who *I* was, so I put down the phone. I need you to find him for me.'

'All right, Frank.'

'Good.'

Connell sounded relieved.

'I'm going to read some more,' he said. 'I think I'm near to the end of their story. Though I still have to find out what happened to Maria, back in Nero's Rome. That's still to come. I have to see how they came to have to hide all their gospels. It was the end of the line, the act of desperate people – perhaps just one person, one last survivor of the Children, after three hundred years.'

'All right, Frank,' she said. 'You read. I'll find al-Masih for you.'

'Thanks. I'll call tomorrow. By the way, you sound better.'

'Yes,' she said, looking levelly out of her window. Her eyes were chill. 'I see everything clearly now.'

Alexandria, A.D. June 386

They hid in the corners where the dark shadows were, close to the basilica in which the bishop led his monks in worship. They could hear his voice raised high and the crash of five hundred voices barking the response over and over again.

'Excise!'

'*Excise!*'

'Destroy!'

'*Destroy!*'

'Reform!'

'Reform!'

There was a pause, and then they heard him howl.

'Away with the temple treasures! Let the fire of our minds and the flames of our smelters roast these gods!'

There was a roar, the thunder of drumming feet and the great doors of the basilica smashed back. Bishop Theophilos, Patriarch of Alexandria, led his monks out, the very spear-tip of a surging black tide, poles and crowbars tossing on the waves, wild eyes glittering. They poured up the street towards the temple of Attis, leaving the raw stench of unmixed wine in their wake.

David and the two girls slipped out from their hiding places, making for the long building with its small, high windows in the cul-de-sac. There was a sudden bellow of triumph in the distance as the massed attack of monks burst upon the temple, the crashing of falling masonry, the high-pitched shriek as a temple priest made the mistake of standing up for his god, abruptly cut off.

David and Maria carried short crowbars not unlike the larger ones being used by the monks, they put the claws behind the hinges of the door and with a concerted heave it came away. They entered at speed, a slave was rising in alarm from his pallet by the vestibule, and as he called out David felled him with a single blow.

They slipped up the narrow staircase and opened the door to the dormitory. It was filled with the smell of children. Holding a lamp in her hand Maria went in. Paulina waited below to gather the children in. In the hills, in the old monastery where the Children of Jeshua had their refuge, safety was waiting. By dawn they would be far from the city.

In simple shifts they padded out, their eyes wary as they saw him outside, but David only smiled, and pointed down the stairs to where Paulina was waiting. They ran down with soft feet, hurrying for the outside world that they had seen only through their barred windows, little children, boys and girls, six and seven years of age.

There came a roar of rage and a shriek for help from inside the room. Three last children burst out of the door, and David rushed in.

Maria was struggling in the grip of Dimitrios, a burly Greek. A slave came the other way, pursuing the fleeing children. David grappled with him, tumbling and crashing among the rough pallets in the half light. He left his opponent moaning in the wreckage and lunged towards the Greek. He abandoned Maria as he saw David coming, teeth gleaming in the gloom, and she ran across the room to the stairs. The two men crashed together, their heads impacting, blood spurting in the darkness.

David knew Dimitrios, he had stood quietly among the spectators and would-be buyers at the slave market, he had seen the little group of pretty children standing there, newly washed, their hair combed and shining, he had seen them called forth one by one, wary gaze flicking over the lizard-eyed men as they disrobed, showing their smooth, unformed bodies, had heard the Greek's recital of the arts in which he had trained them.

He reached between the slavemaster's legs and found his testicles, squeezing them together with a bone-crushing grip. Dimitrios squealed like a pig. He ground them in both of his powerful hands as the Greek beat a tattoo on his back, and felt them burst like overripe plums. Finally he let him fall to the floor, where the man writhed, screaming.

There was the thunder of feet coming up the stairs. He dived towards the Greek's room, pushing the window open and jumping down into the street below.

He crashed into the soldiers coming the other way. The prefect Cynegius was deploying troops to keep the pagans from retaliating as Theophilos destroyed their temple. Men leaned shouting from the window, and they seized him.

'Theft of property is a crime,' Cynegius said briskly. There was always a lot to do the day after a temple-smashing, he wanted to get the cases heard, the sentences passed and the criminals on their way to the mines or the block as quickly as possible.

'You admit to the theft of twenty-five male and female slaves from their owner?'

The tall, powerful man standing below the dais looked up at him without fear.

'He owed me them,' said David, as though he, too, was in the business. At the prefect's side the clerk of his court frowned in thought as he peered at David, and the two young women with him in the dock.

'And more than stealing the property of one Dimitrios, a licensed dealer in slaves, you killed him.'

The blood pumping into the Greek's scrotum had blown it up like a bath-ball. When it burst, it let his life out with it.

'It was not my intention to kill him,' said David. 'He attacked me as I was recovering my property. I was defending myself.'

Cynegius regarded the trio thoughtfully. As a man who had considerable experience of these things, there was something not quite right about them.

'And these two women. They are with you?'

'I have already told the clerk. I know nothing of them. The soldiers captured them by mistake. I alone went to Dimitrios to recover my property.'

The prefect turned to the clerk.

'What say you?'

'They claim to be dancers.'

He reached down and opened a bag.

'The woman Maria was carrying this.'

He pulled out a shimmering dress of many colours. As he held it up, it sang. It was sewn with a multitude of tiny silver and gold bells.

'And there is also this.'

He brought out a small leather bag. Inside were seeds, dried flowers and leaves, small dried fruits like tiny pieces of mosaic.

'It is a part of our art,' said Maria. The clerk was still staring at David, and suddenly, he jumped to his feet.

'I have it!' he cried. 'I knew that I was familiar with this man. He is no dealer in child prostitutes. He is David, of a strange Christian sect called the Children of Jeshua. They make a practice of freeing slaves, and converting them to their doctrines. They are outlawed. This David is wanted on many charges, including heresy.'

The prefect sat thinking for a moment. Slave-theft, murder, even, were run-of-the-mill offences, for the magistrate at least, if not for the captured and about to be punished culprit. Heresy was something else entirely, something feared by both the state and the state's Orthodox Church alike. Dangerous, charismatic preachers like this one in front of him were a threat to both structures. The old tribal gods had not threatened the state, nor now did the Orthodox Christian God, working in harness with it. Christian heresies did. They were by definition anti-authoritarian, they gave men with grievances transcendental and wholly dangerous beliefs with which to pursue those grievances; and they were capable of spreading like wildfire, leaping from one disaffected group to another throughout the Empire. Like a fire, it needed to be stamped on while it was still small, not when it had grown into a roaring conflagration.

He had to know what he was dealing with, he needed the services of an expert.

'Send him over to Bishop Theophilos,' he said to the clerk. 'The women too, for they may be involved. I have heard that he has a guest, an expert upon heresy, one Paul of Avila. When we have such a person in our midst, we should not be slow to avail ourselves of his services. Have them report to me as to the nature of this man's heresy.'

Two guards walked David from the court to the bishop's palace. They passed the site of the temple of Attis where Theophilos's men were sorting through the rubble. There was fine stone there, hundreds of years old, it would come in useful. At the four corners stood teams of exorcists, busy purifying the area for its service to a new god.

Theophilos greeted his guest in the clean fresh stone basilica, new, rising high above them to the glory of God. The two were men of an age and a mission, the bishop and the hunter. They sat in a quiet corner to talk, the building lit by the glow of myriad wax candles, a mark of respect in Roman homes, now multiplied a thousandfold in homage to the Lord. The light shone on the explosion of colour within, on the gold and silver vessels, the elaborate marble *piscinae*, the silver canopies over the altar, the gorgeous hangings and the vestments of the priest. Near where they sat was the deep, dark pool of the baptistry where the bishop himself pushed them under three times, the secret words of the catechism still ringing in their ears, their bodies stark naked, before clothing them in white, and giving them a candle.

Relics were extremely important. Only they could provide protection against the divisions of demons that roamed the earth seeking to steal men's souls. Alexandria suffered from having none such as Peter or Paul, Andrew, Luke or Timothy, but God's divine favour was shown when upon the dedication of the basilica the skeletons of the saints Gervasius and Protasius were found there. Shortly afterwards the actual bodies of the saints Agricola, Vitalis, Nazarius and Celsus were unearthed, and Alexandria was as well protected as any against the depredations of the demons.

They sat amid magnificence, the bishop and the hunter, and from a far corner of the cathedral came the sweet sounds of choristers at practice. The bishop was Theophilos, the hunter the Spaniard, Paul of Avila, the seeker of sin.

Theophilos had a gift for Paul, a small jewelled amulet.

'The very tooth from the head of Saint Nazarius,' he said. 'Wrapped in cloth dipped in his blood, for it was as fresh as if it had been shed that day, and his decapitated head entire, his hair and beard as though it had just been washed.'

'I shall find something of such power most valuable,' Paul said gratefully.

They sat quietly, listening to the pure sounds of the choir, and when the boys came to the end of the psalm Paul nodded in deep approval.

'Perfect,' he said. 'Not a note, not a word, not a pause out of place. Which is proof they are in the service of God.'

'Is that how you can tell?' Theophilos asked.

'Heresy breeds in the minds of men. It seethes there like maggots on a corpse,' Paul said knowledgeably. 'Since it affects the mind it can be identified in the words and actions of the man so contaminated. Once found, it can be brought out, in all its foulness, into the light of day. To detect it in its early stages great rigour, and the study, in minute detail of the man one suspects is necessary.'

'Was this how you uncovered Priscillian?'

'It was hard, as you would expect in one who, though a bishop, had become the captive of Satan.'

'I have heard that to all appearances he led a life of great asceticism, and was considered to be a fine preacher of the word.'

'Both of these things are true, but the one is the camouflage of a sheep's wool when within lurked a ravening wolf, and the other the instruction in the scriptures by Satan himself, from the copy he has stolen. We had strong suspicions of him from the start, for we could judge him by those who arranged his ascent into the office of bishop in Avila. Four years of investigation it took, until we were able to present our charges of Gnosticism, Manicheism and moral depravity to the court at Bordeaux – who found him guilty. The wiles of those in the service of Satan are well known, and he sought to escape through appeal to the Emperor. However, this gave us our chance to indict him under the imperial law of witchcraft, which provides for the right to use rigour in examination. He withstood the *eculeus*, the rack, for the love of Satan was running strongly within him, but under the effect of the iron hooks, and then the red-hot plates applied to the lacerated flesh, he broke, and it all came out, stinking and writhing. He had studied obscene doctrines, held meetings with depraved women at night, had prayed naked – to whom? To Satan, to be sure.'

Theophilos shuddered.

'When does such sin enter a man's soul?' Paul said wonderingly.

'He is born with it,' Theophilos said certainly. 'Mewling babies are immersed in sin, for are they not the fruit of sin, of those organs with which Adam and Eve defiled the garden of Eden? *Ecce unde!* That's the place! That's the place from which the first sin was passed on. Adam defied God, now whenever a man feels the stirrings of lust he feels shame, it is the reminder and most fitting punishment for that original crime. Only baptism – as quick as you can after birth – can purify that sin, and then we all walk a beam, awaiting God's pleasure or wrath. A man I heard of, pious, eighty-four years old, suddenly bought himself a dancing girl for his pleasure, and so lost Paradise. Is that not the hand of God? Thus it was with Priscillian.'

'True,' mused Paul. ' "Say not in thy heart, My strength and the power of my hand has wrought this great wonder – but thou shall remember the Lord thy God, for he it is who gives the strength to do great deeds." When I stood amid the reek of the Satanist, the iron plates burning through the gloves on my hand, and heard him confess I rejoiced, for I knew I was the instrument of God's will.'

'In which level of Hell does he burn now, I wonder?' mused Theophilos.

'The third, and worst,' Paul said certainly. 'For he fell from so great a height. There among usurers boiling in molten gold, among adulterers tearing and eating their own flesh, there will he be, among the hundred million condemned souls packed like grapes in a press, bricks in a furnace, salt sediment in a barrel of pickled fish will he burn, as ferocious fiery animals slowly consume his flesh. Staring up through the flames will he see the heavenly host above rejoicing to see the damned so punished, breathing in their smoking reek as perfume. *Sancti de poenis impiorum gaudebunt.*'

The choir had finished its practice, they could hear the pattering of their feet on the cold stone as they went out. The feast of All Souls was to be held later in the week. Churchmen such as Damasus were aware of the deep and ancient need of man for magnificent ritual and celebration, and donned pagan dress and jewels so that converts would barely notice the change in the nature of their new masters. Did it matter if the ancient feast of the Dead became All Souls? Or the death and resurrection of Adonis and Attis on the twenty-fifth and twenty-seventh of March, be celebrated in the death and resurrection of Christ at Easter, on the same dates?

'Yes,' said Theophilos. 'That is why rigour is so necessary in this world, to save men from eternal damnation in the next.'

'Heretics welcome persecution,' Paul assured him. 'Many is the time I have heard a heretic admit that fear made him become earnest to examine the truth, that the stimulus of fear started him from his negligence. That is why the necessity for harshness must be greater in the investigation of heresy than in the punishment, so as to leave scope for displaying clemency.'

'Rigour,' agreed Theophilos. 'That's the word. Was that not the way of Christ? Did he not by great violence coerce the saintly Paul into belief in him? Did not a certain man make a great supper, and bid many? And did they not all with one consent begin to make excuse? And the man commanded his servant to go out into the streets and lanes, and when there was still yet room, into the highways and hedges, that his house might be filled. So wrote the holy Luke. And what was the commandment of the man to his servant?'

'Compel them to come in,' Paul said softly.

Soft footfalls came along the nave, and the bishop and the hunter looked up. It was the clerk to the prefect.

'Greetings,' he said. 'Prefect Cynegius begs your expert knowledge. He has found a heretic, one David of the Children of Jeshua, and two women who may be his accomplices. He wishes to know the nature of their crimes.'

Paul of Avila slowly stood up and drew himself to his full height, his robes of office falling in long black folds about him. His eyes shone with a terrible light.

'We do not rest from the Lord's work,' he promised. 'Not

by day, nor by night. We shall be glad to provide Prefect Cynegius with what he requires.'

All were sweating in the heat of the stifling room. It was dim in there, lit by the glow of the brazier. Paul of Avila adjusted the setting on the rack, the wheels whirred, the great weights bobbed and the man stretched, gasping in pain. The two women, Maria and Paulina, stood manacled to the wall nearby. A young monk, an assistant to the bishop, wiped sweat nervously from his face.

'Is this necessary?' Theophilos asked. 'He has admitted his membership of an outlawed sect. Cynegius likes them for his mines, you know.'

'*Quaestio tormentorum*,' Paul levelly. 'Only through the rigour of inquisition do we arrive at the truth. Believe me, I know of what I speak. I am experienced in these matters.'

'I did not doubt it,' Theophilos assured him.

Paul picked up his most fearsome weapon, and held it up so that the man could see it.

'Tell me what this is,' he ordered.

From the iron bed where he lay stretched in agony David looked up at him.

'It is a book,' he said, his voice unwontedly strong, for one speaking from where he was. 'It is a book written by people about someone they never knew, with the purpose of persuading others that he existed as they said he did, which he did not. It is a book that should have gone to the fire instead of the ones that did, those which told the truth. It is without any doubt a most skilfully designed and effective political document, and is thus by definition untrue. You call it the Bible.'

Paul shuddered, he could not help it. He held the fine, red goatskin-bound book firm in his hand.

'Listen to me,' he whispered. '*Verbum caro factum est.* The word was made flesh. "In the beginning was the Word, and the Word was with God, and the Word was God. The same was in the beginning with God. All things were made by him; and without him was not anything made that was made." Every word, every syllable in this holy book fell direct from the lips of God. To change even a mark of punctuation would condemn a man to Hell. Do you not know what time this is? It is *Anno Domini*, the year of our Lord, and all that are to come to Eternity are of the Lord, for through his servants he has set up his kingdom upon earth. What wickedness we have here . . .'

He eyed David calculatingly, and twirled a wheel, sending the heavy ropes thrumming.

'So tell me, heresiarch, the ways in which you worship. What rules of Satan you follow. *What documents you own.*'

He bent low over David. He had bitten through his lip with pain and his mouth was filling with blood. He held it, and spat, spraying his tormentor with gore. Quite silently, the hunter went to the table nearby, where water was in a bowl, and washed himself. The young monk handed him a towel, moving fearfully, and he dried himself.

'I wish to know where your documents are,' he said, turning again. Maria and Paulina stood silently by the table, in their manacles. As he turned, the eyes of Paul flicked over them with a strange longing that made them shiver.

'We heard that this sect occupies an old monastery, up in the Jabal mountains,' the clerk said helpfully.

'I thank you,' Paul said politely. He looked at Theophilos. 'You have your monks? An expeditionary force?'

'Certainly,' the bishop assured him. 'I shall arrange it.'

He stood up, bending over David.

'Repent,' said Theophilos. 'Repent of your sin before you

die. For Jesus Christ died upon the Cross to take away our sins, he took them upon himself. His mercy is so infinite that he will take yours, yes even yours, shall you show repentance.'

'He did not die on the cross,' David said contemptuously. 'Not for you, nor me.'

'Enough,' Paul whispered. 'We need to hear no more. The devil shall talk no more in this room through you.'

Iron tongs were in his hand.

'You, Jerome,' he ordered the monk, 'come here.'

He thrust an iron bar into David's mouth. Teeth broke as he wrenched his jaws apart and a moan of horror escaped the young man who stood by him.

'Hold the bar,' Paul ordered.

He thrust in the tongs, and ripped out the tongue, casting it on the brazier to burn. The cell was filled with a hideous gargling as David drowned in the blood gushing from the enormous wound. Metal clanged as the bar slipped from the monk Jerome's hand.

'We shall not know now if his sect is in the monastery,' Theophilos remonstrated.

'Oh, but we shall,' Paul whispered. He turned his gaze on to Maria and Paulina. 'For we have the women. And if sin existed in this heresiarch, then it exists within these two, for sin flourishes sevenfold within a woman.'

He stood before them both.

'There you stand,' he said softly. 'Eve, wife of the noble Adam. Lovely without, and rotten within. The devil's gateway, the unsealer of that forbidden tree, the first deserter of the divine law. The maker of Hell itself.'

'You are mad,' Paulina said clearly. 'Demons breed in your head.'

'So. You have chosen to be first!' Paul cried joyfully. 'Then let us begin.'

He stripped her of her clothes as she stood, and Theophilos's eyes ran over her body with a sudden lust, for she was young and beautiful. He quickly averted his gaze as Paul turned to him.

'Are you familiar with the rules for dealing with witches?' he asked.

'No . . . I don't think so,' the bishop admitted.

'I am *malleus maleficarium*, the hammer of the witches,' Paul explained. 'I myself drew up the code for dealing with them, according to God's will. You, Jerome. Heat the rod in the fire.'

The monk pushed an iron rod into the brazier, long and sharp at the end. The man who commanded him picked up a razor from the array of tools available in the bishop's torture chamber.

'First, the hair. I am myself shaven, out of respect for the Lord. Observe this witch, see how long her hair is. Within those locks, devils may hide from view.'

With swift strokes, he chopped savagely at Paulina's head, and bloody hanks of hair fell about her feet. Then he knelt down in front of her, staring at her loins.

'*Ecce unde!*' he whispered, his voice full of hate. 'There it is, that's the place where all the sin came into the world.'

His voice rose to a sudden howl and he slashed and scraped at the triangle of thick black hair as the girl's body jerked in agony and she screamed.

'*In nomine Patris et Filii et Spiritus Sancti!*'

He stood, and Theophilos saw that his face was slick with sweat. He was stiff, the front of his robes jutted out.

'I have touched her vileness,' he whispered. 'Let me make my hands clean.'

He washed in the water, muttering to himself.

'In the name of the Holy Mary, she who was pure, she who was without sin, remaining a Virgin, *ave Maria, gratia plena*.'

He wiped his hands on his robes, and Theophilus saw that he was still erect.

'Only fire can consume the devils that exist within women,' he said hoarsely. He pulled a rod from the brazier, and it glowed a bright red in the dim room.

'For your violation of Jesus,' he shouted, and clapped it to her breast.

'For your creation of Hell, for robbing your children of Heaven.'

He struck her again and again with the fiery rod, and raw, bloody stripes lashed her body.

Then he paused, regarding her as she flapped against the wall.

'All witchcraft comes from carnal lust, which in women is insatiable. *Ecce unde*, there it is, the mouth of the womb, where women consort with devils.'

His voice rose to a howl.

'*Deo favente!*' he screamed, and rammed the pointed rod up between her thighs. Theophilus closed his eyes, for the girl had been young and beautiful, and when he opened them the hunter was turning away from the lacerated corpse hanging on the wall. His hips ceased to jerk, his eyes were glazed and his robes were stained.

There was a sudden gargling from the corner as the young monk vomited.

'*Deo gratias*,' the inquisitor said thickly. 'Thanks be to God.'

Maria awoke from her sleep of pain, slumped up against the wall where she was shackled. The cell door creaked, she saw its outline dim against the light of a small lamp. Her heart pounded in her chest, she gasped in foul-smelling air, charred and bloody.

The lamp moved towards her, light raced across the darkness, chasing the myriad insects that feasted on the blood. She forced herself to stand up straight on limbs that shook as those of an old woman.

'Who is it?' she called bravely.

'Quiet,' a voice hissed. 'It is I, the monk Jerome. The one who was here when he killed your companions.'

'What is it you want with me?' she said to the dim figure.

'I heard them talking, the mad one and the bishop. I am to be interrogated in the morning. I was sick to my stomach when he slaughtered the girl. He says it is evidence that devils have taken up their abode in me, for I should have been filled with joy at their defeat.'

'The devils are in him,' Maria said quietly. 'So run, monk Jerome, run as far away as you can, else you, too, are whipped with fiery rods.'

'I plan to. But I cannot leave you here . . .'

'Why?'

'I cannot believe in a God that commands us to do these things,' Jerome whispered painfully, 'so I cannot leave you here to die in agony in the morn.'

He came forward and she felt cold metal at her wrists, the clink of a key, and her arms fell down beside her. She tottered forward, and he supported her.

'My sack,' she said. 'That they took. Do you have it?'

'It is here. I took it from the bishop's chambers.'

'I must have it,' she said.

He led her down the stone corridor and she felt cool air on her face. Looking up, she saw a crescent moon, and felt its light flood into her, the light of the goddess. She stood alone and pulled herself up straight.

'I have to go to the mountains,' she said.

'I have horses. Come this way.'

Outside the city, she made him stop, taking her sack from him. She sent him to gather brushwood, and with her tinder she lit a fire.

'We must get on,' he said nervously. 'The bishop has sent on his troops, they march on your monastery in the hills.'

'They cannot go to Paradise if I do not make the way for them,' she said, and he watched in awe as she put on her dress of bells, her robe of glory. The stars of Heaven and moonbeams shimmered and she danced for the dead. Red and yellow flames flashed from the gold and silver bells and they sang in the light as her sable hair shone. She cast on herbs and shining smoke enveloped her. From the fire incandescent sparks flew up into the clear black sky and joined the sparkling stars.

He was not sure how long he had stood there. The fire was low, its embers gleamed on the bells, and they whispered softly.

'We can go on now,' she said, and they mounted their horses.

They climbed into the hills, by the light of the crescent moon. When dawn broke they could see the Nile, brown and muddy, in the distance below.

'There,' she said, as they came over the rise. The monastery lay clear in the morning light, like a very outcropping of the harsh, arid mountains. The sun glinted from its pools and reservoirs, its gardens were clothed in green.

'What's that?' Jerome asked suddenly. Dirty black smoke was rising from the courtyard, staining the eggshell-blue sky. On the breeze came the sound of yelling, shouting and screams.

'They have got here before us,' Maria said bitterly. She turned in her saddle. 'I must rescue the books. Our prayers, our songs. Our history. The words of Jesus. They have never been lost, not since we received our commandments.'

She stared across the valley. The smoke was thickening, the noise of battle on the air.

'There is a way in, through the back. I shall take it. You do not have to come.'

'I am with you, I am one of the Children,' he said simply, and they put their heels to the horses' ribs, cantering down the slope to the battle.

The black-robed monks were killing the wounded. The fighting was over, smoke swirled in the corridors as the monastery burned. She carried a tall earthenware jar with a clay plug, ready for the storage of olive oil, and a pot of ochre varnish. In the smoke she laid them down and pulled the books and scrolls from the shelf by the altar. Jerome had taken a sword from one of the dead, he held the door.

'I hear them come,' he called. 'Be quick.'

She was finished, she lifted the jar and ran for the passageway that led up from the rocks. As she did so she heard a man scream behind her. In the doorway Jerome was wielding his sword against men robed as he was. She ran into the smoke, and saw him no more.

In the cave she dug at the flaking rock, pulling out the shards, tossing them into a pile behind her, until she had a hole deep and wide, ready to take the jar. She crouched in the very mouth, looking back down the valley, and saw the black-robed figures coming, following the footprints she had left in the dust.

She took her pen, and ripped a cover free.

'*They have killed us all. The Children of Jeshua are no more. I, Maria, am the last of the one true faith. They search for me, they will find me soon.*

'*Here lie the words of those who sought to bring the word of*

Jesus to the land of Satan. Whosoever may find them, we who have died command you not to let them die with us.

'*I see them down in the valley. I must seal the jar and bury it. They are coming. The evil ones are coming.*

'*Be there one among you that will put on the robe of glory. Be there one who will say the prayers for me. Be there one who will dance by the fire in the silver smoke as the robe of glory sings for me.*'

When she had written, she put the parchment on top of the scrolls and books. The small bag of holy herbs was in the sack, she tightened its strings and dropped it inside. In the distance, she could hear the coarse shouts of the monks. She pulled her dress over her head, and it sang for the last time as she let it fall into the jar. Then she took her pot of ochre varnish, and painted the clay plug with it, sealing the jar up tight. Her slim fingers left ochre streaks and prints on the pottery. She lowered it into the hole, packing chunks of rock all about it and over it, until it was covered from sight.

There was a hole at the back of the cave, and she climbed out into the open air. It was rocky up there, she left no prints. She ran along the cliff face. They were below in the valley. She saw them coming up the rocky path. They shouted for joy as they saw their prey above them.

High up on the bluff, she stood still. There was no one left to say the prayers; no one left to make the dress sing; no one left.

She ran forward, flying through the air to the ground.

22

Wales

'Mr al-Masih?'

'Dr Connell?'

He recognised the Egyptian's accent, with its faint American overlay.

'Yes,' he said. 'Do you have a decision for me?'

'I have consulted with people in my government. Because we believe you to be innocent of the charges against you, we will give you asylum in Cairo while the matter is explained and concluded with your own authorities. We will do this provided that you bring with you the antiquarian texts in your keeping that are the legal property of the government and people of Egypt, these texts to be given over to the Coptic Museum.'

'I'll do that,' said Connell. 'How will you get me out?'

'A big Chriscraft boat will pick you up from somewhere on the coast. You will have to tell us where. It will take you across the Channel to France. An aeroplane will fly you to Egypt.'

'That sounds all right.'

Connell thought for a few seconds. He was reluctant to mention Wales. The Channel. Sudden memories of childhood holidays on the coast came to him.

'Exmouth,' he said. 'Near Exeter. You can moor in the estuary there, there're always a lot of boats.'

'Very well. Where shall we meet you?'

He remembered standing in the sun in his shorts with sand in his shoes and a crisp green pound note in his pocket, back when a pound could buy you a whole afternoon in the funfair. Standing watching the running men, the great white lifeboat gathering speed down its shining runners, the huge burst of foam as it hit the water; watching its wake as it headed out to sea.

'The lifeboat station,' he said. 'It's near the clock tower. You can't miss it.'

He was late. His Minor Traveller with its latticework of wood encasing the boxy rear, had burst a radiator hose near Weston-super-Mare. Now, as he came down into the town with the river Exe glittering on his right, white craft bobbing on the water, he smelled of antifreeze and radiator rust, and his hands were grubby and sticky from winding black repair tape about the decaying old hose.

They'd built a swimming pool since his day, and done something horrid to the railway station. He remembered taking the mighty Cornish Riviera Express with its coaches headed by the powerful Castle class 4–6–0, all oiled metal muscle and white steam. You changed at Exeter for the little two-coach Thomas the Tank Engine branch line that took you down to the coast. Thirty years on he still felt a prickle of excitement.

He turned on to the esplanade. People were on the beach. Sand-castles and moats were being flung up, pale feet under rolled-up trousers felt the unfamiliar grit of the yellow sand. He could smell hot-dogs, candyfloss and toffee-apples. In the distance he could see the white circle of the big wheel in the fairground. He had his window wound down and on the warm, salty air he could hear people shrieking happily on the roller-coaster.

They had built a multi-storey car park where the old tea-rooms used to be. The small boy inside him felt a stab of anger at the desecration of a splendid world. He remembered sitting in the corner window crusty with sand, with a glass of milk and a very sticky currant bun, slowly unwinding it as he read his dog-eared *Just William* and waited for his auntie to come back from her job in the shop.

He turned in to the car park and took a ticket from the machine. He remembered the old car park, it had had a man who guided people to a place. He'd been in the war, he limped.

On the first floor Connell parked and got out, automatically stuffing the ticket into his pocket. He carefully locked the old car. The texts were packed safely under the rear seat, out of sight. A *frisson* of anxiety brushed over him, sweeping his old memories away. In a little while he would be on a boat, heading out to sea. He was wanted on a murder charge. Men of evil intent were trying to kill him.

The stairs were smelly, someone had vomited over them. Connell turned away and pressed the button for the lift. The doors hissed open, and he stepped inside. As they closed, he could see the lifeboat station, very white in the sun. It was dark inside, the neon lamp flickering fitfully above him.

The lift shuddered faintly as it came to a stop and the doors wheezed open again. He took one step forward, and froze in mid-stride. Two men were standing in the shadow of the park, only a few yards away. They were looking out from the shade into the sun, towards the lifeboat station. He heard them speak.

'He's late.'

'Have patience. The Lord will deliver him up.'

Fox stood calmly, his weight on both feet. He was wearing blue trousers and a light-blue shirt, its sleeves rolled up below the elbow. He had some sort of communicator in his hand, Connell could not see if it was for a radio or simply a mobile phone. He and Giulio watched the station steadily. Giulio had a large oblong plaster on his temple where Connell had hit him.

Connell stood in agony. He reached out a finger and pressed the button to go back up. The doors shook with ague and wheezed. As they closed Connell saw Giulio turn his head to look behind him.

At the next floor Connell slipped from the lift as quickly and quietly as he could. The Minor Traveller was on the other side of the concrete floor, he could see the wood shining in the sun.

Feet were running up the stairs. He dived in between two parked cars and crouched down. Through a tiny gap he saw Giulio emerge, followed closely by Fox.

'He's here,' the younger man said. 'I tell you, I saw him.'

Behind them the lift doors clattered closed.

'Yes,' Fox said calmly, ominously. 'He's here.'

They split up to cover the floor. As quietly as he could, Connell dropped flat and crawled under the car next to him. He could see Giulio's trainers moving steadily and silently over the concrete. On knees and fingers, elbows and toes, Connell shifted under the cars like a crab. His head brushed an engine and oily fragments of dirt fell about him.

The feet were going away. He was under the last car in the row and could see the stairwell. He came out into the open, skittering like a bug for the doorway. He slithered on sick, and was out of sight.

Silently he scampered down the stairs and was on to the street, the fresh sea breeze blowing in his face.

'*There!*'

He saw Giulio hanging over the parapet above him. Fox

whipped the radiophone to his mouth and Connell ran. Way ahead of him a man in a blue shirt and trousers suddenly got off an esplanade bench and began to jog purposefully in his direction.

They had not changed everything. The alley that led up towards the funfair was still there, he went up it and took the old metal stile like a hurdler. As he ran round the corner he heard running feet behind him.

They had not changed the entrance to the fair either. The sun and the salt had faded the red paint, but the old clown still beckoned the fun-loving to come in. He pushed his money into the little kiosk and the girl inside passed him his ticket without looking up from her magazine article on the diets of the stars.

Inside the funfair time had stood still. The young girls still wore silly hats, they still giggled uncontrollably. Young children still ate pink candyfloss, still attempted to break their teeth on virulently coloured sticks of rock. Fathers paid up indulgently and thought about a pint, mothers complained about their feet. Connell slipped among them like a fish seeking shelter in a shoal.

Glancing back over his shoulder he saw the man from the esplanade coming through the gate and heading his way. Suddenly he found himself cornered between the roller-coaster kiosk and a busy hot-dog stand. He could feel the vibration through his feet as the little train did aerobatics on its line in the sky. Girls shrieked happily as it clattered down its last stretch and hit the water with a roar. For a second or two it was blotted quite out of sight, and then it came trundling into the station, dripping from its sides.

He could see the man getting nearer, cutting off his escape. In desperation he joined the queue at the kiosk and bought a ticket for the next ride.

He sat in the last carriage, trying to hide his face from sight as people filled up the seats in front of him. A young man in a satin bomber jacket looked along the train and headed for the back.

'This free?' he asked.

'It's free,' said Connell. He glanced at the young man sitting down next to him. Just a holidaymaker.

There was a jerk as the train caught on the traction gear, and they began to climb up the steep slope that led to the run. Connell could see the whole fairground spread out beneath them, and then the town itself, and the blue sea along the sand. Near the top the young man turned around to look back down. He waved at someone.

Connell glanced behind him. On the little station, Fox stood looking up at him.

He saw Connell and lifted a hand ironically.

'We want the texts, Dr Connell,' the young man said conversationally. The train reached the summit, rolled forward slowly for a second, and then pushed its nose down into the first of the switchbacks.

Fox's man beside him was quite relaxed. He had an arm on the side, he seemed to be enjoying the ride, secure in the knowledge that it would deliver him and Connell to the bottom, where Fox waited with his men.

'No point in making a fuss,' he said, over the roar of the clattering wheels. 'You don't want the police catching you, do you? You just give us the texts and you can go free.'

Connell knew, with a sudden utter certainty, that giving Fox the texts would be the last act of his life.

The train hurtled down a new slope. A ferocious one hundred and eighty-degree bend rushed up at them. Connell reached down and with a savage heave threw the man out of the carriage.

He flew through a gap in the lattice structure. Connell thought that he heard people scream.

The train was losing its impetus. It rolled lightly through a few more bends, saving its best for last. The final slope arrived, and the carriages accelerated downwards towards the water. It hit the pool with a crash and a boom. A huge sheet of white spray blotted everything from view and Connell squeezed from under the safety bar and hurled himself over the back.

The water rushed over him as he tumbled along the rails. Waves crashed against the sides and back again. He lifted his head clear. Water ran out of his ears and he heard people scream. There was horror in the sound, not joy.

The platform was clear. Lifting himself up he saw people running to the back of the ride, where the man had fallen. He got up and dropped down on the other side of the pool. The framework of the roller-coaster was all about him. He ran through it, out of sight. On the far side he pushed his way through a loose piece of hoarding. He was by the gate. Still dripping, he walked swiftly out. On the street, in the warm sunshine, he began to run.

The breath was tearing at his chest, his heart pounded in his ears. His mind had gone blank, all his intelligence and knowledge eradicated by stark elemental terror. He stopped.

He was out of town. His head was down, his hands on his knees as he dragged air into his lungs. Dirt was under his shoes. He looked up. He was on a construction road amongst pine trees and scrub. He could hear the sea. Through the trees he could see piles of tubing, and very large white concrete pipes. Nobody was about.

He heard a car coming and saw it through the trees. A dark

Citroën. He ran again. Behind him he heard the engine rev suddenly, and knew that they had him.

He was in the construction site. A great pipe jutted from the ground and he dived into it, slithering down inside.

He lay in a pool of stagnant water. From the outside he heard the car, heard voices echoing down the tube. From behind him he could hear water, the sea.

Looking up he could still see daylight, white cloud against the sky. He edged backwards, out of sight. There was a circular ridge running around the tube, he eased his knees over it, moving backwards. From above, the voices were harsh.

Beyond the ridge was a slope. He put his foot down to anchor himself and it slipped on slime. He slithered backwards. In the dark he made a wild grab for the ridge and felt it pass under his fingers. He shot into the blackness. For a second he flew, and then he landed with a huge splash. The impact winded him, he floundered about, water filling his mouth, his eyes and his ears. He forced himself to his hands and knees as air retched into his lungs, and he heard someone shout. There was the sound of a man climbing into the tube. A scraping, an echoing.

The water in his mouth was salt. Light glimmered in the distance. He stood up, and cracked his head on the roof, bending low, he began to stagger down the tunnel, splashing and tripping. From behind him he heard the crash as his pursuer fell into the pool he had just left. Almost immediately, he heard him coming after him.

The tunnel was going down, the water was rising. There was a thin quarter-moon of light, only a few inches high. He was crouched over on his hands and knees, his face practically in the water. He took a deep breath, and went under, his feet pushing in the silt, his hands swimming.

Someone grabbed his ankle, pulling him back. The breath

was roaring in his lungs. His hands gripped the tunnel mouth and he kicked viciously with his free foot. He was suddenly free, he heaved and he was out in the sunshine. The sea was all about him and he struck out with hands and feet for the shore, half blind in the light, choking and gasping.

Giulio caught him from behind as he crawled up the beach, dragged him down, ramming his face into the water.

'Where are they?' he cried. 'Where are the texts?'

He pulled him up by the hair, screaming into his ear.

'Where are they, where are the messages of Satan?'

There was something under his hand, sticking out from the sand, something hard. Giulio slammed his head down into the water once again. As he pulled him up Connell dragged the object with him and struck out with it. His attacker screamed in sudden pain. Giulio staggered back across the sand, blood spilling from a wound across his face, and Connell pursued him, hitting him again and again to stop him from running and getting help.

The sand was covered in gouts of blood. The rusty length of angle iron in Connell's hand ran with it. Giulio was on his hands and knees, from somewhere someone was screaming. Connell was insane with fear and rage, no longer a man but a frenzied animal, he clubbed his victim, stabbed him and slashed him until he did not move.

Finally the screaming broke through into his mind Connell looked up from his murder and saw a woman shrieking at the top of the beach. A man stood next to her, something dark on his shoulder. A single black eye stared at Connell. A video-camera.

Connell staggered forward, the woman pulled frantically at her companion and they broke and ran. Connell paused, looking about him at the carnage, then he lurched forward still running.

The house seemed unoccupied. The garden was overgrown, nature was overcoming cultivation. Salt was stripping the windows of paint, streaking the glass. The door was ajar, the brass knocker was green. A creeper was consuming the porch.

Connell went inside, his shoes squelching. The room led on to a kitchen that looked out on to an equally overgrown back garden. A young woman was seated in front of open French windows. A small easel was in front of her, various pots of paints sat on a little table, she was creating a picture. Softly coloured birds hung upon grass stems, cutting free the seeds with their bills. She looked up from her work as he staggered into the room.

'You are covered in blood,' she said unafraid. 'Why?'

'Some people are trying to kill me,' he gasped, into the quiet of the abandoned room.

'I think I've been waiting for you,' she said, and turned back to the painting. Connell came forward, his whole body feeling almost light from shaking so much.

The girl got up and poured some water from a jug. She gave him the cup and he drank it gratefully. The salt was harsh in his mouth.

'Where are you running to?' she asked.

'I'm just running,' he said, and his legs gave way, sinking him to the ground.

'Have you got anywhere to go?'

'Yes. I have a house.'

'A house in a city?' she asked, watching him closely.

'No. A cottage in Wales. It's very old. Miles from anywhere.'

'That sounds nice,' she said. She began to screw lids on to her pots of paint. 'How will you get there?'

'I have a car,' he said, 'but I'm afraid to go and get it.'

'Of course you are,' she said calmly. 'So I'll get it for you. Have a spare room, this cottage of yours?'

'Yes, of course.'

'I'd like to paint in Wales. So where is your car?'

He reached into his sodden pocket, his hand dragging on the material. He emptied it out, and some keys and a parking ticket fell on to the floor.

'It's in the multi-storey car park, an old Morris Minor, the type with wood on the back. Do you know what I mean?'

'Yes. You don't see many now.'

He held out the keys and ticket.

'Can you drive?' he asked. 'It's up on the first floor.'

'I don't have a licence,' she said smiling, and took the keys. At the door she looked about the room.

'They're coming to knock this down next week,' she said.

After she had gone Connell made himself get up. He took off his shirt and washed himself in the sink. Blood and sand and mud swirled on the old porcelain. He dried himself on a worn towel that was hanging from a hook, very thin but clean, with hands that shook like an old man's. Under the sink he found a small camping stove fuelled by a blue gas cylinder. He boiled a little pan of water and made tea, very hot and sweet, with a tube of condensed milk. As he was finishing it he heard the noise of the car outside. He looked up, sudden weary fear bruising him.

The girl came in. She looked at him in intuitive sympathy.

'Did you think it was them?' she said.

Connell nodded.

'It's only me,' she said. 'I saw police in the town. We'd better go before someone finds you.'

Connell lay down on the floor in the back and pulled a blanket over him. The girl got into the front. As she started up he reached out a hand and touched the boxes that held the gospels of the Children of Jeshua.

23

Wales

A man on his knees begged for his life. He held out bloodied hands for mercy. His executioner struck him with his blade and blood flew. He fell backwards, still holding up one hand in a last plea. The man above him hit him again and again until he was still.

The killer looked up from his victim, straight into the camera. His teeth were bared in a rictus of savagery, his fist gripped his brutal weapon. He snarled, he was unrecognisable as a normal human being. He was a psychopathic murderer.

The image froze on the screen and the announcer spoke again, in a voice that had had emotion beaten from it. It was the sound of a man trying to describe something he did not want to recognise.

'Dr Frank Connell is already wanted for the murder of his business associate, the antiquarian book dealer George Abercrombie, in horrifying circumstances. The police suspect satanic ritual. The two latest victims of the serial killer were Catholic seminary students. The police describe Dr Connell as the most dangerous wanted man in Britain today. They said that under no circumstances should he be approached by a member of the public.'

Connell reached out and switched off his small portable television. Outside, Welsh songbirds were singing before dusk.

'That's you,' he said quietly to the girl. 'A member of the public.'

He glanced up.

'You can leave if you want. I won't stop you.'

She stared steadily at him.

'Got anything to drink, here?' she enquired.

'Yes . . . of course.'

'I'll have what you have.'

'I drink wine,' said Connell, 'that's what the Children drink.'

He got up and took a bottle of Australian Shiraz from his rack, pulling the cork and filling two tumblers.

'Why did you kill him?' the girl asked quietly.

'They would have killed me. And they wanted the gospels. We're soldiers in a very long war. We kill each other as a matter of course. I see that now.'

He sat back in his chair, exhaustion flooding over him.

'What war? And how long?'

'Nearly two thousand years,' Connell whispered.

The girl leaned forward and pushed his glass up to his mouth.

'Drink a bit,' she said, 'it'll help you talk. I have to know.'

Connell gulped and the pungent wine stimulated him.

'The Children put herbs in their wine,' he said.

'What children?' she demanded. 'Who are these children?'

Connell drank some more wine, and as always, he revived. He got up. He had put the boxes containing the texts by the door, now he went over and placed them on the table he had set up for himself to work at. He opened one very carefully.

'See,' he said. She got up and looked inside at the ancient papyrus books and scrolls.

'Gospels copied in the fourth century,' he said quietly. 'The history and liturgy of a religious movement that called themselves the Children of Jeshua. Jeshua is Aramaic, it means the same as the Hebrew Joshua, or the Greek Jesus.'

'The called themselves the Children of Jesus,' she said.

'Yes. They believed that they were descended – *quite literally* – from Jesus, and his wife Mary of Magdala.'

'Mary Magdalene?'

'Yes.'

'The sisters told me she was a whore that Christ took pity on.'

Connell looked at her enquiringly.

'Sisters?'

'I have no family,' she said levelly. 'I got left with my auntie and she died. I was put in this home, that the nuns ran. The Sisters of Mercy. Though they weren't . . .'

'No . . .' he said. 'And Mary of Magdala wasn't a whore, she was the foremost disciple of Jesus, and he married her.'

'So why call her that?'

'Are there women bishops?' he asked. 'The Church doesn't like women, except when they are bowing down in worship. It decided at the beginning that it didn't like females, which cut it off from the oldest myth in the world, the myth of the goddess. The Great Mother is missing from Christianity, it's one of the things most wrong with it, that makes it so flawed. Mary, the mother of Jesus, is unrecognised as the mother goddess. The Christian Church treats the Earth as though it were dead matter, which cuts if off again. The Great Mother is goddess of the Earth. For the Children, the Earth and her creatures are a whole, the planet itself is alive, all other life depends upon it.'

The girl looked at him with a faint amusement.

'The wine's done you good. You're talking.'

Connell smiled wryly.

'I'm a Celt,' he said, 'talking's no problem to me.'

She frowned again, looking at the texts in their boxes.

'Why? Why hate women?'

'The Children believed that the Church was the creation of Satan, that he made it in his own image,' Connell said quietly.

She looked at him steadily, with unblinking dark blue eyes.

'What do you think?'

'I . . . well, I'm an academic, it's easy to get carried away . . .' Connell hedged.

'You said you were a soldier,' she reminded him.

'Yes . . . there's something very terrible about the way the Church destroyed every other belief. They acted like some fearful predator . . . they sucked other religions' blood and killed them. Christ has a halo because he's the sun god. He was born on Christmas Day because it's the winter solstice, that's when Mithras was born. He was resurrected at Easter because that's when Dionysus was reborn. Easter falls on the Sunday following the first full moon after the spring equinox, so that the resurrection of Christ, like that of Dionysus, reflects the turning of winter into spring. Although of course the death of the god who descends into Hades for three days before being reborn – the number of days of darkness while the moon is not seen – is even older than Dionysus. The gods and goddesses change names but the story is the same, whether it is Ishtar and Tammuz, Cybele and Attis, Aphrodite and Adonis, or Jesus, son of the Virgin Mother, Mary. That's a fundamental in beliefs. But the Christian Church didn't miss out on detail either. The bishops bless with the sign of Sabazios, their crook is the crook of Attis, the Good Shepherd. The festivals of the Christian Church are all robbed from the celebrations of other gods and goddesses that they proceeded to murder.'

'But what do *you* think?' she said again.

'There is one thing I find strange . . .' he said slowly. 'The

Children fight the Church of Rome all the way. Even when they are reduced to acting as a resistance movement against an occupying power, they fight. Their last member buries their texts and gospels with the written hope that someone will one day find them and take up the cause.'

Connell looked up. Outside a bird was singing in an old, overgrown apple tree.

'They didn't fight *anyone else*. Only the Church of Rome. And they fought them right from the start. That's the strange thing.'

He put down his glass on the windowsill and gazed out at the gathering dusk.

'You see, the world as it was in the first century was simply teeming with beliefs. The cult of Jesus was just one of hundreds, and within it there were hundreds of sects, of which the Church of Rome was only one. And yet it's there, right from the beginning in their gospels. *They are commanded by Jesus himself to fight the Orthodox Church, for it is the Church of Satan.* How did they know? How did they know that the Church of Rome would win, and slaughter all others, centuries later?'

'Perhaps Jesus Christ told them so,' she said quietly.

Connell woke to sunshine streaming through his bedroom window. A bird, perhaps the same bird, was singing in the apple tree. He could smell tea.

He got up and put on his dressing gown, slotting his feet into the slippers by the bed. Downstairs the girl was sitting at the table, reading from a sheet of typed paper. A small pile of them lay in front of her. His fat brown teapot sat in the middle of the table, poking its snout from its knitted woollen cosy.

'Morning,' she said brightly, 'I made tea, is it all right? I found your caddy. Shall I pour you some?'

'Yes, please. A couple of sugars.'

He sat down. He found he liked having this young person with him.

'I love tea,' she said, passing him his mug. The door was open, countryside smells of grass and plants seeped through it.

'My auntie taught me about tea,' he said. 'When I used to stay with her on the coast. That's her pot, she left it to me because I liked tea so much.'

'*My* auntie loved tea!' she exclaimed. 'She would never use a tea bag, only leaves.'

'Only leaves,' he agreed gravely. 'And take the pot to the kettle. You can keep the leaves afterwards, you know, they're good for clematis. You put them about the crown.'

'Are you a gardener?'

'Can't tell a pansy from a petunia. It was George who loved gardens. I kept my tea leaves for him.'

Simply saying his name made his eyes suddenly sting, and he wiped them.

'That was your friend,' she said.

'Yes. The one I am supposed to have murdered.'

He looked up at her.

'I did kill him,' he said. 'I had to. They had nailed him to the wall and set the house on fire. I couldn't leave him to burn . . . I stabbed him with a scissor blade.'

He looked outside, a sudden rush of panic in his stomach, but there was only the bird. It stopped singing and flew off towards the hedge.

'I've been reading this,' she said, holding out the sheet of paper. 'Is that all right?'

He swallowed tea, and the anxiety ebbed away.

'Of course. You're reading one of the texts. That's a translation I made from the Coptic.'

'I do like them, the Children. They're very brave. I like reading about them.'

Behind her he could see her books, the rather shabby, worn second-hand books that she had brought with her from the condemned house. She had set them out carefully on a shelf, along with her box of paint jars and canvases ready to be turned into pictures.

'You like reading,' he said.

'Oh, I love it.' Her face came alight. 'I had my books when I lived with my auntie, because she loved to read. She used to sit with me when I was little, and we'd read together. Stories about animals and people and places and dreams . . .'

Her small face twisted.

'The sisters threw all my books away,' she said bitterly. 'And gave me a Bible.'

She looked at the text she had been reading.

'I hated them, and I hated it,' she said. 'I love the Children, they hate them too.'

'Yes, they do.'

'God loves you,' she said. 'That's what they told me every day. God loves you and you must love him. He knows your every thought, and if you think of sin he will punish you. He will burn you in Hell. One of the sisters burned my finger with a match so that I would know. She told me that was like cold spring water, compared to Hell.'

'What did you do?' he asked.

'It was a book. It could have been a drawing, or a song. Or a dance. I love to dance. But I wasn't allowed to sing, or dance, or paint,' she said. 'And they'd taken my books away. So I used to dance in my head, sing songs in my head, paint pictures in my head, read my books in my head, all the books I'd had as a little girl. If I lay in bed at night – we had to lie straight with our arms out so we wouldn't touch ourselves and think of sin – I could dance and sing and paint and read, all in my head.'

'That's a great talent,' Connell observed.

'It kept me from going mad,' she said, and her mouth turned again. 'There was a little place by the fence where the sisters couldn't see you. Every day a boy passed by there on his way to and from school. He had books; I knew, because sometimes he came by with his nose in one. So I asked him for one and he gave it to me. When I gave it back he let me have another.'

'What happened?' he asked, leaning forward to catch her words.

'They found one. It was about a talking wolf and a witch, it was good. They said God was very angry with me. I said I hated God. They whipped me and put me in a cupboard. I broke out in the night, I climbed over the railing and ran away.'

'How old were you?'

'Twelve. I've been running ever since.'

'How old are you?'

'Nineteen.'

She busied herself with the teapot, milk and sugar.

'One of the sisters, she used to come by my cubicle,' she said, without looking up. 'She used to touch me where we weren't supposed to touch. I hated her. I prayed to God every day to make her stop, but he never did.'

'He never does,' Connell observed. 'Hence the saying of the concentration camps – "God is on leave." He never does intervene. The Church explains it through the doctrine of free will, otherwise known as God Helps Those Who Help Themselves.'

'So what is the point of prayer?' she asked.

'Who is listening to the radio?' asked Connell. 'The Children believed that they were warriors fighting in enemy territory. That the world was controlled by Satan. They fought for God, his wife the Great Mother and their son, who were good, against Satan, who was evil. It was worth doing because it was a free contest between the God and Goddess and Satan, and God and the Great Mother could win. The only problem was that they didn't. The Children, God's SAS commandos, were always outnumbered by the troops of the devil. When people prayed, it was Satan who sat by the radio listening.'

She listened, watching him with intelligent eyes.

'Can I read all this? What you've translated?'

'Of course.'

He hesitated, then spoke.

'This is silly. You save my life and I don't even know your name.'

She shrugged.

'What would you like to call me?'

'Don't you have a name?'

'Yes. But I didn't like it. I don't use it.'

He made a mental leap.

'Mary? Like the Virgin Mary on the wall?'

She nodded, dropping her eyes.

'There was another Mary, Mary of Magdala, the wife of Jesus. They had a daughter called Maria. I'm reading about her now. She has a hard time of it too. She was brave – just like you. You could call yourself after her.'

'I'm not brave. Am I?' she asked, as though the question had not occurred to her.

'Oh, you are,' he said quietly, 'you most certainly are.'

'Tell me about her.'

'She lived with her mother and her younger brother Jeshua in Antioch. Around the year 60 A.D. What we call *Anno*

Domini because the Church counted everything from the birth of Jesus, so it became the year of our Lord, and they got so powerful they could make everyone else do so too. Mary of Magdala was murdered very early one morning as the sun came up, by a man she feared very much. He was the Fisherman. He was Cephas, that we know of as Peter, disciple of Jesus.

'The two children managed to escape, although Jeshua was wounded by a spear thrown by Peter's secretary and minder, Mark. They managed to jump on to a grain-carrying ship bound, as most vessels were then, for Rome. There they fell in with a man with two names.'

'How do you mean, two names?'

'He had two names because he had two personalities,' Connell explained.

'Like Jekyll and Hyde?' she said.

'Yes. Very like Jekyll and Hyde. Most of the time he was Saul, but he could become Paul.'

Connell pointed his mug at the boxes.

'I haven't really met Paul yet. Saul knows he's there waiting, he talks about him. Paul is *the* Paul. Visionary, religious poet, missionary, apostle, inventor of a new belief that was to take over much of the world. Christianity. Those who benefited from his unique creativity, the bishops, were very grateful to him, they made him a saint. St Paul. Saul doesn't get too much of a look in. Saul is who Paul was before his conversion – supposedly on the road to Damascus – a hard-line Pharisee, a persecutor of the Early Church.'

She frowned.

'But if he's in Rome he must be Paul, not Saul. Wasn't he sent there for trial?'

'Supposedly,' said Connell, 'but Saul was a Roman agent, a kind of supergrass, we would say. He's in Rome because his masters got him out. Saul is what you might think, a first-class shit, dangerous, untrustworthy, a nasty piece of work. The last person the two children should have got involved with, as they were to find out. And yet . . . it isn't that simple. Even given the fact that Saul is what he is, Paul won't go away. Paul is real, he lives inside Saul's head, Saul can talk to him, like he was a brother. And Paul really did do that. He is the one responsible for it all.'

'What did Saul do to the children, Maria and Jeshua?' she asked anxiously.

'He betrayed them to the Fisherman – to Peter.'

He paused, thinking.

'I still have to find out what happened. Then I must get back in touch with al-Masih.'

'Who?'

'A man who's going to help me. I think Juliana's phone must be tapped . . . that's how Fox found me . . .'

He put his mug forward.

'Does the pot hold any more? I must read the texts, now that I have them all. Do you want to read my translations?'

'Yes, *please*.'

She filled up the mug.

'I'll take it up while I shave,' he said. 'Then I'll get it all in order for you. There's something else about Maria, the daughter of Mary of Magdala.'

'What's that?'

'She seems to come back, again and again, all through the history of the Children. Sometimes she's Ruth, sometimes Mary, sometimes Maria. But she's the same. Juliana spotted it. She is a reincarnation. Or do you think that's crazy?'

'No, I don't,' she said soberly. 'Did they survive? the first Maria and her brother Jeshua?'

'Maria did. Not Jeshua. . . . I have a mention of Maria with Mark in the *Bellum Judaicum*, the Jewish Revolt of the late sixties. But there's a gap of several years before she gets there. The last I know of her is her being sold into slavery in Rome.'

He found her outside the stone barn, which she had set up as a studio. She was painting the trees of the old overgrown orchard, apples, damsons and plums. Elderflowers splashed their green coats with fading white flowers. He stood behind her, admiring the work, and was struck by the softness of the colours. He peered at her array of pots, and saw that they were without labels.

'Where do you buy these?' he asked.

'You don't,' she said, and flecked the hillside with the golden yellow of the gorse bushes. 'You make them.'

'*Make* them?'

'Of course. The ones you buy are synthetic. Too bright. Harsh, like the world. So I make these.'

Connell had an opened bottle of wine, he poured some into two tumblers.

'You can make this too, if you know how,' he said.

She put down her paintbrush and took the glass, sitting in the dappled shade.

He pointed up on the hillside, at the gorse bushes blazing like molten gold in the sun.

'You can make wine from the gorse flowers,' he said. 'I drank some once. It made me feel quite Olympian. How do you make paints?'

'From plants;' she said, 'from roots and leaves and seeds; from shellfish; clays and minerals, sometimes. I learned how to do it, I worked with some people that had an old water mill, they had people there that knew all the old ways of making things. People from the city used to come and watch us, they liked seeing things done by people. I can make a chair, you know, using a lathe you work with your foot. I can make a boat, a coracle so light you can carry it on your back to the water. I know all the old ways, from when people made things, not machines. And I can make paints.'

'Maria would know how to do it too, she knows all about the herbs,' he said. A thought came to him, and he got up, going to the house.

'I'll be back in a moment,' he said. When he reappeared he was carrying a box, which he put carefully down on the table. Inside were layers of cotton wool, and also a glass jar. He brought it out into the light, and held it up. Little fragments half filled it, a fine silt of multi-coloured pieces like bits of mosaic.

'What is it?' she said. 'It's beautiful.'

'They are the holy herbs of the Children,' he said. 'They used them for their most important rituals. They were in a leather flask in the pottery jar. Maria put them there when she hid it. I don't know what they are made up of.'

She held the jar reverently.

'I might be able to identify them,' she said. 'If I may.'

'They came with something else,' he said. 'When we opened the jar, the scrolls and codices were strewn with them.'

He peeled back the top layer of cotton wool, and she gasped as the sun glistened on row upon row of tiny silver and golden bells.

'What are they?' she breathed. 'Where did they come from?'

'They are the bells of the robe of glory Maria wore. It was sewn with all these tiny bells, so that when she danced, it sang.'

'Where is it? The robe?'

'There was nothing left of it,' he said. 'Only the bells.'

'What would it have been made of?' she asked curiously.

'Muslin, perhaps, or a light wool.'

'Hmm.'

In her turn, she got up and went inside the barn. She reappeared with a bolt of soft, creamy-coloured cloth which she held out for him to see.

'Like this?'

'Oh, yes.'

He stroked the material. It was slightly uneven, light, hand-woven.

'It's lovely,' he said. 'Where did you get it?'

'I made it.'

She took a drink from her glass.

'How?'

'On a loom. When I worked with the ancient crafts people. It's still untouched, I haven't dyed it yet. I don't know whether to make it into a blanket, or clothing, a rug, or what.'

'That's the kind of cloth the Children would have used.'

'The robe of glory,' she mused. 'Would it have been dyed?'

'Not one colour,' he said. 'We have a description of it. It was sewn with bells, of course, but it was coloured. Blue as the sky, woven of the stars of heaven, of moonbeams, sunbeams, of all the flowers of the world.'

She picked up one tiny bell, and rang it softly next to her ear.

'It must sing again,' she said.

24

Rome, A.D. 63

They came into the market, a strange, ill-matched trio, the tall, aristocratic senator, his young wife, his handsome catamite. They were there to purchase a personal slave for Gaia, an attendant to improve her position in the house, for Flavius proved unwilling to send Calenus away.

A young girl caught Gaia's eye immediately, dressed in a white shift she stood up tall, holding her head proudly and looking over the milling throng in disdain, unlike the majority of the craven wretches on the blocks. Her hair was sable black, her piercing eyes stared into a world only she was aware of.

'That one looks suitable,' said Gaia smiling pleasantly at her husband.

'The dealer's Jew,' Flavius grunted. 'A Syrian Jew at that. I know my Jew. We'll look around first. It doesn't do to be too eager, with your Jew.'

They spent some time examining other specimens before passing by the man's stand once more. Gaia stood looking with feigned indifference. She desperately needed an ally, a friend. Even a slave would do.

'What do you think, darling?' Flavius enquired. Gaia knew that it was not she who was being addressed. Flavius's love was for the boy. She was there to provide one thing, an heir, and so far she had not done it. Each month the smile on the face of Calenus grew stronger, and more vicious.

'She looks strong,' the boy said indifferently. 'Although one cannot see with her clothes on.'

'She has no needed to possess the physique of a carthorse,' Gaia said sharply. 'She is to be a personal maid.'

She needed a friend, someone to help her. *Why why why* wouldn't she get with child? What was she doing wrong? She should have asked her mother, she supposed. It was too late now. The old woman had been carried from her house with blood running from her ears, glistening like a sow.

Flavius indicated interest with a raise of his eyebrow and the dealer came over, beaming obsequiously and wiping his hands.

'I need a new maid,' said Flavius. 'What about that one there? Is she strong?'

'You can see for yourself, Lord,' said the dealer. 'You! Take off your clothes.'

Stone-faced, the girl did as she was bid. Standing slightly behind Flavius, Calenus's eyes ran over her body, from her toes to her hair.

'Strong as a mule,' said the Jew.

'And as obstinate?' suggested Flavius.

'No, Lord, as docile as a puppy dog.'

Flavius knew his Jew; he nodded, and moved on once more. The Jew, who knew his Roman aristocrat, his catamite and his wife, watched him go off with a certain confident patience. Gaia paused, still looking at the girl, who was pulling her shift back on. There was something about her that was familiar. She addressed her.

'I am Gaia, wife of Flavius. Do you know me?'

The girl looked down from the slave block.

'I have seen you,' she said. 'Prefect Titillinus held a party for the emperor. He made your husband fight on a raft.'

Gaia's face drained of colour at the memory.

'Then you also saw what happened to me,' she said bravely.

'Yes. I am Maria, I danced amongst the maenads of Dionysus.'

'Ill luck comes to us all,' said Gaia. 'It has visited you, else you would not be standing here with chalk on your feet.'

She was silent for a moment before putting her thoughts and fears into words.

'You are in need of help,' she said in a quiet voice. 'Let me tell you what will happen to you if I do not buy you. You are young and beautiful. This Jew will sell you for a great deal of money. The one that buys you will see you as a business proposition. Some Greek or Jewish *leno* will buy you for his *pervigile* keep-awake bar, or his whorehouse, and want to wring every last breath out of you. You do not look the kind to submit. Either he will kill you, or you him. Either way you will die, for it is the long death of the rods for slaves who kill their masters.'

'I am not meant to die,' said Maria. 'Not yet.'

'You can be my slave instead. I too need help. I do not know what I will ask of you, but I must have it done. Will you do what I ask?'

'Yes.'

'Then let me talk to my husband.'

Gaia went through the browsing crowd to where Flavius stood with Calenus. As he saw her coming, the boy slipped away, back towards the slave dealer.

'That one,' said Gaia.

'She is very expensive . . .' Flavius hedged.

'*Then Calenus's backside must be lined with pure gold by now,*' Gaia whispered savagely. 'You have what you want, give me what I want.'

Flavius stared levelly at his young wife. The scar on his arm was red, vanishing into the sleeve of his toga.

'I do not yet have all I want,' he pointed out.

'You will,' Gaia promised.

'Very well then.' He reached for the *crumella* about his neck. 'Now let us see how far we can drive this Jew down. *Aureo hamo piscari*, after all. Cash on the nail talks.'

Calenus came up to the dealer and lounged against his lectern of records.

'It looks like Uncle will make you a sale,' he drawled, 'for the young bitch there. Tell me, though, aside from being as strong as a mule and as docile as a puppy, is she a good fuck?'

'Ah . . .' The man put back his head and rolled his eyes to the heavens. 'Lord, your nights will be spent in such ecstatic pleasures you will spend all the day longing for evening to fall. See those breasts, like twin roses! That belly, like heaped wheat set about the lilies. Those thighs as white as ivory . . . see her mouth, how pink the lips, how white the teeth, like a flock of sheep, even shorn and fresh from the washing!'

Calenus smiled his small, vicious smile.

'I'll settle for hearing her squeal,' he said.

It was quiet in the villa's small sunlit square. In the bedroom of Gaia Maria had the heavy white shutters nearly closed to keep out the harsh light of midday and its accompanying heat. In the pleasant gloom she sorted through the pile of clothes as she had been commanded. Some she folded away, putting them in the big wooden chest at the end of the bed, some she reserved, after examination, for repair and redyeing at the *infectores*. Clothes had value, even those of the dead. Gaia could put her mother's belongings to some use.

There was a leathery rustle as the heavy curtain was pushed back. She looked up in surprise to see Calenus come into the room. He leaned against the wall and eyed her insolently.

'Your mistress is out,' he observed. 'She has gone off with Uncle.'

'I know,' she said, and continued to work through the clothing.

'I saw you without your clothes, in the marketplace.'

'It is one of the disadvantages of being up for sale, that the least worthy may see one not as one wishes,' she observed.

'You have no wishes,' he snapped. 'You are a slave.'

She picked up a shimmering saffron-yellow *palla* and examined it carefully without response.

'I wish to see you without your clothes,' Calenus ordered.

'I am not *your* slave,' she commented, without looking up. She folded the big square scarf.

'I am a free man,' he said dangerously. 'You are without rights. If I wish to view your body you will do as I say.'

She looked up at him for the first time.

'I know what happens in this house,' she said. 'Do you not take the master in your mouth? Do you not bend over the bed *a tergo*? Is this what a free man does? Slaves work because they must. Prostitutes do what they do because they are paid.'

Even in the dim light she could see Calenus's face whiten with rage.

'I wanted to look,' he whispered. 'But now you will have to do more for what you have said.'

'You wished to look to begin with. Then torment me further. Why? Is it that I help the mistress, that you hate?'

He sprang at her suddenly, forcing her up against the wall with surprising strength. She tried to push him away and her clothing tore as they struggled. She felt his hand inside her tunic, he squeezed her breast savagely and she cried out. His hand was between her thighs, he hurt her as she clamped her legs together. He gripped her throat, crushing the breath from her, and her eyes became dim. She reached down between

465

his own legs, feeling him stiff and hot. With desperate strength she clenched her fist on him and he screamed, a high-pitched howl of agony.

The breath rushed back into her chest. He was on his knees beside the bed, his hands clutched to his groin, moaning. The leather curtain crashed back and Gaia stood in the doorway. She looked at Calenus and her eyes gleamed.

'I should have warned you about *him*,' she said. 'But I see you now know. I'm going shopping. Flavius has been detained on business. Come.'

Calenus looked up at her, his eyes brimming with hate.

'I'll tell Uncle about this,' he promised. 'I'll have your bitch cut up into pieces.'

'Tell *Uncle* what?' Gaia demanded victoriously. 'You're his *bugger* boy. He won't want to hear that you secretly desire women, will he? Come, Maria. I think *I* desire one of the new glass mirrors. And we shall go to the baths.'

The two girls swept from the room, and Calenus very slowly got to his feet, bent and hunched in pain.

'I'll see that you pay,' he whispered. 'I'll see you pay, you see if I don't.'

By the door the attendant of the baths pulled the cords of the pulley. In the roof the bronze dome that closed off the ceiling rose, and mist leaked out into the air. Shafts of sunlight lit up the steam like golden bars. Lying on the marble slab Gaia put her face into the towel and closed her eyes as Maria massaged her.

'I *must* get with child,' she said, her voice muffled. 'I *must*. I've tried everything. I've sat in the lap of Mutinus, I've prayed to Isis, last month I sacrificed a bull, I sent his *vires* to the heavens as sweet smoke, but nothing.'

466

She twisted her head, and one sharp eye peered up at Maria.

'If my belly doesn't swell soon then Flavius will get rid of me and try with someone else. And then we will *both* be in it, because I don't know about you, but I have nowhere to go.'

'*Does* he try?' Maria asked quietly, rubbing oil into the muscles of Gaia's neck, which were as taut as hawsers.

'It is difficult for him . . .' Gaia muttered. 'He is used to buggery, and he is old . . . If it were not for this feeling of honour he has, he would not do it at all, and when he does, he must be drunk first. And when he is drunk, it is difficult to . . . interest him.'

'All your muscles are tight,' said Maria.

'So would yours be! That little bastard Calenus, he sniggers at me . . . He only awaits my downfall. He seems to know when Flavius will try, and he gets to him first. It's like handling boiled asparagus then.'

She turned over restlessly.

'Do my front. Oh, just look at you . . .'

She reached up with a gentle hand and touched Maria's breast. It was swollen, the marks of Calenus's fingers livid against the milky skin.

'The little rat . . . I'd like to ram something sharp up him.'

Her hand moved across to the other side, and stroked her. She glanced around to see if any of the other bathers were visible in the steam.

'Do it to me . . .' she whispered. 'Oh, it's nice. Flavius never touches me . . .'

In the fog there came the hiss of water on the coals, and a wave of fresh hot steam billowed over them. Gaia slipped her hand down Maria's body, and between her legs.

'There. Please do it there. There is an ache . . .'

Maria put the scented oil on her hand, and massaged the soft skin of Gaia's thighs. She moaned in the mist, her whole body shivering, and stuffed the towel into her mouth to stifle her cries. As taut as a bowstring, her body arched. Tears leaked from between her tightly closed lids, and she suddenly slumped on to the marble.

She dragged the towel from between her teeth and opened her eyes.

'Oh, what was that?' she whispered. 'What happened?'

'You will feel better now,' said Maria gently, and Gaia slid herself from the table, standing on shaking legs.

'I'd better get to the cool room,' she muttered.

'A farmer, when the cow does not get in calf, changes the bull,' Maria said.

Theatre of Balbus, Rome

'The actors for the final scene haven't arrive,' Scipio said irritably.

A dawn shower had wet the stone seating outside the three-storey stage structure, now a warm morning breeze was drying it. People placed their cushions down on tavertine limestone, settling themselves comfortably in preparation for the show, exchanging jokes and gossip with their neighbours, their cheerful voices filling the auditorium. A visit to the theatre was a pleasant diversion.

'There was an absolute mob in the streets today,' said Gaia. 'My litter was behind a load of Ligurian stone, it took ages. Where are your actors coming from?'

'From the *ludus magnus* over on the Via Labicana,' the theatrical director said absently, looking at his preparations. 'The *procuratore* promised to have them here by dawn, curse him. Oh well, if they don't arrive Lucius will just have to stay on stage.'

The mime actor and singer performing stretching exercises in a corner laughed. 'I would do anything for my art, but that may be taking it too far.'

'It would go down in history,' Scipio assured him. 'Oh, Valeria, do you have a moment?'

A strikingly handsome and well-formed woman in a reseda-yellow gown altered her course to come to them. Inside the stage building it hummed with the noise of moving actors, stagehands shifting scenery, musicians practising short bars on zithers, flutes and trumpets, the muttering of incantations for good luck and performance.

'Yes, Scipio?'

'Would you take Gaia and show her to our guest seating?'

'Of course. Oh, Hylas says the actors have arrived.'

'Good. Lucius, your finest moment can wait for another day.'

The actress took Gaia past a small forest of foliage and a wood-pile of faggots waiting to go on stage, through an entrance that led out into the dancing-ground, the orchestra, and up to a prime row of seats marked off with small red flags.

'Which part do you play?' Gaia asked.

'I have a number of roles, but I do star once! I'm the one with the swan. Scipio will be down in a moment.'

She hurried away, and Gaia sat down. She soon spotted the director coming through the crowd from the rear of the stage, a handsome man in his thirties. He was an acquaintance of Flavius. Calenus had played upon the stage, it was where Flavius had first conceived his desire for his smooth, unmarked body.

'Are you comfortable?' he asked, sitting down next to her.

'Very,' she said, 'and so looking forward to the show. This is its first production, is it not?'

'Not quite,' he said, his eyes flicking about his theatre. 'The idea was commissioned by Prefect Tigillinus, as a surprise for the Emperor.'

'Oh,' said Gaia, unable to keep the horror from her voice.

'They aren't here today,' Scipio said, not unkindly, 'but the Emperor likes theatrical events and the prefect is always ready to oblige his master.'

'Yes. I went with Flavius to a party thrown by the prefect . . .'

'It is difficult to refuse,' he said. He looked her in the eyes and she saw a depth of knowledge there. He shrugged. 'If I wish to practise my art I must be here, must I not? I must have powerful patrons, must I not? Who is more powerful than the Emperor?'

He glanced around, the automatic reaction.

'But my family, I keep at the farm' he said quietly. 'It is not safe for the young, not here.'

She regarded him with a sudden interest.

'You have children?' she asked.

'Two boys,' he said proudly, and she smiled at him, quite brilliantly. Nonchalantly, she crossed her arms and leaned forward, showing the tops of her smooth brown breasts.

'This is so exciting,' she said.

There was a sudden flourish, a blast of trumpets and a clash of cymbals, a dazzle of colour, of men and women, the *pyrricists* in scarlet and fire yellow. A figure came down from on high, his gown rippling like flames as he flew through the air. Gaia exclaimed with pleasure, and gripped Scipio by the arm.

Lucius sang a *cantica* of tragedy, of the theft of his paternal throne, the loss of his royal rank, and his trained voice filled the amphitheatre, holding the centre of the stage; his eloquent hands translating horror, fear, joy and sorrow; the chorus swaying to his cadence and command; the *symphoniaci* who replied to him taking up his motifs; the orchestra of zithers, trumpets, flutes, cymbals and castanets underlying him, supporting him as he drew breath; and all were entranced.

Then the scene broke up and the awe with which the audience had heard the great idol Lucius sing gave way to humour as they guffawed at the lampooning of those known to be in bad odour at the court of the Emperor, and those with the latest gossip delighted to see it confirmed on stage by the mime actors, who though short on plot were nevertheless highly skilled at improvisation and embroidery on a theme, expertly gauging the mood and temper of their public. Gaia put her head back and laughed. She was very pretty. She let her hand drop on to Scipio's thigh, and a sudden gleam of interest came into his eye.

Two figures were on a stage suddenly bare of people. A running woman, her yellow gown flowing like flame. A pursuing bird, a swan, all in white, powerful, its size betraying its divine reality – the god Zeus in animal form.

'It's Valeria,' Gaia said delightedly, and clapped her hands.

The woman ran left, only to be countered by the swan, its powerful neck striking forward; she ran right, only for escape to be cut off once more. She pressed back against the pillar, trapped, and the swan's strong bill snapped forward, seizing her gown and jerking it from her body to lie as a pool of flame at her feet.

'*Ut mimae nudarentur*' Gaia whispered to Scipio, and looked deep into his eyes.

The swan, bigger and more powerful than Leda, the woman, took her throat in its bill. Gaia leaned against Scipio and felt his arm around her. The sleeves of her gown were wide and loose, his hand slipped up inside, and about her breast. The swan's strong body forced its way in between Valeria's legs, it thrust itself into her. Scipio's hand caressed her and she gasped pleasingly.

The swan Zeus carried his victim away and the play continued apace, with humour, violence, rape, incest and pillage following one hard upon the other. The final act was approaching, it was time for Prince Hippolytus, that Lucius had played so well, to die. The horses were ready, the ropes prepared, they dragged him on, struggling suitably, his features hidden behind the mask. They lashed him to the great beasts and whipped them on.

The chorus was quiet, the orchestra silent for the amphitheatre to be filled with the dying man's last terrible shriek. The horses suddenly charged, wheeling about the great stone stage, bloody spouting fragments of a man tumbling behind them. Orchestra and chorus burst into music.

They gathered the pieces in a pile as Theseus held them up, one by one, attempting to put his son together in a bloody and ghastly jigsaw puzzle.

It was almost done. But the villain still had to die, after all the suffering he had caused.

The centre of the stage was piled high with dry faggots. They dragged him on with his hands tied behind him and the crowd yelled as one for his death, angered by his evil and his arrogance. They roared as he ran desperately about the stage among his erstwhile victims, seeking escape; they cheered as he was trapped; they yelled for the cloak to be brought to wrap him in.

Those whom he had tormented rolled him up, lashed him till he was simply a thrashing log, and passed him hand to hand up the pyre. They had torches in their hands, they plunged them into the dry tinder and the flames reached up towards the sky.

Lucius reappeared from the wings and bowed.

'*Valete ac plaudite*,' he said, and the audience came on to their feet in wild applause to see justice and right triumphant.

As the people streamed out the thing in the fire finally stopped flapping.

Gaia and Scipio got up, gathering their cushions.

'That was wonderful,' she said.

'Thank you,' Scipio said. 'A poor work but mine own.'

Gaia stared him straight in the eyes.

'Oh,' she said softly, 'I enjoyed the play too.'

The muscular arms of the *cursores* swung the litter up on to their shoulders with a practised effort and they stepped forward as one man. Through the *lapis specularis* Gaia saw the walls of the theatre recede as they headed across the piazza. A thin line of smoke trailed up into the sky. Beside her the *tapetia* that covered the swans' down *torus* of the litter moved, and she saw the face of Scipio.

They smiled conspiratorially. He moved to kiss her and she placed a finger on his lips, holding him back. Then she pointed down to her feet and slowly up the length of her body to her mouth. Scipio smiled, his teeth white in the shade of the litter, and moved carefully down. He took off her soft sandals and took her toes one by one in his mouth, licking them like sweet grapes. She felt a tingle run through her ankles up to her back.

In the *acta* the shopkeepers had their *tabernae* open, their wares spilling out over the paving. Tinkers were seated on their stools, hammers tapping, a schoolmaster shouted his lesson to his pupils, crouched behind inadequate screening. A young man was receiving his first shave, the *depositio barbae*. As usual, the *tonsor's* hand had slipped and blood ran among

the down. He was reaching for a spider's web soaked in oil
and vinegar to staunch the wound. A poor man paused outside
the fuller's and hitching up his tunic relieved himself in the
chipped jar provided for the purpose, what he left providing
the fuller with the bleach for his trade. The din of the street
came through the curtained door as though they were outside.

Scipio kissed the insides of her knees, his hand undid the
zona around her waist and she felt the cool air on her thighs
as he pulled up her tunic.

Hawkers from Transtiberina were calling out, bartering their
packets of sulphur matches, the owner of a cook-shop sold
sausages, still sizzling straight from his pan, the spicy aroma
of herb and pork tickled her nostrils. A servant came hurrying
down the *vicus* with a baby bawling in his arms, still bloody
from birth. The slave-dealer stood waiting, *denarii* in hand.
Scipio buried his face between her thighs and she bit down
upon a knuckle to keep from crying out.

Coins jangled on a moneychanger's table, beggers called
out to Bellona for alms. A cart full of builder's rubble creaked
behind them.

She was naked, his mouth caressed her breasts. They kissed,
and her ears were filled with the thumping of a shining hammer
beating dust into gold.

The cursores swung the litter down by the entrance of the
little sun-drenched square where the mosaic said *Cave Canem*
and the powerful wolfhound sat along with Cossus the slave.

She stepped out, the mistress of the house returning from
the theatre.

'I shall be going out again soon,' she said. 'Go inside, all of
you, and have something to eat and drink. Cossus, guard the
litter.'

She went inside. In the atrium she paused, and went to an open shutter. The slave Cossus was standing by the litter, protecting it from any passing *effractores*. She called to him.

'Yes, mistress?' he said, coming up to the window.

Behind him the thick curtain of the litter was pushed back and Scipio stepped into the street.

'Wait for me there. I shall be going to the baths with Maria.'

'Yes, mistress.'

Private life was very public. One might not count the presence of one's slaves any more than birds in the trees, or dogs in the street, but they were there, always, and they talked. Scipio was walking away down the street, past the row of shops, his tall figure easily seen in the scrum. Cossus went back to stand by the litter. Where the *actus* met the *vicus* Scipio paused, and looking back bowed low to her, his blue *pallium* shimmering in the sun.

A.D. 64

Maria placed a soft cushion down on the curving stone seating of the amphitheatre, an Gaia dug her fists into the small of her aching back before setting herself down upon it. Scipio and the actress Valeria, following behind, also sat, as Maria opened up a yellow parasol to shield Gaia from the sun. All about them the rows of marble faced seats were filling with people. Below the sand had been dyed green, the Emperor's favourite colour of the moment, and was raked perfectly smooth. A gentle spring breeze was blowing, the crowd buzzed and mumbled in anticipation, the winters were long without entertainment.

Gaia shifted about on her cushion, attempting unsuccessfully to get comfortable.

'What are we doing here?' she complained. 'I should be at home making arrangements for the baby. My feet swell if I don't put them up. It is all very well for Flavius down in Pompeii to send messages and tickets but I would have been just as happy to stay at home.'

'The tickets were sent by the Emperor,' Scipio said quietly. 'Flavius is commanded, he carried out his commands.'

'Oh, and does the Emperor care if my feet go like unbaked bread?' Gaia grumbled, dropping her voice. A gaunt, sad-faced woman all dressed in sombre grey paused as she passed by their seats.

'My dear,' she said, 'if the Emperor has asked for your presence, then you may be sure that just as I am, you are here for his entertainment.'

Gaia watched the aristocratic old lady moving away with irritation.

'Who might she be?' she demanded.

'Pomponia Graecina,' Valeria offered.

'Why does she wear such drab clothes?' asked Gaia, twitching her shimmering, multi-coloured *palla* about her shoulders. 'She looks so dull.'

'She mourns her son, whom Nero had killed, and her husband. It is said that she belongs to a strange sect, who call themselves followers of Jesus.'

By Gaia's side, holding up the parasol, Maria stared out over the hideous green sand, and said not a word.

'And who might he be?' asked Gaia.

'Apparently this Jesus claimed to be the son of God,' Scipio volunteered.

'Which god?'

'That is the strange thing, he claimed to be the son of the only god.'

Gaia laughed. 'Whoever heard of such a thing? The gods are everywhere. And what of the goddesses? There cannot be just one god. The idea is foolish. What happened to this Jesus anyway, that these strange people worship his memory.'

'They say he was crucified like a common slave. His followers hold strange rites, and practise cannibalism in his honour. They drink the blood of new-born children.'

'And Pomponia does that?'

'Nero accused her of observing foreign superstitions.'

'Well, I don't want anything to do with people who drink the blood of babies,' said Gaia firmly.

'It is what they say,' Scipio said mildly.

Gaia straightened her back suddenly.

'Ooof . . .' she said smiling. 'This one will be a boxer, I think.'

Scipio smiled.

'And what will he look like?' he asked slyly.

'Who knows . . .' Gaia said conspiratorially. Opposite, and then all about, *mappas* burst out like cream butterflies as the people waved to greet their benefactor and host. Scipio glanced up at the *pulvinar* and the portly figure settling himself into his chair.

'Here he is,' he said. 'Let the games commence.'

Gaia frowned, looking up at the crowd of sycophants that swirled about Nero.

'Isn't that Calenus?' she muttered. 'What's he doing there?'

'Oh, young Calenus has ambitions beyond bending over for old men,' Scipio said tactlessly. 'If you'll excuse me. No, Calenus is making his own friends.'

'If it means he stays away from me, then that's fine.'

Maria looked silently up at those in the imperial box. He

was there, as she knew he would be. She turned away. Above her, Saul settled into his seat, smiling and joking with those about him.

The *munera* began as they should, with the magnificent parade of gladiators decked in purple and gold, driving in chariots. They dismounted, so that all might see them properly, slaves carrying their fabulous gleaming armour and weapons behind them. Standing before the *pulvinar* they thrust their right arms forward in salute.

'Ave Caesar, morituri te salutamus.'

Their voices crashed out, the crowd bayed with approval and Nero waved genially. As the fighters marched out the sand was suddenly filled with capering clowns and dwarfs, cripples and fat women engaging in mock combat, and all loosened their belts and guffawed.

'What is it? Are you well?' Valeria asked anxiously. Gaia had gone very pale.

'I see what Pomponia Graecina meant,' she said in a low voice. 'My brother Speculus is one of the gladiators.'

The comic turns ran off, and then there was more. The Emperor varied the entertainment, not wishing to bore his people. Two big black men fought each other and they marvelled to see the sight, and were much intrigued to see that though dark as lava, they bled bright red, like other men. Then a young woman with a dagger fought an older woman with a sword, handicapped by having her feet hobbled. The old woman almost won, hacking off one of the young one's arms, but got too close, and the young one knocked her down, gutting her like a fish before she died. Then two men fought in chariots, which the crowd enjoyed, as both were skilful charioteers. The winner spitted his opponent like a chicken with a shrewd spear thrust, pinning him to the side of the car, but fell out as he did so, and his horses dragged him thrashing around the arena until he died. When they had wiped the tears away they all agreed that the Emperor had treated them well.

It came, as she knew it would. A tall, elegant figure carrying a net and a harpoon danced about a broad, heavily armoured one with shield and sword.

'Flamma,' said Scipio.

Speculus threw his net, his darting tunnyfish trident at the ready. The stocky Flamma in his sparkling silver mail slipped from its clutches with feline speed and agility, and the crowd applauded the skill of the fish that refused to be caught by the fisherman.

The net was slashed. Speculus danced away from Flamma, pulling the edges together in a makeshift knot. She could see him laughing, calling something out to his opponent, and Flamma replied. Then Flamma jumped forward in attack, and as Speculus ran backwards the harpoon tripped him, his hands busy with the repair of his net, and he went down in a flurry of green sand.

Flamma stood over him and Speculus sat up on one elbow. He looked up at the *pulvinar*, and raised his left hand, his face expressionless. Above him, Gaia closed her eyes.

There was a sudden roar.

'*Ave atque vale*,' Scipio said quietly beside her. 'Hail and farewell.'

When she looked up Flamma was taking off his helmet, wiping away the sweat that streamed down his face and soaked his curly black hair with a bloody hand. The slaves brought the palms that symbolised success, and a silver dish, piled high with gold pieces and costly ornaments. He ran across the arena as custom demanded, and all shouted his name. Below Libitina, goddess of the dead, the *libitinarii* were carrying their bloody stretcher through her gate, and Charon was raking the sand green once more.

As the *gnomon* cut the *polos* of the seventh hour they could see the Emperor rising.

'Time for *cena*,' murmured Scipio. 'He's hungry.'

Nero appointed a senator to preside in his place, and disappeared with his entourage.

Nearby, Pomponia Graecina got up and went out along the *vomitoria* to the stairs, and her waiting litter.

'May we go too?' Gaia said quietly.

Scipio looked anxiously at her.

'We must be at the *cena* of the Emperor,' he insisted. 'He expects his guests to be there.'

'Very well,' she whispered.

The Emperor's dining room could have accommodated a villa. A hundred people or more lounged at their ease, to be fed and entertained with the best, for Nero was a gentleman, he could spend his own money as well as that of others.

Gaia rested as well as she could upon the couch, with Scipio and Valeria. Maria waited nearby to be of service, and unobtrusively scanned the gathering. The Emperor was at the head of the room with his cronies. Within calling distance of them she could see Paul, and not far away, Calenus.

The gladiator Flamma was there, reclining on a *lectus* between two glamorous patrician women in high spirits, their blood excited by the proximity of death. The famous mime actor Lucius was there, with actresses, and the *auriga* Crescens, fresh from his chariot at the Maximus, young, handsome and a millionaire. His *amictus* was edged with the scarlet of his team, the *factio russata*.

The cream of the Emperor's society was here at this dinner

– fighters, actors, racing drivers, actresses, whores and courtesans, financiers. The *ministratores* began handing round *colyphae* bread rolls shaped like phalluses. The phallus and its natural partner were much in evidence, from serving dishes to the candelabras that lit the happy occasion. They brought *mulsum* honey wine and oysters, and all was good. As was obligatory, *hilaritas*, good humour reigned amongst the guests.

There was no lack of encouragement to enjoy oneself, and if the guests were short of imagination they could find inspiration from the colourful frieze that ran all around the walls. Long-tailed and long-membered satyrs joyfully persued laughing, half-naked maenads about the room. Occasionally, when one was in the mood, she allowed herself to be caught, and suitably ravished. Otherwise she successfully defended herself with her *thyrsis*, a wand tipped with a pine-cone, the sceptre of the god of wine. The god Pan held down a she-goat, and copulated with her, a strange and rather frightening expression on his face, and those satyrs whom the maenads had rejected joined him, somewhat indifferent to their choice of beast. Bacchus and his beautiful lover Ariadne rode in a chariot pulled by panthers, among a parade of lightly clad, merry followers imbibing and indulging their desires in the grape-hung foliage of the land they lived in. Humour was not absent: a group of revelling satyrs blended wine and water as they got into the mood to satisfy the maenads waiting on tip-toe to run, one skilfully balanced the mixing-bowl on his penis.

As the *ministratores* mixed wine and served it in goblets the shape of phalluses – just in case there was anyone there who had missed the point – Gaia's eyes flicked between the scenes of happy debauchery and the gladiator Flamma, lounging, relaxed and powerful on his *triclinium*. The cloth of his *amictus* was irritating the new wound opened that morning in his shoulder and he had tugged it away. She could see the wound, the lips sliced open by the razor-sharp barbs of the trident, closed by a neat line of flax sutures. The killer's hands glittered with rings of all kinds, twisted bronze wire, jet, gold with glass intaglios, silver, some set with precious stone, some in the shape of snakes, curling themselves about a powerful finger. On his thumb was the largest ring of all, gold with a carved onyx intaglio depicting an armed Mars being crowned by a winged Victory.

She felt no strange thrill from sitting in the penumbra of death, only a sinister fear, but still could not keep her eyes from flicking his way. His eyes were as alert as a dragon's, wide-set and brown in his square olive face.

'What are you looking at, little Miss?' he said, from behind an oyster shell.

'I am a married woman,' she said.

'So what interests you, little Madame?'

'The rings,' she said. 'You wore none in the arena this morning.'

'Neither *scutum* nor *spatha* can be gripped by a hand wearing rings,' he said expertly. 'But these celebrate my victories. I am given them by those who desire my services afterwards. For that bauble on your hand I might bend you over a couch for a few moments.'

'That is my wedding ring,' she said coldly. 'I am a married woman.'

He jerked a thumb at the two women either side of him, drinking wine with one hand and feeling his muscles with the other.

'So,' he said contemptuously, 'are they.'

'Your eyes have lost their keenness since this morning,' she said, 'I am with child.'

Flamma smiled, not unpleasantly.

'My apologies. As you can see, I am distracted.'

She continued to stare at him and he glanced up again, aware of it.

'You would like me to be godfather to the child, perhaps?' he suggested.

'In the arena today,' she said, 'you and Speculus were talking to each other as you fought. What were you saying?'

'At the *cena libera* last night we sat together. We agreed that the victor would screw two women, one for himself and one for the other. He was of good birth, I am from the gutter. He was boasting that he was on his way to Suburra to fuck my sister. But here I am, ready to fuck his.'

'No,' she said, 'you are not. For I am his sister.'

Flamma was silent for a moment, and then he shrugged.

'*Vincam aut moriar.* You conquer or die. It is how it is.'

A whole roast boar, piping hot, baskets of dates hanging from its tusks and surrounded by little suckling pigs made from simnel cake was brought in, and carved like lightning by a man dressed as Ajax, using a sword.

While they were digesting before the next course Flamma called for the *kottabos* to be brought.

A female slave, naked except for a garland in her hair, set it up. At the top of a tall, slim bronze stand was a statuette of a naked Diana, and on her hand held aloft, the slave balanced a slightly concave bronze disc known as a *plastinx*. Below, half-way up the stand was a much larger bronze disc, the *manes*.

'Who's to play?' called Flamma. He took a gold ring from his finger and put it on the table in front of him. 'Winner takes all.'

Very quickly the slave had gathered up a pile of rings, brooches and *aureii*, as all about entered into the spirit of the occasion.

'Room for another?' someone called cheerfully. Gaia looked up to see Calenus, smiling with a boyish charm.

'I never mind how many rings I win,' Flamma boasted, and Calenus tossed a gold circlet into the pile.

Most fell out during the first round. Both Scipio and Lucius threw the wine dregs from their cups with the utmost elegance of movement, as befitted those who earned their way from the stage, and succeeded in hitting nothing. Valeria, whose eye was good, succeeded in splashing the *plastinx* with wine, but not of moving it. Flamma, whose coordination of hand and eye kept him wealthy and alive, succeeded in bringing the bronze dish down with a pleasing clang on to the *manes* below, as did Crescens, the charioteer. Flavia, one of the women at Flamma's side, did likewise, and so did Calenus.

'I would not care to win against either of those,' Scipio murmured to Gaia. 'Flamma is an animal, but Crescens little better. Last week he saw a gold chain on a man and beat him half-senseless to take it. And who is to say nay to one of the *miliarii*, the champion of the *factio russata*? Not Scipio, I think.'

Flamma's girlfriend missed the next time around. When Crescens threw his wine splattered the *plastinx*, but it did not fall. From his couch Flamma threw his dregs with a strong forefinger. The dish teetered on Diana's hand, and fell with a resounding clash. It was left to Calenus. His wine flew scarlet in the air, and missed. The highborn whores and hangers-on around Flamma's square table cheered lustily as the champion gathered in his loot, scattering some of it to his companions.

'Don't hand away my ring just yet, Flamma,' Calenus called. 'I would win it back.'

He took off two more. He looked straight at Maria. 'You,' he ordered, 'bring a pot to piss in. He who hits the target most squarely wins.'

They all applauded in approval. Maria looked at Gaia, and she nodded. The Emperor's court was a most dangerous place to be, and Calenus was reclining closer to him than they.

'Right,' Scipio murmured.

Maria brought a chamber pot. She stood where Calenus indicated. As she passed him he suddenly reached out, and jerked her tunic from her shoulders. They cheered as she stood naked. The distance was measured off, and Flamma hitched up his *amictus*. His life depended upon accuracy, the stream flew directly into the pot with a resonant drumming and the tables resounded to the cheering.

'*Occupavit et vicit*,' he said confidently, and Calenus grinned.

Maria emptied the vessel and once again stood ready. Calenus pulled up his robe. His grin was suddenly savage. The jet flew straight at Maria. They roared, and he hosed it up and down until she dripped from head to toe.

'What do you say, Flamma,' he shouted triumphantly. 'Does that hit the target square?'

He caught the tossed ring and fitted it back over his thumb. He turned, as he strolled back to his couch, and smiled lethally at Gaia. Without saying a word, Maria went out of the room, stone-faced.

There was boiled calf and acrobats, mullet and buffoons, visits to the room next door to make room for more of the same, *vomunt ut edant, edunt ut vomant*. Gaia pushed her food away, unable to eat.

'Are you all right?' Valeria asked, leaning over.

'Perhaps I shall be better in a few minutes,' said Gaia, and brushed a cold sweat from her lip.

There were half-naked Spanish dancing girls and a statue of Priapus, holding up an apronful of phallic marzipan sweets and cakes with his hands and his prick.

The castanets rattled, breasts jiggled and loins moved under flimsy muslin. The two women next to Flamma had pulled up his *amictus* around his waist, with breasts spilling from their gowns they knelt, one each side, mouths meeting each other, tongues flickering.

'You don't look well,' Valeria said, concerned. Gaia was sweating and very pale.

'I think I'm going to have to go,' she said.

'We must stay,' Scipio said nervously. 'The Emperor would not approve.'

'I understand.'

She got up. Flamma lay back with half-closed eyes as Flavia mounted him, her companion watching, her hand moving under her gown. Across the room Calenus sat up, as alert as a hawk, watching Gaia stumble away. He slipped from his couch and came over.

'Is something wrong?' he asked, affecting concern.

'She is unwell,' said Valeria. 'She is going home.'

Maria was coming down the corridor as she left, looking freshly washed.

'Are you clean?' Gaia asked.

'My skin is on fire,' Maria said grimly. Then she looked more closely at Gaia.

'You are not well,' she said immediately. 'We must get you home.'

From behind them came the surging roar, as of the sea, of a banquet in full progress. Maria helped Gaia outside, and did not see Calenus, bending urgently to talk to Saul, nor Saul issuing his commands.

In the street her litter was waiting, and with it the *custos* on his horse, guardian of her virtue. He was the Greek slave Saltus, her husband's steward. She got in, Maria walking beside, and the men carried her home through the streets, noisy with the first carters dragging their loads in and out.

The rhythmic swaying of the litter on the slaves' shoulders stopped. A terrible smell was in the air, the smell of death.

She pulled back the curtain, looking out. Great carts laden high with bloody bone and offal were creaking by. An elephant's dead eye stared sightlessly at her. Bloody fur and scale passed. The gourmets of Rome, for whom rarity was all, would treat their guests to panther steak and barbecued ostrich on the morrow.

Hands there were, and bloodied torsos. Speculus looked her straight in the face, his own set with the determination not to beg any more than a raised hand, the gash through which his life blood had spouted dark across his throat.

'*Saltus!*'

Her voice cracked like a whip and the horseman behind her litter forced a way through, holding up the carts under the oaths of their drivers, letting her pass.

In the litter she suddenly doubled over in pain as a terrible cramp racked her stomach.

'Maria,' she called weakly. 'Quickly, for the baby is coming.'

The rooms were prepared, a wet nurse reserved. The *paedagogus*, the *nutritor* who would offer the child its educational sustenance had been interviewed. A cot made from polished vine wood stood ready, padded with a feather-filled *torus*. Clean and new swaddling bands awaited to constrict the child, make it grow up straight and tall. Small linen and wool tunics lay waiting folded and dry in the chest. Flavius had placed *Genii Cucullati* close, three small cloaked gods each holding an egg in his right hand. Guardians and symbols of both fertility and immortality, they watched over the waiting cot from a ledge in the room. Flavius had placed a small Priapus to stand guard at the doorway, and some metal chimes jingling by the shutter to keep away evil spirits.

Only Flavius was still in Pompeii, for the baby's time was not yet due.

In a high-backed chair Gaia bit on her knuckle as the cramp racked her swollen stomach, and the midwife Aelia methodically finished laying out the tools of her trade on a cloth on the table. The room had been set aside for the purpose, it was curtained off against male eyes.

In the *lararium*, the household shrine in the atrium, the gods stood waiting. Inside it was a model of a temple containing the *Genius Paterfamilias* who guarded over the house, his toga pulled up over his head to keep out sounds of ill omen, his hands holding out a napkin and *patera*, the sacrificial dish.

Saltus the steward stood waiting by the door. There was something furtive, underhand about his manner. There came the knock from the street that he was expecting, and he quickly went to open it.

Calenus stepped inside.

'Is she here?' he demanded. 'The midwife?'

'Yes. The pains have started.'

'Good. Bring her to me.'

Moments later Saltus returned with the crone.

'The master is not here,' Calenus told her flatly. 'In his absence I command. It is his wish.'

The midwife looked to the steward, who nodded in agreement.

'Very well,' she said. 'Now let me go back, for I am needed.'

She shuffled away, and Calenus turned to the steward.

'Go, then,' he ordered. 'Go tell Saul the Chrestian that it is as we have agreed.'

The light from the wicks of the bronze lamp in its iron stand was flickering. The maid would be coming to change it for a fresh one in a minute. It would be the third since darkness had fallen. Calenus shifted in his wicker chair, remnants of a half-chewed supper on the table beside him. There was a shuffling at the doorway. It would be the maid.

He looked up in the dim light. Someone shuffled in the gloom. It was not the maid. It was Aelia, the midwife.

'It is done?' he said. But immediately he knew it was not.

'The wife of the magister is dying,' the woman said bluntly. 'She is tiring, and the baby will not be born.'

'Can nothing be done?' Calenus demanded.

'Little for her,' the midwife said frankly. 'When all else fails, the baby can to be cut out of the womb. But for the infant to live, it must be done while the mother is still alive.'

'Will she die?'

The midwife paused. 'It is not always so. It is said that the mother of Caesar lived, and I have known women live, but not often. They burn up with fever, the wound opens. One does not know why. Using a new knife, suitably blessed by the gods helps, but their favour does not last for long.'

Calenus got up, and going out through the gloom into the atrium he took the bronze knife of sacrifice.

'Use this,' he commanded. 'It is dedicated, and blessed by Mithras himself.'

The woman took it, hefting it and testing its edge expertly with her thumb.

'I shall need some slaves,' she said. 'One for each leg and each arm.'

The woman went quickly back to the room.

'Bring more lamps,' she said to Maria, waiting by Gaia's side. In their light she could see that the woman slumped in the high-backed chair, swollen-bellied with a child who would not be born, was weaker than when she had left. Her breathing was shallow, her eyes rolled back in her head, her entire body slick with sweat. There would be no time to boil mandrake root in wine and administer it to her to dull the pain of the knife. Mother and baby were dying.

The slaves, strong *cursores* whose brawny hands and arms were used to carrying their mistress's litter, came in. They grasped her by wrist and elbow, ankle and knee, and Gaia opened her eyes.

The midwife bent over her belly, the bronze knife gleaming in the light of the lamps.

The hideous screaming had subsided into a rasping moan no less horrible. Calenus stood waiting, he understood the formalities. Footsteps came hurrying up the corridor and the midwife lay a bloody baby on the earth for judgement. It mewled, and waved tiny limbs.

'I must return to the magister's wife,' she said. 'It may be that she can be saved.'

The room was hot from the light of the lamps and filled with the metallic smell of blood. It was spattered everywhere, it pumped rythmically from a severed vessel in the terrible wound in Gaia's stomach. Working quickly the midwife tied off the artery using flax, and sewed the womb together using a curved triangular needle and flax sutures. For the main wound she passed *fibulae* pins through both sides, then drew the lips together by fastening them with thread.

'Bring a door,' she commanded. They did so, and laid Gaia on it, taking her to the room where she was to recover, or die.

'You are the one skilled with herbs?' Aelia asked Maria.

'Yes.'

'Then do your best. I shall return in the morning. There is nothing for me to do now.'

The woman packed her instruments and tools, her probes

and knives and forceps, her needles, bleeding cup and hooks away in a cylindrical oblong case. She closed the two halves and was gone.

Maria called for the cook to boil mandrake root in white wine. While it was being done she washed Gaia's body from head to toe with warm water, and covered her with a wool blanket. When the infusion came she helped her to drink it, and slowly the moaning stopped. She slept.

Maria dressed the dreadful wound with wine. Dawn was approaching, she wrapped a cloak about her and went out of the house to be there when the gates of the city were opened. They swung back and she joined the flood of carts escaping, slipping into the olive and cypress groves of the Campus Martius.

She moved in sun and shade, over meadow and by stream bank, searching with an expert eye. Wild poppies were growing and she visited these, cutting small slits just below the capsule. She found henbane, and gathered both root and bark. She saw the bluey-mauve bells of comfrey flowers and gathered their leaves. Skirret was there, and the dew of the sea, wild rosemary, she took both. Tansy grew by a stream and she took bunches of the saw-toothed leaves. Shiny dark green myrtle grew among the cypress, she stripped its leaves, and inhaled the spicy orange fragrance. She found the long green leaves of eupatorium and dug the plants up for their roots. Yarrow and lady's mantle were there, and she took their leaves. From the poppies she gathered small drying pills of juice, and hurried back into the city.

Gaia was semiconscious in the darkened room, and she gave her three of the poppy pills with a little swallow of wine while she made her preparations. She hung up tansy around the bed to repel flies and set myrtle leaves to infuse while she stripped the rosemary stems of their leaves. She made up a poultice of henbane bark, yarrow, rosemary and comfrey leaves, which she applied to the wound after she had cleaned it with a mixture of wine and the infusion of myrtle. Yarrow was something that helped the blood to clot, but also a herb that helped others, like henbane, rosemary and comfrey, to ease inflammation.

From time to time she burned a rosemary stem in the brazier, and the air of the sick room was magically freshened. She infused the leaves of the lady's mantle and gave it to Gaia in sips throughout the day. As a young girl her mother Mary had instructed her in the art. Lady's mantle was especially good for ladies, for all things feminine.

In the night Gaia began to burn with a fearful dry fever. The midwife Aelia came in the morning, looked and left without saying a word.

The skin over Gaia's face was stretched, the skull visible just beneath. Maria boiled up the eupatorium roots and strained the juice. On the bed Gaia twitched and shook, her teeth chattering with fever. Her hands were tethered to the frame of the bed to stop her tearing at the pins holding the wound together.

The juice of the roots had cooled. She poured some into a small wine cup and knelt beside the bed, propping Gaia's head forward to drink. The heat radiating from her body burned like fire, the skin was dry, it crackled like old leaves.

Her lips had split with fever, blood tinged the yellow infusion as Maria made her drink. She let her head rest back on the cushion and prepared another dose. The sun outside was pushing its way around the gaps where the shutters joined the window. Outside the city bustled and rattled. Men and women shopped, ambled to the baths, argued, bargained, laughed. Children slid nuts down a slide to demolish a tower of them, and played at ball against the wall.

Gaia gasped in her unconsciousness. Her slim muscles drew taut, standing out from the skin like bowstrings. Sweat sprayed from her body, drifting like mist in the room, collecting in puddles, soaking the sheet.

She was very thirsty. The shutter was open, and a pale yellow curtain allowed light to filter pleasingly into the room. The scent of rosemary was in the air. Maria was sitting in the low-backed wicker chair, when she saw her eyes open she got up quickly, bringing a cup with her.

'You are awake,' she said joyfully. 'Drink a little of this, it is skirret water, it will help build your strength.'

She sipped the aromatic liquid. There was something wrong, something very badly wrong.

She pushed the cup away, but was so weak she could not prevent Maria from giving her more.

Something was missing, she felt a terrible sense of loss.

'My baby,' she whispered. 'Where is my baby?'

'Drink a little more,' Maria urged. 'A little more and then rest.'

'I cannot rest without my baby. A little boy or a little girl? Please, bring my baby to me.'

'A little girl,' Maria said slowly.

'What is the matter? Has something happened to her? Why is she not here?'

Gaia looked up at Maria from a face like a skull.

'Calenus was here. He did not raise her up from the earth. He did not recognise her as the daughter of Flavius.

Gaia had Maria bring the comfortable wicker chair from the *cubiculum* out into the *peristyle*, where the air was fresh and the sun shone in among the green plants, and there was the sweet sound of playing water.

One of the *cursores* who carried her litter was standing by the entrance, Septimus by name, young and swift of foot.

'Fetch me Saltus,' she said.

The steward took his time. Slaves could weigh the balance of power within a house to a hair. He strolled towards her, ostentatiously wiping a corner of his mouth clean of the fruit he had eaten for breakfast.

'I was preparing the master's accounts,' he said boldly, thus stating their relative positions of power: he an invaluable servant, no doubt soon to be freedman, she a barren half-cripple, undoubtedly soon to be cast aside.

'I care not for the master's accounts,' she said. 'I have other things to discuss with you.'

From the wing where they had their mess the *cursores* of her litter crew drifted quietly into the *peristyle*, and stood behind Saltus. Two carried a *scamnum*, the bench that they sat on when they ate.

'My baby,' said Gaia. 'My baby that the midwife Aelia cut from me. What happened to her?'

The steward was instantly alert, his small dark eyes, almost hidden in the folds of skin, flickering warily to look at her.

'The master's . . . friend did not raise her up, mistress, he did not acknowledge her as the master's own.'

'I know that. Calenus, you mean,' she said, her voice very cold and precise. 'So after the custom, she was exposed, was she? Who did it, and where was she taken?'

'I do not know where, mistress. I believe it was the new slave, the girl who died of the fever, who took her.'

'How convenient. Maria?'

'He is lying, mistress. I heard the baby cry. When I went to find her she was gone. It was before the dawn, Saltus was not to be found.'

She stared up at him with eyes as chill and unblinking as a snake's.

'Saltus?' she said softly. 'It is not like you to have your sleep disturbed.'

'It was the maid,' Saltus said arrogantly.

'She took the child.'

'Yes, yes.' He held his head up, but sweat was beginning to run out from under his dark, curly hair. Gaia looked behind him.

'Septimus?'

'He lies, mistress. I saw him slip out before dawn was brushing the far sky over the hill. The child was under his arm, crying.'

'So. You took my baby. Where to?'

'To the dung heap, as the master's friend told me to,' Saltus said desperately. 'Where the dogs would eat it.'

'If that was all, you would have smothered it and had it taken away with the carcasses of the roast birds, stale bread and kitchen rubbish. You are not one to put yourself to unnecessary effort.'

Gaia shifted herself in her chair, her healing wound still uncomfortable.

'You are one uncommonly fond of money, though. I have often observed that you would walk to the city gates in a pair of someone else's *caliga* on the promise of two *quadra* at the other end. Which must be why you took my baby out alive. You sold her to a slave-dealer. That is why you have lied to me.'

She nodded to the *cursores* and they had the bench laid in front of her and the steward stretched out along it with his tunic off in a few seconds.

'Let me tell you,' he gasped, stretched taut under the combined efforts of two grinning litter-bearers pulling at each end.

There was ill-feeling between those who had the soft jobs inside, the *servi atrienses*, and those who had to brave the elements no matter what, and the steward was not popular with these men.

'Afterwards,' she said dismissively. 'You have as many lies in you as a Suburra beggar, we shall drive them out with the whip and see what is left.'

The young man, Septimus, held a plaited bull's hide thong in his hand, some three feet long, thicker at the base than at the tip. He swung it through the air, making it moan in anticipation of the steward's cries and his companions grinned. Gaia nodded.

'Make him like a patchwork quilt,' she said brutally, and the whip lashed down.

The sweat was running freely when he had finished, and he wiped his face on the shoulder of his tunic. Blood dripped down from the tasselled end of the whip, a spray of gore marked the mosaic the length of the steward's back on the far side.

'Pretty as a Persian carpet, Mistress,' Septimus said, admiring his handiwork. The *cursores* released their grip and Saltus lay slumped the length of the bench, his chest heaving and breath moaning in his throat.

'So where did you take my baby?' said Gaia, from her chair.

'I did as I was ordered . . .' the Greek gasped through his pain. 'I gave it to one who waited outside the bar.'

Gaia sighed. 'A man of business has no time to wait outside bars for baby slaves who may not come. *Septimus.*'

The thong lashed down again into the welter of blood and Saltus screamed.

'You are afraid to tell me who you sold my baby to,' Gaia

said icily. 'But I can keep this up until the whip cuts you into dog meat. Who has my child?'

'It is Paul the Christian,' Saltus whispered. 'The master's friend Calenus told me to take her to him.'

Maria's eyes suddenly glittered.

'He is a slave-dealer?'

'One who calls himself a Christian, a follower of Jesus.'

A dreadful chill of fear ran through Gaia's body.

'Tell me what you know of these Jesus-worshippers.'

'They hold secret rites, where they drink blood,' Saltus said despairingly. 'And eat the flesh of new-born babies.'

It had been a short walk, one Gaia felt able to make herself, accompanied by her *cursores*. She had not required the company of the steward, only his directions. When she returned he would be gone, his back washed in vinegar and rubbed with salt, to the mines, there slowly to die.

The timber-framed colonnade of shops was filled with life, sound and smell. The baker's slave boy was setting out with his basket of golden loaves made from the finest white flour for his master's best customers, hot from the brick oven. She could not smell their rich fragrance. The poulterer held up a pair of fine guinea fowl, a man felt their plump flesh. On hooks hung game of all descriptions, she was blind to the rich fur and feather. On the corner the butcher sharpened his chopper on the steelyard, a side of bacon awaiting jointing on the block in front of him, his wife sitting at the back with her tablets as she casted up the accounts. Across the street came the tapping of the tinker's hammer as he beat out a cauldron, and the clanging of the smith with his tongs and pincers, she heard them not.

It was an unassuming place, for a site of evil. A carpenter

497

worked in his front room, open to the street, his tools hung up on the wall by his bench. Gimlets, adzes, augers, chisels, punches and gouges were neatly arrayed, together with various straight-bladed saws and planes. A bronze compass and a pair of dividers lay to hand, the carpenter was engaged in fine work. He was finishing the inlay of a cupboard, made from exotic wood with an undulating grain and changing lights, *lecti pavoni*, like a peacock's tail. The cupboard was a place of importance, for the storage of cherished books on their rolled up scrolls. An epigram ran along its top edge: *Unless you provide me with choice books I will let in moths and savage bookworms.*

The carpenter whistled softly between his teeth as he worked. He was a cheerful, balding man of perhaps thirty, with a greying beard and deft, clever fingers. She had paused out in the street, now she went in.

'I am looking for one called Paul. Paul the Christian.'

'Then you have come to the right place,' the man said, without looking up, running glue from the warm pot evenly over the back of a piece of inlay. From somewhere behind the shop she heard the sound of voices, singing a song she did not know. It had a joyful timbre.

'I am Gaia, wife of Flavius.'

He looked up at her from his work and she saw grey eyes, like a winter sky, but strangely warm. They held a hint of amusement, of some sort of pleasure.

'Indeed you are,' he said, 'and I am Cadmus, who is a carpenter; who was a priest of Dionysus, a fallen soul; who is one who follows the Lord Jesus.'

'This Paul has something of mine.'

He pressed the maple letter into its inlay and it fitted without a gap.

'Commissioned and paid for,' he said, and somewhere in his

voice bubbled pure pleasure, like a deep spring. 'Like this cupboard.'

'Then I shall return your money, with suitable interest.'

'The goods are not for resale,' he said, and she knew that her fears were true.

'The man who sold you my child was the steward of my house.'

'I know,' said a voice, and a small man with a large head and only one ear pushed the curtain at the back of the shop aside and came through. He smiled warmly.

'I am Paul,' he said.

'My steward sold you my child. He tells me that you are some sort of priest, of a cult who call themselves Chrestians, or followers of Jesus.'

'We are. And what do you know of us?'

'I am a woman of the world, I know that you follow strange rites, and practise cannibalism.'

'First I am a slave-dealer, who buys babies for later sale, now I eat them with my companions. Tell me, what gods do you worship?'

'We have many gods who help us in our house.'

'The usual? Juno, Minerva, Jupiter, Mars? Isis, Diana, Apollo?'

Gaia nodded, her armed slaves at her back.

'They do not seem to have helped you very much,' Paul observed. He looked her in the eyes. 'Now listen to me. There is God the Father, who made us all in his own divine image. He sent his son Jesus Christ to earth to live with us. Jesus Christ took all our sins, all the sins of the world upon himself, he died upon the Cross for all the sinners of the world. He did that for you, although you do not know him. He asks in return that you believe in him, the Lord Jesus. Worship him and when your mortal flesh is no more you will sit at his right hand with God the Father among the angels.'

More people were slipping into the little shop from the room behind, where they had been singing. They stood quietly, smiling kindly at her. With a shock, she saw the old lady, Pomponia Graecina looking at her with a strange love and understanding in her eyes.

'If this Jesus is so powerful where is his image?' she demanded. 'The streets and gardens and temples of the city bear images of the gods as a meadow flowers after the rain, but I see no Jesus.'

'You see him every day,' a Greek said softly, his face seamed by many years of sunshine. 'For he casts his light upon us, he bathes us in his love.'

He waved a hand to the lane outside, where the sunlight filtered down through the narrow gap between the buildings.

'I am Timothy, who collects the words of Jesus from those who knew him. His glory is so great that one may not look upon him directly with ones' eyes. Yet we see the Lord Jesus every day, for he rides in his chariot across the sky.'

He pushed back the hanging that shut off the workshop from the rooms behind.

'Julia,' he called. 'Julia, Gaia, the wife of Flavius is here.'

There was a light noise from the room and a woman appeared, a woman in her late twenties, olive-skinned and dark-haired. She was herself pregnant. She carried a baby tenderly wrapped in a woollen shawl.

'I am Julia, the wife of Timothy. Jesus has saved me, as he has us all here with you. Now we are your brothers and sisters in Christ, for he has saved your child.'

She smiled as she gave the bundle into Gaia's arms. Gaia looked down, and the little creature fitted into her.

The noise of the hammers, the smell of the bread, the colour of the wood, the feel of the baby in her arms fused into a blazing bolt of light. What had been torn from her had been restored. She stood in his radiance and felt all around her, the presence of the Lord Jesus.

25

Wales

Connell carefully puffed the fine liquid spray over the ancient papyrus, and set it to one side. When he returned the writing that had vanished would be visible as a pale grey script. He got up, stretching himself, and picked up a few sheets of paper from the table. Maria had opened the windows at some time in the morning, a soft breeze was blowing through the room. He thought that he could smell cut corn and chaff. He went outside and could hear her singing, somewhere near the barn.

She had a fresh canvas on her easel. A beautiful woman danced near a fire. It was at night, out in the open, for the flames lit up the green leaves of the trees, in the grass wild flowers were set. She had sable hair that flowed in the breeze and her robe danced with her, its myriad bells flashing in the firelight.

'It's the robe of glory,' he said softly.

'Maria,' she agreed. 'Or Ruth, or Mary, whatever name she had at the time.'

'She's outside.'

'That's where the Children liked to be, out in the fields and woods, by the rivers and streams and seas. They only worshipped inside when they had to, to hide from those who hated them.'

'You have the Children all worked out,' he commented.

'It all comes back to me now,' she said strangely. 'I see them all.'

'When I first met you, you said something strange. You said you thought you'd been waiting for me.'

'Oh, yes. I've always known that someone would come. And you did.'

She applied a few small brush strokes.

'There. I'd better let it dry.'

She turned on her little wooden stool.

'What have you found?' she asked.

'Oh, a lot. I've come to the end of a section. The codex was in pieces, I think I've got the next part, but I've had to raise the ink, it's not easy. I thought I had the right bit before, but it was something else entirely. They're both fascinating, though. Paul has done it again. He seems to have built up his Church by quite powerful conversion techniques – practically imprinting. The people who he acquires – like Gaia and Pomponia Graecina – become quite literally born again. I suppose I can see why, but then again, can I? There is something just . . . sinister about Paul.'

She glanced at the sheaf of paper he was carrying.

'Is that it?'

'No. This is different. Somebody else. He's in the desert. The desert was very important to those who wanted their religious views clarified. The violent cold, the clear sky, the fierce heat, the thirst and the hunger had a way of simplifying their consciousness. It was a kind of phone booth to God. John the Baptist practically lived there, off and on.'

'Who is it? Is it John?'

'No, I don't think so. I think it's Jesus. He experiences some kind of vision. Want to read it?'

She held out her hand.

'Yes, please. I'll come in, I think. It's time for a beer, anyway.'

'George used to say that all life was about arranging what to do in the intervals between drinks,' Connell observed.

They went inside and she sat down at the table to read.

The night was cold. It went through the furred skins he wore, in the fashion of his far-distant ancestors, but Jeshua did not feel it. He walked in the light of the full, white moon that was over the horizon, casting jagged black shadows over the rocky desert ground. When he stopped there was no noise at all.

Jeshua looked up into the depths of the sky and the stars shone savagely down at him. He turned and sat upon a rock, his furs swathed about him. The moon was huge in his face. It filled his eyes, filled his mind, and as he gave himself over to it his vision came to him.

He knew that it was a very long time in the past. The moon looked down upon a young woman. It was a slim crescent moon, waxing. Jeshua felt the vigour of life burgeoning within the woman. In her left hand she held a bison's horn, curved just as the moon above her, that the shaman had carved with the thirteen marks of the swelling moon, the thirteen months of the year. Summer flowers were woven into a garland about her hair, their perfume surrounded her. In her right hand she held a small stone lamp steady. In the glow from its juniper-twig wick her dress rippled with light. It was made from fresh green grasses, from long reed leaves and flowers all woven together, the gift of the goddess.

Music was playing about her in the darkness. Before her was blackness – a tunnel that led into the earth. It was time, and she stepped forward, holding both her polished horn and her stone lamp high.

It was a labyrinth, a narrow passage leading ever downward. Her lamplight glinted off the gold- and silver-speckled rock, the music behind her faded as she walked forward, until she could hear it no longer, only the padding of her softly slippered feet.

The path widened and she could hear the steady pattering of water upon stone. Her lamp lit up long fingers of stone hanging from the cave roof, below them rounded, nippled breasts standing up from the floor, painted with red and black dots.

She squeezed through a tiny gap and burst into light. She was within the womb of the goddess, within a majestic room lit with lamps. The walls were richly engraved and coloured, there to see were all the creatures the goddess gave birth to, the rhinoceros and the mammoth, bison and bear, horse and reindeer. Running amongst them were wolverines and the wild ass, musk ox and the hare. The snowy owl and the swan flew overhead, beneath them silver fish swam in the river. There too were the human animals. Darts flew in the air in the magic ritual of the hunt.

Beneath an engraving of a pregnant mare, set about with plants bursting with leaves, a mask hung from a wooden stand. It was of a doe, made from her skin. She reached out and put it on over her head, and as she did so from somewhere beyond the light of the lamps a drum began to beat.

Animal skins lay in a circle on the ground. She began to dance around them to the rhythm of the drum. From the darkness a figure appeared on the other side of the circle. It was the shaman, in her animal form. The skin of a lioness covered her and gave her her power. Her huge round eyes were the owl's and looked through the woman into the future, into death and rebirth. Her hands were those of a bear, power-fully clawed. Around the great eyes was the mask of the lioness, and from her head thrust the antlers of fecundity. She led the woman in the dance around the skins. Suddenly from the darkness there was a man, naked but for the mask of the great black aurochs over his head. The huge horns shone in the soft gold gleam of the lamps, matching the carved crescent of fertility in her hand.

They danced together and she drew him to her with the horn in her hand. Her body was dusted with red ochre, the colour of life-giving blood. The Great Mother looked down upon them, lying inside her, and the grasses and flowers of her garment scattered about them on the skins of her creatures.

In the cold of the desert the moon still filled Jeshua's vision. He knew that thousands of years were passing, that the seasons were warming, that the vast cliffs of ice were retreating. He saw the woman and her people leaving the caves that had sheltered them from the fearsome cold of the winters.

He saw her and the man with their children, saw the world they lived in, saw her as she became the priestess of the temple. The goddess had come out with the people, now her womb was the very earth itself, and governed by the moon above. As always, its four phases came and went, and now were paralleled by the rhythm of the planting of the seed, its gestation and birth as green and golden corn, its death and rebirth. The woman's people were born of women, of the goddess, they were nurtured by her, taken back by her. The plants about them, the crops they grew, the fruit they gathered, the animals they kept, that gave them milk, eggs, meat, skins and wool were all, like they themselves, children of the Goddess, and all were sacred. Moon and woman and earth were all tied together in a governed, holy and exact rhythm of order and development.

Colour sprang out from their buildings, their homes and shrines and temples. Cunning signs and symbols decorated the walls, circled about the fine pots and vessels they made from the clay, spiralling and meandering like rain and river. They wove into their baskets, patterned their cloth. Bees and butterflies flew about the edges of the temple walls, honey was the nectar of the goddess and of the god who supported her in their sacred marriage. The souls of the children flew as gaily patterned butterflies from the husks of their former bodies.

In the desert, a thin haze had come over the sky. The harsh stars softened and Jeshua saw them as did the people in his vision, the iridescent drops of milk streaming from the life-giving breast of the goddess.

The sky above him was the same as the one the people watched. They lived between the earth and the sky, they saw the moon and the sun and the stars of the goddess, they entered into her earthly and celestial rhythms. Jeshua was there as they gathered the great stones, placing them in the precise swirling patterns of the cosmic dances of the stars, engraving them with the whirling patterns of the inexhaustible energy of the goddess. He watched as the woman in her temple observed the movements of the moon and sun and stars, as the crops about the great hill burst green from the earth to turn golden in the sun. As the summer moon became full she led her people along the processional ways of stones that towered high above them. They gathered in the silvering harvest, the hill, the mound that was the womb of the goddess above them. The moon that bathed them in its light slowly emerged in the still waters of the great moat, the birth of her child. As they entered into their rituals with her the reflection climbed up to her breast, putting into motion the suckling of the baby. The moon climbed higher, and the moat became opaque with creamy light, the milk of the goddess.

Connell went through the kitchen and outside into the sunshine. His garden was filled with the alien sound of a powerful engine on the far side of the field over the hill, where the corn was growing. A slowly moving trail of dust brushed the skyline brown. His apple trees were bearing red and yellow striped fruit, he climbed up on to the stone wall and picked two of them, then brought them inside. He took some beer from the refrigerator, removed the tops with a pleasing hiss, and put one and an apple on the table in front of Maria.

'More and better,' said Connell, and drank, letting the wonderful nut and hops fill his mouth. Maria tapped the manuscript.

'Goddesses, and gods,' she said, looking up. 'From the beginning? That's what he's seen, the woman going down into the cave?'

'You got it the right way round. The goddess is central, her marriage with the god is a sacred union. The myth of the goddess was magic, it produced religions, arts, philosophies, society.'

'So where did it all come from?'

'The relationship between earth and the heavens. The phases of the moon and those of the womb that gives birth. These are the same for us as they were for the palaeolithic Stone Age woman that Jeshua sees in his vision, except that the cave people understood the fundamental importance of it all far better than we do now. We live in a society whose ideal is a woman starved to half her natural weight, who is carved to shape by a surgeon's knife and stuffed with man-made protruberances like a Frankenstein doll, and who is never seen to be pregnant. *They* – as far back as 20,000 or more years ago – made figurines of goddesses who are wholly female, life-giving, nourishing, regenerating. They are imbued with lunar mythology – the thirteen days of the waxing moon, and the thirteen months of the lunar year. The ten lunar months of gestation. The moon was central to their existence, to their entire philosophy. It combines within its movements the two rhythms of permanence and change. From it they could measure, conceive of patterns and connections.

'The moon became their most important symbol, as the great light shining in the total darkness of the night it was the supreme image of the goddess, of the unifying force of the Great Mother of All.'

Connell took a bite of his apple and crunched the tart flesh.

'These are really nice,' he said. 'Sort of scabby on the outside, but they taste lovely. I suppose they haven't been sprayed.'

She was reading what he had written.

'They seem to see everything as a whole,' she said.

'That's right. Everything they observed had a seasonal rhythm. The migrating and returning birds and salmon. The cycle of gestation, birth, growth and death amongst all the animals and themselves. The bud, blossom, fruit and fall of the trees and bushes. Their own lives were an integral part of this world, they could not see themselves in opposition to it. In summer they gathered, and concentrated all their energies upon the hunt. In the arctic winter they made tools, made skins and furs into clothes, told their myths, legends and stories about the fire. They watched the moon, and the circular pattern of the stars. And worshipped the goddess, the Mother of All.

'Take the animals. Read Genesis in the Bible and it will tell you that we – humans – are to "replenish the earth and subdue it, have dominion over the fish of the sea, and the fowl of the air, and over every living thing that moveth upon the earth." Now if you told that to a palaeolithic tribe they would think you the worst kind of howling psychopath! Such an isolated and violent ideology would have been totally repellent, completely sacrilegious. They treated animals with both awe and reverence. They were sacred beings, who provided them with life through their meat, with furs and skins, bones, tusks, antlers and horns to shape their tools and clothes, to carve and paint, to use as needles and calculators, to fashion into jewellery. Their fats illuminated the darkness in lamps. Animals were the embodiment of the divine power of the Great Mother in providing for her children. Animals and human animals existed together, held in unity by a special bond. They moved to invisible rhythms, they held the souls of the tribal ancestors. They were as one with the world.'

'Women seem to be very important,' she observed. 'The one Jeshua sees, she becomes the priestess, she leads the people to the great place of stones, where they watch the moon's reflection.'

'Of course. While the feminine values predominate, women are greatly honoured.'

'And still, as he moves on, in the next phase.'

'Yes. There's a Cretan feel to that – it's how the old world evolved. It's a hymn to Nature itself as the goddess, isn't it? That's what he sees. Everywhere he looks, all about him he sees colour and culture, he hears a hymn to joy and life, the abundance and beauty of the world they lived in.'

'So who are the men on the horses?' she asked sombrely. 'The filthy ones who smash all the lovely things, who kill all the people? Where have they come from?'

In the desert the dawn was coming. The moon had vanished, it was the approaching sun which lighted the sky, leaving black the jagged rock of the mountains where Jeshua knelt in the icy cold of the night.

He saw the woman and her family, her people on a magical island, emerald and gold with spring flowers, with oak and cypress on the hills, snow capping the mountains and feeding sparkling rivers. He saw the woman in her robes of the priestess, holding the double-headed butterfly axes of the goddess, poppies wound about her head, bees and doves in the air around her. He saw the gaiety of the people's rituals, the colour-drenched temples, their grace and elegance, their joy. He saw the young men and women vaulting the crescent horns of the black bull together. He saw a web of life, beautiful and delicate.

In the desert the sun rose over the bleak rocks and smote him in the eyes, sudden and savage. He was blind, the image of the magical land blurred in the hot blast. When he saw again his vision was dim. Smoke was drifting over the land. The temples of the goddess were burning, her golden fields were afire, dirty black smoke discoloured her azure sky. The air was filled with the howling of madness. Through the murk streaked men on horses, men grimed and filthy, savage weapons in their hands running red with blood, and all about in the ruins and the burning fields lay the people of the goddess who they had slaughtered.

In the desert the harsh sun blazed down on Jeshua from a pitiless steel sky. In front of his eyes the murder continued. The people of the goddess were defenceless, the warriors slashed and sliced their flesh with their swords, crushed their bones with their maces, ripped open their bellies with their daggers. They rode their horses over the dead and dying, and Jeshua cried out for it to stop.

The smoke cleared. On the plain a mighty host was drawn up. Their great banners snapped in the wind, there was the creak of harness and the clink of their weaponry, but they were silent. Thousands of fell, unblinking eyes stared at him, and

Jeshua realised that he was not watching, but that he was there on that plain with them. A wind was blowing, bringing with it the stench of corruption. Behind the army was a mountain of bone. Grinning skulls stared eyeless at him and a creature came bounding through the men of war, small and dark, clad in garments of human skin. It took him with a clawed hand and led him forward.

A gleaming chariot stood at the head of the host. Jet black horses stamped in harness, the reins ready, the quivers filled with spears as thick as sheaves. Armour hung waiting, the creature at his side led him to it.

In front of the chariot a beautiful woman lay upon a bed of flowers and sweet grasses. It was the one he had seen in his vision. Now she lay as if asleep, clad in a fabulous robe of gold and azure, of shimmering green, of indigo and violet. Her hair lay about her head, as thick as corn. Her eyes were closed, but her bosom rose and fell.

Robes were waiting for him, the evil creature held them out, priestly robes, but not of linen. Blood oozed from them, they were fashioned from newly flayed skin. The creature smiled, a long dark tongue running over its lips. It pulled him to the side of the woman, and thrust a jagged blade into his hand. From behind him the voices of the warriors shouted, a single, harsh crash of sound. The black, roiling clouds above him opened and rained blood. It ran down his face, through his hair, over the savage knife in his hand, but not on the woman. All were still, all watching him as he stood.

Soft white moonlight lit his way as he came from the desert. It bathed the rampart and defensive towers of the priestly redoubt. They were waiting for him, as he came up a torch of tightly bound twigs crackled into flame, banishing the light of the goddess above. In its glare he saw the beard and long mane of the baptist.

'What did you see?' he demanded.

'I saw Satan,' said Jeshua.

'And how did he tempt you?' said the harsh voice.

'He would give me everything, if I but led the people of Israel into war.'

Those about him stared silently at him, and he walked on and past the citadel, back into the moonlight.

'The warriors,' said Connell. 'Where *did* they come from? The world never knew war and conquest before them. Something terrible happened to the tribes that lived in the harsh places, the steppes and the desert. They acquired gods – not a goddess – gods that were very violent. The gods created the idea of human guilt and of sacrifice. They were sky gods of lightning, wind, fire and storm, the sun. Then they found, or they invented, or they were somehow given bronze, a metal that did not shatter. With it they made the mace, the axe and the sword, and once they had these they found, or invented, or were somehow given the concept of war, of conquest, of slavery and empire. They took over the world. Jeshua, in the desert, is living – like the rest of the people of Israel – in the Roman Empire, which succeeded those of Babylon, Assyria, Persia and Greece.'

'But what of the great goddess?'

'Murdered,' Connell said shortly. 'Instead of unity, we now have slaughter. The Babylonian god Marduk massacres the goddess to create the earth and heavens from her dismembered corpse. He hacks open her son like an insane serial killer and makes mankind from the blood. But even he is eclipsed by Yahweh, sole god of the people of Israel, who institutes genocide and the holy war as a way of life. The Old Testament is a hymn to intolerance, hatred and murder.

'Yahweh's only rival in terms of power was Zeus, father god of the Greeks. Despite his enormous power Zeus was loved for his great love of women and family – he had not only a goddess wife but innumerable gorgeous lovers both mortal and divine, as well as a huge number of daughters and sons. In bitter contrast Yahweh hates women and all things feminine. Zeus marries the goddess, Yahweh murders her, hacks her into pieces. He has no wife, no daughter. He constantly struggles victoriously against the great feminine forces that threaten his dictatorship. Zeus and the goddess Hera have a stormy marriage, but marriage it is – between the new, heroic, solar way of thinking and the old, lunar cyclical one of transformation. The two are not, once experienced, opposed to each other. It was possible for humans to work out how to stay in the Garden of Eden. But Yahweh won. And expelled us. And made Eve take the blame. He has made women pay ever since. And Yahweh, I would remind you, is the god of Judaism, Christianity and Islam. Christians call him Lord, or Almighty.'

'I don't like Yahweh,' she said coldly.

'No, the Children don't like him either,' Connell said mildly. 'They knew who he was. He had to be Satan.'

'But she is the goddess,' she argued. 'You can't kill the goddess.'

The smell of chaff, torn earth and diesel fuel had become stronger, through the window they could hear the sound of a big machine at work.

'*Doctrinally*, you can. The text of the Bible is, if you think that way, dictated by Yahweh, Father God, King of Kings and God of gods, who is, as he makes clear, a jealous god – "Thou shalt have no other gods before me." No gods, and certainly, no goddess. But as you say, it isn't necessarily so. If the goddess is Gaia, Mother of the Earth, then while the Earth is herself living so must be the Goddess, however much noise Yahweh makes.'

'So where has she gone?' she asked eagerly.

'She hides in the unconscious of us all, whatever culture, whatever race, in the myths and legends, in stories and fairy-tales, in our dreams. She is Sleeping Beauty, who waits for her prince to come, to restore her rightful place, in sacred union. She is Cinderella, grimed in the soot of what we have made according to Yahweh, the bright and shining one who keeps the fire alight. She too is waiting to be reunited with the prince. She is waiting for us to wake up from our nightmare so she may be dressed in her robe of glory, tinkling with the sound of bells.'

'So that's the real answer. The goddess is real.'

'Real in our dreams,' said Connell, 'but still suppressed by Yahweh.'

She tapped the paper she had read.

'But isn't she the woman there, who lies sleeping in front of the army. She is Sleeping Beauty. The one the evil creature wants Jesus to kill?'

'That's it,' Connell said quietly. 'Jesus lives in the Roman Empire. His people are enslaved, they are yearning for the Messiah, the one who will lead them in battle, the descendant of David, their mightiest warrior. It's clear. Satan offers Jesus the opportunity to do just that, but he must murder the goddess first. And he won't do it.'

'The Children knew who the Almighty is,' she said, 'but if we rejected him too, it is *he* who would vanish, like a nightmare goes in the morning. Leaving nothing behind but sunshine.'

She got up, looking out of the window. Beyond Connell's overgrown garden a huge blue machine was moving, cutting the corn and stacking the straw in its wake. It left a thick haze of dust behind it.

'I hate machines,' she said absently.

'They make life easier,' he said, 'that's why we invent them.'

'Easier for what?' she demanded, her voice suddenly sharp. 'And do they? Do we invent them?'

'They don't just appear.'

'Don't they? They seem to.'

She turned her back on the giant harvester and leaned against the windowsill, holding her bottle of beer in one hand.

'I like *some* machines,' she said. 'I like a well like that one out there. That's a good machine. It's simple, someone made it with their hands. I like a loom, that makes cloth, I like barrels and jugs and yeast and hops that make beer. I *don't* like things like that.'

She turned back to gesture at the combine, and glanced up at the sky, where high above a jet was leaving a spreading white contrail against the sun.

'And I don't like that either.'

'Agricultural productivity?' Connell suggested.

'People still starve,' she said obstinately, 'and machines like that mean people rot on city streets instead of living on the land here.'

'Ah. But all governments hate the peasantry, because they are independent.'

'Back when people worshipped the goddess they didn't. Isn't that right? Not until the warriors came. These places, Sumer, Babylon, didn't everything grow there?'

'Yes. They were very fertile. The goddess was queen of the Earth, goddess of the vine and of the grain – their wine and beer were famous – of the date palm and the corn, the cedar and the fig, the sycamore, the apple and the olive, she was the Green One, queen of stall and fold, the shepherdess who kept the cow byre and sheepfold. She was queen of the sparkling waters, her fertility made the very reeds that the scribes used to write with, so she became queen of writing, of literature, art and the interpretation of dreams.'

'Very nice,' Maria said dryly, 'and what are these lands like now?'

'Desert,' Connell said shortly. 'War swept through the whole great land, first one way then back again like the tide. Whole populations were transplanted, taken into slavery or simply slaughtered. It was an age of insanity and massacre.'

'The gods approved. Yahweh thought it was wonderful,' she pointed out. 'When did it stop, all this war?'

'It hasn't.'

'Yahweh approves.'

She picked up her apple from the table and bit into it.

'This is really nice,' she said approvingly. She looked up at Connell with sharp eyes. 'Did you use a machine to grow it?'

'Of course not.'

'No. You don't *need* machines, do you? Not really complicated ones like that thing out there. You can grow food with simple tools. You can catch fish with a line and a little boat, you don't need a great steel ship.'

She looked about her.

'You could make a house like this yourself.'

'Yes, you're right, it was made without machines,' said Connell, 'local stone and slate, local wood. See the inglenook fireplace, they'd have sat round the fire in the winter.'

He went over to the table where the papyrus was showing the marks of writing. Glancing down, he could see the names of Paul, and of Nero.

'But you can't make a great glass building without the machines.'

She looked out again at the cornfield.

518

'It's the wrong colour,' she said. 'It ought to have flowers in it. In the land of the goddess flowers are everywhere. The goddess loves flowers.'

She was standing in the sunshine, it lit up the colours of her face.

'Do you know what she hates?' she asked.

'What?'

'Machines. When she comes back, when she overthrows Yahweh, she's going to get rid of all the machines.'

26

Rome, July A.D. 64

'I like you,' said Nero, affably.

He put a silk-clad arm around Saul and they walked together down the Egyptian porphyry marble corridor.

'Thank you, Imperator,' Saul murmured pleasantly.

'I mean it. You're my sort.'

They were on their own as they strolled down the great palace corridor towards the courtyard. Saul could hear the musical sound of water falling in multiple cascades from the *nymphaeum*. The very air of the summer residence was pleasingly cool from the effects of the massed fountains and lush gardens.

For once, the formidable entourage of the Emperor, the carriages and the silver-shod mules, the Mauritanian horsemen and outriders, the hordes of beautiful youths trained to sing out his praises upon sight, all were elsewhere, and Nero wandered down his corridor alone, accompanied only by Saul. They came to the lovely courtyard and there the Emperor paused, looking peevishly out over his creation. A pleasant breeze rippled the flowered silk of his dressing gown.

'It's very poky,' he said discontentedly.

'Hmm,' Saul grunted, noncommittally.

'Oh it is,' said Nero, turning to him. 'For ordinary people, beyond dreams, of course. For an ordinary Emperor, I suppose it would suffice. For me . . . mere torture.'

'I see. Of course, it is much too small. Too drab.'

'I thought you would. Too small, indeed. Certainly, yes, too drab.'

Nero threw his arms wide.

'I just want to live like a human being,' he said exasperatedly. 'Is it too much to ask?'

He turned, capturing Saul's shoulder again, and they went back into the apartments of the palace.

'Let's relax a little,' Nero said. 'I want you to tell me a little more about the Jesus of yours. An interesting fellow, you say. Tigillinus seems to think he might be useful.'

They went through a gilded, twenty-foot-high door, and into a grand room, indirectly lit and aired from the courtyard, its walls richly decorated with detail in red and blue, gold and purple, the costly, imperial colours. On a gold, silk-covered couch a young girl was waiting, she rose as they came in.

'Ah . . .' Nero said in approval, and waved a hand about. 'Now this is a taste of what is to come. Famullus did these for me. I want him to do more, in the new palace.'

'Which palace is that, Imperator?' Saul enquired politely.

'The new one I'm having built. The *Domus Aurea*.'

'The golden house. A fitting home for an Emperor such as yourself.'

'I thought so,' Nero agreed contentedly. 'It will have an arcade a mile long, rooms studded with jewels and gold overlays. Ivory ceilings! I shall slaughter thousands of elephants simply to decorate the ceilings. The dining room will be circular, a bowshot wide with a revolving roof synchronised to the movements of the very heavens. All shall be surrounded by a great lake and a lovely park, filled with vineyards, orchards, forests and meadows, and populated with animals from the four corners of the Empire.'

'Wonderful,' breathed Saul. 'Where are you to build it?'

'I don't know,' Nero said, once again peevish. 'Outside Rome, I suppose, though why I should have to be stuck out there I can't imagine. Oh, and a three-hundred-foot statue of myself, completely covered in gold. The people must be able to see me.'

'Of course,' he agreed.

Nero threw himself extravagantly on to the couch, and the beautiful girl sat down next to him, as light as a feather. The Emperor cast his arm about her, and she began to fondle his groin.

'This Jesus. He wants a new world. Well, he did, he's dead, isn't he. But the ones who believe in what he preached. They think a new world's coming.'

'Yes.'

'Well, so do *I*. They call me debauched. I know that. But they have to see that I, their Emperor, am leading them out of the bonds and fetters that have held them down, imprisoned. They are restricted and held back from fulfilling themselves, physically and spiritually. I am leading them to a salvation that only I know.'

The girl delicately stripped back Nero's gown, exposing him to the air, her hands caressing him. The Emperor looked calculatingly at Saul.

'Isn't that what your Jesus wants?'

'It is.'

Nero turned to the girl.

'Well, don't keep my guest waiting,' he said reprovingly.

The girl smiled without saying a word. Leaving the seat she came around, dropping her dress to the floor and bending herself naked over its padded arm. She was slim, with smooth buttocks and long legs. Nero sprawled at his ease, and the girl took him in her mouth.

'Nobody in the world is pure,' said Nero philosophically, 'nor chaste, not in any single part of their body.'

He looked up at Saul, suddenly aggrieved.

'They just hide it! Hypocrites! They perform obscene acts in the dark. Not I. Not you, friend Saul.'

'Not I.'

'Are you forgiven, then? Does your Jesus forgive?'

'Jesus the Christ died so that I might live, he forgives my sins.'

'Well, get on with it, then,' Nero said amiably, waving at the bobbing rear of the girl. 'Give him something to forgive you for.'

Saul hesitated for a second. Nero laughed.

'She isn't a *woman*, you know. It's all snipped off. Go on, have a feel.'

Saul slipped his hand between the legs of the creature and it was as Nero had said, all cut away and smooth. He ran his hands over the boy's bottom.

'Like a peach,' Nero said approvingly. 'Like a peach.'

Saul hitched up his tunic and entered him, the three swaying and bumping together in a strange harmony.

'You want me to approve of your Jesus,' Nero grunted.

'A new world is coming, the old gods are dying,' said Saul, gripping the hips of the youth. 'It can be your world, your god. Jesus is waiting for you, where you lead your people.'

'Only Jesus? Must they believe in him?'

'He commanded us. Compel them to come in. We need you, the Emperor to compel them, and then we, your servants of your Church, will bring you your willing servants.'

'One god?' Nero mused.

The boy rocked to and fro to the slapping of flesh.

'One God, one Church, one Emperor,' Saul promised. 'You

shall be god's vicar upon earth, he shall speak to his people through your mouth.'

Nero grunted like a boar and fell back upon the cushions. Gasping, he watched approvingly as Saul finished buggering the youth.

'*Deo gratias*,' Saul gasped, and let the youth go.

'I like you,' Nero murmured. 'I told you I did.'

As the boy slipped away Nero pulled himself upright, tugging his gown about him.

'I have it,' he murmured. 'This god, he must have the finest temples.'

'The finest,' Saul assured him. 'The highest, the grandest, the most beautiful, to the glory of God.'

'Yes, yes. I see it all. You shall be my chief priest.'

He pulled Saul down next to him, and looked searchingly at him with his blue, protruberant, insane eyes.

'Forget about Jesus,' he said dismissively. 'Dead on a cross, who needs him. Put him out of your mind. God is already here. I shall build a temple for him the like of which has never been seen on earth before. There shall be a statue to him, three hundred foot high, all covered in gold, it shall be visible to all in Rome, and all shall bow down in worship.'

'And I shall be chief priest.'

'Oh, yes. I like you, I told you so.'

'Where is this god?' Saul asked carefully.

'Right here,' Nero beamed. 'He is right next to you.'

He sighed with pleasure.

'They shall have no gods but me!'

'Jesus is coming,' Paul said softly, and they all cried out with joy at the very sound of his name.

'He is coming to us, he has told us so.'

Gaia clasped her hands together, shaking them, beside her Cadmus held his arms up, ready to embrace the Saviour. It was warm in the room, they felt the heat of his love. A single, thick beeswax candle burning on the altar illuminated them, chased shadows into the dark corners.

' "Fear not," he said!' Paul exclaimed. ' "I am the first and the last: I am he that lives, and was dead; and is alive forevermore. I have the keys of Hell and of death." '

'Ohhh, yes,' Gaia whispered. 'Praise him, praise him.'

'He looks down upon us,' Paul assured them all. 'He tells us, "I know your works, and labour, and patience, and how you hate those who are evil. That for my name's sake you have laboured and not come faint. Furthermore you hate the Nicolaitans, the Jews, the unbelievers, whom I too do hate." '

He paused and frowned, and the congregation were suddenly filled with trepidation.

' "Nevertheless, I shall have something against you, should you leave your first love. Remember now from whence you might fall, and repent, and do the first works; or else I will come to you quickly." '

'No, no!' cried out Pomponia Graecina. 'We shall never leave the Lord!'

'Do you not fear?' Paul asked them all.

'We fear nothing!' Cadmus shouted.

'We fear only that the Lord Jesus will not love us,' Julia, the wife of Timothy, called out.

'You are wise,' Paul agreed. 'For the punishments of God far exceed those of man in both terror and length. But for those who love the Lord, and do his will, his protection is infinite, his punishment of his enemies both swift and severe. No one, not the Emperor himself can escape the wrath of God. For we are at war with the dragon, he that was expelled from Heaven and fell to earth. And when he let loose a seven-headed beast, and another, whose number was three sixes in a row. We know who he is, for are we not in that city that is his . . .'

'*Nero!*' Pomponia Graecina hissed savagely.

'Yes,' said Paul. 'We know who bears the number of the beast. But what of those who worship the beast? The same shall drink of the wine of the wrath of God, which is poured out without mixture into the cup of his indignation; and they shall be tormented with fire and brimstone in the presence of the holy angels.

'The angels shall pour out their heavenly vials and the seas and rivers will run with blood of the sinners. The wicked shall be scorched with the sun, the seat of the beast shall plunge into darkness. All who dwell there shall gnaw their tongues for pain. When God gathers them all together at Armageddon, then shall the seventh angel pour out his vial. Then shall the great city, home of the beast be split asunder. The great Babylon shall come to God to taste the wine of the fierceness of his wrath, to be judged.

'And a woman shall sit on the seven-headed beast in the wilderness, decked in purple and scarlet, drinking from a golden cup filled with abominations. Upon her forehead is written Mystery, Babylon the Great, the Mother of Harlots and Abominations of the Earth. And I saw the woman drunk with the blood of the saints and with the blood of those who love Jesus.'

Paul looked around, seeing the unblinking eyes reflected red in the candlelight.

'We know who the whore is, for we must taste her abominations every day.'

'Rome!' cried out a dozen voices. 'Home of the beast!'

'The ten horns of the beast, these shall hate the whore, and shall make her desolate and naked, and shall eat her flesh, and burn her with fire.'

They cried out with joy.

'A mighty angel shall descend, lighting up the world in his glory, and he shall say, "Babylon the great is fallen, and is become the habitation of devils and the hold of foul spirit . . . Double unto her double according to her works; in the cup which she has filled fill to her double."'

Yes, the Lord would do it back to them, twice as hard, twice as long, twice as agonising.

'Therefore shall her plagues come in one day, death and mourning and famine; and she shall be utterly burned with fire, for strong is the Lord God who judges her.'

'Yes, yes!' Gaia screamed. 'Hallelujah!'

'And the kings of the earth, who have committed fornication and lived deliciously with her, shall bewail her and lament for her, when they see the smoke of her burning, standing far off for the fear of her torment, saying "alas, alas, that great city Babylon, that mighty city! For in one hour is your judgement come."'

'Come!' Cadmus cried, and saliva ran from the corner of his mouth. 'Come, oh Redeemer, come, our Saviour!'

Paul stood at the head of the little church, and was silent. In that silence, they all stared at him with growing anxiety.

'He cannot come,' Paul said again. 'Not until we show him our love.'

He moved amongst them, he had a word for each, the word of the Lord.

'Did he not give you back your baby?' he murmured to Gaia, and stroked her hair with the hand of Jesus.

'Ohhh, yes. Yes, yes.'

'Did he not save you from torment, and bring you to the

life of God?' he asked Cadmus, and the priest could see the red-hot tongs in the brazier.

'Who killed your son?' he asked Pomponia Graecina. 'Who torments you? Who laughs at your pain?'

'The beast and his servants,' she whispered bitterly.

Paul moved amongst them, bringing them the word of Jesus, and then he went back to the altar and picked up the candle, holding it high. In the corner of the room they saw a great pile of torches, dry, twisted twigs wrapped into brands, and Paul picked one up.

'Jesus is coming,' he promised them once again. 'He will come, when we show him his love, when we defeat the beast, when we burn the whore.'

Paul dipped the end of the torch into the candle flame.

'If we do not light a beacon for him, if we do not show him our love, he shall cast us into outer darkness for all time.'

Paul blew the candle flame and they were suddenly plunged into black gloom. They cried out in fear. Then the twigs crackled, there was sudden, brilliant light, and Paul held up the brand high in the air.

'Come!' he shouted. 'His love shines upon you. Come love the Lord!'

They howled their assent, sobbing for joy. They seized their torches, dipping them into the flame of Jesus, and ran out into the hot night, to do his will.

Domus Aurea, Rome

The slaves had finished carting away the thick black ash, the ground lay fresh and open, and already brick and stone were sprouting all the way from the Palatine Hill across the valley to the Esquiline and on to the Caelian Hill as well. No sooner had the last load of debris made its way to the Ostian marshes than they were back, laying and digging and setting, and the beginnings of the pavilions, temples, fountains, porticoes, baths and gardens that were to make up the fabulous place sprang up under their hands like magic. Ten days of wind-whipped inferno had cleared the Roman hills of habitation better than any demolition squad.

Tigillinus always knew where to find the Emperor, he would be somewhere in the two hundred acres of his new estate, usually with either Severus or Celer, sometimes with both architects, planning the glories of his future palace.

He found him down in the valley, where the slaves were digging out the site for a large artificial lake, and hauling away the spoil. The artist Famullus was there, making notes and small working sketches on some sheets of papyrus he carried, while the Emperor talked.

'Ah, Tigillinus,' he said affably, as the praetorian prefect approached. 'Famullus is going to decorate some of the rooms in the palace. He's been showing me some sketches.'

'I'm sure his work will be most beautiful. He has done work for me at my Aemilian estate.'

The artist murmured something polite and shifted away, pretending to work out some detail on his papyrus. Only those with sensitive antennae got to survive close to the Emperor and his immediate advisors. The predecessor to the grim man who had walked down the hill towards them, good Burrus, was given poison for a cough mixture, and forced to drink it. Had the Emperor not had the young Aulus Plautus strangled and buggered the thrashing victim as he died? Had he not murdered his own mother, evil bitch though she was, had his lovely young wife tied up in a hot bath and sat watching as they opened her veins? And when she wouldn't die, had her dragged out and into a room where they steamed her to death like a lobster, and removed her head? That was to show to his mistress, at whose instigation she had been murdered, and who married him. Not that she would make old bones, he'd be bound. No, life about the Emperor was dangerous, the artist hoped merely to complete his painted stuccowork for the palace and avoid being incorporated into its foundations as some kind of good luck charm.

'What do you think, Tigillinus?' Nero demanded. 'About the lake will be grottoes, woods and gazebos. Truly *rus in urbes*. A fitting setting for such an artist as myself. A theatre is to be built for my plays.'

'Wonderful,' Tigillinus said shortly. 'That is, if the populace don't come and burn it down.'

'Why would they do that?' Nero demanded, his blue eyes bulging angrily.

'They say that that is what you did to their houses.'

'Have I not ordered the construction of new *insulae* for the plebs? And new roads and open spaces?'

'And a new palace, taking up a big piece of the best part of the city,' Tigillinus said dryly. 'To be paid for by the Fire Relief Fund.'

'I am Emperor . . . Am I not a god? I have to have a fitting place to live. And did I not hurry back from Antium to supervise the firefighting?'

'The story is going round that at the height of the blaze you went to the Tower of Maecenas in your tragedian's costume and sang *The Sack of Ilium* from beginning to end.'

'The flames were so beautiful,' Nero muttered. 'How could I not make the comparison between modern disaster and the past? I am an artist, I tell you.'

'There are other artists about, making up *their* songs. Shall I quote one?

> The palace is spreading and swallowing Rome!
> Let us all flee to Veii and make it our home.
> Yet the palace is growing so damnably fast
> That it threatens to gobble up Veii at last.

'Doggerel,' Nero said dismissively. 'Mere doggerel. Let me get my lyre and I'll sing you a new one of my own.'

'*Imperator*,' Tigillinus said grittily, 'nobody cares if it was written by Homer or by Datus. It is what the people believe that matters. They are saying that you want to rename the city after yourself.'

'Why not? Have you seen the new statue I have commissioned of myself, to stand in front of the palace? Gilded bronze and twice as high as the tallest tree. You'll be able to see it shine from Sabinim.'

'Not unless we do something about these stories that are raging,' Tigillinus said bluntly, his coarse Sicilian accent making the words hang in the air.

Nero stared at his first minister and guard commander for a long time, his attention finally captured. Madness had not yet completely claimed him for its own.

'Very well,' he said. 'Why don't you go and sort it out with Saul? He's my . . . priest. He'll help you.'

'Is he here?'

'I saw him earlier. Up near the statue. Now. I feel a song coming on. Let me to my lyre and I can sing it to my guests during *cena*.'

Tigillinus hurried grimly back up the hill. He found Saul in conversation with Calenus, amidst the building work.

'The Emperor's in trouble,' he said without preamble. 'All

over this bloody palace. They – them out there who used to live right here, before the fire – are saying he burned all their homes down to build it.'

'I know,' said Saul. 'Would it not be best to bring the culprits to trial? To make them pay for what they did?'

The prefect's eyes narrowed.

'You're saying it *was* started deliberately?'

'Of course.'

'Who did it then?' Tigillinus demanded.

'The Christians,' Saul said softly.

'What? *Your* bloody lot?'

'Yes.'

'*Why?*'

'Because I told them to.'

Tigillinus's eyes bulged in disbelief. Saul pointed down the valley, to where Nero was strumming.

'*He* wanted it done. This palace is a temple. A temple to him.'

The prefect was silent, acknowledging the truth of what Saul was saying, that the Emperor was insane.

'But now, no problem. Bring out the Christians. Make them pay.'

'The *munera*, you mean? A special event?'

'That's it. It'll make the people feel better, see if it doesn't.'

'Yes,' Tigillinus said thoughtfully. 'That could work. So where can I get hold of these blasted Christians?'

'Well, you'd better make it look good,' Saul said reasonably. 'Pick one of them up and interrogate them. Then go from there.'

'I know how to go from there,' Tigillinus promised. 'So who do I start with?'

'I heard that the Emperor is looking for money,' Calenus interjected boldly. Tigillinus turned to him.

'The Emperor is *always* looking for money,' he said bleakly. 'True gentlemen, of which he claims to be one, always throw their money around, or so he says.'

'I am keen to help the Emperor,' Calenus said unctuously, 'and I too would like some money. Is it not also true that a part of the estates of those who commit treason against the Emperor is given to those who denounce them – the majority going to the Emperor, of course.'

'That is correct.'

'And surely, being one of these Christians must count as treason?'

'It certainly does.'

'Then I can tell you where to start your search,' Calenus said triumphantly. 'And remember it was I who told you, when the estate comes to be shared out. Go to Gaia, wife of Flavius. She is a Christian.'

Basilica Julia, Rome

They played games here, the magnificent marble of the hall's floor was marked out in squares for them. Caesar had paid for it, with his Spanish gold. The crowds who watched the games liked to come for the other type of entertainment the great building had to offer, they were here now, shoved around the edges of the *corona* where the *decemvir* sat in his curule chair among his assessors; they hung over the tribunes on the first storey, craning their necks and cupping their ears against the din of four law courts operating at full blast in one great hall, only separated by inadequate curtains and screens.

Gaia waited with Maria. Then it was her turn. The guard

held back the curtain and they went in. It was hot in there, stuffy and stifling. The judge was wiping his face with a corner of his *amictus*. The water in the *clepsydra* water clock had dripped through into the bowl beneath, he motioned for the clerk to refill it. He looked wearily up to see what new group of felons confronted him on the benches below and his expression was filled with horror. He was Flavius.

'Gaia!' he said. He composed himself. 'Well, at least a mistake has been made here. Let us get it out of the way.'

Gaia stood by the bench as the charge was read out. The clerk's voice was drowned out by a blast of synthetic applause from the paid *laudiceni* earning their supper next door as the advocate who had hired them stated his case with no less histrionics. As the clapping claque quietened Flavius cleared his throat. The water dripped steadily through the little hole.

'You are charged with being a member of a criminal group that observes foreign superstitions, that is, followers of Jesus the Nazarene, himself a convicted and executed criminal. It has been proven that these Nazarenes, acting *en masse*, for evil purposes of their own, began and spread the fire of July that has caused so much damage to our city. They are therefore to be brought to justice.'

Flavius sipped a little lukewarm water from a cup as he peered at his wife, and in his glance over its rim she saw fear. She stood up straight, and was calm.

'All that is necessary –'

Booming oratory rolled over his strained voice from the third chamber and he paused.

'Rot Galerius Tracalus,' he muttered irritably. 'All that is necessary, Gaia, as proof that you are innocent, is a simple sacrifice to the gods and the Emperor. A chicken will do. I have a priest waiting at the altar, it can be done in a moment and you can go home. Now, what do you say?'

'I cannot sacrifice to any gods, nor the Emperor. I have but one Lord, who is the Christ Jesus.'

She spoke out clearly, her soprano voice cutting through the booming and babble of those about the building.

Flavius winced as though lashed by a thong.

'Gaia, Gaia, don't say these things . . . listen, the *clepsydra* is running out, by the last drop I must pass judgment. It is just a little sacrifice. It is proof, you see? Without sacrifice, some god will be angry, and the anger of the gods is hard to bear. What say you? Look, if not a chicken, how about a simple pinch of incense? Yes? A pinch of incense and a simple little oath to, to – the health of the Emperor. Yes? What could be more reasonable than that?'

He looked down on her, his anxiety beginning to turn to terror.

'No one can know what you keep in your heart,' he urged quietly, leaning forward.

'My Lord Jesus will know,' she said steadfastly.

'Gaia, do not think that your rank will protect you,' he said, desperate now. 'Nor that you are married to me. It is not a question of forfeiture of estate, or banishment for a while. The Emperor has decided that membership of this little cult is *capitalia et atrociora maleficia.* Its members are *vilitas*, and without rights. You will *die*.'

'We all must die,' she said steadfastly. 'Flavius, I stand under a greater authority than yours. My Jesus said that anyone on this earth who dared denounce him before men would be denounced by him before God. Whatever suffering may be inflicted upon me here on earth will be nothing compared to the suffering I shall endure by being banished from the presence of my Lord.'

'We have no time for this,' Flavius said urgently. 'Listen to me, merely sacrifice and the fact that you . . . mistakenly came into contact with these people can be forgotten. You can go free.'

'Flavius, Flavius, you should not be trying to corrupt me, but thinking of your own soul,' Gaia said gently. 'Do you not know that Jesus is coming? Very soon the trumpets will sound, the cymbals clash and the gates of Heaven will open. The mightiest walls on earth will fall down and the Lord will reveal himself to his people once again. But only if you believe in him will he take you with him up to his palace in the sky. Will you not believe in my Lord Jesus too?'

An expression of pure horror came over Flavius's face.

'Where have you got these mad ideas from?' he screamed, suddenly breaking. 'Who has infected you with this mental debauchery?'

He turned furiously upon Maria, standing quietly behind Gaia.

'Is it you? Are you the one who has perverted my wife's mind?'

Maria looked steadfastly up at the howling judge.

'Not I, Magister. I do not worship this Jesus.'

Gaia turned, and for the first time pain entered her eyes.

'Maria, Maria, you do not know what you say . . . Do not turn away from him who loves you . . . For the eternal fires of Hell shall be your reward.'

'I know nothing of this Jesus,' Maria said again.

'Very well,' Flavius muttered. 'Get you to the altar and make sacrifice.'

Maria turned without a word, and walked out of the court.

'Gaia,' Flavius said once more, his tones pleading. 'Do not make me do this. Think what you will do to me as well as yourself. Is it not a pleasant autumn day?'

The clerk bent and whispered in his ear and she saw him blanch with fear.

'*Tigillinus is in the building.* Gaia, once he is here I will not be able to save you. Come, quick. Did you pay attention to the air as you rode in? Was it pleasant? Quickly now, sacrifice to the air.'

'I paid no attention to the air,' she said. 'Only to him who made it, who rides across it in his chariot every day, in the heavens above.'

'But the day is pleasant,' Flavius persisted. 'And no pleasure will come your way if you insist on killing yourself. Just do as I say and you will be saved.'

'The death which awaits me is more pleasant than the life that you would give,' she said, 'for I shall be with Jesus.'

The courts were temporarily quiet. The peace was broken by heavy, slow, ironic clapping from the curtained entrance. She turned to see the Sicilian standing there.

'Then get you to him,' said Tigillinus, 'for the clock is dry.'

It was hot in the gloomy stone room, stuffy and dark after the walk down from the hills through the leafy woods in the cool of the morning, and Julia was drenched in sweat. It was not, however, ordinary perspiration, for it dripped from her on to the floor, cold as ice, and she shivered. She was afraid.

The heavy weights shifted under the command of Tigillinus's man, the ropes thrummed under the sudden strain and Gaia screamed, a gasping, gurgling scream of someone who has very little breath left with which to do it.

'This is *quaestio per tormenta*, you said so,' Julia said bravely. 'So ask your questions and take her from the machine.'

'I have asked my questions before you were brought here,' Tigillinus said, his rough provincial voice like gravel in the grim room. He had taken off his cloak and hung it over his arm in the heat. The nails of his *calcei* scraped on the stone floor.

'This one has freely confessed to being a Nazarene, a follower of the criminal Christus. She is the wife of a senator, would you believe. She ought to know better. But she won't tell us the names of any of her other conspirators, which is unreasonable of her. But we shall see. Quintus! You aren't stretching the creases from your toga, put some effort behind it.'

The man at the head of the rack, resting on its trestles, grinned, comfortable in his work. He made an adjustment to the complex system of weights and ropes fastened to the woman's hands and feet and the machinery moved, stretching all the joints, from one end of the body to the other. Blood ran down both sides of her mouth, where she had bitten through her lip against the pain.

'When you're ready, you can tell Quintus where your criminal friends are,' Tigillinus remarked. He took Julia's elbow and began to walk her around the room. Within her womb she felt her baby thump vigorously, unhappy with his mother's state of mind, and she tried to send reassuring messages down to him.

'I wouldn't normally be doing this,' Tigillinus said, and his avuncular manner made her very skin crawl, 'but it's serious, the crimes are *capitalia et atrociora maleficia* and the law clearly specifies the use of *quaestio tormentorum*. The law is right, for this woman Gaia has admitted to illegal worship, and is thus among the *vilitas*. No better than queers, pimps and gladiators. Oh, have I said why you're here? No, no, of course I haven't. You see, we searched her place and found some texts to do with this Jesus, nicely written they were, by a professional, I could tell that, and he'd signed his name on them, Timothy the scribe. One of my lads, thought he knew a Timothy the scribe, which is why we sent for you up on the hill. There's a couple of lads waiting for your Timothy, when he comes home, and we'll have a word with him too.'

He put out a hand and touched some metal hooks hanging by ropes from the wall.

'Ever seen these used? No, what am I saying, a lady of quality like yourself would never have been down in a place like this, let alone seen them used. It's ordinary chaps like me that have to do the dirty work of keeping Rome safe from harm.'

The ferocious hooks, sharp and barbed, clanked, giving off a terrifying message. Julia had not thought it possible to be more afraid than she already was, but a fresh flood of adrenalin gushed into her stomach and her baby once again kicked angrily.

'*Ungulae*,' said Tigillinus with professional approval. 'You get them inserted into the flesh and pull them with weights, very slowly. You can see, they're cleverly designed, they won't come out. Originally a method of capital punishment, but one of our predecessors tried it out as a method of *quaestio tormentorum* and it worked well. You find the person you're questioning is nearly always guilty so you can move on to their execution without changing method! Now that's what I call efficient.'

He moved on, taking Julia with him by her elbow.

'I do take it you're not one of these Nazarenes, are you?' he asked, casually. A brazier was burning in a corner, adding its heat to the foul air in the room.

Her baby thumped.

'No. I am not,' she said.

'I'm so glad to hear it. Now here we have the hot irons.'

Her stomach rebelled and Julia bent over as far as her baby would let her, vomiting on to the stone floor.

'Quintus! Cup of water for the lady. Taken a bit queer. She's with child, you know.'

Julia leaned against the wall, breathing heavily, and some chains rattled against her.

'Ah, those are useful,' said Tigillinus. 'They're for use in interrogatory torture, along with the castigation by rods.'

She gulped some water.

'Sorry, where were we? Oh, you were saying you weren't one of these followers of Christus, isn't that right?'

She saw Gaia, lying stretched on the track looking at her.

'Not I,' she said again.

The eyes closed.

'That's good.'

Tigillinus peered down at the floor. 'Well, what did you have for dinner? What's this? Bread, wine, and fish, by the look of it. Now there's a coincidence. Gaia, here, she chucked up when we gave her a little stretch, and that's what *she* had. Sort of a ceremonial rite, she said. She's been free with her information, except for the names, and you know, we have to have names. Are you sure you aren't one of them, Julia?'

'No.'

The terrible eyes opened again.

'Oh, well. Was your fish and bread and wine nice, Julia?'

'Yes,' she whispered. Vomit and fear were sour in her throat.

Tigillinus was looking at her through the gloom, and she remained silent.

'But you're not one of them. So that's all right. Very well, Quintus, you can take that one off now.'

The fat man tripped the mechanism, the wheels whirred, the ropes slapped slack, blood spouted from the wounds they had made. He unhitched the loops expertly and tipped the gasping, naked body off the rack with a practised shove. Unable to put out her hands to protect herself she fell to the stone floor with a crunch of bone. Blood began to trickle across the slabs and Julia moved to help her.

Tigillinus held her by the elbow.

'Leave her be,' he said.

They were standing by the fearsome flat body of the machine, wet and sticky with sweat and blood.

'Get on.'

They had not yet applied the weights, she simply lay stretched out on her back, the bulge of her baby pushing high up in the air.

'So this Christianity has spread into the body of the upper classes like Gaia here,' said Tigillinus, 'the Emperor will be very worried. There must be lots more of you. Better give me their names now. Save a lot of trouble. I've got guests coming, I need to call by at the baths.'

'I know nothing.'

He leaned on her, using her protruding stomach as a rest.

'When's the baby due?'

'In a month,' she gasped.

'Boy or a girl?'

'I don't know. How could I?'

He had moved out of her vision, down by her legs, she heard him picking through pieces of metal.

It was cold, he put it up between her thighs.

'Want to find out now?' he asked.

Anno Domini

The Gardens of Nero, Ager Vaticanus

He had a permit from Sabinus, prefect of the *urbs*, who was the brother of the general, Vespasian. He was on the Emperor's business, the wagon train forced its way through the crowded city streets in daylight; the people cursed them and the *catabolenses* lashing the mules cursed back.

They had gone to the *horrea* of Ostia, armed with Nero's writ, and from the warehouses had taken what they needed. In the wagons were stacks of stout wooden poles, and sisal rogue's yarn from the ropemaker. Naval rope was superior to all other, it was smuggled out of the dockyards for resale, when possible. Their possession of the coils with their telltale red jute markings would have been questioned had it not been for the authority Flavius carried. They had bundles of dry faggots and iron fittings commissioned from the naval smithy; blocks of tar and resin pitch; braziers and cauldrons in which to melt them; tall trestles and planks, to make ready platforms; *amphorae* of wine, without which the job could not be done at all.

Sabinus, brother of Vespasian, who was sensibly keeping out of sight in the country after falling asleep during an interminable recital by Nero, was waiting for them.

'I have a map here, Flavius,' he said, holding a sheet of papyrus. He was a solid, good-humoured man not unlike his brother. Today he was agitated. The papyrus trembled in his hand.

'The Emperor wants to be sure the gardens are properly lit. He is holding a banquet tonight. He has issued instructions to me as to the sitting of the torches.'

The workmen were unloading the supplies, lighting the braziers.

'You were in Palestine all those years ago,' Sabinus muttered. 'Isn't that where all this started? Perhaps that is why the Emperor appointed you to this task. You have some expertise, possibly?'

'I do not know why I am here,' Flavius said. '*Mannius!*'

A slave had opened an *amphora* and had poured the contents into a large bowl. He brought two beakers, filled high.

'Drink it,' he said to the prefect. Sabinus sniffed it.

'Neat?' he said, in horror. 'We are *gentlemen*.'

Flavius drained his in a draught.

He stared at the melting pitch beginning to trickle around the sticky cauldron, the hot smell of tar and coarse resin tickling his nose. The gardens began to clang to the beating of the fitters' hammers as they set up the brackets.

Sabinus looked at the pitch, and swallowed his beaker at a gulp.

They had been to the baths, there was no one there who could not spare a *quadra*, most, tactfully, at the new *thermae* of Nero on the Campus Martius, a few, like Gallus the senator, in their own *balneum* at home. They were well-heated, anointed with oil, scraped with *strigils*, cooled in the great pool of the *frigidarium*. 'Well washed, well washed,' they called and drawled at one another, as they emerged dripping, after the fashion of the time.

Freshened, perfumed, dressed, the pinnacle of society, they made their way to the Emperor's palace in the gardens set out by his mother, before he had had her beaten to death by some sailors, the drowning he had arranged having proven ineffective. In his vast *triclinium*, amid the gleam of gold and the glitter of glass they lounged on their couches. Famullus's exquisite murals decorated the walls. He had pleaded pressure of the work on Nero's Golden House to avoid being present. Pimps, panders, actresses and whores were there, however; gladiators from the arena, charioteers from the circus, stage directors, financiers and swindlers; eunuchs, freedmen, government ministers, extortionists, torturers and killers, it was difficult to tell which role any of them were playing at any time.

Gallus was one of the dwindling band of patrician families left from the republic. He sat among the throng in the feeling that he was bathing in dung. His father would have had any of them thrown out of his presence, his grandfather would not even have recognised their existence. Gallus smiled, laughed at their jokes, winked and nodded. He was a survivor, it was a family trait. The ancestor who had founded the family fortunes had deserted Pompey in time to put his sword to Caesar's use on the plain of Pharsalus.

His young wife Terentia took her cue from him, the pallor of her fear hidden behind the raiment of her make-up, and seated between two actresses, or harlots, smiled and chattered like a pretty bird.

The *ministratores* were efficient and skilled, lack of care at this table led to worse than demotion to the messengers' *decuria*; the guests were reclining, nibbling on the *hors d'oeuvres* and sipping their sweet *mulsum gustatio* within moments of being shown their place by the *nomenclator*. Scorpus the charioteer was there, of the Greens, the *factio* that Nero favoured, still with the strapping on his arm from the bloody shipwreck on the thirteenth turn that had snatched victory from him, and the life from Crescens, who had thought it his. Scipio from the theatre was there, for it was his production in which the Emperor was to star as Canace, and be violated by her own brother, Macaris. Tiberius's catamite Vitellius was there, the Spintra, lizard-eyed and sardonic. Tigillinus too, it was said that he was planning a further spectacular to cap his previous triumph. Supervising all was the corpulent figure of their genial host.

It was getting dark. In the gardens bands were playing. The lovely grottoes and arbours came to life from the dusk as great torches were lit, one by one. Vitellius, lounging at ease, peered out. A gang of firemen were igniting the illuminations under Flavius's command. He watched him lurching about in the incandescence.

'I say, old Flavius has been celebrating,' he drawled maliciously, 'I didn't think that he had it in him.'

' "Bathing, wine and Venus wear out the body, but are the real stuff of life," ' Scipio quoted. A gentle shower of scented water brushed over them from the cunning sprinklers in the ceiling and the *ministratores* brought in fresh dishes.

Flavius vanished, weaving into the glare and they turned their attention to the arriving food. Nero was ever a generous host, and boned dormice rolled in honey and poppy seed, together with spiced boar sausages hot from the grill were circulating, with special dips to bathe them in.

'Try this new brew, Spintra,' Nero called to Vitellius, and Scipio's companion on the *lectus* smiled pleasantly, unbothered by his master's description of him as a pervert, and plunged a mouse head down into the strong-smelling pot, munching it thoughtfully.

'Wonderful,' he called. 'What is in it, Imperator?'

'Saffron, malobathre, grilled dates, pepper and resin boiled up in wine and honey. I have a new Syrian cook. *Ut nemo agnoscet quid manduces.* A wonder.'

Scipio noticed Vitellius's eyes watering, and how he grasped for a quick gulp of wine.

'What's it like?' he asked in amusement.

'A trifle heavy on the pepper.'

'Nero likes that. Strong flavours.'

'I can take it,' said Vitellius, watching them bring in the first roast, 'I survived dining with Caligula.'

An entire female wild sow from the Ciminian forest took up the length of a great silver platter, small stripy piglets of sweet fruits and marzipan sucking on the teats. The server opened its side with an expert slash of his knife and thrushes flew out and about the room, to cheering from the guests.

There were dishes in profusion, hares miraculously sprouting hawk's wings, looking like Pegasus, slices of lobster *flambéed* alive and served in *assafoetida* sauce, a great and rare mullet. Such rarities as boiled crocodile, roasted ostrich and stewed giraffe were available to the Emperor, and anxious not to disappoint, he served them all.

In between courses there was entertainment, for as a good host he did not want his guests bored. The stand-up comedian Datus had them in fits with his lampoons of those in bad odour at court, Spanish dancing girls, almost naked beneath filmy gowns, performed a slick routine. A nude Egyptian woman armed with a whip and a dagger prepared to fight a Gaulish dwarf in a leather jerkin, hefting chain and hand-axe. While they were getting ready bets were laid. On the top couch Nero presided over all, beaming and in good humour, seated next to a very beautiful young girl, whom he fondled from time to time.

'Who's his little friend?' said Scipio curiously.

'Ah, that's Pythius,' Vitellius's eyes gleamed, the courtier with a good piece of gossip.

'That's a boy's name,' Scipio objected.

'*Exactly.* When Nero saw him he thought that he was so beautiful he should have been a girl. So he's made him into one!'

'No?' said Scipio.

'That's right,' Vitellius chuckled. 'Clean off.'

'There are some who think the world would be a better place if our Emperor's father had married a woman of that sort,' Scipio murmured, and Vitellius laughed.

'I see Saul's not here,' he said.

'That little priest fellow? I don't know what the Emperor sees in him.'

The fighting pair were squaring off.

'Which do you fancy?' he asked.

'Oh, I'm one for the women,' said Scipio. 'I always have been.'

He leaned forward, picking up an exotic apricot from the Caucasus and the two struck simultaneously with their flails. Gore spattered his fruit as he was about to bite into it, and he fastidiously stopped a passing slave with a bowl of rose-water to wash it.

'That was your girl's blood,' Vitellius observed. 'Might have been tasty.'

'I work in the theatre,' said Scipio. 'Blood I can taste any time.'

They wheeled about the impromptu arena in front of the couches, feet feeling for a grip on the fabulous mosaic, the dwarf with a livid, bleeding slash from temple to jaw, the woman dripping blood from a serrated gash from shoulder to breast. She sprang forward, toes gaining purchase on the stone's of Apollo's face, whip slashing at her opponent's chain arm. With incredible agility and strength the hump-backed creature bounded back like one of the apes at the games, clearing the wooden barrier, and the girl followed up, using the barrier to launch herself in a tremendous scything slash of her dagger.

Old Atticus the freedman was scrambling from his *lectus*,

she opened his paunch like a tunnyfish as the dwarf leaped away once more, and he splashed to the floor, where he lay flopping. The dwarf jumped up on to the barrier as the roar of sincere mirth rocked the room, seeing the advantage it gave; as he jumped the woman lashed at his dangling private parts with her whip, he hit the mosaic with a scream and she was on him, slashing and stabbing until the floor ran red.

She stood up in the gore, holding her hand, where she had chopped off two of her own fingers in her frenzy, and Nero tossed her a bag of gold. Then she staggered out, dripping, gasping with terror and pain, and the slaves came in to clear up the mess. Old Atticus had finished flapping like a landed fish and they dragged him out with the rest of it.

The guests wiped the tears from their eyes, those spattered with gore called for fresh *amicti*, they got up to pay visits to the *foricae* and *vomitorium*, to prepare themselves for the next bout. Eventually they settled back on their couches and a small orchestra played a not unpleasing air written by Nero; rose-petals scented with sweet-smelling oil fell like rain from the ivory-fretted ceiling and little but expensive gifts were distributed.

'Send one to Atticus's widow. She likes fine things.' said Nero.

He got up, and stretched, then scratched his paunch. The boy without genitals eyed him warily.

'I feel a song being born, with which I shall regale you all in a little while,' he announced, and picked up the lyre that was ever close to his side.

He swept from the room, strumming.

'Send Flavius to me,' he called over his shoulder. 'I shall need some illumination.'

Outside, the firemen were changing the spent torches for fresh.

Nero sat down, hitching up his *amictus*. The room was open
to the sky, above, stars glittered. A few moments later the
door to the room opened, letting in some light, and the noise
of the orchestra and guests. Flavius paused in the doorway.

'Imperator?'

'Light.'

Nero lounged back, picking at the strings of his lyre. A *cena*
was a leisurely affair, it might last eight or ten hours. A team
of fireman from outside came in. They carried lamps, they set
up trestles and planks to fit four great torches into brackets
that had been created off the walls.

Nero had ceased his picking, more interested for the time
being in the preparation of the illuminations. The scrape and
clink of metal echoed off the walls as the torches were fitted
in place. The men were clumsy, they dropped things. A torch
moved. It talked, it made a low chanting.

'Christians,' Nero said brightly. 'The ones who started the
fire. Well, from fire to fire they shall go.'

In the light of the burning faggot Flavius held in his hand
he could see that the torches on the wall were made from a
core of a man and a woman, lashed together naked. Around
them was dry wood, heavily seasoned with pitch.

'Very good, Senator.'

Flavius stepped forward, moving unsteadily, the brand
waving in his hand. He peered desperately into the gloom,
looking at the couple.

'What are you staring at?' Nero said into his ear. He had
got up and padded quietly over the floor. 'Are you looking for
someone?'

'No, Emperor,' Flavius whispered. Fumes of uncut wine
drifted about him.

'Then light the torches,' Nero whispered dangerously. 'Give me light.'

Flavius shut his eyes and plunged the brand into the tar. '*Hallelujah, Hallelujah.*'

'They tell me they're different, but they sound just like any other Jew,' Nero said, and began to strum his lyre.

The room was filled with glare. When the screaming stopped Nero looked up at Flavius through the drifting smoke.

'She isn't here, Flavius,' he said, in a friendly voice. 'I've got her in the cells under the circus. Tigillinus wants to keep a good supply for the games.'

Flavius stood silent.

'They tell me you're an honourable man,' Nero said interestedly.

'Yes, Imperator,' Flavius whispered.

'Now there's a thing you don't see many of these days. Honourable men. But since you are one, I can trust you. You're married to one of these filthy Jesusers.'

He jerked a thumb at the charring horrors on the walls.

'These things. Treason, you see. So get yourself back to your villa and open your veins, there's a good fellow.'

The room was quiet. Maria ceased pacing the room, and sat down on the bed. The sense of dread she had felt all the long, silent day came to a head. Gaia would not be coming back. She knew it. The baby Valeria was with the nurse, she would never know her mother. The workings of evil that had killed her brother Jeshua had reached out and gathered her in. If she waited any longer it would be her own turn. With a sudden sense of relief she jumped up, and began to gather together her few things, stuffing them in a bag.

There was a brushing of cloth at the doorway and she

glanced up. In the light of the small oil lamp she saw the *cursore*, Iphicrates.

'The master is back,' he said, his face impassive. 'He wants you.'

She put the bag on the bed.

'Where is he?'

'In the bath.'

The little lamps sent yellow-tinged shadows chasing along the corridor. The *balneum* was cold, no hot coals sent friendly steam surging through its marble-coated walls. There was a slow swirl of water from the oblong tub as she came in. She put the little lamp down on a ledge, and Flavius looked up at her from the water.

'I want you to see that things are done properly,' he commanded. 'With *honestum*, with honour, without *turpe*, without shame.'

'Done properly . . .' she said, puzzled, and then she saw that the water was dark, it was dark-red from the blood flowing from Flavius's wrists. A small, sharp knife rested on the flat edge of the bath in a little pool of bloody water.

'Why?' she whispered.

'My wife has committed treason, I am tainted with her shame.'

'*Why kill yourself?*'

'The Emperor commands me.'

'The Emperor is mad!'

Something moved in the shadows behind her.

'He *will* be interested to hear you say that,' a voice said mockingly.

She turned quickly, but a tremendous blow from a club, singing out of the darkness, knocked her flying across the room. She slammed into the wall, and fell into a heap.

Calenus strolled forward to stand over the bath.

'Well, well, well,' he grinned mockingly, 'what are you doing there in all that gore, Uncle?'

'Calenus, Calenus . . .' the old man protested. 'This is not decent . . . What are you doing here?'

'Checking the valuables,' the youth laughed. By the wall, Maria tried to stand up. She was dizzy and weak, her balance had deserted her. Calenus stepped forward with a few swift strides, and gripping her light tunic in one hand, ripped it from her, sending her flying with a powerful jerk.

'Calenus . . . for shame . . .' Flavius cried.

'Shame, shame, shame,' Calenus called out, laughing. He lashed out at Maria with his boot, kicking her across the room. The sight of her blood seemed to excite him, quite suddenly he was on his knees between her legs.

'No!' Flavius cried out. With a tremendous effort he pushed himself up in the bath, blood spraying scarlet from his wounds.

Calenus pulled up his clothing, straddling Maria as she lay half-conscious, feebly struggling. Behind, the dying man fell from the bath to the marble floor.

When she woke, in the dim light of the dawn filtering through the tiny barred window of the cell, she found herself sprayed with his blood.

27

Rome, September A.D. 64

Calenus moved methodically through the villa. The rooms were lit by the golden afternoon light falling into the open *peristyle*, where Flavius's fountain still played, cold water all the way from the mountains tinkling musically, cooling the warm air.

Calenus had a leather bag, moving slowly through each room he trawled in the small but valuable objects that he had marked down in his time as the old man's catamite. The Emperor would acquire the house itself to be put into his portfolio for sale or gift, but it was understood, by the rules of the day, that the one responsible for so replenishing his coffers might gather up as much of the denounced and deceased's belongings as he was able to pick up and carry away with him. So amber and gold, ivory and jet all made their way into Calenus's sack, and a little pile of paintings by the wall grew, for Flavius had been a man of culture, Calenus had them marked down for a gallery he knew.

In the *triclinium* he checked that the slaves were making it clean, strewing the floor with petals and setting the tables, in the kitchen he saw to it that the cook was busy, for he was entertaining that evening, friends of his were coming round to share his hospitality and congratulate him on his good fortune.

In the bedroom stood the lovely table of exotic wood, of undulating grain and changing colours almost like a flame, *lecti pavoni,* a peacock's tail that he had eyed covetously so many times as he bent over the bolster for Flavius's pleasure. He had always intended it to be his. Now he hesitated for a moment. The Emperor had a keen sense of what might belong to other people, and what was his, by right. The colour purple being one of them. Riding in his carriage he had spotted an aristocratic lady walking with her maids in a robe of that colour and had had his guards strip her on the spot. Her husband's estate he acquired the same day, it went to settle a gambling debt. He was not without heart, however. Realising he had left her homeless he arranged for Tigillinus to give her a job in one of his whore houses.

Calenus eyed the beautiful, and very valuable table thoughtfully. He decided to present it to Nero personally. As he was moving on Statio, the doorkeeper, came in.

'Some fellow at the door for you,' he said.

'If it's one of Uncle's cronies tell him he can find him with the rest of the offal out on the marshes, the kites won't have picked him clean yet.'

'No,' the man said stolidly. 'Some fellow asking after the slave girl, Maria. I said I'd get you.'

Calenus slowly turned, straightening up, a strange expression on his face.

'This man,' he said softly. 'What does he look like?'

'Big fellow. Tall. He's wearing good clothes, but he looks like he's been travelling for a while.'

'His face?'

'Difficult to see, he has a cowl over his head, the kind of thing you wear when the wind's blowing the dust about.'

'A cowl . . .' Calenus whispered. 'That you might wear, travelling.'

'Yes,' the doorkeeper looked at the youth curiously. 'You know him?'

'I know someone who does. Listen, send him to me, out in the *peristyle*. And when you have done so, hurry to the house of Paul, that some know of as Saul. The priest of the Emperor. You know the man, and where he lives?'

'I know him.'

'Tell him that a man with a cowl has come.'

The doorkeeper hurried away and Calenus put down his bag of goods, walking out into the bright sunshine of the *peristyle*. Statio appeared, ushering forward a tall figure in a fine quality Nervian *byrrus* cloak that could keep out all weathers. The green cowl was up over his head to protect him from the sun. On his feet he wore stout, double-soled *galliculae* walking boots, and over one shoulder a strong leather sack of his belongings.

'Hail!' Calenus called out cheerfully. 'I am Calenus, how may I help you?'

He saw the doorkeeper hurry away upon his errand.

'Sit you down,' said Calenus. 'Are you thirsty?'

'I am,' the man said, in a deep voice. 'I have come from the port, and the day, as you see, is warm.'

Calenus called out for water, and a slave brought a jug and beaker. When the man poured the glass and drank from it, the sleeves of his tunic fell back, and Calenus saw that he wore fingerless leather mittens on his hands.

'I thank you,' the man said, when he had quenched his thirst. 'That was good.'

'Do you have a name, Sir? Or shall I call you thirsty?'

'No,' the man said with a chuckle. 'My name is Jeshua.'

'You are from Palestine?' Calenus enquired, and a strange gleam came into his eye.

'Galilee. A long time ago. I am one who has business all over the shores of the Great Sea.'

'So how may I help you, Jeshua?'

'I am seeking the master of the house. Are you he?'

'The master has . . . gone away. But you may deal with me.'

'It concerns a maid that works here. I have need of a reliable slave. One told me of her. I thought to come by and see if her master wished to sell her to me.'

'What name would this maid have?' Calenus asked casually.

'Maria.'

'Oh, yes, Maria. She is . . . out at the moment. But I shall bring her to you when she returns.'

'I have gold to purchase her with.'

'I did not doubt it,' said Calenus, getting up. 'Rest you here a while after your journey.'

Calenus went into the house, and Jeshua sat for a few moments before rising himself. Flavius's *peristyle* was planted with greenery and flowers; after his sea voyage he felt the need to be surrounded by growing things, and he walked slowly about, appreciating the scents of the plants and the sounds of falling and flowing water.

The old villa was a nest of suntraps and shady spots, nooks and crannies. In a tiny courtyard where geranium fell in a crimson sheet down the wall, a voice spoke to him from the ground.

'Who is there? I see feet.'

It was a girl's voice, it spoke from a narrow, barred grille at the base of the wall. He bent down and knelt on the tiles. His eyes could not see inside for a moment, but a hand came out, reaching frantically for his.

'Father!' Maria cried. 'Father!'

The darkness ebbed away as he clasped his daughter's hand, and he saw her in the dank cell.

'My darling, they told me you were here,' he said. 'I have come to save you.'

'No, you haven't.'

There was a clatter of feet behind him.

'Here he is!' Calenus cried triumphantly.

Paul stood there, with armed slaves at his back.

'It is the Cowled Man,' he cried, softly and joyfully. 'At last, the Cowled Man.'

When the darkness flowed in through the grating like ink, filling the tiny room where she was incarcerated, they brought an oil lamp and set it on a ledge. The stolid Statio carried in a large bowl of warm water, in which a cloth floated.

She stood up, crossing her arms over her naked chest.

'What of some clothes?' she asked.

He shook his head, not meeting her gaze.

'The master's boy, Calenus, is entertaining,' he said, and seemed to feel it was sufficient explanation. He went out and she began to wash herself. Her back and head were bruised from the blows she had received, and when she cleaned her hair the water became dark with blood.

They came for her, leading her out and up the stairs. She could hear music and coarse laughter from the *triclinium*. They pushed her through the leather curtain and she stood naked in the lamplight.

The guests lolled on their couches, filled with fine food and wine. The wreckage of a banquet lay about the tables. They yelled with hideous delight as she stood there. She made herself keep her hands down and stood as impassive as stone.

Calenus reared up, smiling with dreadful satisfaction.

'Well, here she is,' he cried. 'Here's the entertainment.'

He reached down to the hem of his *amictus* and pulled it up over his waist, exposing himself to her.

'You can see,' he crowed, 'I've been waiting for you.'

'Guests first!' one of the cronies cried.

'Oh, no,' Calenus said softly. 'Not with this one. You boys can have her afterwards.'

She walked forward towards Calenus, and stopped by his couch. He jerked his hips obscenely.

'So do it,' he whispered, his eyes glittering as he stared up at her.

She bent over him as his companions roared, and took him in her mouth.

Circus of Gaius and Nero

The Fisherman was strong, but they were many, and they were experienced in the struggles of those about to die. They lashed his hands to the high tripod, he ground his teeth and screamed curses at the man he could not see, who beat him with the rod again and again, as from behind the wall of the pen came the laughter of the crowd at the antics of the clowns.

When the blood ran down from his back to his heels, pooling on the lava stone cobbles, he hung from the ropes, unable to stand, and the man who had done it to him came around.

'You,' he whispered.

Paul smiled.

'I am about the Lord's work,' he told Peter. 'I am commanded to do his will.'

They took him down, unafraid of his struggles, for he was weak. They held him up and Paul jammed a crown made from thorns over his head.

'Did you not wish to be king of the Jews?' he mocked. 'Did you not betray your master for me?'

'My Lord Jesus has forgiven my sins!' Peter barked, as they

lay him down on the heavy wood of the cross. 'He rose from the dead, he died for me.'

'Yes, yes,' Paul agreed. 'And now you are to die for *him*.'

The centurion in charge was experienced at that kind of work, he tapped the large-headed nail through a wide wooden washer, to avoid it pulling through when it took the weight. Then they held Peter's arm to the wood and he drove it through at the wrist, as the Fisherman jerked like freshly caught tunnyfish. They secured him at the wrist and ankle, and looked to Paul for instructions.

'You can take him through when they're ready,' he said. He began to walk off, then turned back. Bending over Peter, he took a small knife out of his pocket.

'You owe me something, I think,' he said, and sliced off his ear. As he tossed it to the ground, he tapped the scarred stump of his own.

Peter had closed his eyes against the agonies he endured, now he opened them to stare up at Paul with unremitting hatred.

'I go to be with my Lord Jesus,' he gasped. 'And that you cannot take from me.'

Paul straightened up.

'Not your Jesus,' he said, walking away. 'Mine.'

Nero had finished the work begun by Caligula, his was the imperial *pulvinar* where they sat. It was the best place in the circus to be. Comfortable padded couches replaced the hard marble seating suffered by the rest of the spectators, shade from the heat of the sun was provided by a team of sailors from the Misenum fleet, expert in the handling of canvas, who could rig a striped awning over them in seconds. A private *forica* was behind the box, airy and with a fountain playing, slaves were to hand to provide refreshment. It faced the short end of the arena, where the view was excellent, and naturally, the best of the entertainment took place on the hard yellow sand beneath. For a foreign guest a place on one of the silken couches was an honour, for professional courtiers such as Tigillinus and Vitellius a token of their expertise at remaining atop the greasy pole. For professional entertainers such as Flamma, it was dangerous, if well-rewarded.

The *mappas* waved like flocks of butterflies, and they rose, for the Emperor had arrived, fresh from driving his chariot among the crowds thronging through his garden to the show.

He was in good spirits. As the animals were driven up the ramps from their masonry cages beneath and the *venatores* provided the crowd with an *hors d'oeuvre* of sport and suffering, he settled into his couch, joking with his cronies, clear-eyed even after his debauch the previous night. He enjoyed the best of health.

'How many of these Christians have we left?' he enquired of Tigillinus. 'I used a lot last night, to light up the gardens.'

'Enough, don't you worry. We must have cleaned the city of most of them. I've filled them out with a few batches of criminals. The people will have a good show. And remember who gave it to them.'

A roar of laughter came from the crowd and they looked down. A huge ostrich cartwheeled below the *pulvinar*, ablaze from claw to beak. The *venatore* whose witticism it was watched grinning with hand on knee, his torch ready to repeat the joke. The incandescent bird hurtled about the sand before subsiding into a kicking bonfire, smouldering as it died.

Paul came through the door of a small, stone-walled box. Two men sat there under guard of armed soldiers who stood at the back. He hitched up his tunic with blood-flecked hands and sat next to them. The younger of the two was Mark, the older, Jeshua, the Cowled Man.

'I'm Paul.'

'I know who you are,' the man said in his deep voice. 'Much of your work have I undone, about the shores of the Great Sea.'

'You hate me.'

'I hate your instruction. Vile, narrow and evil are your doctrines.'

'I am instructed by the Lord Jesus,' Paul said dreamily, watching the slaves clearing the great open arena below.

'Jesus,' said Jeshua. 'That is my name, if spoken in Greek.'

Mark exclaimed, as they carried out a man nailed to a cross, and set it up in a hole that had been dug for it.

'There is Peter,' he cried. He turned to Paul.

'What is this? Are you paying back old scores?'

Paul glanced at him, indifferent to his protest.

'I do the work of Jesus, that I am commanded to,' he said again. 'What are the words of the Lord? "Thou shalt have no other God but me," I am the instrument of his will. I hasten those who worship the wrong god towards their perdition.'

They were bringing out others nailed to crosses, in the holding area below men and women were gathering under guard. They were singing hymns, the sound of their voices rose up in harmony.

'Those down there,' said Jeshua. 'Those who are about to die, they do not worship the wrong god.'

'No,' Paul agreed. 'There they are, my own Christians.'

'Why do you sacrifice your own people?' Mark demanded angrily.

Paul was watching them with a strange, terrible glitter in his eyes.

'It is the proof of God,' he whispered. 'The Lord Jesus died upon the cross for them. He died and on the third day he rose again. He died to forgive their sins. Now they, who love him, give up their lives for him. See if it is not so.'

Jeshua tugged at his stitched leather mitten, and pulled it off. He turned his hand, so that they could see the fearful, puckered white scar that indented both back and palm.

'I am the Jesus you have made them worship,' he said grimly. 'I did not die.'

The slaves worked efficiently, clearing the remains of the dead beasts. A small herd of deer appeared, driven up one of the ramps. Their skin bloody, and they moved strangely. It was when a pack of dogs, big Irish hunting hounds, appeared from the other end that everyone realised that they were not real deer at all, for as the dogs loped baying across the sand the deer scattered, running, each and every one, on their hind legs. They were but men and women stitched into freshly flayed deer-skins. They ran like rabbits, screaming, as the huge dogs, the resident circus pack, hunted them down among the greenery placed in the arena for the purpose.

'They're criminals, actually,' Tigillinus muttered. 'Raptores and some old whores, mainly. The Jesusers don't run very well, they tend to stand there and sing hymns.'

The dogs converged on a last deer, trying to dig itself under a bush, and they pulled it out in pieces. This was their territory, they knew every last trick of the prey released there for them. The huntsman's *cornu* sounded, and they obediently trotted back to their kennels to the applause of the crowd, which liked to see expertise.

'We shall not put them on,' Gaia said firmly.

'We shall not,' Julia echoed.

The tribune stood at the cell door with the blue robes over his arm.

'It is traditional. All condemned women such as you wear the costumes of the goddess Ceres, and the men those of priests of Saturn.'

'*Exactly*,' said Gaia crisply. 'And thus appear to be offering our lives as sacrifice to those gods. Had we been willing to sacrifice to them we should not be here now, but back at home. We are here of our own free will, for we worship Jesus, and are ready to go to him, but not wearing such garments. Take them away, and bring plain white shifts.'

'I have never known anyone make so much trouble as you Jesusers,' the man said, grumbling. He went off, taking his gowns with him and returned with plain, coarse white shifts. They put them on, and he led them out of the cell and up the ramp into the sunlight.

It smelled up there. It reeked of blood, the sand was dark with it, it caught metallic in the throat. It smelled of singeing flesh and smoke. They waited by the turnstile to be told to go on.

In the middle of the arena coals glowed, for a giant barbecue. On a great griddle bodies charred; in a big metal roasting pan two naked bodies screamed and flapped, frying slowly to death. Purple and swollen, it was impossible to say whether they were men or women.

'Slaves,' the tribune said laconically. 'Infected by this Jesusism of yours.'

'Soon they shall bathe in cooling springs,' Gaia said certainly. 'But the fire in which they bake shall seem as cold as snow compared to the furnaces of Hell that await you and those who have put them here.'

'When you die, you are dead,' said the tribune. 'I fear no fires when I am gone.'

'Tell that to Jesus, when you see him,' said Julia, and the two women held each other close.

A row of crosses had been erected, and men and women were nailed to them. In the centre an old man had been crucified upside down, his white hair hung like a halo. Vultures had been tethered to the cross beams, an anguished groaning came from the line.

A man knelt on the sand, his hands clasped, his lips moving in prayer, an executioner standing by with a heavy military sword in his hand.

'It is Timothy,' Julia whispered.

The swordsman looked up at the *pulvinar*. He received a signal, the sword glittered in the sunlight, the head flew through the air, tumbling over the ground, and Julia clasped Gaia, her eyes tightly shut.

'Be happy,' Gaia urged gently. 'He is with Jesus. We shall be reunited so soon, all of us, even the baby in your womb, all shall live in the glorious light of Heaven.'

'Yes . . .' Julia whispered. 'Of course we shall.'

'He was a Roman citizen,' the tribune commented. 'It was his right.'

He looked at them anxiously. 'You didn't want to be beheaded, did you? I forgot to ask.'

'We are a living *eucharista*,' Gaia said proudly. 'The savage claws that open our bodies will spill blood that is the wine of Christ, their terrible jaws will grind our flesh into the pure flour of Jesus.'

The tribune shook his head, unwilling to talk anymore with mad people. There was a coughing, a snarling, a howling, and the efficient mechanism of the circus ejected the next group of players into the arena.

'You're on,' said the tribune, and without waiting to be pushed the two women stepped forward. They were beautiful, and Gaia was well-born. There were those there who knew her. It was a treat the crowd was not given very often, and they roared their approval. From other exits other Christians were advancing into the arena.

A tremendous blow knocked Gaia flying. She picked herself up off the sand, and turned to see a bull burying its horn into Julia's stomach. It jerked its massive black head and sent her flying high in the air, tumbling like a doll.

A bear was there, brown and furry, coming towards her with its rolling gait. She saw its little glinting eyes, the huge yellow teeth.

She put out her arms in the shape of a cross, and held her head up high.

It blotted out the sun, rearing up on to its back legs, and a massive paw slashed.

She had come apart, she lay on the sand, scarlet with spouting blood, and the roar of the crowd crashed in her ears: *well washed, well washed.*

The sun blazed in her eyes, and she saw the face of God.

Mark stared at the terrible scars of crucifixion that disfigured the hands of Jeshua. Below, the Christians were being led out to death, their voices raised high in songs of praise.

'How came you to survive from the cross?' he asked urgently.

'I was betrayed,' Jeshua said grimly. 'By him who dies down there, who like this one, mistook me for a god of his own invention. I was taken from my people, the oppressed, the enslaved, the women that men tread upon like matting. I was delivered up to those who hated me. He knows, this Saul who now calls himself Paul, for was he not there?'

Paul sat, ignoring them, as below those he had instructed went joyously to die.

'My wife Mary was still free,' Jeshua continued. 'She whom Peter hated. She was an aristocrat, she gathered those she knew. Pilate was a corrupt man, Judas Iscariot, who served me, gathered together the money, he whom Peter had hanged. I was crucified, so that the priests of Judah, who hated me and my works, might believe me dead. As I hung there, on the cross that had been set up on the land of Joseph, they held a draught up to me of a sponge, that they placed upon a spear. I drank from it, and then I knew no more.

'When I awoke, my wife Mary was with me, and I was upon the cross no more. She tended my wounds, and when I was well again I moved once more among my people. There were some who saw me and believed me risen. Then I left the land of Israel, to spread my word throughout the world. I am the one that this Saul hates.'

Mark turned to Paul.

'Here he is, the Jesus you believe in.'

Paul pulled his gaze from the dying.

'He cannot be,' he said with ultimate certainty. 'For Jesus reigns in Heaven. He will not return until all the world bows down in his name.'

'You're doing well,' Nero said approvingly to the Sicilian.

'That's it, Imperator. They'll soon forget all about the golden house.'

The crowd shifted in their seats, adjusted dress and cushion, tested the sun with their parasols, the air with their peacock-feather fans. They visited the *forica*, checked their make-up in their mirrors, examined the programme of the day's events set out on the posters freshly stuck on the walls, placed bets with the bookies doing business down by the bronze balustrade that separated voyeur from victim.

The *hors d'oeuvres* were over, it was time to sink their teeth into some meat, for the roast to be brought on. They were ready for the gladiators.

'A bit of entertainment, here, Imperator,' Tigillinus said, as the *nomenclatores* came out to describe the event.

'You too, Flamma,' he said, and the gladiator listened to him politely. 'You'll be interested in this one, you being a fighter.'

A beautiful young woman had emerged from the gate. She wore a simple skirt and her ankles were chained together by a loose shackle. She was naked from the waist up and they all admired her physique.

'Who's that, then?' Nero asked amiably. 'Good-looking wench.'

'Yes, that's what Calenus thought,' Tigillinus agreed. 'She's Maria, the maid of Gaia, old Flavius's wife.'

'Oh, yes. Didn't I have her at your party? Became one of these Jesusers, didn't she? I had old Flavius open his veins for it. Calenus was his bugger-boy, wasn't he?'

'That's it. Anyhow, there was some bad blood between Gaia and Calenus, and the maid Maria, too. So after Flavius slit himself open Calenus held a party for his mates, and decided to have some fun with the maid.'

'Good idea,' Nero said approvingly.

'When they were all merry he had her brought in. He'd decided they'd have her service them all *con bucco* first, and by the time she'd finished with the last they'd be ready to enjoy her in other ways.'

Nero nodded. On the sand a man had come out and was standing some yards away from the woman, staring at her in hate.

'There he is,' Flamma murmured. 'That's Calenus.'

'So Calenus lies back,' Tigillinus continued, 'while his mates cheer him on, and pulls up his *amictus*. Down you get, he says, and the bitch does just as he asks. *And she bites the top of his cock off.*'

A bellow of laughter went through the box and the spectators nearby glanced across, wondering what was amusing the Emperor and his guests.

'So there he is. He wants justice. He wants to slash her into ribbons and cut her into bits. He'd have done it after the party only he was too busy having his mates tie a cord round the stump. I said he could do it here, where we can all see it, and he seemed to think it a good idea.'

Nero beamed, and rubbed his hands together.

'Excellent, excellent. You're an artist, Tigillinus. A picture painted in one shade of gore is boring. A melody requires more than one instrument. Liven it up, give it notes from the harp as well as music from the water-organ.'

Calenus was looking up at the *pulvinar*, awaiting permission to begin. He wore a short tunic, suitable for fighting, carried a plaited bull-whip in one hand and a short curved *sica*-style dagger in the other. Nero raised a hand in assent, and leaned forward to watch.

'Right off, you say, Tigillinus?'

'Clean through,' he assured him. 'I saw the stump. He couldn't get her off, and she was moving her jaw from side to side like a saw.'

'Must have teeth like razors,' Nero remarked. 'I'm glad that little wife of Gallus didn't have the same idea the other night.'

'That's Maria! My daughter!' Joshua shouted suddenly. He

rose up in anguish and as he stood the two soldiers shoved him back down, their swords drawn.

'Is it?' Paul said indifferently. 'Oh, yes, it is. Some amusement of Tigillinus's, no doubt.'

Down on the sand the two were circling about each other. Calenus drew back the long plaited whip and lashed it forward. His strategy was clear. Once she had tasted enough strokes she would turn to run, and then the whip would curl around her legs, bringing her to the ground, and dismemberment.

A strange thing happened. Maria did not flinch from the slicing blow, but went into it, seizing it with both hands as it cut into her. With a terrific jerk she tore it from his grasp, and the crowd roared with approval.

In the Emperor's box, Flamma gave a strange, half-amused grunt.

'Calenus doesn't seem to have understood where he is,' he remarked.

Maria had the whip turned around. It was clear that she was familiar with weapons, for she began to cut the advancing Calenus into ribbons with expert blows, one after the other. He turned to run and she wrapped it around his ankles, pulling him to the ground like a heifer. She was on him, her hand in his hair, heaving his head back, and the whole circus heard his terrible gurgling shriek as she sliced him from ear to ear.

Flamma actually laughed.

'Fool,' he said contemptuously.

Then the crowd cheered again as a number of young men scrambled over the bronze balustrade and dropped down into the arena. They ran over the sand towards the *pulvinar*.

'Imperator, we are friends of Calenus who lies dying. We ask your permission to kill the woman for him.'

'Granted,' Nero said genially. 'Give them weapons.'

In the box where Paul sat, Jeshua tensed like a great cat.

'I am going down,' he said, very quietly, so that only Mark could hear him.

'I will come with you,' said Mark. 'For you are the true Jesus.'

'*Now!*'

The two men jumped forward, scrambling down the seats. They paused for a second on the parapet, then jumped down on to the sand. At the sight of fresh contestants the crowd cheered even more.

'Better and better,' Nero said genially. 'Well, this is turning out well. Give *them* swords too.'

The sand was hot, Mark could feel it burn through the soles of his sandals. He saw Maria embrace Jeshua, gripping her whip and dagger in one hand.'

'Father,' she murmured. 'Oh, Father.'

She looked up, as alert as a wild animal as he trudged over the sand.

'What are *you* doing here?' she demanded. 'This is the henchman of the Fisherman.'

'The Fisherman has paid,' said Mark, glancing up at the cross where a dreadful, bloodied figure raved in the sun. 'I wish to atone, for I have met Jesus.'

She looked over his shoulder at the crew of young toughs that waited for them, and at the instructors from the *ludus* bringing swords.

'You'd better be able to fight,' she said bleakly.

'I can fight,' Mark promised.

Swords were brought for them. The young men stood, heads together. Maria watched them, and coiled up her whip, blood streaming down her side from its blow.

When the *spathae* were brought, long and glittering in the sun, an approving murmur went through the crowd. The cockless Calenus had been a fool, his friends had some planning. Two picked out Mark, one took on Jeshua, and the last two Maria.

When the *cornu* sounded the combatants swirled about each other. Three joined into a wedge of slashing steel, and Maria was suddenly cut off from Jeshua and Mark, who found themselves back to back. Keeping well out of the whip's reach, the last two ran around Maria until one was at her right, and the other to her left, so that the three formed a line. Then they began edging in.

'She's had it,' said Tigillinus, watching from above.

'Fifty *aureii* on the woman,' said Flamma, and Tigillinus grinned.

'Taken,' he said.

The man on the right was in range of the whip. She slashed, and he caught it on his sword blade, slicing it through. The crowd grunted, and leaned forward to get a better view of her being cut up.

Without hesitating she leaped forward at him, discarding the whip, jumping with both feet. He swung the sword, but she had hurled herself down feet first, the chain taking him across both knees, knocking him backwards. She slashed the tendons of his sword hand with her dagger and whirled to face his partner. Her hand was at her waist, she threw her long skirt up into his face and sprang behind it, dagger outstretched. There was a brief thrashing and screaming and when she got up the youth lay flapping his life away, his guts strewn over the sand.

His companion had got up, blood spurting from his wrist, and was holding his sword in his left hand. She picked up the spare *spatha* and in a few expert strokes chopped him into pieces.

'See how she uses the cutting edge of the blade,' Flamma

commented professionally, as parts of the youth flew in the air.

Mark and Jeshua had moved to the wall, defending themselves from the three. Running silently behind them Maria whirled her blade, and a head flew in the air. A man screamed in panic, Mark skewered him like pork. The last turned and ran, he tripped and Mark hacked him to death on the sand.

The three embraced each other, their chests heaving with exertion, and walked to the *Sanavivaria*, the gate for the living.

'I suppose you want your money,' Tigillinus said grumpily, but when he looked round, Flamma had gone.

It was dark in the tunnel.

'What now?' Maria asked.

Mark gripped his *spatha*.

'I'm keeping my sword,' he promised.

'*Here!*' called a strong voice. Peering through the gloom, they could see a broad figure beckoning from a small door. It was Flamma.

'Come on, quickly,' he called, and they ran through the door and down a little corridor. An iron door was at the far end, the gladiator took a key from his belt, unlocking it. He pushed, and sunlight flooded in. They looked out through porticoes, the river glittering across the square.

'Get you gone,' Flamma urged. 'Get out of Rome.'

They paused, the tall man and his daughter, the young man from Jerusalem.

'Why?' Maria asked. 'Why do you help us, Flamma?'

The gladiator shrugged.

'I hate amateurs,' he said. 'You were professional.'

'I fight Satan,' she said. 'When he is killed I shall fight no more.'

28

Gulf of Kutch, India, A.D. 64

'There are three kinds of people in the world,' Mark said, 'the living, the dead, and those who go to sea.'

He groaned, and shut his eyes as he lay on the canvas sail folded on deck, hoping that blotting out the sight of the rising and falling coastline would help quell his nausea.

'The dead are at least fortunate in that they do not feel so ill,' he continued, and Maria, sitting beside Jeshua, smiled. A spume of spray coated their hair, the storm was chasing them as they scurried for land, the square latitudinal sail bellied out, Georgios the helmsman working at the quarter-rudders.

'I'm hungry,' she said. 'Gyas is baking *biscoctum*, I'll see if it's ready.'

'I'm going to die,' Mark said unhappily.

Jeshua, who like his daughter was a good sailor, smiled, not unsympathetically.

'It just *feels* that way,' he said.

They were sitting up in the prow, among the collection of wood and lead anchors. Maria set off down the deck to the galley at the stern, her bare feet gripping the planks. Beneath her in the hold of the fifty-tonne freighter were *amphorae* of wine from Terracina, and rich Sicilian olive oil, stacked in three layers, beneath them the millstones of the ballast. She went past the hatch where the smith, doubling as shipwright, kept his tools, and by the crewmen manning the sails. The approaching storm was sweeping in, whipping up the waves; she saw Georgios eyeing both, and the far shore where green trees were bending, conning his craft to safety. They were a long way from Rome.

The galley was down some vertical steps. Here were stored the crew's provisions, the flour for the biscuit and bread, the wine, beans, cheese and salt pork, together with whatever fresh fruit and vegetables they had managed to buy at their most recent port of call. They ate fish too, caught with net and line, but no one was fishing today.

The galley was empty, filled only with the smell of the baking biscuit in the clay oven. The door to the hold was open, however, and she could hear the noise of Gyas shuffling along the gangway that ran along the middle. He came out, and looked warily at her, a small man with a big paunch.

'What are you doing here?' he grumbled. 'I've been checking the cargo, I heard something break, they ought to pack it better, we've lost some olive oil.'

His feet were leaving golden prints on the decking of the galley, and she could smell the rich oil, but she also saw the wine thief in his hand, saw him slip the siphon away, and knew that he had developed a taste for the fine first-grown Terracina vintage; she could smell it on his breath.

She supported herself with one hand against the side of the ship as it rolled in the increasing swell.

'I came to see if the biscuit had baked,' she said neutrally. The ship was a partnership, the profits divided by the ancient maritime codes. The others would find out if Gyas had been cheating them by drinking from the sealed *amphorea*, they could decide what to do with him. By then, they would be gone.

For now, the only thing that mattered was some biscuits. The rolling sea made Mark's stomach heave, but hers hungry.

'It should be done,' he said.

She was there, she saw it happen. As the cook opened the oven, exposing the bright red coals, the ship ran into the first of the heavy waves conjured up by the storm outside. Gyas was drunk, his feet slow, he stumbled and in falling knocked down the stopped pottery jug of his cooking oil from its rack.

The crack of it breaking and the flash of flame were instantaneous. It ran liquid, the roll of the ship carrying it all over the dry timber of the galley, and down into the hold. It caught the clothing of Gyas on the floor and he screamed.

She scrambled up the steps and on to the deck.

'*Fire*,' she yelled. She grabbed a canvas bucket and ran to the side to fill it.

'Fire in the galley,' she shouted, and they all ran, for conflagration was feared above all. She heaved the bucketful of water in on its rope and ran across the deck. A blazing torch shot out of the galley, knocking her over and spilling the water. Screeching like a fiend, Gyas vanished over the side.

The painted timber of the ship, colourfully decorated to ward off evil, was blazing. Charis had been her name, though little grace had the freighter had. Life and bread she had brought to those who sailed in her, she had become sacred. The oil of her cargo made her into her own pyre.

The fire ran down the hold, erupting through the decking like fingers from Hell. Jeshua and his daughter stared at each other from the far ends of the ship, they shouted through the flames. Mark stumbled to his feet. The fire licked them, they threw themselves into the seething sea, and did not see each other again.

The noise of the birds greeting the rising sun awakened Mark. He crawled out from under the pile of palm fronds that had sheltered him and bent in a prayer of thanksgiving to the Father and the Great Mother of All, who had saved him from the raging sea. The hands of the goddess had reached down as the water threatened to overwhelm him, picking him up in a great breaking wave of her ocean to spill him high on the beach.

His mouth and throat burned, his entire body was encrusted with salt, his clothes scraped his skin. The sea was now calm, gentle waves patted the sandy shore, a drowned sailor rolled to and fro like a log.

He trudged down the beach, looking for signs of life. A stream flowed down from the hill into the sea, he bent and scooped up a palmful, it was brackish. He followed it up, and where it tumbled over some rocks a pool had formed. He waded in, and the water was sweet and cool.

When he had done, he wrung out his tunic as best he could. He was without shoes, money or weapons. In the pounding water the slightest extra weight would have been sufficient to sink him, wash his body up against the shore where the crabs waited to feast.

He went back down to the beach, looking for Jeshua or Maria, but it was deserted except for the corpse, and reluctantly, he went back to the stream, following it inland. The overhanging trees thinned as he climbed, and he came to an area of hillside that had been cleared of vegetation. In the distance he could see some form of town, with brightly painted buildings, but dominating the hill was a temple. The stream flowed out from under steps of blue stone. Elaborately carved pillars, painted red and black held up a heavily eaved roof of gold and green. It was deserted, and he cautiously went up the steps. A strange smell of decay was on the air. He peered into the temple interior. It was very dark, and he went in.

As he did so, the far wall began to glow with light and he

could see before it a huge carved statue, jet black in colour. A hideous goddess grinned down at him. Surrounded by baying she-jackals the monster had four arms, two bearing an iron hook and a noose, the other pair a sword and a decapitated head. The bodies of two children hung from her ears as pendants, around her neck was a necklace of skulls. The black body was smeared with blood, more ran down from her mouth, in which rested the mangled body of a man. The statue was stone, the victims human.

A howling mob of young women suddenly emerged from the dark. They overpowered him, trussed him up with ropes, and carried him away.

From the trees Maria saw a band of small brown women in brightly coloured gowns bearing a man tied up with rope, hurrying towards the town, making glad cries like birds. She retreated into the undergrowth and kept watch. The city of the Indian king, Meghaduta, to whom the Charis had been travelling, had been a further two days sail to the south; she did not know where she was, nor who these people were.

After a while the young women came back from the town, singing a high-pitched, trilling song. On the journey she and Jeshua had sat with Georgios by the quarter-rudders, they had learned some of the language. She was pleased to find she understood the words. It was a song both comforting and fertile, grim and deadly. Nectar dropped down from the moon and anointed the bodies of maidens, a goddess snared men and women with a hook and throttled them before chewing on the bodies she had created.

Maria hid patiently and watched. After some while, one of the girls emerged from the temple, carrying a wicker basket. Maria shadowed her as she strode purposefully into the woods.

She was gathering wild herbs, placing them in careful bundles in the basket. When the temple was far behind them, Maria came forward.

'Greetings,' she said quietly, and the girl started in alarm.

'Don't be afraid,' she said. 'I only want to talk to you.'

The girl stared fearfully at the strange, well-built young woman.

'Who are you?' she asked, pulling her yellow robe about her.

'I am Maria. Who are you?'

'My name is Bhadra, servant of Shakti Chandi.'

'You are gathering herbs, for medicine?'

'No, for the fires of Chandi.'

'That is her temple, back there? She is a goddess? I saw you and others carry a man from it, and take him away.'

'We found him in the temple. We found another, by the sea shore and so we have taken them both to be with the others who wait in the king's cells.'

'Wait for what?'

'For Chandi's great day. It is clear to us that she has sent them to make up the sacred number.'

'There were many of you. Is there not one who rules in Chandi's name?'

'It is Guyha, the high priestess.'

'Who decides who shall be the high priestess? The king?'

'No, Chandi decides. On a day of sacrifice she sends one who would be her servant. The old and the new must fight, and Chandi chooses which one pleases her best.'

'How do they fight? What weapons do they use?'

'With no weapons but their hands, their feet, their teeth. When Chandi has chosen, the winner uses her sword to take the heart from the one Chandi rejects and eat it.'

'The men,' Maria said, 'the ones you found. I want them, they are my companions.'

Flat black eyes looked at her.

'You cannot have them. They belong to Chandi.'

'What if I go to the king, whose cell they are in?'

'The king belongs to Chandi too.'

The cell was airy, made from thick clay brick walls, the window that looked out over the woods strongly protected with iron scrolled bars. It was large, with room to walk about on the tiled floor, there was a jug of fresh water and cups to drink it from. A guard had brought a tray of fruit, bread and roasted fowl. Two young men squatted on a bench, in a corner of the room Jeshua sat cross-legged. Mark drank from the jug, and went over to sit next to Jeshua.

'You survived,' he said with relief. 'I was looking for Maria, but I couldn't find her. Then a lot of girls rushed me.'

'They captured me too.'

'What do you think they want with us?' Mark asked tentatively.

'Why are we here? You and I, and these two boys who sit as if dreaming? I think we are here to make sure that the people of this kingdom enjoy good crops, good seasons and good health for the next five years.'

'Why five?'

'It appears to be Chandi's sacred number. Chandi is the goddess whose temple you made the mistake of entering.'

'There are only four of us here,' Mark objected.

'There is the king. I too, have been a king. The king is always required, either on his own, or to make up the sacred number that will bring good fortune to his people.'

'How are we to provide this fortune?'

Jeshua looked steadily at him. 'You cannot guess?'

'I think I can,' Mark said bravely. 'How did you realise this so quickly?'

'I have been here before,' Jeshua said quietly. 'There were those that required this of me, for the people of Israel. That I die, to take on their sins.'

He looked at the two young men.

'Do they know of this?'

'Yes, they do.'

'They are not upset.'

'They are pleased. The moment they are sacrificed to Chandi, they will be reborn, better and richer than they are now. So dying is no more important than snuffing the life from a gnat. It is the same evil doctrine of Yahweh that Saul, who calls himself Paul, preaches to the little ones. That those who suffer here are rewarded in Paradise. They do not know that the Paradise he offers is the home of Satan.'

'But here they have a goddess.'

'Once she wore a robe of glory, woven from the stars of Heaven, from the oceans and the sky, from all the flowers of the earth. All the creatures of the earth were hers, hers were the meadows and woods, the streams and rivers, hers the cool refreshing rain, hers the sun that ripened the crop, the moon that brought the dew. Once when she danced her robe sang for joy, and her people sang with her. Now she is draped in black and steeped in blood. She stinks of corruption, she carries a sword, she eats raw flesh. Her people fear, and the land about her is made waste.'

The sacred grove of the goddess was situated outside her temple, tall trees untouched by axe, carefully and lovingly tended by the acolytes and, in this night of worship, lit by torches. They brought out Jeshua and Mark, and the two youths. Jeshua and Mark they had bound tightly, to prevent their escape.

The king was waiting, seated upon his throne. His favourite wife they had taken away, having stripped her of her clothes and jewels, his first-born son sat nearby, staring tranquil into the smoky darkness.

The king wore robes of the deepest red, dyed from the finest tumeric of his fields, on his head he wore a gold circlet. The head gleamed in the lights, he was bald, they had led him about his kingdom that day, and in each village the headman had plucked out a clump of hair.

Guyha the high servant of the goddess stood on the platform by the throne, tall and strong, in robes of jet, her face blackened. She held up her arms and all the waiting people fell quiet.

'Great goddess Chandi, whom we worship. Giver of life and death. Our king comes before you.'

She took off his ornate gold necklace.

'The king loves his people.'

She took off his red robes.

'The king takes upon him all the sins of his people.'

She took off his gold circlet.

'He takes our sins away that you may grant us good crops, seasons and health.'

About his plucked head she thrust a circle of spiky thorn, and the blood ran down.

A long lane had formed among the people and the king slowly came down from his throne to walk down it. While he did so his subjects screamed abuse at him, spat on him, slapped and cuffed him as he went by.

When he came to the end of the lane he stood, naked except for his mockery crown, with Guyha beside him. One of the acolytes handed her a blazing torch, and she held it high.

'Great goddess Chandi, our king comes to you.'

She thrust the torch into the king's groin. He screamed and turning, ran back along the lane of people. There each had a small knife, and as he passed they slashed at him.

Fountaining blood, he fell within the sacred grove. They fell on him and hacked him into a thousand tiny pieces.

When they were done, the bloody fragments were given to Guyha, who gathered them up into a pile. Those who had taken part in the sacrifice then lined up, leaving the gory, twitching skeleton on which they had been soaking handkerchiefs, to act as relics and charms, and received their part of the king's flesh. Within minutes, the darkness was lit by the light of bobbing torches as the runners brought the blessing of Chandi to the villages of the kingdom. There priests were waiting, and the offering would be divided in two. Half would be burned at the altar, the other half divided among the heads of household of the village, to be burned and buried on their land, so that the king's death would bring health and prosperity to all his subjects.

The head they had left despite their frenzy, Guyha took it, and went inside the temple while the acolytes prepared the king's son.

Mudra, the aphrodisiac grains, had been ground up in a sacred pestle, and the ceremonial bread made from them. *Madya*, fine wine, was poured into a golden goblet. A living fish was brought from the stream, it slapped on the altar beside a living goat. The chief acolyte put a torch to the faggots and the fire licked up about them.

The son was given the bread to eat and the wine to drink. He took the bread and broke it, to symbolise the crushing of his father, he drank the wine for his blood. They took off his robes and naked acolytes rubbed sacred oil into his skin with their own bodies. He was blessed, and walked forward, stiff and erect, to satisfy the goddess.

Smoke was drifting across the grove of trees, the air that Chandi breathed. From the temple came the sound of women singing hymns. It seemed a very long time. People were coming through the smoke, acolytes.

'Chandi awaits you,' they said. They smelled of oil and herbs, blood and smoke, and led Mark and Jeshua into the temple.

The vast stone statue towered against the far wall. Fresh victims adorned it, the king's wife was impaled upon its sword, his son hung by the neck from its noose. The king's head was about its throat.

A terrible figure stood at the foot of the statue, waiting. Tall, black-faced, and in robes of jet. A bloody sword dangled from one hand.

It was Bhadra who had led the king's son into the temple. Her body had glistened with holy oil, her hair was rubbed with the sacred herbs.

Guyha lay on the altar, her robes of office draped over the goddess's feet. She was naked except for a yellow silk scarf in her hand, Bhadra brought the king's son to her, they lifted him up to make the ritual complete.

As the youth coupled with the goddess the acolytes sang sacred hymns. The priestess raked his back with silver claws and he shuddered. She slipped the noose of the scarf around his neck and strangled the still jerking body, and they pronounced the prayers that would bring good fortune to the kingdom for the next five years.

They hung him from the statue, and as they did so, a strange figure stepped forward out of the darkness, tall, black-faced and dressed in the jet-black robes of office.

'The king is dead,' it cried out in a harsh voice. 'Now Chandi asks for the blood of her priestess.'

The figure threw back her robes, letting them fall to the floor, and the acolytes saw that the woman was black all over. Bhadra bent and gathered the robes of the priestess, and the two women faced each other.

They were both as black as midnight, they sprang at each other like panthers. Silver claws glittered in the torchlight, blood spattered the temple floor. Like a huge cat one struck at the other's throat, her jaws closing, and a terrible gurgling scream echoed about the walls. One fell to the ground, the blood ran out in a pool.

Dead bodies hung from the huge stone statue, hundreds of years' worth of blood encrusted its surface. The priestess stood waiting, a body lying at her feet. As Jeshua came up, the acolytes who had led him there fell back. In the light of the torches he could see that the woman who lay on the temple floor had her throat torn out. Blood was sticky about the mouth of the victor and on her hand where she had wiped it. Her chest still heaved with the exertion of her victory.

They did as Jeshua bid them, they pulled down the temple of Chandi and burned it. The dreadful, encrusted statue they smashed with hammers, into gravel. Where it had stood they sowed the seeds of grasses and flowers, and the little stream that had run red sparkled clear.

'The goddess is the Great Mother of All,' he told then, standing tall in front of them. 'She asks for no temple. Her temple lies all about us. She asks for no high priest, no high priestess. She loves her children, she gives them life, she takes them into her when they die, she makes them live again. She loves to hear her children sing, to see them dance.

'When you worship her, you will find her in each sacred place. Each shining pine needle, each flower of spring. On every sandy shore and in the midst of the morning. She lives in the humming insect, in the prowling bear. Her voice is to be heard in the tumbling river, in the thunder on the mountain. She whispers in the breeze that bends the rushes, she laughs when the rain washes her clothes clean.'

They were quiet, as they listened to the tall man.

'If there comes one among you that says follow me, worship as I do, bow down as I tell you, for I am the priest of the goddess, then shun him. If there comes one who would have priests across the land, and new temples, and sacrifice, drive him out. If one comes who says I shall be your king, let us make weapons of war and conquer our neighbours, in the name of the goddess, then drive him out.'

He spread his hands to encompass the land about them.

'The earth is our Mother. What befalls her befalls all the sons and daughters of the earth. The earth does not belong to us, but we to the earth. We did not make the web of her life, we are a part of it, and what we do to the web, we do to ourselves.'

Then they brought the priestess forward, all black, as black as night, and where all could see her they took her jet robes and burned them. With water scented with flowers they washed her clean, and she was black no more. Then they brought the robe that Jeshua had had them make, it shimmered like the reflection of the sky in a mountain lake and they dressed Maria in its folds. It was sewn with myriad tiny bells of gold and silver, and when she danced for the goddess, it sang.

29

Oxford

She looks like a crow, thought Maria. A strange, thin black crow.

She watched Juliana come down the street from her flat. She looked for anyone with her, anyone following her, as Connell had told her to.

Juliana was alone. She came down the street, walking with a strange, pinched walk, clutching a string shopping bag to herself like a spinster far older than her years. As she watched her Maria felt a sudden prickle of alarm run over her body. It vanished, leaving a simple sense of unease. When you lived on the streets, you instinctively knew the ones to avoid.

Juliana turned into a brown-painted shop. Maria waited, watching for anyone else, but she was alone. She crossed the road, following her.

It was an organic food hall: rice, lentils and pulses of many colours and shapes stood in coarse-fibred sacks on the wooden floor. Juliana was filling a paper bag with brown rice from a scoop. Some string beans, as thin and pale as herself, were in the shopping bag. Maria went over to stand by her, and pretended to examine some bars of scentless soap on the shelf.

She was entirely without make-up, dressed in a black skirt, a black jersey. Her hair was gathered up and pinned into a bun. The skin of her face was taut and had a worn sheen to it, as though it were much scrubbed.

'Connell says to say hullo,' she said quietly, and Juliana froze in the act of pouring her rice.

'Where is he?' she whispered.

'He wants to talk to you. Not on your telephone, not at your flat. He says that Fox must have tapped your line. That's how Fox knew he was meeting al-Masih down on the coast.'

Juliana said nothing, but the scoop in her hand had started to tremble. Small grains were falling, they made a pattering on the floorboards. Maria noticed her fingers, they were scraped red about the nails.

'Do you remember his old room at the college?' Maria asked.

'Yes.'

'There's a payphone in the corridor there. He'll call you on that number. At noon. He wants you to contact al-Masih. You must have a number for al-Masih which he can call. Connell still has the texts, he wants to make them safe.'

'Yes, safe,' Juliana said, and her voice was so quiet Maria could hardly hear it. She stood almost unmoving by the sack, not looking up at the unknown person who was talking to her, the grains of rice sliding from the scoop and pattering about her feet.

'A number for al-Masih that he can call,' Maria repeated.

'Yes,' said Juliana.

The younger woman reached out, making the scoop level. Juliana looked up for the first time. The eyes did not focus on her face, they seemed to look through her, at a terrible object of desire.

'Why are you doing this to yourself?' Maria asked quietly.

'I have to be cleansed,' she whispered. 'I hunger to be pure.'

Maria went out of the shop. At the doorway she turned back, and saw that Juliana had replaced the scoop in the rice and was placing the bag on top of it. From across the road she watched Juliana come out, and with her strange, stiff gait walk towards the high stone walls of the colleges.

Maria went the other way. She could not call Connell until the appointed time. She found a large bookshop and slipped in through the wide glass doors. The books absorbed her, and her sense of unease went away. When she peeped out from the corner where she had hidden to read for free, she saw from the clock outside that it was past midday. With the money in her pocket she bought *Great Expectations*, and went off to a restaurant to read it while she ate.

When she had finished her meal she went to the payphone on the wall and dialled Connell's number. It was still earlier than he had said she should phone, but her anxiety had returned.

'It's me.'

'Al-Masih's coming here,' said Connell. 'I'm not risking being seen. He's coming tonight and we're driving down to the coast near Llanelli while it's dark. The Chriscraft will be waiting to take us over to France. We'll be in Cairo by midday.'

'She's strange, Frank,' Maria said urgently. 'Her head's not in the right place.'

'What . . . who is?'

Connell sounded distracted.

'That woman, Juliana.'

'Oh . . . that business – you know what I mean – it shook her up a great deal. When I spoke to her afterwards she was nearly hysterical.'

'There's something wrong with her. I mean really wrong. You should see what she looks like, what she says . . .'

'Yes, well, look, I can't sort her problems out for her. I have a few of my own. I'm sorry if she isn't well.'

'I didn't say – '

'Maria, I have to get back to the texts, I haven't got long.

Will you get yourself back? al-Masih'll be here once it gets dark.'

'Frank, I – '

'I'll see you then.'

'*Frank, she's got religion!* I don't trust her.'

The line was empty, Connell had gone. She put more money in and redialled. The phone rang steadily. Connell had switched it off. Slowly, she put the receiver down.

A sense of urgency enveloped her as she left the restaurant and hurried to the railway station. She missed the first train by minutes, and had to wait, walking up and down the platform, smoking one cigarette after another, as trains she did not want pulled in and out.

Eventually it came, a small affair of a few carriages and a little locomotive. She had to change at Didcot. Then they rattled at an easy pace through the English countryside towards Wales. Somewhere short of the Severn the train stopped and a friendly driver apologised for the points failure that prevented him continuing. They sat waiting, and Maria felt her anxiety grinding her teeth.

The sun fell towards the horizon, slanting through the windows on her left, walking across the floor away from her. After an age, the diesel suddenly burst into life under her feet, and a few moments later the train began to move once more.

She was the only one who got off at the little station with its troughs and tubs of flowers, and signpost in Welsh and English. As she gave up her ticket she heard the train rattle away up the valley, its engine humming in the dusk.

She walked away past the nearly empty car park, and the lights became a glow that cast a wobbling shadow in front of her. Wild flowers were scenting the warm air, moths fluttered against the last of the blue in the sky. She hurried on along the winding lane, her shoes pattering on the hard road. As she passed, small animals scurried in the undergrowth.

As she approached the little crossroads with its white-painted signpost, pale light suddenly spattered the foliage about her, and in the distance she heard the sound of a car's engine coming up the road. Instinctively she pushed herself into the undergrowth, crouching down out of sight.

The car came round the corner, its gears whining softly, its lights splashing white. It slowed at the crossroads, and stopped, its engine purring only feet away from where Maria was hiding. She could see two dim figures inside. Suddenly, they were lit up as they put on an interior light. They were consulting a map.

The light snapped out, and the engine growled as the driver accelerated up the valley, towards Connell's cottage. The red and white lights blinked as the car was hidden by the trees. Maria came out, and began to run along the road in its wake.

Wales

Connell had lit his oil lamps, their soft yellow glow was momentarily blotted out by the harsh white lights of the car as it turned off the lane. It stopped by his stone barn, and the driver switched off. He stood waiting in the buttery light of the lamps.

The door creaked, and she came in. She was dressed in a long, pale raincoat, buttoned up to her throat.

'It's you, Juliana,' he said. 'Where's al-Masih? I'm waiting for him. When I saw your lights I thought it was him.

'He's on his way.'

'Has he got everything arranged?'

'Yes,' she said, in a flat monotone. 'It's all arranged.'

'That's all right then. The texts of the Children have to be kept safe. That's what matters . . .'

The little house was untidy, in the kitchen old coffee cups and a couple of crumb-covered plates told the tale of Connell's eating habits that day. He was rumpled and unshaven.

'You've been working,' she said. She reached inside her bag. 'I brought something to drink.'

She went through to the kitchen and found glasses inside the glass-fronted cupboard.

'I've been reading,' he said, from outside. 'I found out what happened, Juliana . . .'

She had pulled the cork earlier, now it was hand tight. She pulled it out and poured red wine into two tumblers. The plastic phial was in her hand, she twisted its soft top off as she had been shown, and squirted it into Connell's glass.

'Here,' she said, emerging. 'Have a drink before al-Masih comes.'

'Why not?' he murmured. He had picked up a transcript he had made, and was looking at it.

'Cheers,' he said, and took a swig of wine. 'I haven't had a drink all day.'

She had been watching him with pale eyes, she held her own glass in her hand, still untasted.

'Drink up,' she said. 'There's plenty more.'

'I got it wrong at the beginning,' he said. 'Everything else was easy, all the other texts, it was the very first one I got wrong.'

He took another swallow of wine, still looking at the text. He looked up at her and smiled wryly.

'I can't be blamed. Jesus – Jeshua – was supposed to have been dead twenty years earlier. You come across someone called

Zaddik, the Righteous, in the Jerusalem Temple around 66, you immediately think of James the Just, and say to yourself, well, the dates are out a bit. But of course they aren't, and James was murdered in 62 just as we always thought he was. I knew that "the woman with Zaddik" shouldn't have been there, not in that part of the Temple, but that's explained too. Jesus knew there could be no God without the goddess, no man without woman. He wore the robes of the high priest in order to take them off, he was in the temple because he knew the goddess needed no temple, they would have had it torn down. He was preaching of the Law because he knew the goddess needed no law. He and Mary, Maria and Jeshua, they should have won, it would all have been much different, and much better . . .'

He passed the few pages over to her.

'I found the piece that was missing,' he said. 'Jeshua that came to be called Jesus went to India, as we thought. But he came back to Jerusalem, and that's where Paul finally caught up with him again.'

The courtyard was filled with smoke and the cries of battle. From by the altar Paul threw the spear at Jeshua, standing high on the step, he saw him fall. He ran up the stone stair and Tigillinus's men blocked the way behind him.

He had his sword in his hand, he found Jeshua on one knee in the smoke, the bishop's mitre he had discarded in front of them all burning. Jeshua looked up at him unafraid as he raised the weapon high.

'I am the one you seek,' he said clearly. 'I am the true Jesus they put upon the cross.'

The sun ran down the blade like fire as Paul stared down at him.

'*I know*,' he whispered. '*I know*.'

He swung with all his might, and the steps were red with blood.

A woman screamed below him, he looked down and men were dead on the steps. Maria came running, her blade whistling in her hand. She hit out and his weapon shattered in his grasp.

'*Satan!*' she howled. 'I see you at last.'

Her sword was raised high, she brought it down with both hands, and cleaved him through to the teeth.

She put down the papers. Connell had slumped in his chair, he seemed unable to move. His eyes flickered, looking up at her.

'What have you done?' he whispered. His shoulders hunched feebly as he dragged air into his chest.

She stripped off the raincoat, dropping it on to the floor. Underneath she was all in white. There was a rosary about her neck.

'We were snared by the devil,' she said. 'You were still in his clutches.'

'You stupid bitch,' he said hoarsely. 'You haven't understood who's in charge.'

The yellow of the lamps was suddenly washed away by the harsh white of a car outside.

'It's cold,' Connell whispered. 'So cold. He must be close. The Children always knew when he was close.'

Juliana had bent her head in prayer, her fingers obsessively caressing the rosary beads, her eyes closed. She did not open them as Fox and al-Masih came into the room. They were in uniform, long black robes that buttoned up to the throat, tight-sleeved, with the scarlet sash of the order wound about their waists. On the breast of each hung a cold, glittering cross, silver as ice on its wrought chain.

They glanced at Connell indifferently, assured that he was dying, and went straight to the table where the boxes lay. Fox ripped open one lid and thrust in a hand. He held up a fistful of papyrus and shook it in triumph. Ancient dust and fragments rained about his head.

'We have it!' he howled. 'It is here, all the lies are here . . .'

He turned to Masih.

'Take her outside,' he ordered. 'By the tree. Take a chair.'

Al-Masih took her by the arm and she went with him as uncomplainingly as a zombie, her nun's habit rustling as she moved.

On the kitchen step Connell kept a row of large plastic jugs of kerosene for his lighting and heat. Fox found them, and began to empty them about the rooms, drenching the floorboards, the furniture and the boxes containing the scrolls. Then he went into the room where Connell had worked, and picked up one of his oil lamps. Holding it high, he saw Connell's lips move. He bent his head down to hear what he said.

'Don't you feel it?' Connell whispered. His dying eyes glittered as he stared at Fox in the light.

'Don't you feel the cold?' Connell asked again. 'Your master is here, he is waiting for you.'

Fox put his head back, laughing, his eyes insane with triumphal joy.

'You won't feel the cold now,' he promised. He went to the door with swift strides, and turned. The lamp in his hand flew through the air in a golden parabola. It hit the table where the texts lay and the room exploded into flame.

Outside Juliana stood by the apple tree, chanting softly, her eyes closed, fingers gripping the rosary beads. The white of her habit began to take on a shifting yellow and orange hue as the fire inside the house took hold. Al-Masih stood beside her, a soft, flexible rope coiled in one hand. Fox took it from him and threw it over a stout branch above their heads, holding on to the end with the noose.

He slipped it over her head, as light as a velvet choker, and pulled the knot to behind her ears. They had the chair ready, one at each side they lifted her up as she prayed, and Fox had the rope taut, lashed to a gnarled toe root poking up from the ground. Al-Masih had the rosary off her neck, as she gasped in sudden shock, feeling the rope tighten, he used it to lash her hands together behind her.

She stared at the house without recognition. The lower floor was an inferno, its flames were poking up into the upper rooms like greedy fingers. It roared as it sucked in air.

'What is it?' she whimpered.

'*Hellfire*,' a voice howled in the night.

She shook with a sudden ague, as the freezing cold enveloped her. She felt the terrible, vast presence behind her. The house suddenly exploded with light, something red and green with gold shot high into the black sky, travelling faster and faster away from her.

'*Frank!*' she screamed. '*Take me with you. Take me to the Children.*'

'Too late,' said the voice. Below her she saw the two priests prostrated upon the ground in worship. Something tipped her from the chair, and the rope closed off her throat. She swung from it, dying, and felt the terrible icy fingers behind her reach inside like knives to gather her soul.

The roof of the house crashed in and Fox got to his feet. His face was as blank as that of a sleep-walker. He wiped some foam from his mouth. The body hanging from the rope was still and empty, lifeless as a sack.

'The Lord be with you,' he said.

'Worship the Lord,' al-Masih muttered.

The two priests got into their car, driving quickly away, and from the bushes lining the lane, where the yellow flame still washed away the dark, Maria watched them go.

30

It was done. The robe of glory shimmered like the sun dipping into the sea, like stars in the heavens, like the sky on the water. When Maria put it on, the tiny bells from the jar that she had sewn to it sang softly, as they had for the Children.

Moonlight bathed the glade she stood in. All about her were the creatures of the Great Mother, and amongst them, the people of Jeshua, the poor, the enslaved, the downtrodden and the suffering. She could not see them, she felt their presence.

She knelt, lighting the fire, and the flames flickered yellow and red. She danced, and the dance was as she had danced of old. She sang, and the song was the song of old. She cast the holy herbs into the coals and the silver smoke enveloped her as it had always done. The sparks of life flew high in the air, gold and azure, amethyst and ruby, swirling away on the wind without ever going out, and the Children lived once more.